IS TWO-TIER HEALTH CARE
THE FUTURE?

IS TWO-TIER HEALTH CARE THE FUTURE?

Edited by Colleen M. Flood and Bryan Thomas

University of Ottawa Press
2020

University of Ottawa Press
Les Presses de l'Université d'Ottawa

The University of Ottawa Press (UOP) is proud to be the oldest of the francophone university presses in Canada as well as the oldest bilingual university publisher in North America. Since 1936, UOP has been enriching intellectual and cultural discourse by producing peer-reviewed and award-winning books in the humanities and social sciences, in French and in English.
www.press.uottawa.ca

Library and Archives Canada Cataloguing in Publication
Title: Is two-tier health care the future? / edited by Colleen M. Flood and Bryan Thomas.
Names: Flood, Colleen M., editor. | Thomas, Bryan, 1973- editor.
Description: Includes bibliographical references and index.
Identifiers: Canadiana (print) 20200193406 | Canadiana (ebook) 20200193457 | ISBN 9780776628073
(softcover) | ISBN 9780776629414 (hardcover) | ISBN 9780776628080 (PDF) | ISBN 9780776628097
(EPUB) | ISBN 9780776628103 (Kindle)
Subjects: LCSH: Medical care—Canada—Evaluation. | LCSH: Medical policy—Canada. | LCSH: Medical
care—Law and legislation—Canada. | LCSH: Medical policy—Case studies. | LCSH: Public-private
sector cooperation—Case studies.
Classification: LCC RA395.C3 I8 2020 | DDC 362.10971—dc23

Legal Deposit: Second Quarter 2020
Library and Archives Canada
© Colleen M. Flood and Bryan Thomas 2020

Production Team

Copy editing	Robbie McCaw
Proofreading	Transforma Pvt Ltd
Typesetting	Counterpunch Inc./
	Linda Gustafson
Cover design	Steve Kress
Cover image	Balanced stone art photography
	by Peter Juhl.
	www.temporarysculpture.com

This book was published with the help of a grant from the Canadian Federation for the Humanities and Social Sciences, through the Awards to Scholarly Publications Program, using funds provided by the Social Sciences and Humanities Research Council of Canada.

SSHRC ☰ CRSH

The University of Ottawa Press gratefully acknowledges the support extended to its publishing list by the Government of Canada, the Canada Council for the Arts, the Ontario Arts Council, the Social Sciences and Humanities Research Council of Canada and the Canadian Federation for the Humanities and Social Sciences through the Awards to Scholarly Publications Program, and by the University of Ottawa.

ONTARIO ARTS COUNCIL
CONSEIL DES ARTS DE L'ONTARIO
an Ontario government agency
un organisme du gouvernement de l'Ontario

Canada Council   Conseil des arts
for the Arts   du Canada

Canadä

u Ottawa

Table of Contents

List of Figures

List of Tables

Introduction:
The Courts and Two-Tier Medicare

Colleen M. Flood and Bryan Thomas

Canadians are greatly concerned by long wait times for health care within their public health care system, medicare.[1] Internationally, Canada's relative performance on this score has fallen in recent years,[2] with Canadians reporting some of the longest wait times across comparator countries. But rather than spurring significant government action to improve health care for *all* Canadians, wait time concerns are sparking constitutional challenges to overturn laws restricting private finance, so some Canadians can more easily "jump the queue." Of course, though these challenges are framed around the rights of patients, they are as much about the rights of physicians—led and financed by private clinics and doctors who stand to profit from an expansion of privately financed care in Canada.

---

1   Mario Canseco, "Wait Times, Red Tape Are Main Health Care Snags for Canadians" (30 January 2019), online: *Research Co.* <researchco.ca/2019/01/30/health-care-canadians/>.

2   Canadian Institute for Health Information [CIHI], "How Canada Compares Results From The Commonwealth Fund's 2016 International Health Policy Survey of Adults in 11 Countries" (2017), online: *CIHI* <www.cihi.ca/sites/default/files/document/text-alternative-version-2016-cmwf-en-web.pdf>; CIHI, "Wait times longer for joint replacements and cataract surgeries in Canada" (April 2018), online: <www.cihi.ca/en/wait-times-longer-for-joint-replacements-and-cataract-surgeries-in-canada>.

These court challenges, grounded in the *Canadian Charter of Rights & Freedoms'*[3] section 7 right to "life, liberty and security of the person" and the section 15 right to "equal benefit of the law without discrimination," seek to overturn a variety of laws that exist across Canadian provinces, limiting opportunities for privately financed care. Current laws, which we describe below, restrict (but don't completely eliminate) a two-tier system, wherein doctors can treat patients who are willing to pay for faster access and higher quality care. These laws vary across provinces but include:

i.   restrictions that stop a doctor who bills medicare from charging a patient an additional amount (referred to as "extra-billing");

ii. restrictions that force doctors to choose between exclusively billing the public system or exclusively billing privately, forbidding simultaneous billing in both streams (i.e., dual practice);

iii. restrictions on doctors, in the private sector, charging prices for medically necessary care that are higher than those permitted in the public plan; and

iv. restrictions on private health insurance for services that are covered by medicare.[4]

All Canadian provinces have a mix of some or all of these restrictions, enacted to meet the requirements of federal legislation, the *Canada Health Act*,[5] and thereby qualify for a federal contribution to the operation of their respective health care plans. Consequently, a finding of unconstitutionality of one or more of these laws in a province like British Columbia will have an enormous impact across Canada, as similar laws in other provinces may be then quite quickly overturned on the grounds they are not compliant with s. 7 of the *Charter*.

The reason Canada has legal restrictions on private finance is to ensure that health care is, to the extent possible, accessed based on need and not ability to pay. And as Greg Marchildon describes in his

---

3   *Canadian Charter of Rights and Freedoms*, s 7, Part I of the *Constitution Act, 1982*, being Schedule B to the *Canada Act 1982* (UK), 1982, c11 [*Charter*].

4   *Canada Health Act*, RSC 1985, c C-6.

5   *Ibid.*

contribution to this volume, "Private Finance and Canadian Medicare: Learning from History," overcoming the many barriers and interest groups opposed to universal medicare was a hard-won political war waged over many years against medical associations, which fought tooth and nail to prevent a universal public health care system, and against some politicians who were ideologically in favour of maintaining a significant role for private finance. The mix of different laws that exist across the provinces, and the *Canada Health Act* itself, are thus a product of the particular history and context of Canadian medicare, including political accommodations necessary to bring doctors into the public plan (e.g., doctors are not public employees but independent contractors mostly paid on a fee-for-service basis with relatively little governmental control over their clinical decision making).

Critics of Canada's single-payer model often overlook this history and argue that equality in "mediocrity" is not an equality worth pursuing. They assert it is "common sense" that allowing wealthier patients to jump the queue will free up resources for those left behind in the public system—the trickle-down effect being better, if unequal, access for all. And while this assumption may be true in many markets, as Jerry Hurley comprehensively explains in chapter 3, "Borders, Fences, and Crossings: Regulating Parallel Private Finance in Health Care," health care markets do not function like most markets. Market failures, the limited number and high cost of training health care professionals, and the difficulty of attracting medical manpower into remote and rural areas across Canada, mean that there are health-professional shortages in many critical areas *already*. If a two-tier system is permitted to flourish, it seems most likely that more health professionals will move at least some of their time from the public to the more financially lucrative private sphere. And in a country the size of Canada, this will likely prove to be most problematic in places where it is already hard to attract medical labour, such as in the North, rural areas, and small cities.

Canadians need not look far for examples of how fairness in the allocation of health care can be skewed by private financing: this is visible already with the country's patchwork coverage of pharmaceuticals,[6] and for long-term and home care services, as Sara

---

6   Health Canada, *A Prescription For Canada: Achieving Pharmacare For All* (Final Report) by Advisory Council on the Implementation of National Pharmacare (Ottawa: Health Canada, June 2019).

Allin and colleagues detail in chapter 5, "Experiences with Two-Tier Home Care in Canada: A Focus on Inequalities in Home Care Use by Income in Ontario." The concern then is that permitting a two-tier system will not improve wait times in the public system but in fact worsen them, and there is evidence to demonstrate that where permitted in two-tier systems, medical labour is drawn away from the public to the private tiers. Further, as Vanessa Gruben explains in chapter 6, "Self-Regulation as a Means of Regulating Privately Financed MediCare: What Can We Learn from the Fertility Sector?," a larger privately financed sector in Canada will also mean an even larger role for delivery by for-profit providers with attendant concerns about the quality and safety of care delivered.

Despite these worries, in the face of increasingly long wait times and the struggles Canadian governments have faced in managing these, those Canadians with resources may conclude that equality of access must be sacrificed to ensure their own access to timely care. In the context of a *Charter* challenge, debate over two-tier care could be seen as a contest between the "rights" of patients with resources to access a market without impediment and the interests of patients who continue to rely on the public system. The choice is usually not put so bluntly; instead, most who argue for greater private financing couch it as win-win (i.e., despite inequality, both rich and poor will be made better off). Canada's single-payer system has long enjoyed strong public support and continues to do so despite its problems; perhaps, then, it is no surprise that those seeking to expand the role of private finance and open up broader opportunities for a two-tier system have bypassed electoral politics and have turned to the courts.

The first major judicial attack on restrictions on two-tier care came in 2005, in what is arguably one of the Supreme Court's most controversial decisions ever, *Chaoulli v Quebec*.[7] There, the court struck down a Quebec law banning private health insurance for services covered by medicare. The reasoning was that, were it not for this restriction, patients facing lengthy wait times could obtain quicker care in the private sector. Writing for the majority in *Chaoulli*, Justice Deschamps found that, given unreasonable wait times in the public system, patients' rights in Quebec were unjustifiably infringed by a law prohibiting private insurance for hospital and physician services. Lawyers for the Quebec and Canadian governments had

---

7   *Chaoulli v Quebec*, 2005 SCC 35 [*Chaoulli*].

argued that restrictions on private insurance were necessary to ensure an adequate supply of doctors' services within the public system, as a large private market would lure the limited number of doctors away from the public to the private sector to receive higher rates of pay and to treat patients requiring less complex care. The majority did not respond directly to this argument, but did rely on a brief and superficial review of international evidence to conclude that most Western European countries (it seemed to the majority) manage to maintain high-performing public systems while permitting a two-tier system.[8]

Although successful, the *Chaoulli* decision did not lead to the runaway private financing of health care in Canada that the applicants hoped for, due to three factors:

i.   The impugned law overturned in *Chaoulli* prohibited duplicative private health insurance, but this is only one of *several* laws restricting two-tier care in Quebec and other provinces, including, for example, restrictions on dual practice.[9] Consequently, the impact of *Chaoulli* in opening up two-tier care was not as dramatic as one might have imagined.

ii. The majority decision rested upon the Quebec *Charter of Human Rights and Freedoms*[10] as opposed to the *Canadian Charter of Rights and Freedoms*, and thus technically applied only to Quebec—necessitating re-litigation in other provinces to spread the *Chaoulli* precedent nationwide.[11] The fact of Quebec's long wait times at this time was pivotal to the

---

8   Colleen M Flood, "*Chaoulli*: Political Undertows and Judicial Riptides" (2008) (Special Edition) Health LJ 211.

9   Colleen M Flood & Tom Archibald, "The illegality of private health care in Canada" 154 CMAJ 825.

10   *Charter of Human Rights and Freedoms*, RSQ c C-12 [Quebec *Charter*].

11   Notice as well that the outcome in *Chaoulli* turns on specific findings of fact concerning wait times within Quebec's health care system. Under Canadian federalism and the terms of the *Canada Health Act*, the administration of medicare falls to the provinces. Expanding the *Chaoulli* precedent across Canada will require (*inter alia*) province-by-province litigation establishing that patients are endangered by unreasonable wait times. This point was emphasized in a 2015 decision, when the Alberta Court of Appeal rejected a plaintiff's request for a summary declaration that Alberta's restrictions on two-tier care are invalidated by the *Chaoulli* precedent. See *Allen v Alberta*, 2015 ABCA 277 at 13.

           success in *Chaoulli*, and would need to be demonstrated for other provinces.

iii. Quebec's Liberal government at the time responded to *Chaoulli* not by completely striking the ban on private health insurance, as would seem to have been required, but only liberalizing the law with respect to private health insurance for hip, knee, and joint replacement whilst simultaneously establishing wait time guarantees within the public system for those same health services. Although the guarantee was not enshrined in law it seems—as Amélie Quesnel-Vallée and colleagues discuss in chapter 4 ("*Chaoulli* v *Quebec*: Cause or Symptom of Quebec Health System Privatization?")—it was nonetheless effective, at least in part, in quelling the growth of a significant private insurance market and, in turn, a significant parallel private tier, at least in the short term.

Although *Chaoulli* did not singularly ring in a new era of two-tier care in Quebec or across Canada, in our view it had a normative impact, which is to say it helped popularize the idea of private finance and, indeed, cast it not only as a legitimate policy option but as constitutionally mandated when "monopoly" governments fail to deliver timely care. Amélie Quesnel-Vallée and colleagues argue in their chapter that *Chaoulli* was more a *symptom* than a cause of privatization, growing out of the slow encroachment of private clinics in Quebec—an encroachment visible in other provinces, more so today than ever. Another way to see the case in context is that changes in Canadian society, including the growing income inequality and aging baby boomers who are anxious to use personal wealth to access care, are combining to soften up society at large and political institutions for a break from single-payer medicare. Mark Stabile and Maripier Isabelle document rising income inequality within Canada, and hypothesize that it becomes more difficult as a result for publicly funded care to satisfy the median voter.[12] Their model predicts increased political pressures for a greater role for private finance as a by-product of growing income inequality.

       Building off of *Chaoulli*, interest groups who want to benefit from the expansion of private finance in the Canadian system, as well

---

12   Mark Stabile & Maripier Isabelle, "Rising inequality and the implications for the future of private insurance in Canada" (2018) 13:3 Health Econ, Pol'y & L 406.

as patients distressed by increasing wait times,[13] have launched law-suits in other provinces (Ontario,[14] Alberta,[15] and British Columbia[16]) which expand far beyond the *Chaoulli* precedent. Of most signifi-cance, as Martha Jackman explains in chapter 2 ("*Chaoulli* to *Cambie*: *Charter* Challenges to the Regulation of Private Care"), is an ongo-ing case that went to trial in September 2016 in British Columbia.[17] Launched by Cambie Surgeries Corporation (a private for-profit clinic) and led by its owner, Dr. Brian Day, the challenge is to the constitutionality of laws in British Columbia that

   i. ban private health insurance for medically necessary hospital and physician services (as in *Chaoulli*) [s. 45 (1) of the *Medicare Protection Act* (*MPA*)];[18]

   ii. ban extra-billing so that doctors cannot charge patients above and beyond what they receive from the public plan [s. 17(1) of the *MPA*];

   iii. ban dual practice so that doctors must choose to bill exclu-sively to the public system ("enrolled") or "un-enroll" and bill exclusively to private payers.[19]

Cambie, then, is a much broader challenge than *Chaoulli*, reflecting their claim that in order to have a flourishing two-tier system in Canada—to make it much more economically viable for doctors to provide these services—it may be necessary not only to overturn

---

13   CIHI, "Wait times for joint replacements and cataract surgery growing in much of Canada" (28 March 2019), online: <www.cihi.ca/en/wait-times-for-joint-re-placements-and-cataract-surgery-growing-in-much-of-canada>.

14   *McCreith and Holmes v Ontario* (5 September 2007) (Statement of Claim filed at ONSC).

15   *Allen v Alberta*, 2015 ABCA 277.

16   *Cambie Surgeries v British Columbia (Attorney General)* (23 November 2018), Vancouver S090663 (BCSC) [*Cambie*].

17   *Ibid.*

18   RSBC 1996, c 286 [*MPA*].

19   The language is quite confusing in the BC legislation. Physicians who are "enrolled" in the public system have two options: they can "opt in" (bill the government directly) or "opt out" (bills patients directly but not more than the public plan permits; the patient can then claim this sum from the public plan). Physicians who choose not to participate in the public plan ("unenrolled") are free to bill patients for services at whatever rate the market will bear, in private clinics.

restrictions on the sale and purchase of private health insurance but also to facilitate a two-tier system by striking down restrictions on dual practice and extra-billing. If the ban on extra-billing were struck down altogether, then all enrolled physicians would be entitled to bill what they wanted to the patient or her insurer on top of what they bill the public system. However, *Cambie*, in its closing arguments, say that they do not seek to fully strike down the ban on extra-billing and, indeed, grant that enrolled physicians should not be entitled to tack on private fees to medicare services, as this would create a financial barrier to accessing a public service. But they insist that enrolled physicians—that is, those billing the public plan—should also be allowed to treat private patients provided medicare funding is *not* involved. As written, the *MPA* bans enrolled physicians from extra-billing and wholly private billing in one fell swoop. *Cambie* asks that these sections be struck altogether, leaving it to government to respond with more tailored legislation that bans extra-billing while allowing wholly private billing by enrolled physicians.

It is worth noting that the *Cambie* challenge itself has come about as a defence to a determination that doctors at the Cambie clinic in Vancouver were breaking the law by extra-billing. Nonetheless, perhaps because extra-billing is so clearly in contravention of the *Canada Health Act*, the *Cambie* claim seems to have become more nuanced on this point over the course of the multi-year trial, focusing on the restrictions on private insurance and dual practice. Despite muting their attack on extra-billing in their final arguments, *Cambie* still asks that the court issue a "suspended declaration of invalidity" over all of the provisions, requiring government to enact response legislation within a fixed period of time—legislation that, in their claim, must liberalize dual practice but could maintain restrictions on extra-billing. However, should government fail to enact response legislation during the period of suspension, the entire suite of protections—including the ban on extra-billing—would be deemed invalid. Needless to say, this is a high-stakes game, given the challenges governments face in enacting structural reforms to health systems.

Cambie, if successful in whole or in part, has the potential to rapidly accelerate the development of two-tier care across Canada and if the BC laws banning dual practice or extra-billing are overturned, in whole or in part, this would strike at the heart of the *Canada Health Act*. To forestall this, provincial governments will have to demonstrate that wait times in their provinces are "reasonable" or that there are measures in place to make sure that section 7 rights (life, liberty and security of the person) and section 15 rights are not infringed unreasonably, a topic we return to in the conclusion.

In determining whether existing BC laws restrictive of two-tier health care can survive a *Charter* challenge, what will be crucial is how a court treats evidence of Canada's approach to the public-private mix relative to other jurisdictions. In short, a court is more likely to be persuaded that Canada's legislative restrictions on two-tier are justified for the protection of medicare if there is evidence of a similar approach in other countries. In *Chaoulli*, the majority found that Quebec (and the other provinces that similarly restrict private health insurance) is alone among comparator health care systems in prohibiting parallel private health insurance, and this finding grounded their ultimate conclusion that the prohibition was arbitrary and unconstitutional. However, as hinted earlier, the court's approach to comparison was remarkably brief and superficial, failing to note that private health insurance *serves very different purposes* across jurisdictions.

For example, in a number of countries, private health insurance is not primarily used for the purposes of queue-jumping but, instead, provides coverage for user charges and extra-billing charges that are mandated or permitted within the public system. Zeynep Or and Aurélie Pierre's discussion in chapter 9, "The Public-Private Mix in France: A Case for Two-tier Health Care?," well illustrates this problem. In France, private health insurance is mainly needed to cover the copayments that all patients must pay for all health care, and further, this "private" health insurance is heavily subsidized, if not directly paid for, by the state (the latter being for low-income individuals). Moreover, one finds a completely different flavour of "two-tier" in Germany, where self-employed individuals have the option of withdrawing *completely* and *almost irreversibly* from the country's social health insurance scheme and securing coverage in a regulated private health insurance market (see Achim Schmid and Lorraine Frisina Doetter's chapter 8, "The Public-Private Mix in Health Care: Reflections on the Interplay Between Social and Private Insurance in Germany.") In other jurisdictions, such as the Netherlands, private health insurance is mandatory, heavily regulated to ensure comprehensiveness and accessibility, and, again, is not primarily used for the purposes of jumping queues in the public system; mandatory and regulated private insurance *is* the universal "public" system.[20]

To the extent that these French, German, and Dutch systems are "two-tier," it is not in the sense being pursued in the *Cambie* litigation. Indeed, Canadians in favour of expanding private finance are pursuing something altogether different: retaining medicare coverage for all, while allowing those with the financial means to "go private" when confronted by long wait times for specific episodes of care. In this regard, what they hope for is more similar to systems like that of Ireland, New Zealand, England, and Australia, the first three of which at least have historically struggled with long wait lists *despite* the existence of a two-tier option. The Irish experience with a two-tier system, as Stephen Thomas and his colleagues explain in chapter 11, "Embracing and Disentangling from Private Finance: The Irish System," has been so destabilizing that it is driving major reform to strengthen and protect the Irish public health care system. Despite this, advocates of privately financed care insist on the logical fallacy that because some high-performing European systems allow "two-tier care"—a concept defined so loosely as to be almost meaningless—there is no drawback in Canada's abandoning its hard-won commitment to single-tier care. This kind of magical thinking has gained increased popularity in political discourse. Thus the fair resolution of upcoming constitutional challenges will depend on how courts understand comprehensive evidence of comparative health policy, including how the BC health system truly compares in regulating two-tier care relative to other health care systems.

We had two major objectives with this book. Our first objective is to test whether Canada is in fact (as contended by those in favour of privatization and endorsed by the majority in *Chaoulli*) an aberration in the Western world in having legislative provisions that dampen the potential for a two-tier system. We explain the extent to which OECD countries employ different mixes of regulation and policies to limit two-tier care and show how countries that do not directly ban two-tier care through law may achieve a comparable effect through other policies. We also explore the impacts of two-tier in those countries that have more fully embraced it in the sense

20   Colleen M Flood & Bryan Thomas, "A successful Charter challenge to medicare? Policy options for Canadian provincial governments" (2018) 13:3 Health Econ, Pol'y & L 433.

advocated by the claimants in *Cambie*—that is, maintaining universal health care but permitting people to buy faster or higher quality care. For example, as explored by Stephen Thomas and colleagues in chapter 11, "Embracing and Disentangling from Private Finance: The Irish System," the difficulties of access to care in Ireland suggest that two-tier certainly does not solve the problem of wait times in that country. Likewise, Fiona McDonald and Stephen Duckett, in chapter 10, "Embracing Private Finance and Private Provision: The Australian System," unpack the Australian experience with two-tier care, explaining the significant (and regressive) tax subsidies that flow to those purchasing private insurance. Moreover, they discuss the regulatory mandate in Australia that forces higher-income individuals to buy private health insurance—a feature that reportedly results in many Australians acquiring "junk" policies, thus fulfilling the legislative requirement but not providing substantive coverage.

Apart from understanding the regulation and impact of two-tier care in different jurisdictions, our second objective in writing this book is to anticipate how the BC provincial government—and ultimately all Canadian governments—might respond in the event that the *Cambie* challenge succeeds. They will, in the wake of a successful challenge, have the opportunity to pass alternative laws and policies that are constitutionally compliant.[21] As Canadian governments consider their options here, a deeper understanding of how other jurisdictions *actually* regulate the public-private divide will help them make better policy choices. The debate over the adoption of regulations more permissive of private finance often stumbles over assumptions about the experiences of other countries and the translation of foreign experiences to the Canadian context. Indeed, comparative health policy is generally fraught with misdirection and superficiality.[22] For example, as Bryan Thomas discusses in

---

21   The example of Quebec's shrewd legislative response to *Chaoulli* was mentioned above; for more information, see the detailed description by Quesnel-Vallée, McKay, and Farmanara in this volume. On dialogue theory generally, see Kent Roach, *The Supreme Court on Trial: Judicial Activism or Democratic Dialogue* (Toronto: Irwin Press, 2001).

22   Ted Marmor, Richard Freeman & Kieke Okma, "Comparative Perspectives and Policy Learning in the World of Health Care" (2005) 7 J Comparative Pol'y Analysis: Research & Practice 331; Ted Marmor & Claus Wendt, "Conceptual frameworks for comparing healthcare politics and policy" (2012) 107 Health Pol'y 11.

chapter 12, "Contracting Our Way Around Two-Tier Care? The Use of Physician Contracts to Limit Dual Practice," the English system is portrayed as allowing two-tier care and having lower wait times than the Canadian system.[23] However, in translating the English experience to the Canadian system it is critical to appreciate that English physicians are generally full-time salaried employees, whereas Canadian physicians bill medicare on a fee-for-service basis.[24] Indeed, having doctors work on a salary within pubic hospitals is a feature of many systems that appear two-tier (e.g. New Zealand, Australia, Ireland) so that, at least within public hospitals, care remains free for patients. Requiring physicians to be paid a salary and to work normal hours also puts a natural constraint on their ability to practice privately. In contrast, if Canadian provincial laws banning dual practice and private insurance were overturned, it seems more likely that the lure of the private sector will result in greater diversion of physicians from the public system than occurs in England—threatening its sustainability.

With constitutional challenges to medicare underway, now is the time for Canadians to think carefully about the potential impact of two-tier care, looking beyond shallow comparisons to other systems. With this book, we look to advance the research base, fusing understandings of constitutional law with evidence and analysis from health policy research. In particular, we ask for a careful consideration of the historical, economic, political, and geographical factors particular to the Canadian health care system that impact the viability of transplanting foreign approaches to the Canadian context. We hope this research is of use to the courts as they consider these constitutional challenges, to policy-makers as they revamp medicare and respond to a court decision that allows private financing of medically necessary care, and to Canadians as they grapple with the sometimes counterintuitive world of health policy.

---

23 Brian Day, "30 Years of health care dysfunction," *National Post* (1 April 2014) online: <nationalpost.com/opinion/brian-day-30-years-of-health-care-dysfunction>.

24 Séan Boyle, "United Kingdom (England): Health System Review" (2011) 13 Health Systems in Transition 1 at 117–119.

PART I
THE CONTEXT AND CONTESTATIONS OF PUBLIC AND PRIVATE IN THE CANADIAN HEALTH CARE SYSTEM

CHAPTER 1

Private Finance and Canadian Medicare: Learning from History

Gregory P. Marchildon

From the time that medicare was conceived to the present day, there has always been a polarized debate on the issue of private finance in Canadian medicare. Initially, in the early decades of medicare, the ongoing negative view of medicare by the medical profession, despite medicare's growing popularity in the general population, was perpetuated by perceived constraints on the ability of physicians to maximize profits, especially the restrictions on extra-billing introduced by the federal government through the *Canada Health Act* and the banning of extra-billing by some provincial governments.[1] In recent years, the debate has been spurred by the less-than-satisfactory performance in terms of timeliness and quality in the provision of health services, especially Canada's relatively poor performance in successive international surveys published by the Commonwealth Fund, a health policy think tank based in the United States.[2]

---

1   Carolyn J Tuohy, "Medicine and the State in Canada" (1988) 21:2 Can J of Pol Science 267 at 279–81; S Heiber and R Deber, "Banning Extra-Billing in Canada: Just What the Doctor Didn't Order" (1987) 13:1 Can Pub Pol'y 62 at 62–64.

2   The Commonwealth Fund's 2017 international survey comparing eleven high-income countries ranked Canada ninth overall, largely due to its relatively poor performance on access, equity, and health care outcomes. See Eric C Schneider et al, *Mirror, Mirror 2017: International Comparison Reflects Flaws and Opportunities for Better US Health Care* (New York: Commonwealth Fund, 2017). Numerous

It needs to be emphasized that the debate on private finance is limited to medicare. For all other areas of health care aside from hospital, diagnostic, and medical care, defined as "insured services" under the *Canada Health Act*, there is no government regulation of private finance. Indeed, Canadians pay for a considerable amount of their health care through private health insurance (generally through employment benefit plans) and out-of-pocket payments, such that these forms of private finance constitute roughly 30 per cent of total health expenditures, one of the highest private shares among the higher-income countries of the Organisation of Economic Co-operation and Development (OECD).[3]

When it comes to medicare, however, provincial and territorial governments regulate private finance in order to live up to the universality requirement under section 10 of the *Canada Health Act* that all their respective residents have access to these insured services "on uniform terms and conditions." The single-tier nature of Canadian universality—a strong form of universality—has been upheld by provincial and territorial governments through banning or discouraging private health insurance (in some provinces); preventing physicians from practicing public (medicare) and private medicine simultaneously (in most provinces); and banning hospitals and clinics from imposing user fees, as well as physicians from extra-billing their medicare patients (in all provinces).[4]

The rules on these practices have evolved in different ways and at different times over the decades since medicare was first implemented. While there are both significant and nuanced differences among the thirteen provincial and territorial regulatory regimes on

---

journalists and popular authors have used the Commonwealth Fund results, and Canada's relatively low rankings on timeliness of service and quality, to draw a causal link between the performance and the failure of medicare. See, e.g., Jeffrey Simpson's many columns in the *Globe and Mail* since the end of the 1990s and his book *Chronic Condition: Why Canada's Health Care System Needs to be Dragged into the 21st Century* (Toronto: Penguin, 2012) at 157–159, 165, and 200. A more recent example is Stephen Skyvington's *This May Hurt a Bit: Reinventing Canada's Health Care System* (Toronto: Dundurn, 2019).

3   Canadian Institute for Health Information, *National Health Expenditure Trends in Canada, 1975–2017* (Ottawa: Canadian Institute for Health Information, 2017).

4   Gregory P Marchildon, "The Three Dimensions of Universal Medicare in Canada" (2014) 57:3 Can Pub Admin 362 at 364 ["The Three Dimensions of Universal Medicare in Canada"]; Colleen M Flood & Tom Archibald, "The Illegality of Private Health Care in Canada" (2001) 164:6 *CMAJ* 825 at 826–829.

private finance, the intent remains the same: not to allow one group of residents privileged access to medicare services based on ability to pay or the preferential terms of private health insurance relative to all other residents. It is this policy objective in general—as well as the particular regulatory regime in place in British Columbia—that is the issue under litigation in the Cambie Surgeries case.[5]

This chapter examines the history of the regulation of private finance in terms of key decision points that would establish this regulatory regime in two key areas. The first was the active contestation among provincial governments over a single-payer design versus a multi-payer design, and the ultimate selection of the latter as the dominant design. The second key area concerns hospital user charges and physician extra-billing as part of the medicare policies of selected provincial governments and their eventual elimination.

The Historical Contest between Single-Payer and Multi-Payer Financing

Although the main conflict between single-payer versus multi-payer approaches occurred in the 1960s, when universal medical coverage was introduced, the debate over the best approach to achieving universal coverage can be traced to the immediate postwar period. In January 1947, Saskatchewan implemented universal hospital coverage on a single-payer design in which the provincial government paid directly on behalf of patients for all necessary hospital care and diagnostic services.[6]

While this design feature was similar to general tax-based financing as implemented eighteen months later for the National Health Service (NHS) by the British government, there were important differences between the Saskatchewan plan and the NHS. The most important of these differences was that, unlike the NHS, where

---

5   *Cambie Surgeries v British Columbia (Medical Services Commission)*, (2015) Vancouver S090663 [*Cambie*]. In his interlocutory ruling in *Cambie Surgeries v British Columbia (Medical Services Commission)* 2015 BCSC 2169 at paras 14–28, Chief Justice Cullen provides summary of the proceedings in the case to that date. A complete timeline and links to key legal documents in the *Cambie* case has been compiled by the BC Health Coalition, online: <http://savemedicare-bchealthcoalition. nationbuilder.com/court-documents>.

6   This plan was based on *The Saskatchewan Hospitalization Act, 1946*, ss 1946, c 82, and the regulations thereunder.

hospitals were publicly owned and operated, hospitals and their boards in Saskatchewan remained independent of the provincial government. In other words, the Saskatchewan plan changed financing but kept the multiplicity of delivery arrangements—a public-payment but private-practice system.[7] The term "single payer" only came into general use decades later, and mainly to distinguish a Saskatchewan/Canadian style of universal health coverage and its private delivery from a NHS-style system.[8]

In 1950, three years after the Saskatchewan plan came into operation, a very different hospital-insurance plan based on a multi-payer design was implemented in Alberta. Contrary to Saskatchewan, the Alberta government subsidized the purchase of private health insurance by residents who could demonstrate their inability to pay market-rate hospital insurance premiums. Unlike the compulsory scheme in Saskatchewan, where all residents were expected to be registered in the program, Alberta residents could choose to go without health insurance. In addition, since the cost of the subsidies were shared with municipalities, local governments could also choose whether or not to participate in the program. Finally, although the Alberta plan, similar to the Saskatchewan plan, was financed through general taxation and fixed premiums (a particular form of taxation known as poll taxes), additional revenues were generated through a hospital user fee based on days spent in hospital.[9]

Until the federal government passed the *Hospital Insurance and Diagnostic Services Act* (*HIDSA*) in 1957, these two plans were the main alternatives. However, federal cost sharing of provincial hospital-insurance plans were conditional on accepting key national standards in *HIDSA*, which, in turn, supported—even if they did not require—a single-payer approach. In particular, the definition of universality required that all residents have access to hospital services

---

7   C David Naylor, *Private Practice, Public Payment: Canadian Medicine and the Politics of Health Insurance, 1911–1966* (Montreal and Kingston: McGill-Queen's University Press, 1986).

8   Carolyn Hughes Tuohy, "Single Payers, Multiple Streams: The Scopes and Limits of Subnational Variation under a Federal Health Policy Framework" (2009) 34:4 J Health Pol Pol'y & L 453 at 453–454.

9   For more details on these differences, see Gregory Marchildon, "Douglas versus Manning: The Ideological Battle over Medicare in Postwar Canada" (2016) 50:1 J Can Stud 129 at 133–140 ["Douglas versus Manning"].

"on uniform terms and conditions."[10] This wording implied that (1) all provincial residents be registered for coverage, thereby making a scheme based on voluntary enrollment ineligible for federal cost sharing; and (2) all provincial residents would have the same coverage, thereby preventing major differences in coverage based on price, risk (e.g., pre-existing conditions), and insurance company.

With 25 per cent of provincial residents uninsured, and an infinite variation in the scope and cost of individual health insurance policies, Alberta's scheme was deemed ineligible under *HIDSA* for federal cost sharing. As a consequence, the Alberta government converted its decentralized, multi-payer financing model into a (solely) provincially administered single-payer plan. Although a few other provincial governments, in particular the government of Ontario under Progressive Conservative Premier Leslie Frost, would have preferred multi-payer financing, between 1958 and 1961, they eventually accepted the single-payer design in order to be deemed eligible for federal cost sharing under *HIDSA*.

The Multi-Payer Alternatives: Manningcare, Bennettcare, and Robartscare

The real battle over single-payer would come in the 1960s with the expansion of coverage from hospital care to physician services. Although Saskatchewan again took the lead in being the first province to establish universal medical coverage in 1962, this time it would find itself almost alone in promoting the single-payer approach, and in enduring a bitter twenty-three-day doctors' strike when first implemented.[11] Between 1963 and 1966, three provincial governments set up rival, multi-payer universal health plans in a bid to convince the federal government to legitimate multi-payer plans

---

10 Under section 5(2)(a) of the *Hospital Insurance and Diagnostic Services Act*, SC, c. 28, provincial governments were required "to make insured services available to all residents of the province upon uniform terms and conditions" in return for federal cost sharing.

11 *The Saskatchewan Medical Care Insurance Act*, ss 1962, c 1, inelegantly subtitled *An Act to provide for Payment for Services rendered to Certain Persons by Physicians and Certain other Persons*. See Malcolm G Taylor, *Health Insurance and Canadian Public Policy: The Seven Decisions that Created the Canadian Health Insurance System and their Outcomes*, 2nd ed (Montreal and Kingston: McGill-Queens University Press, 1987) at 285; Gregory P Marchildon & Klaartje Schrijvers, "Physician Resistance and the Forging of Public Healthcare: A Comparative Analysis of the Doctors' Strikes in Canada and Belgium in the 1960s" (2011) 55:2 Med Hist 203 at 207–219.

in any future federal standards and cost sharing. These provincial plans—providing a level of coverage for physician services—became known by the names of their respective premiers—Manningcare in Alberta, Bennettcare in British Columbia, and Robartscare in Ontario—were supported by organized medicine, most other provincial governments, the insurance companies, and the business establishment.

Almost identical to the design of the Alberta multiplayer hospital-insurance plan of the 1950s, Manningcare provided public subsidies to low-income residents to pay the premiums for private health insurance. Premier Ernest Manning held the strong belief that providing subsidies for the poor would address the problem of access without damaging the principle of individual responsibility, while universality on a single-payer model would eliminate both choice and individual responsibility. In keeping with this philosophy, coverage was voluntary, unlike the compulsory coverage in the Saskatchewan plan of 1962. Manning's government worked closely with the Alberta Medical Association and the insurance industry on the design of the plan.[12] After the plan became operational, in 1963, Manningcare was continually advocated by organized medicine and the health insurance carriers as the model for the federal government and all other provincial governments in Canada.[13]

Like Premier Manning of Alberta, Premier W. A. C. Bennett of British Columbia ideologically preferred a multi-payer model and also worked with organized medicine in his province to design a plan that would be acceptable to the doctors. However, unlike Manning, Bennett was prepared to compromise to increase the probability of his program complying with any future national standards for federal cost sharing of the program. As a consequence, his plan was limited to non-profit health insurers, including a physician-owned insurer. Although Bennett did not want the government involved in providing insurance, the non-profit health insurers resisted the idea of taking on the poor risks and insisted the provincial government provide medical coverage through its own plan for these individuals. As a consequence, a governmental insurance plan—the British

---

12   Ronald Hayter, "'Manningcare' cheered by Alberta Doctors," *Toronto Star* (29 March 1963) 1–2.

13   Cam Traynor, "Manning against Medicare" (1995) 43 Alta Hist 7 at 7–19; Marchildon, "Douglas versus Manning," *supra* note 9 at 143.

Columbia Medical Plan (BCMP)—was established in order to cover higher-risk individuals and families. However, Bennett insisted on a common, comprehensive package of medical services, which all the non-profit health insurers were required to offer, a contrast with Manningcare. Bennettcare became law through a series of regulations passed under an already existing law in June 1965.[14]

In comparison to Manningcare and Bennettcare, Robartscare took a longer time to gestate. Carefully observing the Saskatchewan doctors' strike in July 1962, Robarts's government decided to adopt an approach that would be acceptable to both organized medicine and the powerful insurance carriers in Canada, many of which were headquartered in Ontario. The bill that would eventually become the *Medical Services Insurance Act* was sent out for consultations in late 1962 and early 1963 before being presented in the provincial legislature.[15] When the bill went to second reading, in April 1963, the provincial minister of health, Dr. Matthew Dymond,[16] laid out the ways in which it would differ from the Saskatchewan approach.

First and foremost, it would be a multi-payer plan based on subsidizing the purchase of existing private health insurance contracts. In Dymond's words, the private insurance carriers had "done an outstanding job" in covering "some 70 per cent of the people of Ontario" with "some type or degree of coverage." He stated that there was "no sound evidence" that the "monopolistic control" of a single-payer plan could deliver coverage at a "lower cost" than the type of multi-payer plan his government was introducing. He further argued that a multi-payer model, through the "competition of the open market-place" would "put a better, more effective check on rising costs" than single-payer financing. Dymond also pointed

---

14   Gregory P Marchildon & Nicole C O'Byrne, "From Bennettcare to Medicare: The Morphing of Medical Care Insurance in British Columbia" (2009) 26:2 Can Bull Med Hist 453 at 460–467.

15   This bill would not become law until 1965: *Medical Services Insurance Act*, RSO 1965, c 56. See *Table of Public Statutes and Amendments: R.S.O. 1960; 1960–1961; 1961–1962; 1962–1963; 1963; 1964; 1965; 1966; 1967; 1968; 1968–1969; and 1970* (Toronto: Queen's Printer for Ontario, 1970), online: *Statutes at Osgoode Digital Commons* <http://digitalcommons.osgoode.yorku.ca/ontario_statutes/vol1970/iss1/174>.

16   Matthew Bulloch Dymond (1911–1996) was Ontario's minister of health from 1958 until 1969 and, as such, was responsible for the implementation of universal hospital coverage in the province, first introduced on 1 January 1959, and the chief architect of Robartscare. Ontario Legislative Assembly parliamentary history, online: <https://www.ola.org/en/members/all/matthew-bulloch-dymond>.

out that his government had "very closely collaborated" with both the Ontario Medical Association and the Canadian Health Insurance Association on the drafting of the bill.[17]

Although welcomed by organized medicine[18] and the insurance industry, the bill was heavily criticized in some of the Ontario media as a sellout to these same pressure groups.[19] The editor of the Kingston *Whig-Standard*, for example, charged that the government was using "public funds" to "underwrite a medical scheme which" would "profit the private insurers (who, of course, would never agree to assume the risks of the comprehensive, all-inclusive coverage guaranteed under the proposed bill)." The *Whig-Standard* then pointed out how the Beveridge report in the United Kingdom had stated many years before "that the insurance principle was not a sound method of financing medical services, and that the broader the services provided, the more difficult it would be to retain that basis." For this reason, Lord Beveridge had concluded "that the ultimate solution would be to finance medical benefit in the same manner as all public health activities—from public funds."[20]

The bill was a strategic effort on the part of the Robarts administration to convince the federal government to reject the single-payer approach that marked the *HIDSA* of 1957 and instead propose cost sharing for multi-payer plans for physician services. Robarts and Dymond were able to play for time while they negotiated with the federal government. Although the Ontario government waited until 1965 to get Robartscare passed into law, it had still not finished

17   John P. Robarts fonds (Statement made by MB Dymond on second reading of the *Medical Services Insurance Act*, 25 April 1963), Toronto, Archives of Ontario (RG 3-26, Apr.–Dec. 1963, file Premier Robarts general correspondence: Medicare).

18   AO, John P. Robarts fonds, RG3-26, file Premier Robarts general correspondence: Medicare (Apr.–Dec. 1963), clipping from article entitled "Doctors' Group Favours Plan for Health Care" in *Globe and Mail* (14 May 1963).

19   AO, John P. Robarts fonds, RG3-26, file Premier Robarts general correspondence: Medicare (Apr.–Dec. 1963), clipping from article entitled "Half-Baked Medical Plan is Effort to Resist Progress" in the *Toronto Star* (15 May 1963): in this respect and in contrast to the *Globe and Mail*, the *Toronto Star* consistently favoured single-payer Saskatchewan-style medicare over Robartscare in a series of editorials, including "A Test for Medicare" (16 May 1963) and "Caricature of Medicare" (13 January 1964).

20   RA O'Brien quoted in *Kingston Whig Standard* (25 April 1963) 1. O'Brien sent this article to Premier Robarts: AO, John P. Robarts fonds, RG 3-26, file Premier Robarts general correspondence: Medicare (Apr.–Dec. 1963).

writing all of the administrative regulations under the law by March 1966.[21] However, by 1966, the federal government, under Liberal Prime Minister Lester Pearson, was beginning to better specify the areas where it would be flexible and the overarching design principles on which it would not bend.

The Federal Government's Response

Highly influenced by the recommendations of the Royal Commission on Health Services (commonly known as the Hall Commission) delivered two years earlier, the Pearson government followed the reasoning in the commission's report in its negotiations with the provinces and in the legislation establishing national medical coverage.[22] After carefully weighing the advantages and disadvantages of a non-universal subsidy model compared to a universal tax-based approach, the Hall Commission concluded in favour of the latter for three main reasons. First, universality avoided the need for a stigmatizing means test. Second, single-payer tax financing eliminated the expensive overhead involved in insurance risk rating. And third, it would take far less time to achieve close to 100 per cent coverage of provincial populations through a compulsory, publicly administered, and universal enrollment than on a voluntary approach through the subsidy of private health insurance.[23] At the same time, the Hall report did not foreclose the possibility of a multi-payer plan as long as it was carefully regulated in the public interest and report to the provincial minister of health.[24]

---

21 AO, John P. Robarts fonds, RG3-26, file Premier Robarts general correspondence: Medicare (Apr.–Dec. 1963), clipping from article entitled "Easy Adjustment to OMSIP" in the *Toronto Telegram* (26 March 1966).

22 PE Bryden, "The Liberal Party and the Achievement of National Medicare" (2009) 26:2 Can Bull Med Hist 315 at 324; Canada, *House of Commons Debates*, 27–31, vol 7 (12 July 1966) at 7544–7545 (Hon Allan J MacEachen).

23 Royal Commission on Health Services, *Royal Commission on Health Services: Volume 1* (Ottawa: Queen's Printer, 1964) at 723–745. A recent version of this debate (as well as trade-offs involved in relying on private health insurance originally identified by the Hall commission) continues to play out in the Netherlands: see Robert AA Vonk & Frederik T Schut, "Can Universal Access be Achieved in a Voluntary Private Health Insurance Market? Dutch Private Insurers Caught Between Competing Logics" (2019) 14 Health Econ Pol'y & L 315.

24 See Royal Commission on Health Services, *supra* note 23 ("Administration at the provincial level should be a Commission representative of the public, the health professions, and Government, reporting to the Minister of Health, and it should

Allan MacEachen, the federal minister of health who had recently taken over the portfolio from Judy LaMarsh, exhibited more flexibility than his predecessor on two key points in order to expedite the acceptance of national medical coverage. The first was his willingness to consider voluntary schemes as eligible for federal cost sharing as long as a minimum of 90 per cent of residents were enrolled in the program. The second compromise—aimed at appeasing Bennett in British Columbia—involved relaxing the definition of public administration so that private not-for-profit insurers could be part of the provincial scheme as long as these carriers were answerable and accountable to a public authority. Previously, LaMarsh had said that private carriers could not be part of eligible provincial plans.[25] This new position opened up the possibility of a multi-payer plan along the lines of Bennettcare but required major changes in the cases of Manningcare and Robartscare.

At the same time, MacEachen held firm on the principle that eligible provincial governments had to demonstrate that their plans offer comprehensive medical coverage to all residents on uniform terms and conditions. The federal government insisted that eligible provincial plans would have to provide comprehensive medical coverage and meet the definition of universal in the sense of access based on uniform terms and conditions for coverage of physician services, as had been required under the national insurance plan for hospitalization. When asked about the eligibility of Robartscare by the media, MacEachen said that it was "not readily apparent" that the plan, based largely on private for-profit insurers, could meet these criteria.[26] While Manning was opposed to national medicare on the level of basic religious and political values,[27] Robarts felt that universal medicare on the Saskatchewan model was a bad idea from a more pragmatic standpoint. Indeed, he failed to understand why

---

also assume administration of the hospital-insurance plan in the province. In a province where a voluntary prepayment agency operates, we recommend that such an agency may be used as the administrative vehicle augmented by additional representation of the public, the health professions and the Government" at 20).

25   Taylor, *Health Insurance and Canadian Public Policy, supra* note 11 at 369.

26   MacEachen quoted in article entitled "Medicare won't Drive Us Out: Insurance Men" in the *Toronto Star* (21 May 1966): AO, John P. Robarts fonds, RG3-26, file Premier Robarts general correspondence: Medicare (Apr.–Dec. 1963).

27   Marchildon, "Douglas versus Manning," *supra* note 9.

Ottawa would not agree to what he viewed as a far more practical, less expensive, and less complicated subsidy model than a government-administered single-payer plan.[28]

When the federal *Medical Care Act* went to first reading in the House of Commons on 12 July 1966, MacEachen stated the basic principle upon which the bill was based—"that all Canadians should be able to obtain health services of high quality according to their need for such services and irrespective of their ability to pay," and "that the only practical and effective way of doing this is through a universal, prepaid, government-sponsored scheme."[29]

When the bill was passed into law, in December 1966, the Alberta and Ontario governments realized they had lost the war to get their respective multi-payer schemes accepted for federal cost sharing. Section 4(1)(a) of the *Medical Care Act* required that, to be eligible, provincial plans had to be "administered and operated on a non-profit basis by a public authority appointed or designated by the government of the province," which, in turn, had to be answerable to the "government of the province or to a provincial minister." In addition, under section 4(1)(b), the provincial plan had to provide medical services "upon uniform terms and conditions to all insurable residents of the province."[30] This strong form of universality[31] blocked the eligibility of any provincial multi-payer plan that permitted variable forms of coverage under different prices through individual insurance carriers, a problem avoided in BC through setting the terms constituting the basic (yet reasonably comprehensive) package of universal medical coverage.

If the governments of Alberta and Ontario wanted plans that would be eligible for federal cost sharing, then Manningcare and Robartscare were dead in the water, and, indeed, these multi-payer plans were soon abandoned in favour of single-payer plans that met the federal criterion of universality. However, due to its non-profit design and the existence of a government-administered insurance fund offering a public coverage option, Bennettcare was able to

28   AK McDougall, *John P. Robarts: His Life and Government* (Toronto: University of Toronto Press, 1986) at 168.
29   Canada, *House of Commons Debates*, 27–31, vol 7 (12 July 1966) at 7545 (Hon Allan J MacEachen).
30   *Medical Care Act*, 1966–1967, c 64, s 1 (RSC 1970, c M-8).
31   Marchildon, "The Three Dimensions of Universal Medicare," *supra* note 4 at 364.

rapidly adapt its non-profit plan to meet the requirements of the *Medical Care Act*.[32]

On 1 July 1968, the date set for the implementation of the *Medical Care Act*, British Columbia and Saskatchewan were the only jurisdictions deemed ready and eligible for federal contributions. The government of Alberta would take an additional year to establish a regulatory and administrative structure acceptable to the federal government. Ontario needed more time and did not implement its plan until 31 October 1969.[33]

While this was the end of the story for Manningcare and Robartscare, it was not the end for the multi-payer program in British Columbia. The non-profit insurance carriers provided to their subscribers free coverage for physician services but, over time, they found it increasingly difficult to live off the thin profit margins provided through government subsidies. Moreover, members of the general public increasingly obtained comprehensive medical coverage through the BC government's public plan, the BCMP. By 1972, only two of the non-profit plans operated as licensed carriers of medicare insurance. Before the end of the decade, only the BCMP remained, and Bennettcare had officially morphed into a single-payer plan no different than any other provincial plans in Canada.[34] In 1992, many years after the BCMP had become the de facto single payer in British Columbia, the provincial government introduced a blanket prohibition on the sale of private health insurance for all medicare services (hospital and physician services).[35]

---

32 Gregory P Marchildon, "Canadian Medicare: Why History Matters" in Gregory P Marchildon, ed, *Making Medicare: New Perspectives on the History of Medicare in Canada* (Toronto: University of Toronto Press, 2012) 3 at 13–14.

33 Taylor, *Health Insurance and Canadian Public Policy*, *supra* note 11 at 375.

34 *Cambie Surgeries Corporation et al v Medical Services Commission of British Columbia et al (British Columbia Supreme Court)* (Expert affidavit of Gregory P Marchildon on the Evolution of Medicare in Canada at 55–7) (3 March 2014).

35 Section 39(1) of the *Medical and Health Services Act* stated that "[a] person must not provide, offer or enter into a contract of insurance with a resident for the payment, reimbursement or indemnification of all or part of the cost of services that would be benefits if performed by a practitioner," and section 39(3) stated that any such contract "is void." These sections were replicated in section 45 of the *Medicare Protection Act*, RSBC 1966, c 284. See Gregory P Marchildon, "Private Insurance for Medicare: Policy History and Trajectory in the Four Western Provinces" in Colleen M Flood, Kent Roach & Lorne Sossin, eds, *Access to Care, Access to Justice: The Legal Debate over Private Health Insurance in Canada* (Toronto:

User Charges and Extra-Billing

Similar to the question of single-payer government financing versus multi-payer public-private financing, the policy of user fees in health care has long polarized both researchers and decision makers, particularly in jurisdictions where there are significant populations that cannot afford even the most modest user fees easily affordable by the broad middle class in higher-income countries.[36] Although there is considerable evidence that user fees are, in fact, ineffective in reducing the *inappropriate* use of such services, the policy of user fees was advocated, and continues to be advocated, by governments, policy advisors, and think tanks.[37] Although there is evidence to support the logical proposition that the more patients have to pay directly for medical care, the less they will use it, the problem is that a portion of this reduction is for *needed* care as demonstrated in the multi-year, large-scale RAND Health Insurance Experiment and other studies.[38]

In other words, while user fees can save public plans in the short run, they can generate higher downstream costs for governments by discouraging necessary care—particularly preventative care—and result in poorer outcomes for those who have been

---

University of Toronto Press, 2005) 429 at 438. I was unable to determine the government's reasons for this change, although it is perhaps significant that the NDP, a party dedicated to preserving the single-payer and single-tier aspects of medicare, won a landslide electoral victory in October 1991.

36   Mylene Lagarde & Natasha Palmer, "The Impact of User Fees on Access to Health Services in Low- and Middle-Income Countries" (2011) 4 Cochrane Database Syst Rev, online: <https://doi.org/10.1002/14651858.CD009094>.

37   This literature is summarized by the Canadian Foundation for Healthcare Improvement: "Myth: User Fees Ensure Better Use of Health Services" (2012) Canadian Foundation for Healthcare Improvement Mythbusters, online (PDF): <https://www.cfhi-fcass.ca/sf-docs/default-source/mythbusters/Myth_User_Fees_EN.pdf?sfvrsn=47dfa44_0>.

38   For an exceptional empirical and conceptual summary, see Ray Robinson, "User Charges for Health Care" in Elias Mossialos et al, eds, *Funding Health Care: Options for Europe* (Buckingham, UK: Open University Press for the European Observatory on Health Systems and Policies, 2002). For a concise summary of the multi-million-dollar RAND Health Insurance Experiment on user fees conducted between 1971 and 1986, see Robert H Brook et al, "The Health Insurance Experiment: A Classic RAND Study Speaks to the Current Health Care Reform Debate" (2006) *RAND Research Brief*, online: <https://www.rand.org/pubs/research_briefs/RB9174.html>.

discouraged from seeking appropriate care at an earlier stage of their illness. Given that they prevent the poor from accessing needed services (while not blocking access for those able to pay), the presence of user fees invariably reduces equity of access. As discussed below, the debate over two types of user fees—particularly hospital and clinic user charges and physician extra-billing—has a long history in Canada. As a matter of legislative language in Canada, user fees are divided into two sub-groups: (1) user charges—facility fees imposed on patients by hospitals as well as diagnostic and surgical clinics, and (2) extra-billing—physician fees imposed on patients that are in addition to the rate set by provincial governments for medicare services.

Since the introduction of the *Canada Health Act* (*CHA*) in 1984, with its penalties for provinces who permit user fees and physician extra-billing by hospitals, clinics, or physicians,[39] the assumption has been that the Canadian model of medicare requires all provincial governments to provide first-dollar coverage on all *CHA*-insured services. In fact, in its negotiations with provinces leading up to national implementation of universal hospital and medical coverage in the mid- to late 1950s and 1960s, the federal government did not insist on the elimination of modest user fees as a condition of eligibility for federal cost sharing. This was despite that there is legislative language in both the *HIDSA*[40] of 1957 and the *Medical Care*

---

39   See *Canada Health Act*, RSC 1985, c C-6, ss 18 (extra-billing), 19 (user charges), 20 (deductions and process for extra-billing and user charges). The question of user fees is also partially addressed in the accessibility criterion of the *CHA* in section 12(1)(a): "In order to satisfy the criterion respecting accessibility, the health care insurance plan of a province must provide for insured health services on uniform terms and conditions and on a basis that does not impede or preclude, either directly or indirectly whether by charges made to insured persons or otherwise, reasonable access to those services by insured services." Of course, those arguing in favour of user fees have generally proposed modest user fees, with built-in exceptions, which they feel do not impede *reasonable* access to insured services, the same argument made by some provincial governments in the pre-*CHA* era of medicare.

40   See the definition of insured services in the *Hospital Insurance and Diagnostic Services Act*, SC, c 28, s 2(g) [emphasis added]: "'Insured services' means the inpatient services to which residents of a province are entitled under provincial law *without charge* except a general charge by way of premium or other amount not related to a specific service and except authorized charges... ."

Act[41] of 1966 which could have allowed the federal government to withdraw some of its cash transfers to those provincial governments with user fees for hospital, diagnostic, or physician services.

In the pre-*CHA* medicare era, the question of user fees, including physician extra-billing, sharply divided provincial governments, and this, from the earliest days of medicare. While the universal hospital- and medical-coverage plans in Saskatchewan originally excluded patient fees at the point of service, the plans in Alberta and British Columbia insisted on the use of such fees as a way to reduce what the governments in those provinces defined as "unnecessary" utilization of hospital or physician services, a position grudgingly accepted by the federal governments in the pre-*CHA* period.

The most interesting aspect of this early history is that Saskatchewan reversed its position on user fees after a change in government in the 1960s. In 1964, the provincial Liberal Party under Ross Thatcher defeated the social-democratic government that had been in power for two decades, in part because of the controversy surrounding the implementation of universal medical coverage. Although organized medicine and much of the business and professional community expected Thatcher to undo medicare once elected, the new premier kept the program in order to avoid a backlash from the large number of residents who supported the change.

However, fixated on the growing cost of medicare, Thatcher concluded that user fees were needed to reduce what he perceived as overutilization of health services. Although the problem was linked to an increase in the use of hospital and physician services, as well as major increases in the physician fee schedule, Thatcher felt that, unless residents paid a price at the point of delivery for these services, utilization would spiral out of control. As a consequence, in April 1968 his government introduced user fees. Hospitals were thereafter required to charge $2.50 per day for hospital stays. If a hospital stay extended beyond thirty days, hospitals charged patients

---

41 Section 4(1)(b) of the *Medical Care Act, 1966–1967*, c 64; RSC 1970, c M-8, has a provision that is almost identical to the accessibility criterion in the *CHA*: an eligible provincial is "operated so as to provide for the furnishing of insured services upon uniform terms and conditions to all insurable residents of the province, by the payment of amounts in respect of the cost of insured services … and that does not impede or preclude, either directly or indirectly whether by charges made to insured persons or otherwise, reasonable access to insured services by insured persons."

$1.50 for each day after the thirtieth day. Doctors were required to charge $1.50 for each office visit, and $2 for any out-of-office consultation, including those at the hospital (including emergency departments) or the patient's home.

Officially labelled "deterrent fees" by the Thatcher government, these user fees remained in place until August 1971, when they were eliminated by a newly elected New Democratic Party (NDP) government under leader Allan Blakeney. This is the only experiment in the application of user fees during the medicare era that has been extensively analyzed in Canada. The experiment was studied by two academic economists, R. Glen Beck from the University of Saskatchewan and John Horne from the University of Manitoba. Their time-series analysis spanned slightly more than a decade, from 1963, one year after the introduction of universal medical coverage, to 1977, six years after the user fees were eliminated.[42] Although there are numerous analyses of user fees in jurisdictions beyond Canada, including major analyses such as the RAND study in the United States, the very different institutional context of these user fees means that these studies are of limited application to the context of Canadian medicare. In contrast, the Beck and Horne study is directly relevant in assessing the likely impact of current policy proposals to introduce user fees in the Canadian context.

As stated above, it is only logical to expect that user fees, in the form of directly charging patient copayments at the point of service, will—holding everything else constant—reduce utilization. And, in fact, Beck and Horne found that the user fees reduced the total number of physician services per resident in Saskatchewan in the 1968–1971 period relative to the periods before (1963–1967) and after (1972–1977) the imposition of user fees.[43] The only question was whether user fees blocked at least as much needed care as unneeded care among those mainly lower-income residents who could not afford the fees.

Hospital services were a very different matter. Beck and Horne examined changes in the length of hospital stays for seventeen

---

42   RG Beck & JM Horne, "Utilization of Publicly Insured Health Services in Saskatchewan Before, During and After Copayment" (1980) 18:8 Med Care 787.

43   Relative to the average trend line from 1963 until 1977, total physicians' services per eligible Saskatchewan resident dropped 8.1 per cent in 1968, 10.5 per cent in 1969, 5.9 per cent in 1970, and 6.4 per cent in 1971. Beck & Horne, "Utilization of Publicly Insured Health Services," *supra* note 42 at 789.

discrete diagnostic and surgical procedures. For fifteen of these procedures, there was no appreciable change in length of hospital stay. However, even in these two outlier procedures, the shorter stays were not related to the imposition of user fees. In their words, there was no "compelling evidence that the introduction of user charges shortened lengths of stay or that the elimination of such charges increased lengths of stay."[44]

Although Beck and Horne did not speculate on why patient user fees produced at least some decline in utilization of outpatient physician services without a corresponding decline in diagnostic and hospital services, it is worthwhile suggesting a hypothesis. An individual has to make his or her own decision as to whether to see a physician. If individuals are unsure about whether it is necessary, they are more likely to wait to see if the condition or concern they are experiencing disappears if they are concerned about the cost of the visit.[45] Patients, however, do not make independent choices concerning diagnostic and hospital care, particularly in Canada, where physician referrals are generally required for diagnostic tests and assessments by specialists for hospital-based treatments. Primary-care physicians, including those in emergency departments, are much more in control of making such decisions than individuals, and few patients are prepared to refuse a test or undergo surgical treatment recommended or demanded by a doctor.[46]

---

44 The study compared patients who paid the user fees to a control group of patients not required to pay user fees: Beck & Horne, "Utilization of Publicly Insured Health Services," *supra* note 42 at 806.

45 Of course, all bets are off after the initial visit. If a physician recommends or insists that the individual come back for a follow-up visit, once again the individual is likely to defer to the physician's expertise rather than rely on his or her own judgement as to whether a follow-on appointment is necessary.

46 A typical patient pathway in Canada is described in Gregory P Marchildon, *Health Systems in Transition: Canada*, 2nd ed (Toronto: University of Toronto Press, 2013) at 103–04. There is some debate over the gatekeeping role in Canada. These differences are reflected in the literature. See, e.g., Benjamin TB Chan & Peter C Austin, "Patient, Physician and Community Factors Affecting Referrals to Specialists in Ontario, Canada" (2003) 41:4 Med Care 500 at 501 (gatekeeping role) and Marie-Dominique Beaulieu et al, "Family Practice: Professional Identity in Transition. A Case Study of Family Medicine in Canada" (2008) 67:7 Soc Sci & Med 1153 at 1155 (no gatekeeping role). Although there do not appear to be specific provincial laws formally stipulating a gatekeeping role, provincial governments have established strong financial incentives to encourage referrals, while administrative systems for hospitals and diagnostic clinics are designed

If this hypothesis is correct, then user fees would likely only be effective (in terms of reducing utilization) for primary medical care. The question then becomes one of whether the user fees are effective in preventing inappropriate care; and, if so, to what extent. In particular, is the amount of inappropriate care being blocked greater than the amount of appropriate care being prevented through user fees? This question cannot be answered definitely without understanding the level and distribution of income and wealth in any given society. However, if we accept that in a relatively prosperous country such as Canada, with a relatively large middle class, modest user fees would not likely reduce potentially inappropriate use of primary-care services by a large percentage of individuals because they would not be deterred by user fees. At the same time, these same fees would deter low-income individuals and families from seeking primary care—while some of this might be inappropriate care, a majority of this care could be quite needed and appropriate in the circumstances.

In summary, therefore, a regime of user fees for primary care in Canada might create the worst of both worlds: it would not significantly reduce overall utilization given the large percentage of the population that can easily afford modest user fees (the healthy, wealthy, and most of the middle class) while blocking the working poor (assuming those on social assistance are exempted from user fees), who, on average, are more likely to suffer from medical problems than higher-income Canadians. The minimal savings obtained through such a program, given the high cost of administration, including managing exemptions, would hardly seem worthwhile. Given this, the decision to impose user fees would have to be based on the idea of moral hazard and the ideological principle that only individual payment for medically necessary health care at the point of service is effective in generating sensible stewardship of resources.[47]

---

in ways that virtually require referrals by general practitioners/family-medicine specialists: Dominika Wranik, "Health Human Resource Planning in Canada: A Typology and its Application" (2008) 86 *Health Pol'y* 27 at 31.

47   Collége des économistes de la santé, "Utilisation Fees Imposed to Public Health Care Systems Users in Europe" (Roundtable report of presentations for the Commission on the Future of Health Care in Canada, Paris, 29 November 2001). The countries covered in this report included Germany, Austria, Switzerland, Belgium, the Netherlands, Italy, Demark, Norway, Sweden, Spain, and France. This report formed a key part of the evidence upon which the Romanow com-

One specific type of user fee—physician extra-billing—is currently the focus of a constitutional challenge by Cambie Surgeries Corporation, a private surgical clinic, in the Supreme Court of British Columbia. In this case, the plaintiff, as represented by Cambie and Dr. Brian Day, the founder and medical director of Cambie, alleges that prohibition against extra-billing in the *Medicare Protection Act*[48] in British Columbia means that a private facility is limited to charging "the fee that the doctor alone would be paid for providing the service in the public system." In the plaintiff's view, this restriction makes "it economically impossible for an enrolled doctor to perform any medically required services in a private facility, and also economically impossible for the private clinic to allow the doctor to do so."[49] The logic of the argument is questionable given the requirement that independently contracted doctors working within provincial medicare systems are also expected to pay their overhead costs, and this understanding is built into the fee schedules negotiated between provincial governments and provincial medical associations. While medicare physicians will generally use the surgical operating theatres in public hospitals, provincial governments have worked with opted-in physicians to cover the capital costs of niche surgical facilities in a number of provinces. The key is whether the physicians are working under the rules of medicare or not. If they are, they agree to respect the provincial laws on extra-billing. In most provinces, including British Columbia, physicians have the right to opt out of medicare and charge patients directly.[50]

The plaintiffs in the Cambie Surgeries case have argued that extra-billing in a parallel private system (with physicians allowed to practice in both sectors simultaneously) can, by providing patients

---

mission relied to recommend against the lifting of the Canada Health Act's restrictions on extra-billing and user charges in order to reduce utilization and thereby reduce cost or to raise new revenues. See Roy Romanow, *Building on Values: The Future of Health Care in Canada* (Ottawa: Commission on the Future of Health Care in Canada, 2002) at 28–30.

48 The prohibition on physician extra-billing is in ss 17(1)(b) and 18(3) of British Columbia's *Medicare Protection Act*, RSBC 1996, c 286.

49 Opening Statement of the Plaintiffs, Between Cambie Surgeries Corporation, Chris Chiavatti et al (plaintiffs), and Medical Services Commission of British Columbia, Minister of Health of British Columbia, and Attorney General of British Columbia, 6 September 2016, p. 92.

50 See Flood & Archibald, "The Illegality of Private Health Care in Canada," *supra* note 4.

who can afford to pay the extra fee, reduce the pressure on the public system and reduce wait times. Surgical wait times are mainly associated with elective surgical procedures such as cataract surgeries and orthopaedic hip and knee procedures. Manitoba actually provides an example of the impact of extra-billing in the case of cataract surgeries. In that province, cataract surgery was available in both the public and private systems for most of the 1990s, with patients being required to pay out of pocket for the extra fee if they chose to go to a private clinic, a practice discontinued by the NDP government under Premier Gary Doer first elected in 1999. In a study of wait times during the period when extra-billing was permitted, the Manitoba Centre of Health Policy "found that waiting times for cataract surgery in the public sector were the longest for surgeons who also had a private practice."[51] While the study could not determine the precise reason for this outcome, the authors could still conclude that a parallel private system "does not result in shorter waits in the public sector."[52]

Conclusion

The current debate on the limited private financing of medicare in Canada has long historical roots. Single-payer financing moved Canada from an insurance-based model of health care to a public-service model of health care. Those arguing in favour of allowing the purchase of private health insurance for medicare services want a return to an insurance-based approach, with multiple, private insurers so that individuals have choice in the depth and breadth of coverage as well as in the provision of services.[53] However, if this is permitted, it will raise all the equity issues that existed before medicare and will ultimately create barriers to access for the poorer members of society, likely the working poor if governments continued to protect those individuals receiving social assistance. In addition, two-tier public and private insurance coverage will inevitably lead to two tiers of services; that is, public services for those residents

---

51   Carolyn DeCoster, Leonard MacWilliam & Randy Walid, *Waiting Times for Surgery: 1997/98 and 1998/99 Update* (Winnipeg: Manitoba Centre for Health Policy and Evaluation, 2000), at 35.

52   *Ibid* at 35.

53   See Åke Blomqvist & Colin Busby, *Rethinking Canada's Unbalanced Mix of Public and Private Healthcare: Insights from Abroad* (Toronto: CD Howe Institute, 2015).

limited to medicare coverage and a private tier of services for those with private insurance coverage or the ability to pay out of pocket.

Those arguing in favour of the continuation of single-payer financing emphasize the right of access by all citizens to the same health coverage. While the federal government does not directly impose a single-payer model on provincial governments—and historically permitted at least one version of a multi-payer approach—it will no longer be possible for Ottawa to insist that all provincial medicare coverage be on "uniform terms and conditions" as currently defined under the *Canada Health Act*. Although the government of British Columbia managed its multi-payer program for a few years, it did so under regulations that forced all non-profit carriers to offer identical coverage packages. This constrained profitability to the point that all private insurers eventually exited the sector to focus on more profitable supplementary health insurance.

User fees on patients are an additional way to inject private finance into medicare. Before the *Canada Health Act*, user fees, either in the form of hospital user charges or physician extra-billing, were a regular part of medicare in provinces such as British Columbia, Alberta, and Ontario. However, from an analytical standpoint, the most interesting user-fee experience was in Saskatchewan from 1968 until 1971. The results of this experiment demonstrated the ineffectiveness of hospital user charges in reducing utilization. Physician extra-billing did reduce the utilization of primary care; these user fees just as likely blocked care that was needed as care that was not necessarily required. As a result, physician extra-billing, while it may have saved the provincial government some money in the short term, would likely have increased the downstream costs due to lack of adequate upstream prevention and treatment. Finally, all user fees have negative equity implications. Even modest user fees, while not a serious deterrent for middle- and high-income earners, can prevent low-income individuals from seeking needed care. Extra-billing can also drive up physician remuneration in wealthier, urbanized areas more generally, making it even more difficult for smaller centres, much less rural and remote communities, to attract physicians. For all of these reasons, a policy that once again permits physician extra-billing would be a regressive step.

CHAPTER 2

Chaoulli to *Cambie*:
Charter Challenges to the Regulation
of Private Care

Martha Jackman

Unlike the *Universal Declaration of Human Rights*,[1] the *International Covenant on Economic, Social and Cultural Rights*,[2] and many other twentieth-century constitutions,[3] the *Canadian Charter of Rights and Freedoms*[4] does not contain an explicit right to health or to health care services. Instead, section 7 of the *Charter* guarantees everyone in Canada "the right to life, liberty and security of the person and the right not to be deprived thereof except in accordance with the principles of fundamental justice." Section 15 of the *Charter* promises every individual "the equal protection and equal benefit of the law without discrimination."[5] It is these two *Charter* rights that

---

1   *Universal Declaration of Human Rights*, GA Res 217A (III), UNGAOR, 3rd Sess, Supp No 13, Un Doc A/810 (1948) 71, art 25(1).

2   *International Covenant on Economic, Social and Cultural Rights*, 16 December 1966, Can TS 1976 No 46 (entered into force 3 January 1976, accession by Canada 19 May 1976) [*ICESCR*].

3   See generally Colleen M Flood & Aeyal Gross, eds, *The Right to Health at the Public/Private Divide: A Global Comparative Study* (New York: Cambridge University Press, 2014).

4   *Canadian Charter of Rights and Freedoms*, Part I of the *Constitution Act, 1982*, being Schedule B to the *Canada Act 1982* (UK), 1982, c 11 [*Charter*].

5   For a more in-depth discussion of sections 7 and 15 in the health care context, see Martha Jackman, "*Charter* Review of Health Care Access" in Joanna Erdman, Vanessa Gruben & Erin Nelson, eds, *Canadian Health Law and Policy*, 5th ed (Markham: LexisNexis Canada, 2017) 71 [Jackman, "*Charter* Review"];

Dr. Brian Day has invoked in his constitutional challenge to British Columbia's single-payer health care system in *Cambie Surgeries Corporation v British Columbia (Attorney General) (Cambie)*.[6] Dr. Day is arguing, on behalf of Cambie Surgeries Corporation, the Specialist Referral Clinic (Vancouver) Inc. (SRC), and four individual plaintiffs, that restrictions on private health care and funding in British Columbia are unconstitutional.[7] Like the medicare regimes in most other provinces, the impugned provisions of British Columbia's *Medicare Protection Act*[8] prohibit duplicative private insurance and physician dual practice, and cap private medical fees to the level of public fees in order to ensure compliance with the conditions of the *Canada Health Act*.[9]

The arguments in *Cambie* draw directly on the Supreme Court of Canada's highly criticized 2005 decision in *Chaoulli v Québec*

Martha Jackman, "The Future of Health Care Accountability: A Human Rights Approach" (2015–2016) 47 Ottawa L Rev 437 [Jackman, "Health Care Accountability"]; Martha Jackman, "Health Care and Equality: Is There a Cure?" (2007) 15 Health LJ 87.

6   *Cambie Surgeries v British Columbia (Medical Services Commission)*, (2015) Vancouver S090663 [*Cambie*]. In his interlocutory ruling in *Cambie Surgeries v British Columbia (Medical Services Commission)* 2015 BCSC 2169 at paras 14–28, Chief Justice Cullen provides a summary of the proceedings in the case to that date. A complete timeline and links to key legal documents in the *Cambie* case has been compiled by the BC Health Coalition, online: <http://savemedicare-bchealthcoalition.nationbuilder.com/court-documents>. See also Colleen Fuller, *Cambie Corp. Goes to Court: The Legal Assault on Universal Health Care* (Ottawa: Canadian Centre for Policy Alternatives, April 2015) [Fuller, *Cambie Goes to Court*].

7   *Cambie* (Fourth Amended Notice of Civil Claim) [*Cambie* (Civil Claim)]; *Cambie* (Plaintiffs' Opening Statement of the Plaintiffs, 6 September 2016) [*Cambie* (Plaintiffs' Opening Statement)].

8   *Medicare Protection Act*, RSBC 1996, c 286 [*MPA*], s 17(1), 13(6).

9   *Canada Health Act*, RSC 1985 C-6; *Cambie*, Statement of Defence at paras 66–71 [*Cambie* (Defence)]; *Cambie* (Opening Statement of the Defendants) at 10–21 [*Cambie* (Defendants' Opening Statement)]; Cambie (Opening Statement of the Coalition Interveners) at para 13 [*Cambie* (BC Physicians and Patients Coalition Opening Statement)]. See generally Collen M Flood & Bryan Thomas, "Modernizing the Canada Health Act" (2017) 39 Dal LJ 397; William Lahey, "Medicare and the Law: Contours of an Evolving Relationship" in Jocelyn Downie, Tim Caulfield & Colleen M Flood, eds, *Canadian Health Law and Policy* (Markham: LexisNexis, 2011) 43; Colleen M Flood & Tom Archibald, "The Illegality of Private Health Care in Canada" (2001) 61 CMAJ 825.

(Attorney General).[10] Four of seven justices ruled in *Chaoulli*[11] that Quebec's prohibition on private health insurance violated the right to life, personal security, and inviolability, guaranteed under section 1 of Quebec's *Charter of Human Rights and Freedoms.*[12] Three justices found that, by preventing timely access to medical treatment, limits on private insurance under the *Health Insurance Act*[13] and *Hospital Insurance Act*[14] also violated section 7 of the *Canadian Charter.*[15] In contrast, the three dissenting justices in *Chaoulli* concluded that the ban on private insurance was "a rational consequence of Quebec's commitment to the goals and objectives of the *Canada Health Act.*"[16]

In this chapter, I consider the significance of the *Chaoulli* decision for the outcome of the constitutional challenge in the *Cambie* case. The first part summarizes the *Charter* arguments advanced by the plaintiffs in *Cambie.* In the second part, I briefly review the lower and Supreme Court of Canada decisions in *Chaoulli.* In the third and fourth parts I focus on two aspects of the *Chaoulli* decision that are of particular significance for the outcome of the *Cambie* challenge: first, the courts' approach to evidence about private health care funding; second, their attitude toward the substantive equality objectives of

---

10　*Chaoulli v Québec (Attorney General)*, 2005 SCC 35 [*Chaoulli* (SCC)]; rev'g [2002] RJQ 1205 (CA) [*Chaoulli* CA]; aff'g [2000] RJQ 786 (SC) [*Chaoulli* (SC)]. For critical commentary on the *Chaoulli* case, see, e.g., Marie-Claude Prémont, "L'affaire *Chaoulli* et le système de santé du Québec: cherchez l'erreur, cherchez la raison" (2006) 51 McGill LJ 167 [Prémont, "Cherchez l'erreur"]; Bruce Porter, "A Right to Health Care in Canada—Only if You Can Pay for it" (2005) 6:4 ESR Rev 8 [Porter, "Right to Health Care"]; Jeff A King, "Constitutional Rights and Social Welfare: A Comment on the Canadian *Chaoulli* Health Care Decision" (2006) 69:4 MLR 619; Martha Jackman, "'The Last Line of Defence for [Which?] Citizens': Accountability, Equality and the Right to Health in *Chaoulli*" (2006) 44 Osgoode Hall LJ 349 [Jackman, "Last Line of Defence"]; Robert G Evans, "Baneful Legacy: Medicare and Mr. Trudeau" (2005) 1:1 Healthcare Pol'y 20; Colleen M Flood, Kent Roach & Lorne Sossin, eds, *Access to Care, Access to Justice: The Legal Debate Over Private Health Insurance in Canada* (Toronto: University of Toronto Press, 2005) [Flood, *Access to Care*].

11　*Chaoulli* (SCC), *supra* note 10 at para 101 (per Deschamps J), para 159 (per McLachlin CJ, Major & Bastarache JJ).

12　*Charter of Human Rights and Freedoms*, RSQ c C-12 [Quebec *Charter*].

13　*Health Insurance Act*, RSQ, c A-29, s 15 [*Health Insurance Act*].

14　*Hospital Insurance Act*, RSQ, c A-28, s 11 [*Hospital Insurance Act*].

15　*Chaoulli* (SCC), *supra* note 10 at paras 123–124, 159 (per McLachlin CJ, Major & Bastarache JJ).

16　*Ibid* at para 164 (per Binnie, LeBel & Fish JJ).

the single-payer system. In conclusion I suggest that, even if this were desirable, governments and the health policy community can no longer maintain that wait times and other systemic barriers to care are beyond the purview of the courts. I contend that those seeking to defend medicare must instead advocate for a reading of the *Charter* that reinforces rather than undermines the publicly funded system and the domestic and international human rights principles it reflects.

1. The *Cambie* Challenge

In December 2008, Mariël Schooff and four other BC patients filed a petition in the BC Supreme Court[17] alleging that the BC Medical Services Commission and the provincial Ministry of Health were failing to enforce the provincial *Medicare Protection Act* (*MPA*) prohibitions against direct and extra-billing for medically required services.[18] The petitioners were among thirty patients who had complained to the commission that Cambie Surgery and the SRC had direct-billed them amounts ranging from $400 to $17,000 between 2001 and 2007 for health care services that were included as insured benefits under the *MPA*.[19] The *Schooff* petition, which sought an order of *mandamus* compelling the commission and the ministry to enforce the *MPA*, followed an unsuccessful attempt by the BC Nurses' Union to obtain public interest standing to bring a similar legal claim.[20]

A year and a half earlier, in May 2007, the commission had written to Vancouver orthopedic surgeon Dr. Brian Day about possible extra-billing at Cambie Surgery and SRC, of which Dr. Day is the president.[21] In September 2008, the commission advised Dr. Day it would be conducting an audit of both clinics.[22] In response, in January 2009, Cambie Surgery, SRC, and several other private Vancouver clinics launched an action against the commission, the minister of health, and the attorney general of British Columbia,

---

17 *Schooff v Medical Services Commission*, 2009 BCSC 1596 [*Schooff*].

18 *Ibid* at paras 1–2.

19 *Ibid* at para 51; *Canadian Independent Medical Clinics Assn. v British Columbia (Medical Services Commission)*, [2010] BCJ 1323 at para 5.

20 *British Columbia Nurses' Union v British Columbia (Attorney General)*, 2008 BCSC 321; *Canadian Independent Medical Clinics Assn. v British Columbia (Medical Services Commission)*, 2010 BCSC 927 at para 7.

21 *Schoof, supra* note 17 at para 45; *Cambie* (Defence), *supra* note 9 at paras 49–59.

22 *Schoof, supra* note 17 at para 54; *Cambie* (Defence), *supra* note 9 at para 57.

seeking to have sections 14, 17, 18, and 45 of the *MPA* declared unconstitutional.[23] The impugned provisions prohibit extra-billing, user charges, dual practice, and duplicative private health insurance, and impose fee caps for physicians who have opted out of the public system.[24] When the Ministry of Health's audit of Cambie Surgery and SRC finally took place, in 2012, the auditors reported "limited cooperation from the President, management and staff"[25] of the two clinics, and "significant evidence" of "frequent and recurring" extra-billing, direct billing, double billing, and charges by opted-out physicians exceeding the MPA fee caps, "contrary to the [*Medicare Protection*] *Act*."[26]

Dr. Day and his legal counsel have since admitted that Cambie Surgery and SRC are engaging in illegal billing practices.[27] Their defence is that provisions of the *MPA* prohibiting such practices are unconstitutional and should be struck.[28] In their opening statement at the 6 September 2016, hearing on the substance of the *Cambie* claim, the plaintiffs start from the position that there is "absolutely no doubt that people in the province are being harmed every day by the inability of our public health care system to provide timely medical services."[29] The plaintiffs point to the example of Walid Khalfallah, a thirteen-year-old boy suffering from scoliosis/kyphosis who, fourteen months after an urgent referral by his pediatrician, met with an orthopaedic surgeon at the BC Children's Hospital only to be advised there was a two-year wait for the surgery he needed.[30] While Khalfallah's surgery was ultimately scheduled for

---

23   *Schoof, supra* note 17 at paras 1–12; Fuller, *Cambie Goes to Court, supra* note 6 at 14–17.

24   *Schoof, supra* note 17, Appendix A; *Cambie* (Response to Fourth Amended Civil Claim) at paras 26–29 [*Cambie* (Response to Amended Claim)]; *Cambie* (Defendants' Opening Statement), *supra* note 9 at 15–18.

25   Ministry of Health, Billing Integrity Program, Audit and Investigations Branch, *Specialist Referral Clinic (Vancouver) Inc. and Cambie Surgeries Corporation Audit Report* (June 2012) at 5.

26   Ministry of Health, Billing Integrity Program, *Audit and Investigations Branch, Specialist Referral Clinic (Vancouver) Inc. and Cambie Surgeries Corporation Audit Report* (June 2012) at 4; Fuller, *Cambie Goes to Court, supra* note 6 at 12–13.

27   *Schoof, supra* note 17 at paras 63–64; *Cambie, supra* note 6 at para 24.

28   *Schoof, supra* note 17 at para 4; *Cambie* (Civil Claim), *supra* note 7 at para 98; *Cambie* (Plaintiffs' Opening Statement)], *supra* note 7 at para 1.

29   *Cambie* (Plaintiffs' Opening Statement), *supra* note 7 at para 5.

30   *Cambie* (Civil Claim), *supra* note 7 at paras 54–56.

November 2011, the family decided to proceed with an earlier offer of free surgical care at the Shriners Hospital for Children in Spokane, Washington.[31] Due to complications during that surgery, which took place in January 2012, Khalfallah was left a paraplegic.[32]

Khalfallah's experience is contrasted to that of the three other individual plaintiffs in the case who, the *Cambie* claim alleges, obtained timely private care that "enabled them to avoid further harm from waiting for care in the public system."[33] For example, the *Cambie* claim describes the positive outcome for fourteen-year-old Chris Chiavatti who, in January 2009, suffered a knee injury in Grade 9 physical-education class.[34] At the end of October 2009, with Chiavetti still on a waiting list for a diagnostic consultation within the public system, his family booked an appointment with Dr. Day at the SRC.[35] Based on a clinical evaluation and an MRI done at the BC Children's Hospital, Dr. Day diagnosed a tear in Chiavetti's meniscus and, in mid-November 2009, performed day surgery at the SRC.[36] Chiavetti underwent physiotherapy for several weeks and returned to normal functioning within one month.[37] According to the *Cambie* claim, able to sleep, engage in extra-curricular activities, and focus on his studies again, Chiavetti's "academic achievements helped him to obtain an offer for placement at Yale University."[38]

Against the backdrop of these individual cases, the *Cambie* claim contends that the BC government must ration care to meet its health care budget, resulting in lengthy wait lists.[39] It characterizes private care as "a much needed safety valve"[40] for those who would otherwise be suffering physical and psychological harm waiting for care in the public system. The plaintiffs argue that, by restricting BC patients' ability to make decisions about their bodily integrity, to take steps to alleviate their pain and suffering, and to ensure their health and survival through timely access to private

---

31   *Ibid* at paras 60–63.
32   *Ibid* at para 64.
33   *Ibid* at para 17.
34   *Ibid* at paras 17–23.
35   *Ibid* at para 23.
36   *Ibid* at para 23.
37   *Ibid* at para 25.
38   *Ibid* at para 25.
39   *Cambie* (Plaintiffs' Opening Statement), *supra* note 7 at paras 5–6, 224–227, 292.
40   *Ibid* at para 19.

care, the impugned provisions of the *MPA* violate section 7 of the *Charter*.[41] They contend that allowing private care would improve rather than harm the public system, rendering the prohibitions under the *MPA* arbitrary and, therefore, fundamentally unjust.[42] In their submission:

> The prohibition or severe restriction on access to private medical care for ordinary citizens by the operation of the ... [*MPA*] are not necessary or related to the objective of the Government in preserving a publicly managed health care system in which individual access to necessary medical health care is based on need and not on an individual's ability to pay ... There are options available which allow maintaining a vigorous public health system supported by private health services which, together, would allow the provision of reasonable health care within a reasonable time, and thus ensure the protection of *Charter* rights of all British Columbians.[43]

The plaintiffs further argue that regulatory exemptions for certain classes of patients,[44] such as those being treated for workplace injuries under the province's workers' compensation regime, are further proof that the *MPA* restrictions on private insurance and funding are not only arbitrary but discriminatory, based on disability and age, contrary to section 15 of the *Charter*,[45] and should be struck down.[46]

In their response to the *Cambie* claim, the Medical Services Commission, the Ministry of Health, and the attorney general of British Columbia reject the plaintiffs' arguments that British Columbia's prohibitions on private care violate sections 7[47] or 15[48] of the *Charter*. They contend that the "purpose of the *Act* is to preserve a publicly managed and fiscally sustainable health care system for British Columbia in which access to necessary medical care is based

---

41   *Cambie* (Civil Claim), *supra* note 7 at paras 103–117.
42   *Ibid* at paras 118–131.
43   *Ibid* at paras 119–120.
44   *Ibid* at para 86.
45   *Ibid* at paras 141–145.
46   *Ibid* at paras 98–99.
47   *Cambie* (Response to Further Amended Civil Claim) at Part 3 paras 3–4 [*Cambie* (Response)].
48   *Ibid* at Part 3 paras 19–23.

on need and not an individual's ability to pay."[49] "Were the Plaintiffs granted the relief they seek," the defendants warn,

> this would divert into a private system, available only to some, the resources needed to continue the effort to provide timely care for all in British Columbia's public health care system. It would negate much of what has been accomplished over many years creating and continually working to improve a public health care system supported by all according to their means and providing needed care to all residents in the province without regard wither to means or to medical history.[50]

In their intervention in the case, the BC Physicians and Patients Coalition, representing two patients and two physicians, the BC Health Coalition, and Canadian Doctors for Medicare, also contest the *Cambie* plaintiffs' claims about the consequences of striking down restrictions on private funding. Pointing out that "the *most vulnerable* beneficiaries of BC's health care system ... would be disproportionately burdened by any weakening of the publicly funded health care system that would likely result from the development of a parallel private tier,"[51] the coalition argues that:

> Many of [the Coalition's] members would face insurmountable health and income barriers to accessing the kind of privately financed health care system the plaintiffs seek to impose. They are also very concerned that the shift to a parallel for-profit private system would reduce resources and capacity in the public health care system to provide for patients, would establish harmful incentives for longer wait time in the public system, and would make it even more difficult to implement the necessary reforms we need to improve the public system.[52]

---

49 *Cambie* (Response to Amended Claim), *supra* note 24 at para 11; *Cambie* (Response), *supra* note 47 at Part 3 para 34.
50 *Cambie* (Defendants' Opening Statement), *supra* note 9 at 1.
51 *Cambie* (BC Physicians and Patients Coalition Opening Statement), *supra* note 9 at para 5.
52 *Ibid* at para 10.

2. The *Chaoulli* Decision

As suggested at the outset of the paper, the *Charter* challenge being pursued by Dr. Day in the *Cambie* case draws directly on the reasoning and outcome in the 2005 *Chaoulli* case.[53] The appellants in *Chaoulli*,[54] Georges Zéliotis, an elderly patient who faced delays obtaining two hip replacements in the mid-1990s, and Dr. Jacques Chaoulli, a Montreal-area physician unable to obtain Quebec Ministry of Health approval for a twenty-four-hour ambulance service, a twenty-four-hour house-call service, and a private not-for-profit hospital, challenged the prohibition on private insurance under section 15 of Quebec's *Health Insurance Act*[55] and section 11 of the province's *Hospital Insurance Act*.[56] The appellants argued that, given serious delays within the publicly funded system, the ban on private health insurance put them at risk of significant physical and psychological harm, and even death, thereby violating their Quebec and *Canadian Charter* rights.[57]

At trial,[58] Quebec Superior Court Justice Piché accepted the appellants' claim that health care waiting lists in the province were too long. In her view, "même si ce n'est pas toujours une question de vie ou de mort, tous les citoyens ont droit à recevoir les soins dont ils ont besoin, et ce, dans les meilleurs délais."[59] However, Justice Piché concluded that Quebec's prohibition on private insurance was necessary to protect the publicly funded system.[60] In her words: "Les dispositions attaquées visent à garantir un accès aux soins de santé qui est égal et adéquat pour tous les Québécois ... et, de ce fait il est clair qu'il n'y a pas de conflit avec les valeurs générales véhiculées par la Charte canadienne ou de la Charte québécoise des droits et

53 The following discussion of the *Chaoulli* case draws on Jackman, "Last Line of Defence"; Martha Jackman, "Misdiagnosis or Cure? *Charter* Review of the Health Care System" in Colleen M Flood, ed, *Just Medicare: What's In, What's Out, How We Decide* (Toronto: University of Toronto Press, 2006) 58.
54 *Chaoulli* (SC), *supra* note 10 at paras 19–39; *Chaoulli* (SCC), *supra* note 10 at para 5.
55 *Health Insurance Act, supra* note 13.
56 *Hospital Insurance Act, supra* note 14.
57 *Chaoulli* (SC), *supra* note 10 at paras 193–196; *Chaoulli* (SCC), *supra* note 10 at para 5.
58 An unofficial edited English-language translation of Justice Piché's decision can be found in Flood, *Access to Care, supra* note 10 Appendix A at 531–558.
59 *Chaoulli* (SC) *supra* note 10 at para 50 ("Even if it isn't always a question of life or death, all citizens have the right to receive the care they need, and within the shortest possible time." [author's translation]).
60 *Ibid* at para 258.

libertés."[61] On that basis, Justice Piché decided that the ban on private
insurance respected section 7 principles of fundamental justice[62] and
section 15 equality rights guarantees,[63] as well as being justifiable
under section 1 of the *Charter*.[64]

Justice Piché's decision was upheld by the Quebec Court of
Appeal in three concurring judgments.[65] Justice Forget agreed with
Justice Piché's section 7 analysis.[66] In Justice Brossard's view, having
failed to show that restrictions on private insurance had imperilled
their rights to life or health, the appellants' section 7 claim could not
succeed.[67] Justice Delisle found that, while access to a publicly funded
health care system was a fundamental right, the purely economic
right to contract for private insurance being claimed by the appellants
was not protected under section 7.[68] As he put it:

> Il ne faut pas inverser les principes en jeu pour, ainsi, rendre
> essentiel un droit économique accessoire auquel, par ailleurs,
> les gens financièrement défavorisés n'auraient pas accès. Le
> droit fondamental en cause est celui de fournir à tous un régime
> public de protection de la santé, que les défenses édictées par les
> articles [contestés] ont pour but de sauvegarder.[69]

---

61   *Ibid* at para 260 ("The impugned provisions are designed to guarantee equal and
      adequate access to health care for all Quebecers ... and it is therefore evident
      there is no conflict with the general values promoted by the *Canadian Charter*
      or by the Quebec *Charter of Rights and Freedoms*" [author's translation]).

62   *Ibid* at para 267.

63   *Ibid* at paras 305–306.

64   *Ibid* at para 268. Section 1 provides that: "The Canadian Charter of Rights and
      Freedoms guarantees the rights and freedoms set out in it subject only to such
      reasonable limits prescribed by law as can be demonstrably justified in a free
      and democratic society."

65   *Chaoulli* (CA), *supra* note 10 at para 5. (An unofficial edited English-language
      translation of the Court of Appeal decision can be found in Flood, *Access to Care*,
      supra note 10 Appendix B at 559–564.)

66   *Ibid* at paras 55, 60.

67   *Ibid* at para 66.

68   *Ibid* at para 25.

69   *Ibid* at para 25 ("The principles at issue must not be inverted so as to make an
      ancillary economic right essential, and further, one to which economically
      disadvantaged people would not have access. The fundamental right at issue
      is that of providing a public health protection system to all, a right which the
      prohibitions set out under the abovementioned provisions are designed to
      safeguard." [author's translation]).

On appeal to the Supreme Court of Canada, the majority of the court overturned the trial and Court of Appeal judgments in a 4–3 split decision.[70] Limiting her analysis to the Quebec *Charter*, Justice Deschamps accepted the appellants' argument that the prohibition on private insurance, and the resulting limits on patients' ability to obtain private care, violated the right to "life," "personal security," and "inviolability" under section 1 of the Quebec *Charter*,[71] and were not in accordance with "democratic values, public order and the general well-being of the citizens of Québec" under section 9.1 of the Quebec *Charter*.[72] To the question "whether Québeckers who are prepared to spend money to get access to health care that is, in practice, not accessible in the public system because of waiting lists may be validly prevented from doing so by the state,"[73] Justice Deschamps's answer was no.[74] As she declared: "Governments have promised on numerous occasions to find a solution to the problem of waiting lists. Given the tendency to focus the debate on a sociopolitical philosophy, it seems that governments have lost sight of the urgency of taking concrete action. The courts are therefore the last line of defence for citizens."[75] The appropriate judicial response, she concluded, was to strike down the ban on private insurance.[76]

Chief Justice McLachlin and Justices Major and Bastarache agreed with Justice Deschamps ruling under the Quebec *Charter*. They also found that "prohibiting health insurance that would permit ordinary Canadians to access health care, in circumstances where the government is failing to deliver health care in a reasonable manner, thereby increasing the risk of complications and death" interfered with the right to life and security of the person under section 7 of the *Canadian Charter*.[77] The majority concluded that, since other OECD countries with multi-payer systems "have successfully delivered to their citizens medical services that are superior to and more

---

70 *Chaoulli* (SCC), *supra* note 10 at para 101, per Deschamps J; at para 159, per McLachlin CJ, Major & Bastarache JJ; at para 279, per Binnie, LeBel & Fish JJ, dissenting.

71 Quebec *Charter*, *supra* note 12; *Chaoulli* (SCC), *supra* note 10 at para 45.

72 *Chaoulli* (SCC) *supra* note 10 at para 99.

73 *Ibid* at para 4.

74 *Ibid* at para 100.

75 *Ibid* at para 96.

76 *Ibid* at para 100.

77 *Ibid* at para 124.

affordable than the services that are presently available in Canada,"[78] the prohibition on private insurance was an arbitrary measure that did not accord with section 7 principles of fundamental justice[79] and that could not be justified under section 1 of the *Charter*.[80]

In their dissenting opinion, Justices Binnie, LeBel and Fish noted that section 7 does not protect the right to practice medicine or to deliver private health care services.[81] But they concurred with the majority's view that Quebec's prohibition on private insurance was "capable, at least in the cases of <u>some</u> individuals on <u>some</u> occasions, of putting at risk their life or security of the person."[82] Given the objectives of the single-payer system, the dissenting justices agreed with Justice Piché that Quebec's ban on private insurance was a rational measure.[83] As they explained: "The consequences of a quasi-unlimited demand for health care coupled with limited resources, be they public or private is to ration services ... In a public system founded on the values of equity, solidarity and collective responsibility, rationing occurs on the basis of clinical need rather than wealth and social status."[84] In concluding that the impugned provisions were demonstrably justified under both the Canadian and Quebec charters, the minority cautioned that

> Those who seek private health insurance are those who can afford it and can qualify for it ... They are differentiated from the general population, not by their health problems, which are found in every group in society, but by their income status. We share the view of Dickson C.J. that the *Charter* should not become an instrument to be used by the wealthy to "roll back" the benefits of a legislative scheme that helps the poorer members of society.[85]

---

78   *Ibid* at para 140.
79   *Ibid* at paras 152–153.
80   *Ibid* at paras 154–159.
81   *Ibid* at para 202, per Binnie J.
82   *Ibid* at para 200 [emphasis in original].
83   *Ibid* at paras 242, 256.
84   *Ibid* at paras 221, 223.
85   *Ibid* at para 274.

3. The Evidence Relating to Private Funding

With the retirement of Chief Justice McLachlin, none of the Supreme Court justices who participated in *Chaoulli* remain on the court. Unlike Dr. Chaoulli's challenge, which flew largely under the radar outside Quebec until it reached the Supreme Court of Canada, *Cambie* is being litigated in English and, thanks to ongoing publicity by pro-medicare groups such as the BC Health Coalition[86] and Canadian Doctors for Medicare,[87] and Dr. Day's own efforts,[88] the case has attracted widespread attention in and outside the province. The government defendants in *Cambie* have underscored the fact that the evidence in *Chaoulli* related to the health care system in Quebec almost twenty years ago,[89] and that the Supreme Court's section 7 jurisprudence has also evolved in the intervening period. In their opening statement in *Cambie*, the defendants contend that "the decision in *Chaoulli* provides the backdrop to the present case, but that case involved a significantly different challenge to a different legislative scheme in the context of a very different approach by government to the problems of wait times, and it was decided on the basis of a very different *Charter*."[90]

This attempt to distinguish *Chaoulli* draws support from the Alberta Court of Appeal's 2015 decision in *Allen v Alberta*.[91] The appellant in that case was in severe pain after injuring his knee and lower back playing hockey. Facing a possible two-year wait in Alberta, he underwent surgery in Montana at a cost of over $77,000.[92] Relying on *Chaoulli*, he applied for a declaration that Alberta's ban on private health insurance violated section 7 of the *Charter*.[93] The

---

86   "The Legal Attack on Public Health Care" (2017), online: *BC Health Coalition* <www.bchealthcoalition.ca/what-we-do/protect-medicare/case-backgound>.

87   "Cambie Trial: Frequently Asked Questions," online: *Canadian Doctors for Medicare* <www.canadiandoctorsformedicare.ca/Table/Cambie-Trial/>.

88   "Former BC Premier Campbell believes more private access will improve health outcomes" (2016), online: *Dr. Brian Day* <www.brianday.ca/>.

89   *Cambie* (Defendants' Opening Statement), *supra* note 9 at 54.

90   *Ibid* at 47.

91   *Allen v Alberta*, 2014 ABQB 184 [*Allen* (QB)], aff'd *Allen v Alberta*, 2015 ABCA 277 [*Allen* (CA)]. The *Allen* case was supported by Alberta's Justice Centre for Constitutional Freedoms. See "Access to Health Care: Darcy Aleen's Story" (2013), online: *Justice Centre for Constitutional Freedoms* <www.jccf.ca/access-to-health-care-darcy-allens-story/>.

92   *Allen* (QB), *supra* note 91 at paras 2–21; *Allen* (CA), *supra* note 91 at paras 2–7.

93   *Allen* (QB), *supra* note 91 at para 39; *Allen* (CA), *supra* note 91 at para 7.

Alberta Court of Queen's Bench dismissed the appellant's claim on the grounds he had failed to provide any evidence that the ban on private insurance created or exacerbated wait times or impeded access to care.[94] With reference to *Chaoulli*, Justice Jeffrey affirmed: "I am not bound to apply a conclusion of mixed fact and law from a Supreme Court of Canada case to another case that merely shares a similar allegation but offers no evidence."[95] The Court of Appeal agreed with Justice Jeffrey's analysis. Justice Slatter explained:

> The result in *Chaoulli* is dependent on the factual findings. Notwithstanding the Supreme Court's usual insistence on deference to fact findings of trial judges, the majority of the court came to the opposite conclusion on the fundamental issue of the potential impact of private insurance on the public system. The existence, length and reasonableness of wait times in Québec were also a key to the decision. It cannot be said that the same factors are so obviously present in Alberta in 2015 that *Chaoulli* can be applied.[96]

Notwithstanding significant differences in factual and doctrinal context, two aspects of the *Chaoulli* case remain particularly relevant to the *Cambie* claim and its likelihood of success. The first, as the decision in *Allen v Alberta* illustrates, is the courts' approach to the evidence relating to the implications for the single-payer system of allowing private funding, including as a solution to wait times for care. As outlined below, Justice Piché's findings at trial and Justice Deschamps and Chief Justice McLachlin's reading of the same evidence at the Supreme Court produced irreconcilable differences in reasoning and outcomes in *Chaoulli*, with major consequences for the publicly funded system in Quebec.[97]

Justice Piché began her lengthy review of the evidence in *Chaoulli*[98] with a summary of the evidence provided in support of the appellants' claim by several Quebec medical specialists in the fields of orthopaedics, ophthalmology, oncology, and cardiology. These experts described the difficulties they faced delivering care

---

94   *Allen* (QB), *supra* note 91 at para 53.
95   *Ibid* at para 48.
96   *Allen* (CA), *supra* note 91 at para 442.
97   See generally Marie-Claude Prémont, "Clearing the Path for Private Health Markets in Post-*Chaoulli* Québec" (2008) Health LJ 237.
98   *Chaoulli* (SC), *supra* note 10 at paras 44–121.

within the publicly funded system: long waiting lists; shortage of operating-room time, hospital staff, and equipment; erratic decision making; and lack of planning.[99] As Justice Piché summarized it: "Tous ces médecins ont témoigné sur les difficultés qu'ils avaient, sur les listes d'attente trop longues, sur les délais d'opération, sur les efforts qu'ils font à tous les jours pour tenter de régler les problèmes, pour tenter de trouver des solutions au manque de cohésion, d'organisation et, disons-le, de vision du Régime de santé du Québec aujourd'hui."[100]

Justice Piché went on to review the evidence submitted by the Quebec and federal government respondents, including the testimony of Yale University health policy expert Dr. Theodore Marmor, whom she quoted at length.[101] Dr. Marmor argued that allowing the development of a parallel private health insurance system would lead to decreased public support for medicare and, most significantly, to a loss of support from more affluent and thus politically influential groups most likely to exit the public system.[102] Dr. Marmor also pointed to the problems of unfair subsidies to the private system and providers resulting from past and future public investment in hospitals, capital improvements, and research; diversion of financial and human resources away from the public system; increased government administrative costs required to regulate the private health insurance market; and increased health spending overall, with no clear improvement in health outcomes.[103] Other experts called by the respondents cited the relative efficiency of the Canadian system; the reality that rationing occurs in all health care systems—in private systems like the United States, based on ability to pay; the problem of "cream skimming" in two-tier systems, where private providers "siphon off high revenue patients and vigorously try to avoid providing care to patient populations who are at financial risk"; and

---

99   *Ibid* at paras 45–49.
100 *Ibid* at para 44 ("All of these physicians testified about the difficulties they faced, about waiting lists that are too long, about delayed operations, about their daily efforts to deal with these problems, to try to find solutions to the lack of cohesion, of organization, and let's be frank, of vision in Quebec's current health care regime." [author's translation]).
101 *Ibid* at paras 102–115.
102 *Ibid* at paras 108–109.
103 *Ibid* at para 107.

the overall contribution of the medicare system to social cohesion in Canada.[104]

Lastly, Justice Piché summarized the evidence of Dr. Edwin Coffey, a Montreal OB/GYN specialist and executive member of the Quebec Medical Association, called by the appellants.[105] Drawing on his own experience and a review of the situation in other OECD countries, Dr. Coffey argued that prohibitions on private health insurance create a "unique and outstanding disadvantage that handicaps the health system in Québec and Canada" and "have contributed to the dysfunctional state of our present health system."[106] Having earlier noted the appellants' other experts' unwillingness to endorse the view that allowing parallel private care would provide a solution to wait times and other access problems,[107] Justice Piché determined that Dr. Coffey's opinion on the advantages of allowing private funding was inconsistent with the weight of expert evidence in the case. In her assessment, she said, "le Dr. Coffey fait cavalier seul avec son expertise et les conclusions auxquelles il arrive."[108]

Justice Piché accepted the appellants' claim that health care waiting lists in Quebec were too long.[109] She did not, however, find that the ban on private insurance had an adverse impact on wait times. Rather, the evidence presented at trial suggested the converse: that eliminating the prohibition on private insurance would, by diverting energy and resources away from the public and into the private system, result in increased wait times for publicly funded care.[110] These evidentiary findings led Justice Piché to the doctrinal conclusion that Quebec's ban on private insurance was fully in accordance with section 7 principles of fundamental justice, as well as section 15 *Charter* equality guarantees. She explained: "La seule façon de garantir que toutes les ressources en matière de santé bénéficieront à tous les Québécois, et ce sans discrimination, est d'empêcher

---

104   *Ibid* at paras 89, 91–93, 95, 101.
105   *Ibid* at paras 116–120.
106   *Ibid* at para 119.
107   *Ibid* at para 51.
108   *Ibid* at para 120 ("Dr. Coffey is a lone ranger in his expertise and the conclusions he arrives at." [author's translation]).
109   *Ibid* at para 50.
110   *Ibid* at para 93, 107.

l'établissement d'un system de soins privés parallèles. Voilà précisé-
ment ce que font les dispositions attaquées en l'espèce."[111]

At the Supreme Court, Justice Deschamps came to the opposite
conclusion on the key evidentiary question of whether Quebec's
ban on private insurance was justified by the need to safeguard the
single-payer system.[112] Looking to the expert evidence at trial on
the impact of a loss of support from those exiting the public system
if the ban on private insurance were lifted, Justice Deschamps said:
"The human reactions described by the experts, many of whom came
from outside Québec, do not appear to me to be very convincing."[113]
On the other harmful effects of allowing parallel private insurance,
Justice Deschamps concluded: "Once again, I am of the opinion
that the reaction that some witnesses described is highly unlikely
in the Québec context."[114] Noting that not all provinces ban private
insurance,[115] and that other OECD nations have adopted a variety
of measures to protect their public systems,[116] Justice Deschamps
concluded, in direct contradiction to Justice Piché's findings at trial,
that "the choice of prohibiting private insurance contracts is not
justified by the evidence."[117] The consequence, in Justice Deschamps
view, was that the ban on private insurance must be struck down.[118]

In her analysis of whether Quebec's ban on private insurance
was arbitrary, and so contrary to the principles of fundamental justice under section 7 of the *Canadian Charter*, Chief Justice McLachlin
also disregarded the expert evidence adduced at trial. In her view:
"To this point, we are confronted with competing but unproven
'common sense' arguments amounting to little more than asser-
tions of belief."[119] Following a summary review of the experience of
other OECD countries drawn from a report by the Standing Senate
Committee on Social Affairs, Science, and Technology chaired by

---

111 *Ibid* at para 264 ("The only way to ensure that all health resources benefit all
     Quebecers, and this without discrimination, is to prevent the establishment of
     a parallel private system. That is precisely what the impugned provisions in
     this case do." [author's translation]).
112 *Chaoulli* (SCC), *supra* note 10 at para 14.
113 *Ibid* at para 64.
114 *Ibid* at para 14.
115 *Ibid* at para 74.
116 *Ibid* at para 83.
117 *Ibid* at para 66.
118 *Ibid* at para 100.
119 *Ibid* at para 138.

Senator Michael Kirby,[120] the chief justice concurred with Justice Deschamps that "the evidence on the experience of other western democracies refutes the government's theoretical contention that a prohibition on private insurance is linked to maintaining quality public health care."[121] Although the appellants submitted no direct evidence on this point, Chief Justice McLachlin, like Justice Deschamps, attributed waiting lists in the public system to the ban on private insurance and Quebec's single-payer system.[122] Noting at the outset of her judgment that: "This virtual monopoly, on the evidence, results in delays in treatment that adversely affect the citizen's security of the person,"[123] the chief justice closed her section 7 analysis by reiterating that "the denial of private insurance subjects people to long waiting lists and negatively affects their security of the person."[124]

Neither Justice Deschamps's insistence on the specificity of the situation in Quebec, nor her and Chief Justice McLachlin's reliance on the Kirby Committee's review of the comparative experience in other OECD countries,[125] remove from the fact that the majority in *Chaoulli* set aside Justice Piché's findings on the actual evidence presented by the parties at trial. The majority dismissed Justice Piché's conclusion that Quebec's ban on private insurance was necessary to protect the integrity of the publicly funded system and its objective of ensuring equal access to health care services without barriers based on ability to pay. The majority in *Chaoulli* also found, in the absence of any supporting evidence, that the single-payer monopoly was itself the cause of unacceptable delays, and that striking down

---

120 Canada, Senate, Standing Committee on Social Affairs, Science and Technology, *The Health of Canadians—The Federal Role, Volume Three: Health Care Systems in Other Countries, Interim Report of the Standing Senate Committee on Social Affairs, Science and Technology* (Ottawa: Standing Senate Committee on Social Affairs, Science and Technology, 2002).

121 *Chaoulli* (SCC), *supra* note 10 at para 149.

122 *Ibid* at para 111.

123 *Ibid* at para 106.

124 *Ibid* at para 152.

125 For a critique of this aspect of the decision see Colleen M Flood, Mark Stabile & Sasha Kontic, "Finding Health Policy 'Arbitrary': The Evidence on Waiting, Dying and Two-Tier Systems" in Flood, *Access to Care, supra* note 10 at 296. See also Colleen M Flood & Amanda Haughan, "Is Canada Odd? A Comparison of European and Canadian Approaches to Choice and Regulation of the Public/ Private Divide in Health Care" (2010) 5:3 Health Econ Pol'y & L 319.

the ban on private health insurance was the appropriate remedy for the *Charter* violations created by undue wait times.

The submissions in the *Cambie* case about the need to strike down provincial limits on private care in British Columbia as a solution to wait times, and about the consequences of allowing private funding generally, parallel the arguments that were rejected by Justice Piché but accepted by the majority of the Supreme Court in *Chaoulli*. First, like in *Chaoulli*, the *Cambie* claim contends that restricting private payment harms the public system and the patients who rely on it. In particular, the *Cambie* claim draws a direct link between the ban on private funding and wait times in British Columbia, arguing that "the prohibition on private insurance overburdens the public health care system, increasing wait times for everyone and decreasing the overall quality of care."[126] Like in *Chaoulli*, the *Cambie* plaintiffs contend that, because British Columbians "are prohibited from obtaining insurance, they are forced to languish on a waiting list, with the resulting physical, psychological, emotional and economic harm that this entails."[127]

Second, the *Cambie* claim repeatedly asserts that restrictions on private funding under the *MPA* are unnecessary because allowing private payment and care will not harm the public system[128] or impair access for those who rely on it.[129] Like the majority justices in *Chaoulli*, the *Cambie* claim points to the experience of health care systems elsewhere as evidence that removing restrictions on private care in British Columbia will in no way threaten its single-payer system:

> Based on comparison with other health systems in Canada and internationally, allowing individuals to choose to obtain private insurance and permitting and facilitating access to a private healthcare system does not jeopardize the existence of a strong public healthcare system. The experiences in other jurisdictions demonstrate that a hybrid private-public health care system allows the public system to thrive and provide better care to patients.[130]

---

126   *Cambie* (Plaintiffs' Opening Statement), *supra* note 7 at para 1772.
127   *Ibid* at para 40.
128   *Ibid* at paras 20, 49, 194, 208, 426, 1942–1945.
129   *Ibid* at paras 185, 300.
130   *Ibid* at paras 20, 197, 200, 413, 457–458, 468; *Cambie* (Civil Claim), *supra* note 7 at para 120.

Noting that "the Supreme Court of Canada in *Chaoulli* held that it was neither legally acceptable nor necessary for Québec to prohibit people from accessing private health care,"[131] the *Cambie* claim makes the same argument that "the guiding principles of the health care system of British Columbia ... do not require, as a matter of law or fact, that patients be restricted or prohibited from accessing private health care."[132]

Third, the *Cambie* claim suggests that allowing private funding will in fact help the public system. The plaintiffs insist that, with a parallel private regime in place, access to the public system "can only be improved by having fewer patients to deal with."[133] The *Cambie* claim goes even further in positing the positive impact of private funding on the public health care system:

> Private medical facilities are beneficial for overall health care in the Province. They provide needed additional assessment, consultation, operating and diagnostic facilities; attract specialist doctors to the Province and help retain them by providing them with additional access to operating time, which is rationed in the public hospitals, offer flexible work hours to nurses and have helped to attract nurses back into the workforce and retain them in the Province, encourage improvements and efficiencies in the public health care system and provide patients with speedier access to health care, resulting in reduced pain and disability, improved health outcomes and increased life expectancy.[134]

In *Chaoulli*, Justice Piché concluded, based on the evidence, that allowing private funding would threaten the viability and effectiveness of the public system to the detriment of all residents of the province. As she explained:

> La preuve a montré que le droit d'avoir recours à un système parallèle privé de soins, invoqué par les requérants, aurait des répercussions sur l'ensemble de la population. Il ne faut pas jouer à l'autruche. L'établissement d'un système de santé

---

131   *Cambie* (Plaintiffs' Opening Statement), *supra* note 7 at para 322.
132   *Cambie* (Civil Claim), *supra* note 7 at para 130.
133   *Cambie* (Plaintiffs' Opening Statement), *supra* note 7 at para 185.
134   *Cambie* (Civil Claim), *supra* note 7 at para 14.

> parallèle privé aurait pour effet de menacer l'intégrité, le bon
> fonctionnement ainsi que la viabilité du système public. Les
> articles [attaqués] empêchent cette éventualité et garantissent
> l'existence d'un système de santé public de qualité au Québec.[135]

The majority of the Supreme Court's rejection of these evidentiary findings met with widespread criticism, within both the legal and health policy communities.[136] As Hamish Stewart described it, the majority reversed Justice Piché's evidentiary conclusions "without making clear the basis on which, in its view the trial judge erred in her fact-finding ... [embarking] on a fresh fact-finding process, based largely on evidence that was ... not tested in an adversarial context."[137] In his estimation, the "decision may well be bad for medicare; it is certainly bad for constitutional adjudication in an adversarial trial system."[138] Marie-Claude Prémont also points to the lack of any evidence before the court to support striking down the ban on private insurance as a remedy for undue wait times: "Rien n'indique que les listes d'attente qui affligent le réseau de santé trouvent leur origine dans l'interdiction de l'assurance privée pour les soins assurés. *A contrario*, rien n'indique que l'introduction de l'assurance santé pour ces mêmes services pourrait apporter une quelconque solution au problème que retient l'attention du tribunal."[139] For his part, Morris Barer captures why the absence of a sound evidentiary

---

135　*Chaoulli* (SC), *supra* note 10 at para 263 ("The evidence has shown that the right to access a parallel private health care system invoked by the claimants would have consequences for the entire population. We can't stick our heads in the sand. The creation of a parallel, private health care system would threaten the integrity, the effective operation, and the existence of a quality, public health care system in Quebec." [author's translation]).

136　See, e.g., Ted Marmor, "An American in Canada—Making Sense of the Supreme Court Decision on Health Care" (September 2005) Pol'y Options 41; Charles J Wright, "Different Interpretations of 'Evidence' and Implications for the Canadian Health Care System" in Flood, *Access to Care, supra* note 10 at 220; Prémont, "Cherchez l'erreur," *supra* note 10.

137　Hamish Steward, "Implications of *Chaoulli* for Fact-Finding in Constitutional Cases" in Flood, *Access to Care, supra* note 10 at 207, 212.

138　*Ibid.*

139　Prémont, "Cherchez l'erreur," *supra* note 10 at 181 ("Nothing suggests that waiting lists afflicting the health system can be attributed to the ban on private insurance for insured services. Conversely, nothing suggests that allowing private insurance for the same services would bring about any kind of solution to the problem that attracted the court's attention." [author's translation]).

basis for the decision in *Chaoulli* was so problematic from a health policy perspective:

> Claims about the wonders of private insurance have been around for half a century at least, and have repeatedly shown to be specious. Yet they persist, they are promoted, and the Supreme Court justices, or at least enough of them, bought the story, hook, line and sinker and evidence be damned ... In this, the majority were simply irresponsible. But ... [i]t is the rest of us who will pay, and pay, and pay. ...[140]

Examining the evidence since *Chaoulli*, Colleen Fuller affirms that "private provision and financing of care have not made a significant contribution to wait time reductions in the public system—anywhere,"[141] but, according to numerous studies, have had the opposite effect.[142] Nevertheless, the plaintiffs in *Cambie* have built their case around the same highly contested evidentiary claims accepted by the majority in *Chaoulli*, that private funding offers a solution to wait times, and that striking down restrictions on private care will have a benign impact on the public system. Like in *Chaoulli*, the BC courts' approach to these evidentiary claims will no doubt have a decisive impact on the outcome of the constitutional challenge to British Columbia's single-payer system in the *Cambie* case.

4. The Substantive Equality Objectives of the Single-Payer System

A second important aspect of the *Chaoulli* decision, of direct relevance to the *Cambie* challenge, is the weight accorded to the substantive equality objectives of the single-payer system in the courts' assessment of the constitutionality of the ban on private funding. The trial court and Supreme Court of Canada's differing approaches to this issue in *Chaoulli* and, more specifically, to the overarching principle that access to health care should not depend on individual economic

---

140 Moris Barer, "Experts and Evidence: New Challenges in Knowledge Translation" in Flood, *Access to Care, supra* note 10 at 216, 218.

141 Fuller, *Cambie Goes to Court, supra* note 6 at 22.

142 *Ibid* at 20.

means, had a direct bearing on the outcome in the *Chaoulli* case, and the same will likely be true in *Cambie*.

Justice Piché prefaced her judgment in *Chaoulli* with a reminder that "Le présent débat concernant la santé et ses problèmes actuels d'accessibilité nous fait oublier parfois le passé pas si lointain où les gens maladies ne se faisait pas soigner, car ils n'en avaient tout simplement pas les moyens. La société Canadienne dans un élan de générosité et d'égalité, a voulu que ceci n'arrive plus."[143] In deciding whether Quebec's restrictions on private insurance were arbitrary, Justice Piché noted that no health system in the world has unlimited resources, and that all must engage in some form of rationing, which in Quebec occurs based on need.[144] Justice Piché was of the opinion that the impugned restrictions on private funding under Quebec's health- and hospital-insurance legislation were designed to guarantee equal access to health care services for all, without discrimination based on individual economic circumstances.[145] She therefore found no conflict between the ban on private insurance and section 7 principles of fundamental justice.[146]

Measured against the *Charter*'s section 15 equality guarantee, Justice Piché held that "ces dispositions ne servent aucunement à dévaloriser certains individus ... elles servent plutôt à promouvoir des intérêts sociaux légitimes et à rehausser la dignité des Québécois en leur garantissant des soins médicaux."[147] In sum, Justice Piché concluded:

> Les dispositions attaquées ont été adoptées en se basant sur des considérations d'égalité et de dignité humaine et elles ne sont pas en conflit avec les valeurs véhiculées par la *Charte*. Il est pleinement justifiable qu'un gouvernement ayant les meilleurs

---

143 *Chaoulli* (SC), *supra* note 10 at para 2 ("The current debate over health and problems of access sometimes causes us to forget the not-so-distant past, when people who were ill weren't treated because they simply didn't have the means. Canadian society, in an impetus of generosity and equality, wanted to ensure this no longer happened." [author's translation]).

144 *Ibid* at para 306.

145 *Ibid* at para 258.

146 *Ibid* at para 267.

147 *Ibid* at para 306 ("The provisions in no way devalue certain individuals ... rather they promote legitimate social interests and enhance the dignity of Quebecers by guaranteeing medical care" [author's translation]).

> intérêts de la population à cœur adopte une solution visant à favoriser le plus grand nombre d'individus.[148]

In dissent at the Supreme Court, Justices Binnie, LeBel, and Fish agreed with Justice Piché's characterization of the government's objectives in limiting private funding to protect the single-payer system:

> Quebec wants a health system where access is governed by need rather than wealth or status. Quebec does not want people who are uninsurable to be left behind. To accomplish this objective endorsed by the Canada Health Act, Quebec seeks to discourage the growth of private-sector delivery of "insured" services based on wealth and insurability ... Quebec bases the prohibition on the view that private insurance, and a consequent major expansion of private health services, would have a harmful effect on the public system.[149]

In contrast, the majority justices rejected Justice Piché's finding that the underlying objectives of the single-payer system justified a violation of the *Charter* rights of the appellants and others seeking access to private care. Justice Deschamps saw no individual or collective benefit from the ban on private insurance. In her view: "Some patients die as a result of long waits for treatment in the public system when they could have gained prompt access to care in the private sector. Were it not for [the impugned provisions] they could buy private insurance and receive care in the private sector."[150] Remarking that the *Canada Health Act* "has achieved an iconic status that makes it untouchable by politicians,"[151] Justice Deschamps characterized the dissenting justices' concerns over the impact on the poor of striking down the ban on private insurance as "indicative of [the] type of emotional reaction" generated by "any measure that

---

148 *Ibid* at paras 311–312 ("The impugned provisions were adopted based on considerations of equality and human dignity and they are not in conflict with the values conveyed by the *Charter*. It is entirely justifiable that a government with the best interests of the population at heart adopts a solution that will benefit the greatest number of individuals." [author's translation]).

149 *Chaoulli* (SCC), *supra* note 10 at paras 239–240.

150 *Ibid* at para 37.

151 *Ibid* at para 16.

might be perceived as compromising" the principles of that legislation.[152] While insisting that "no one questions the need to preserve a sound public health care system,"[153] she declared that "[t]he courts have a duty to rise above political debate"[154] and that the appellants had proven their rights had been infringed.[155]

Chief Justice McLachlin was also unqualified in her criticism of the province's ban on private insurance and the resulting "virtual monopoly for the public health scheme."[156] Having found, contrary to the evidence accepted by Justice Piché at trial, that such "a monopoly is not necessary or even related to the provision of quality public health care,"[157] the chief justice rejected the Quebec government's argument that the ban could be justified as a reasonable limit under section 1 of the *Charter*. In her view, "the benefits of the prohibition do not outweigh the deleterious effects ... The physical and psychological suffering and risk of death that may result outweigh whatever benefit (and none has been demonstrated to us here) there may be to the system as a whole."[158]

In the final report of the Royal Commission on the Future of Health Care in Canada, delivered in 2002, Roy Romanow, the former premier of Saskatchewan who chaired the commission, explains that "our tax-funded, universal health care system provides a kind of "double-solidarity." It provides equity of funding between the "have" and "have-nots" in our society and it also provides equity between the healthy and the sick."[159] Unlike Justice Piché's trial decision, the majority judgment in *Chaoulli* fails to take into account the degree to which, by rationing care based on need rather than ability to pay, the single-payer system reflects and promotes these substantive equality objectives.[160] In the words of Justices Binnie, LeBel, and Fish: "Apart

152 *Ibid.*
153 *Ibid* at para 14.
154 *Ibid* at para 89.
155 *Ibid* at para 100.
156 *Ibid* at para 106.
157 *Ibid* at para 140.
158 *Ibid* at para 157.
159 Canada, Commission on the Future of Health Care in Canada, *Building on Values: The Future of Health Care in Canada—Final Report* (Saskatoon: Commission on the Future of Health Care in Canada, 2002) at 31 (Chair Roy J Romanow) [*Romanow Commission*].
160 See generally Porter, "Right to Health Care," *supra* note 10; Prémont, "Cherchez l'erreur," *supra* note 10; Jackman, "'Last Line of Defence," *supra* note 10; Lorne

from everything else, it leaves out of consideration the commitment in principle in <u>this</u> country to health care based on <u>need</u>, not wealth or status, as set out in the *Canada Health Act*."[161]

Like in *Chaoulli*, the plaintiffs in the *Cambie* case take issue with the underlying premise of the single-payer system: that it is necessary to prohibit private funding to ensure equal access to care, and that it is legitimate to prohibit rationing based on ability to pay, even for those who have the means to bypass the public system. Instead, they make the startling claim that "[e]quity will be improved by allowing more British Columbians, instead of just the wealthy as is currently the case, to access private health care," [162] and that "[w]hile Canadians pride ourselves on our ability to provide for those in need ... prohibition on private health care does not contribute to a just health care policy."[163] Like the majority in *Chaoulli*, the plaintiffs in *Cambie* discount any equality-based concerns that allowing private funding will adversely affect less-advantaged patients, who must rely on the publicly funded system. They counter that "[f]or those who cannot afford private insurance ... they still have a universal public health care system ... they lose nothing by allowing BC residents to make a personal choice relating to their own health about whether to acquire private insurance."[164]

Similar to *Chaoulli*, the *Cambie* plaintiffs emphasize that "they are not seeking to compel the government to provide more and better medical services to prevent harm, they ask only that the Government stop interfering with their right to act and choose for themselves how best to address their own health care needs."[165] Characterizing British Columbians as "captives"[166] of the single-payer system, the *Cambie* claim affirms that "[c]learly, it is necessary for the Courts to step in to protect BC residents from the harm they're suffering from a monopoly health care system, as they did in *Chaoulli*."[167] In calling for all restrictions on private funding and care in British Columbia

---

Sossin, "Towards a Two-Tier Constitution? The Poverty of Health Rights" in Flood, *Access to Care, supra* note 10 at 161.

161 *Chaoulli* (SCC), *supra* note 10 at para 230 [emphasis in original].

162 *Cambie* (Plaintiffs' Opening Statement), *supra* note 7 at para 187.

163 *Ibid* at para 465.

164 *Ibid* at paras 185–186.

165 *Ibid* at para 1628.

166 *Ibid* at para 499.

167 *Ibid* at para 501.

to be struck down, the *Cambie* claim decries what it describes as the "fanatical commitment to some pure form of equality of suffering" animating the single-payer system:

> The justification for the drastic restrictions in the *Act* ... is based on a dogmatic commitment to a perverse ideological position: that because the Government has not and cannot take steps to ensure that everyone has access to necessary and timely medical treatment in the public system, everyone should be forced to suffer equally ... that it would be better to ensure that no one is advantaged, even if it means everyone must be made worse off.[168]

The debate over the privatization of medicare does indeed reflect two competing ideological conceptions of equality and its role as an animating principle within the health care system. The plaintiffs in *Cambie* rely on the majority's inference in *Chaoulli* that the *Charter* imposes no obligations on governments to ensure access to timely care based on need but only access based on ability to pay. As the many critics of the *Chaoulli* decision have underscored, this interpretation reflects what the Supreme Court itself has characterized as a "thin and impoverished" vision of equality,[169] entirely at odds with the *Charter's* guarantees of equal protection and benefit of the law.[170] The BC Physicians and Patients Coalition summarize what is at play in *Cambie*:

> [T]he challenged protections comprise the central tenets of a complex socio-economic benefit and protective regulatory scheme. These protections operate ... a universal, sustainable and publicly funded health care system available to all British Columbians on *equal* terms and conditions. This legislation is intended to protect the right to life and security of the person of all British Columbians, including the vulnerable and silent rights-holders whose equal access to quality health care depends upon the challenged protection.[171]

---

168 *Ibid* at para 1946–1947.
169 *Eldridge v British Columbia (Attorney General)*, [1997] 3 SCR 624 at para 73.
170 See generally Porter, "Right to Health Care," *supra* note 10; Andrew Petter, "Wealthcare: The Politics of the *Charter* Revisited" in Flood, *Access to Care, supra* note 10 at 116; Jackman, "Last Line of Defence," *supra* note 10.
171 *Cambie* (Opening Statement of the BC Physicians and Patients Coalition) at para 20.

As outlined above, in making the case for the blanket repeal of all restrictions on private funding and care in British Columbia, the *Cambie* claim relies on the evidentiary approach as well as the reasoning and rhetoric of the majority judgment in *Chaoulli*. Whether or not the BC courts are convinced by the *Cambie* plaintiffs' evidence and arguments about the positive impact of private funding, or the logic of striking down restrictions on private care as a solution to wait times in the province, judicial attitudes toward the single-payer system and its substantive equality objectives are likely to be as significant a factor in *Cambie* as they were in *Chaoulli*.

Conclusion

The Supreme Court has repeatedly affirmed that "the *Charter* should generally be presumed to provide protection at least as great as that afforded by similar provisions in international human rights documents which Canada has ratified."[172] While referring to the comparative health care systems of other OECD countries, the majority judgment in *Chaoulli* completely ignored the international human rights regime to which Canadian governments are accountable in relation to the health care system: the *International Covenant on Economic, Social and Cultural Rights (ICESCR)*.[173] Ratified by Canada in 1976, article 12(1) of the *ICESCR* recognizes "the right of everyone to the enjoyment of the highest attainable standard of physical and mental health." [174] Article 12(2)(d) sets out Canada's obligations to take all steps necessary for "the creation of conditions which would assure to all medical service and medical attention in the event of sickness."[175] And Article 2(2) of the *ICESCR* requires Canadian governments to ensure that the right to health is enjoyed "without discrimination," and, in particular, without discrimination based on "social origin, property, birth, or other

---

172 *Reference Re Public Service Employee Relations Act (Alberta)*, [1987] 1 SCR 313 at 349; *Slaight Communications v Davidson*, [1989] 1 SCR 1038; *Health Services and Support—Facilities Subsector Bargaining Assn v British Columbia*, 2007 SCC 27, 2 SCR 391 at para 70; *Divito v Canada (Public Safety and Emergency Preparedness)*, 2013 SCC 47 at para 19.

173 *ICESCR, supra* note 2.

174 *Ibid.*

175 *Ibid.*

status."[176] The UN Committee on Economic, Social, and Cultural Rights explains: "Health facilities, goods and services must be accessible to all, especially the most vulnerable or marginalized sections of the population, in law and in fact, without discrimination on any of the prohibited grounds."[177]

Notwithstanding Canada's explicit obligations under the *ICESCR*, federal, and provincial governments have consistently maintained that the *Charter's* life, liberty, security of the person, and equality guarantees do not protect the right to health or guarantee access to health care at the domestic level.[178] In rebutting the appellants' *Charter* claim in *Chaoulli*, for example, the Quebec government submitted that "les prétentions constitutionnelles des appelants portent sur des enjeux sociaux qui relèvent essentiellement du domaine politique et n'ont pas de lien de rattachement suffisant avec les système judiciaire."[179] Underlining that "the state has to deal with complex social policy issues and undertake the allocation of limited resources,"[180] the attorney general of Canada declared in *Chaoulli* that "[g]overnments are best equipped to make these complex, sensitive choices the appropriateness of which does not lend itself to judicial debate."[181] Likewise, the BC government's position in *Cambie* is that "s. 7 cannot apply in the context of this case, because the provisions that are challenged by the Plaintiffs do not in any way engage the justice system and its administration."[182] The government defendants

---

176 *Ibid.* In similar terms, Article 26 of the *International Covenant on Civil and Political Rights*, 16 December 1966, Can TS 1976 No 47 (entered into force 23 March 1976, accession by Canada 19 May 1976), requires Canada to ensure that all persons enjoy the "right to life," under Article 6(1) of the *Covenant*, without discrimination based on "social origin, property, birth or other status."

177 Committee on Economic, Social and Cultural Rights, *General Comment No 14: The Right to the Highest Attainable Standard of Health*, UN ESCOR, 2000, UN Doc E/C.12/2000/4 (11 August 2000) at para 12(b). See also Committee on Economic, Social and Cultural Rights, *General Comment No 5: Persons with Disabilities*, UN ESCOR, 1994, UN Doc E/C.12/1994/13 at para 5.

178 See generally Jackman, "*Charter* Review," *supra* note 10; Jackman, "Health Care Accountability," *supra* note 5.

179 *Chaoulli* (SCC), *supra* note 10 at para 110 ("The appellants' constitutional submissions relate to social issues falling within the political realm and that do not have a sufficient connection with the judicial system." [author's translation]).

180 *Chaoulli* (SCC) (Factum of the Respondent (Mis-en-cause) Attorney General of Canada) at para 4.

181 *Ibid* at para 6.

182 *Cambie* (Defendants' Opening Statement), *supra* note 9 at 23.

in *Cambie* further contend that section 7 "does not guarantee a right of access to necessary and appropriate health care within a reasonable time."[183]

The presumption that individual rights are not implicated, and that the *Charter* should not apply to the publicly funded system, also prevails within the broader Canadian health policy community. Christopher Manfredi maintains, for example, that "[t]he question of what kind of health care system Canada should have is simply not amenable to resolution through the language of legal rights."[184] Health care, according to Romanow, "is not a legal construct but rather, a political construct."[185] Not surprisingly, as Donna Greschner observes, the Romanow commission's final report[186] "omits almost completely any discussion of one primary method of regulating relationships between governments and citizens: rights."[187]

There is, however, no doubt that life, liberty, security of the person, and equality interests of both individuals and disadvantaged groups are affected by health care decisions and choices to which the *Charter* directly applies.[188] In the words of Justice Piché, "s'il n'y a pas d'accès possible au système de santé, il est illusoire de croire que les droits à la vie et à la sécurité sont respectés."[189] If wait times and other systemic barriers and inequities in access to care threaten the lives and the physical and psychological security of people who are ill, governments and the health policy community

---

183 *Cambie* (Response), *supra* note 47 Part 3, para 3.

184 Christopher P Manfredi, "Déjà Vu All Over Again: *Chaoulli* and the Limits of Judicial Policymaking" in Flood, *Access to Care*, *supra* note 10 at 154.

185 Roy J Romanow, "In Search of a Mandate?" in Flood, *Access to Care*, *supra* note 10 at 528.

186 *Romanow Commission*, *supra* note 159.

187 Donna Greschner, "Public Law in the Romanow Report" (2003) 66 Sask L Rev 565 at 568.

188 Section 32(1) of the *Charter* states that the *Charter* applies "in respect of all matters within the authority" of federal and provincial/territorial legislatures and governments. In its decision in *Eldridge v British Columbia*, [1997] 3 SCR 624, the Supreme Court ruled that the scope of *Charter* review in the health care context extends beyond government health ministries, authorities, and service providers to the provision of publicly funded care by non-governmental entities. See generally Martha Jackman, "The Application of the Canadian *Charter* in the Health Care Context" (2001) 9 Health L Rev 22.

189 *Chaoulli* (SC), *supra* note 10 at para 304 ("If access to the health care system is not available, it is a fiction to believe that rights to life, liberty and security of the person are respected." [author's translation]).

cannot continue to proclaim that these are simply matters of social policy, falling within the sole purview of legislatures, and beyond the ambit of *Charter* review by the courts. This position is incompatible with Canada's *ICESCR* and other international and domestic human rights obligations.[190] Even if it were defensible from a human rights perspective, the *Chaoulli* and *Cambie* cases show that this argument is no longer a tenable one. As the advocacy groups Charter Committee on Poverty Issues and the Canadian Health Coalition affirmed in their intervention before the Supreme Court in *Chaoulli*, Canadian courts are "constitutionally mandated to remedy *Charter* violations in health care as in any other area of law or policy":

> Where the publicly funded health care system is found to violate the right to health under the *Charter* ... the appropriate remedy is to order governments to take whatever measures are required to respect, protect and fulfill the right to health for all members of Canadian society ... [C]onstitutional remedies can be fashioned to provide effective remedies for *Charter* violations while respecting the legislature's competence to choose the most appropriate means of providing necessary services.[191]

Commenting on the outcome in *Chaoulli*, Andrew Petter posited that, "by handing the imprimatur of constitutional rights to advocates of private medicine and two-tier health care, the court has dealt a serious blow to the legitimacy of the single-payer model of health insurance and the values of collective responsibility and social equality that it seeks to uphold."[192] Dr. Day and his supporters are counting on this in the *Cambie* case, attacking the "very structure" of

---

190 United Nations Committee on Economic, Social and Cultural Rights, *Concluding Observations on Canada*, E/C 12/1993 (10 June 1993) at para 21; United Nations Committee on Economic, Social and Cultural Rights, *Concluding Observations on Canada*, E/C.12/1/Add.31 (10 December 1998) at para 14, 15; see generally Jackman, "Health Care Accountability," *supra* note 5; Porter, "Right to Health Care," *supra* note 10.

191 *Chaoulli* (SCC) (Factum of the Interveners the Charter Committee on Poverty Issues and the Canadian Health Coalition) at paras 46, 48. The author represented CCPI and the CHC in *Chaoulli*.

192 Andrew Petter, "Wealthcare: The Politics of the *Charter* Revisited" in Flood, *Access to Care*, *supra* note 10 at 131; see Peter H Russell, "*Chaoulli*: The Political versus the Legal Life of a Judicial Decision" in Flood, *Access to Care*, *supra* note 10 at 15.

the single-payer system[193] and alleging that the government of British Columbia "is politically incapable of doing more to reform the system to protect constitutional rights without an order from the court to do so."[194] But instead of ceding the *Charter* to Dr. Chaoulli, Dr. Day, and others pursuing *Charter* litigation as a means of dismantling the single-payer system, those who believe in medicare, and want to make it better, must call on governments and the courts alike to interpret the *Charter* in a way that reflects and reinforces the systemic equality and other human rights objectives of the single-payer system. As Kent Roach observed in his critique of the majority's decision to strike down limits on private funding as the remedy for undue wait times in *Chaoulli*:

> The majority of the Court may have simply opened the system to more private health insurance that may benefit those who can afford it while doing nothing for the less advantaged who must rely on the public system. From the vantage point of those who cannot or do not contract out of the public system in the new world created by *Chaoulli*, the problem may actually be too little judicial activism.[195]

Rather than arguing that constitutional rights are not engaged by government funding and other health care choices, we must advocate for an approach to the *Charter* that is animated by the same principles as the medicare system itself—in the words of Justice Binnie in *Chaoulli*, one that is "mindful and protective of the rights of all, not only of some."[196] Contrary to the regressive reading of the *Charter* put forward in the *Cambie* case, we must demand that governments and courts affirm and protect the life, liberty, security of the person, and equality rights of every person in Canada to access health care based on need and not ability to pay.

---

193 *Cambie* (Plaintiffs' Opening Statement), *supra* note 7 at para 1979.
194 *Ibid* at para 1960.
195 Kent Roach, "The Courts and Medicare: Too Much or Too Little Judicial Activism?" in Flood, *Access to Care, supra* note 10 at 186.
196 *Chaoulli* (SCC), *supra* note 10 at para 278.

CHAPTER 3

Borders, Fences, and Crossings: Regulating Parallel Private Finance in Health Care

Jeremiah Hurley

Motivated by equity concerns and the desire to avoid adverse effects on the publicly financed health care system, Canadian provinces have implemented a remarkably effective set of regulations that limit parallel private finance and delivery of core medicare physician and hospital services in Canada. Without necessarily prohibiting parallel private finance itself, these regulations reduce physicians' economic incentive to provide privately financed medicare services, patients' incentive to demand them, and private insurers' ability to insure them, effectively shutting down the market for privately financed parallel services. These regulations, however, are under threat by court challenges. In 2005, the Supreme Court of Canada in *Chaoulli* struck down Quebec's prohibition of private insurance that would duplicate that covered by public medicare, and in the ongoing case of *Cambie*, a private-clinic claimant is not only challenging British Columbia's prohibition of private insurance but also the other restrictions on physician billing options. Should the courts strike down one or more of these latter regulations, Canadian provinces will face greater regulatory challenges as they pursue their health policy goals in the presence of a less restricted parallel private sector.

Although analysts debate whether the overall effect of parallel private finance on a public system is positive or negative, no one disputes that the parallel private and public health care sectors unavoidably interact in ways that can have adverse effects on the public system. To mitigate these adverse effects, countries internationally adopt quite different regulatory approaches to parallel private finance, ranging from grudging tolerance to active promotion. Even countries such as Australia, which promotes parallel private insurance in the belief that overall it can benefit the public system, regulate the private sector so as to protect the public system. Indeed, such promotion of parallel private finance generally leads to even more regulation given the expanded opportunities for adverse effects on the public system. Countries regularly tinker with their regulations in an attempt to strike the right regulatory balance, and occasionally we see countries adopt quite radical changes to regulatory regimes (e.g., recent policy changes in Ireland, discussed by Thomas et al in chapter 11).

Regulating parallel private finance is hard. Private and public systems interact in complex, often nuanced ways, but the regulatory tools available are limited and often can't be deployed in correspondingly nuanced ways. Conflict among policy goals forces difficult choices when advancing one set of goals detracts from another. The impact of commonly found regulatory tools for private health insurance—for example, premium regulation and benefit design— can differ when insurance provides secondary coverage than when private insurance is the primary source of coverage. And effective regulation must encompass in a coordinated way both health care insurance markets and health care service markets.

This chapter examines the regulation of parallel private finance, emphasizing features of health care insurance and health care service markets, and the interactions between the private and public sectors that motivate regulation, to identify regulatory options for Canadian provinces in a context in which parallel private insurance is allowed and/or physicians face fewer restrictions on providing privately financed services—that is, the regulatory context the provinces will face if the courts strike down some or all of the key components of Canada's current regulatory approach.

Two prefatory comments are in order. First, parallel private finance is defined as patients paying privately to obtain services *for which they are covered by the publicly financed health care system*. Patients may pay directly out of pocket or by purchasing private insurance that pays some or all of the cost of obtaining services privately. Parallel private finance is sometimes called "duplicative" finance or "supplementary" finance.[1] Parallel private finance contrasts with complementary private finance, which is when patients pay privately for services excluded from the publicly financed system. While parallel private finance is highly restricted in Canada, complementary private finance predominates for drugs, dental, and other health services excluded from public coverage, and a large share of Canadians hold complementary private insurance.[2]

Second, private finance should be distinguished from private delivery: the two raise distinct analytic, policy, and regulatory issues.[3] Publicly financed health care systems may opt to deliver services through private organizations, such as private physician practices or private clinics; and publicly funded delivery organizations may deliver health care to private-pay patients, such as occurs in the United Kingdom, Australian, Ireland, and other countries.[4] This chapter focuses on *financing*, regardless of the nature of the organization (public, private not-for-profit, or private for-profit) delivering the service.

Parallel Private Markets in Health Care

Interactions between the public and private sectors under parallel finance are unavoidable: it is not possible to fully isolate the two sectors from each other. Regulation can limit the nature and amount of such interaction but it cannot eliminate it. The two sectors, for example, compete for the time and talents of the same physicians, nurses, and technicians, among other inputs, needed to deliver care—competition that increases wages and prices for these inputs and reduces the real purchasing power of a given nominal public budget. Services produced by the two sectors are both substitutes and complements: sometimes a patient's privately financed care

---

1   Anna Sagan & Sarah Thomson, *Voluntary Health Insurance in Europe: Country Experience* (Copenhagen: European Observatory on Health Systems and Policies, 2016) at 2.

2   Canadian Institute for Health Information, *National Health Expenditure Trends, 1975–2017* (Ottawa: Canadian Institute for Health Information, 2017) online: https://www.cihi.ca/sites/default/files/document/nhex2017-trends-report-en. pdf; Jeremiah Hurley & G Emmanuel Guindon, "Private Insurance in Canada" (2008) McMaster University Centre for Health Economics and Policy Analysis Working Paper 08-04.

3   Jeremiah Hurley, *Health Economics* (Toronto: McGraw-Hill Ryerson, 2010).

4   Sagan & Thomson, *supra* note 1.

substitutes for care they otherwise would have obtained through the public system; other times, demand for private services generates an associated demand for public services, such as when private-pay patients experience complications that must be treated in the public system. Because these interactions raise both efficiency concerns (e.g., inefficient risk selection) and equity concerns (e.g., unequal access and queue-jumping), regulation of the markets in health care insurance and health care services seeks to mediate the interactions so as to achieve key policy goals.

Private Insurance Markets

People demand privately financed services already covered by public insurance because they perceive a shortcoming in the public system. The precise shortcoming differs across individuals and systems, but four dominate: long wait times in the public system, perceived lower quality of clinical care in the public system,[5] restrictions on choice in the public system, and lesser amenities in public facilities.[6] The dominant driver of demand for parallel private care in most systems is a desire to avoid long waits in the public system.[7] This is true in Canada, where concerns about wait times have been used to galvanize court challenges to overturn regulatory restrictions on private finance. Differences in quality of clinical care across the public and private systems can be large in many low- and middle-income countries but they do not figure prominently in most developed countries, especially given that private care is usually delivered by the same providers who work in the public system, is often obtained in publicly funded facilities, and evidence indicates that private for-profit facilities provide lower quality of care in some settings.[8]

---

5   I distinguish two aspects of quality: (a) quality of the clinical care, which depends on the clinical skills of the provider, the nature of the facilities and equipment used, and related matters; and (b) performance of the system of care, which is influenced by factors such as wait times. By "clinical quality," I mean only the former.

6   Sagan & Thomson, *supra* note 1.

7   Jeremiah Hurley & Malcolm Johnson, *A Review of Evidence Regarding Parallel Systems of Public and Private Finance* (Hamilton: McMaster University Centre for Health Economics and Policy Analysis, 2014), online: <www.chepa.org/docs/documents/14-2.pdf >.

8   PJ Devereaux et al, "A Systematic Review and Meta-Analysis of Studies Comparing Mortality Rates of Private For-Profit and Private Not-for-Profit Hospitals" (2002) 166 CMAJ 1399; PJ Devereaux et al, "Comparison of Mortality

Choice-related demand is particularly common in the inpatient sector when the public system restricts one's ability to choose a provider or care facility: paying privately enables a person to choose their provider or facility. Canadians do not face such restrictions on their choice of provider or facility. Amenities refers to non-clinical aspects of care, particularly in an inpatient setting, such as the degree of privacy, quality of food, entertainment options, and so forth. Private facilities commonly have better amenities than public facilities, and while public facilities have an obligation to provide reasonable levels of amenities, it would be a poor use of scarce tax dollars to provide a level of amenities akin to high-end private facilities. Thus, overall, concerns about wait times appear to be a prime driver in Canada of demand for parallel private services.

The cost of private care creates an associated demand for parallel private insurance. Indeed, a market for parallel private insurance is necessary for a parallel private sector to flourish. In the absence of private insurance, the demand for privately financed care will remain limited to a small set of high-income or high-wealth individuals. This reality motivates provincial prohibitions against parallel private insurance.

The demand for private insurance is directly related to socio-economic status—internationally, those of higher socio-economic status are consistently more likely to hold private insurance.[9] Greater demand by those of higher socio-economic status is driven substantially by their greater ability to pay but also reflects differences in the value of time, tastes/attitudes, and the increasing tendency in many countries for high-ranking employees to obtain private insurance as an employment benefit.[10] This socio-economic gradient means that the relatively well-off can best take advantage of the private options and the associated preferential access to care. Differential access to care by those with and without private insurance prompts some countries to try to create broader access to private insurance through regulations that mandate community-rated premiums (the same premium must be charged to all individuals in a defined risk pool, regardless of their actual risk status) or, in the case

---

Between Private For-Profit and Private Not-for-Profit Hemodialysis Centers: A Systematic Review and Meta-Analysis" (2002) 288 JAMA 2449.

9   Hurley & Johnson, *supra* note 7; Sagan & Thomson, *supra* note 1.

10   Mark Stabile & Maripier Isabelle, "Rising Inequality and the Implications for the Future of Private Insurance in Canada" (2018) 13 Health Econ Pol'y & L 406.

of Denmark, favourable tax treatment when employers offer parallel private insurance as a benefit to all employees rather than only to senior management.[11] Ironically, such efforts to equalize access to parallel private insurance can produce larger system-wide inequities by supporting a stronger parallel private sector.

Demand for parallel private insurance does not automatically induce a corresponding supply of insurance. The viability of a private insurance industry depends on an array of factors, such as a risk-pool sufficiently large to spread risks effectively and an ability to avoid crippling adverse risk selection, the nemesis of health insurance markets. Adverse selection, whereby costly high-risk individuals disproportionately purchase insurance, can undermine an insurance market. It can be a particular challenge in secondary insurance markets, such as those for parallel private insurance, for in the presence of a reasonably functioning public system, parallel private insurance is attractive primarily to high users of care. Adverse selection is thought, for instance, to have contributed to the premium spiral, shrinking beneficiary base, and unprofitability that threatened the Australian private insurance sector during the 1990s, prior to the introduction of public subsidies and regulations to support the industry.[12] Adverse selection can be exacerbated by regulation designed to improve access and equity, such as community-rated premiums, which makes insurance particularly attractive to high-risk individuals for whom the community-rated premium makes insurance a bargain. For this reason, community rating in these markets is sometimes accompanied by risk-equalization or risk-sharing arrangements among insurers, such as in Ireland and Slovenia, and strategies such as offering insurance through group policies to attract a sufficiently diverse mix of risks to the insurance pool.[13]

Private health insurers themselves strive for the opposite type of selection—favourable selection—whereby they selectively enroll low-risk, profitable individuals. Except where regulation prohibits them from doing so, private insurers commonly deny coverage based on age, exclude coverage for pre-existing and chronic conditions, and

---

11   Maria Olejaz et al, *Denmark: Health System Review* (Copenhagen: European Observatory on Health Systems and Policies, 2012) at 70.

12   Jane Hall, Richard De Abreu Lourenco & Rosalie Viney, "Carrots and Sticks— The Fall and Fall of Private Health Insurance in Australia" (1991) 8 Health Econ 653.

13   Sagan & Thomson, *supra* note 1 at 25.

more generally exclude health conditions and health care services that place the insurer at risk of moral hazard, whereby consumers might purchase the insurance strategically when they anticipate using care (e.g., care for pregnancy and childbirth) or use of services is thought to be highly sensitive to the presence of insurance (e.g., mental-health care), and services that can be especially resource intensive (e.g., accident and emergency services).[14] Private insurers in more than half of the thirty-four EU countries examined by Sagan and Thomson (see note 1), for example, impose age-related coverage exclusions, and in twenty-nine of thirty-four EU countries, private insurers can exclude pre-existing conditions.[15] Fundamentally, without regulation, parallel private insurance will cover a narrow range of acute health conditions and health care services, with a focus on uncomplicated, elective surgical procedures targeted at a relatively healthy (and wealthy) population.

Parallel private insurance is regulated in many countries exclusively as a financial service, with regulation falling under an insurance regulator or similar body. Such regulation is aimed at a narrower set of policy goals pertaining to ensuring solvency (e.g., sufficient reserves) and related matters rather than the broader set of policy goals related to access and equity often associated with health insurance.[16] The industry is highly concentrated in most countries; in three-quarters of the EU countries examined by Sagan and Thomson, the market share controlled by the three largest insurers exceeded 50 per cent, which has attracted the attention of antitrust regulatory bodies in some cases.[17] And deceptive, or at least highly confusing, marketing and administrative practices has heightened the calls for greater consumer protection to simplify policies and make it easier for consumers to compare policies in a meaningful way. Canadian regulation of the complementary private insurance sector matches this, with regulation largely limited to financial matters that apply to all insurance products.[18]

Broader regulatory attention to parallel private insurance occurs particularly in countries that embrace parallel private finance as an

---

14 Thomas Foubister et al, *Private Medical Insurance in the United Kingdom* (Copenhagen: European Observatory on Health Systems and Policies, 2006) at 27.

15 Sagan & Thomson, *supra* note 1 at 62.

16 *Ibid* at 89.

17 *Ibid* at 60.

18 Hurley & Guindon, *supra* note 2.

integral part of their overall system of health care financing, such as in Australia and Ireland. The greater regulatory role arises in the first instance, to encourage uptake of private insurance through tax subsidies, community-rating schemes, and related policies to broaden access. This regulation—and the associated commitment of public resources—then spurs greater regulation, such as regulation of premium increases for private insurance, since premium increases translate directly into greater public expenditure on premium subsidies, regulation to ensure risk equalization and risk-sharing among insurers, and related efforts. Regulation in Australia and Ireland exemplify this pattern.[19]

Health-Services Markets

More common across countries is regulation of the health-services market to mitigate negative spillovers from the private to the public system. In the presence of parallel finance, the behaviour of individuals, who can obtain services in both sectors, and providers, who can work in both sectors, can create adverse effects across the public and private sectors. These effects and the associated need for regulatory response can be understood best by considering separately the demand- and supply-sides of the health-services markets, and the kinds of regulations that can be targeted at each.

Demand Side of the Health-Services Market

Expanding the role of parallel private finance would change the total demand for health care, the demand in each of the public and private sectors, and the composition of people who demand care. The demand for a health care service depends on its full cost to individuals, including both monetary and non-monetary costs. A public system with wait times does not charge patients a fee, but it does impose other non-monetary (e.g., pain, anxiety) and monetary (e.g., lost income) costs associated with waiting. Advocates of private finance emphasize private care as a substitute for public care. An expansion of privately financed care and the opportunity for quicker treatment will unquestionably cause some of those waiting in the

---

19   Judith Healy, Evelyn Sharman & Buddhima Lokuge, *Australia: Health System Review* (Copenhagen: European Observatory on Health Systems and Policies, 2006); David McDaid et al, *Ireland: Health System Review* (Copenhagen: European Observatory on Health Systems and Policies, 2009).

public system to seek private treatment, forgoing public care. But this is not the only effect on demand—the expansion would also generate *new* demand in both the private and public sectors, increasing the total demand for health care.

New demand arises, for instance, when expanded parallel private options enable individuals to access specialist care directly rather than only through referral by a family physician.[20] Some of this direct demand for specialist care would never have been expressed in a public-only system with gatekeeper family physicians, who would triage the patient at the primary-care level. Expanded opportunities for private care may also alter referral patterns and treatment thresholds for private care as physicians weigh more heavily the non-clinical preferences of patients compared to the prioritization criteria in the public system. New private demand would also occur when investors in private facilities promote their facilities and services to ensure a good return on their investment, prompting the "worried well" to seek tests and treatments they may not need.

New public demand arises because public and private care are sometimes complements, so increased demand for privately financed care can also increase demand for publicly financed care.[21] New complementary public demand occurs, for instance, when an individual considering private care first consults their primary-care physician, or when individuals privately obtain an assessment or diagnostic test and then subsequently demand publicly financed services on the basis of the private assessment or test, and/or when a complication develops during private treatment that must then be treated in the public system.

An expanded privately financed sector will alter the characteristics of those who obtain care. The "switchers" who substitute private care for public care will be those with high sensitivity to the costs of waiting and low sensitivity to the money price of private care (or

20   Ma Luz González Álvarez & Antonio Clavero Barranquero, "Inequalities in Health Care Utilization in Spain Due to Double Insurance Coverage: An Oaxaca-Ransom Decomposition" (2009) 69:5 Soc Sci Med 793.

21   Mark Stabile, "Private Insurance Subsidies and Public Health Care Markets: Evidence from Canada" (2003) 34:4 Can J Econ 921; Sherry Glied, "Universal Public Health Insurance and Private Coverage: Externalities in Health Care Consumption" (2008) 34 Can Pub Pol'y 345; Sara Allin & Jeremiah Hurley, "Inequity in Publicly Funded Physician Care: What is the Role of Private Prescription Drug Insurance?" (2009) 18 Health Econ 1218.

private insurance), such as high-income, working individuals. Hence a system with expanded private finance devotes more resources to those with higher incomes. Further, to the extent that new demand is from individuals with relatively lower levels of clinical need but a high degree of impatience and risk aversion, the share of care devoted to those with lower needs would increase.

In sum, these demand-side effects generate two types of concern that underlie calls for regulation. First, the changed mix of demanders exacerbates socio-economic-related inequality of access to health care. Second, increased private and total demand can divert resources from the public sector, reducing access to the public system for those who must rely on it. As described below, the ultimate impact of parallel private finance on access to the public system depends on the net effect of changes in the demand for care and changes in the supply of care.

Supply-side regulation under parallel finance targets the interactions between the two systems that can have a negative impact on the public system. These interactions can be particularly problematic when providers are permitted to work in both the public and private sectors—dual practice—and so that is a particular focus of regulation (and explains why dual practice is restricted in a number of Canadian provinces). But interactions arise even in the absence of dual practice.

As noted already, expanded parallel private finance increases competition for shared inputs into the delivery of care, driving up the prices of those inputs (e.g., the fees paid to physicians), and reducing the real value of the nominal public budget. These price increases can be implicit or explicit. Implicit higher wages arise when physicians are allowed to collect a full public salary but work more than the officially sanctioned hours in their private practices at the expense of time spent on public care, implicitly raising the public-sector hourly wage. Such implicit wage increases have been particularly problematic in mixed health care systems with salaried hospital-based consultants.[22] Evidence from tax records, care audits, surveys, case studies, and anecdote indicates that in England, for instance, specialist consultants in the NHS commonly devoted more

---

22   Ariadna García-Prado & Paula González, "Whom Do Physicians Work For? An Analysis of Dual Practice in the Health Sector" (2011) 36:2 J Health Pol Pol'y & L 265.

time to the delivery of private care than was officially allowed by their contract.[23] The problem has been less severe in recent years because, among a number of changes, the 2003 consultant contract explicitly increased NHS pay rates by approximately 25 per cent, enhancing the attractiveness of NHS work—precisely the kind of wage increase that exemplifies how competition between the sectors can lead to higher prices for inputs to care.[24] The UK experience is not isolated. In an effort to combat brain drain from the public to the private sector, in 1996 the Norwegian government increased hospital physician wages for overtime and extended work by approximately 11 per cent so as to increase the allocation of physician time to public sector work.[25] Nor are such competitive wage effects isolated to the physician sector. In presenting to the Standing Senate Committee on Social Affairs, Science and Technology, Dr. Brian Day of the Cambie Clinic observed that:

> We are not a unionized facility because if we were, we would have the same trouble getting nurses as the hospitals have. We pay our nurses 15 percent higher than the highest level they can achieve after 12 years in the public system, because we need these nurses ... Again, to attract those people [central sterile technicians], we have to pay higher than union wages.[26]

In addition to its effects on costs, such competition tends to bid away from the public sector more senior, experienced physicians, leaving

23 John Yates, *Private Eye, Heart and Hip: Surgical Consultants, the National Health Service and Private Medicine* (London: Churchill Livingstone, 1995); Audit Commission, *The Doctor's Tale: The Work of Hospital Doctors in England and Wales* (London: HMSO, 1995); Stephen Morris et al, "Analysis of Consultants' NHS and Private Incomes in England in 2003/4" (2008) 101 J Royal Soc Med 372.

24 National Audit Office, *Managing NHS Hospital Consultants* (London: The Stationary Office, 2012), online: <https://www.nao.org.uk/wp-content/uploads/2013/03/Hospital-consultants-full-report.pdf>.

25 Karl-Arne Johannessen & Terje P Hagen, "Physicians' Engagement in Dual Practices and the Effects on Labour Supply in Public Hospitals: Results from a Register-Based Study" (2013) 14 BMC Health Serv Res 299.

26 Dr. Brian Day, Evidence Government of Canada, Proceedings of the Standing Senate Committee on Social Affairs, Science and Technology, First session Thirty-seventh Parliament, 2001, Thursday, 18 October 2001, quoted in Teresa Healy, "Health Care Privatization and the Workers' Compensation System in Canada" (Paper delivered at Canadian Political Science Association meetings, Saskatoon, 1 June 2007).

a disproportionate share of public care to junior, less-experienced consultants, a phenomenon that also likely applies to other types of health professionals.[27]

Probably the most contentious question in relation to parallel private finance is its impact on access to the publicly funded system by those who continue to rely on the public system for care—the problem that is captured by the term "two-tier care" in the title of this book. The impact depends on the relative magnitudes of various counteracting effects. Current empirical evidence on these effects is contestable, often derived from observational studies that suffer measurement problems, possible sources of bias, and challenges to establishing causation. Despite these analytic and empirical challenges, we know a considerable amount about many of the most important determinants of the ultimate impact.[28]

The expansion of parallel private finance will change the total supply of a service, the supply offered through the public sector, and the supply offered through the private sector. Such supply-side changes depend importantly on the institutional details of the system design. For this discussion, I assume that the rate of pay offered in the private sector would be higher than that in the public sector (the norm internationally); dual practice is allowed and feasible; that there is a positive relationship between physician labour supply and service supply, and an increase in physician labour is required to produce more services;[29] and that the supply of care is not limited by some factor (e.g., the restricted amount of some inputs) for which the expansion of private finance would have no impact.

The expansion of parallel private finance, and the associated opportunity to earn additional income at a higher rate of pay, influences two types of work decisions for physicians: the decision whether to work, and, among those who do work, decisions regarding the total number of hours to work and the allocation of

---

27   García-Prado & González, *supra* note 22.

28   Hurley & Johnson, *supra* note 7.

29   Physician time and effort are the primary but not the only inputs into the production of most health care services. Physicians combine their labour with non-physician personnel (e.g., receptionists, nurses, other non-physician professionals) and capital (office space, equipment). By substituting these other inputs for their own time, in some circumstances physicians can simultaneously increase the supply of services while reducing their own labour supplied.

time across the public and private sectors and among professional activities such as patient care, administration, teaching, and research.

By affecting retirement and migration decisions, parallel private finance could influence the number of active physicians in Canada. In the short-term, new private-sector opportunities for practice could cause some currently retired physicians to re-enter the workforce, though such an effect would be temporary. More generally, on an ongoing basis it could alter the retirement decisions of working physicians, and this impact could cut both ways: the ability to earn higher income could cause physicians to delay retirement, thereby increasing the overall supply of physician labour relative to what it would have been in the absence of parallel finance, but the ability to earn higher income throughout their career could cause some to retire earlier than otherwise would have been the case (having achieved the required retirement savings at a younger age). In addition, if the current restricted options for private practice causes some physicians to choose not to work in Canada, less restrictive regulation could induce some of these physicians to practice in Canada. If these factors expand the supply of physicians providing patient care, private provision could expand without diverting resources from the public system; otherwise, it could draw net physician resources away from the public sector. We have no reliable evidence regarding the magnitude of these possible effects on the supply of active physicians.

Among those physicians in active practice, a new opportunity to earn private-sector income at a higher rate of pay creates counteracting incentives regarding the total hours of work, and changes incentives regarding the allocation of work effort across the two sectors and across professional activities. A higher rate of pay in the private sector means that, for the same total work effort, physicians can earn a higher income (the income effect). If the demand for leisure time increases with income, as is commonly true, then this income effect would induce a physician to decrease the overall amount of time spent working. At the same time, the higher rate of pay in the private sector increases the opportunity cost of not providing private-sector patient care. This creates incentive to reallocate time by working more overall (and taking less leisure; the substitution effect), and, within the time spent working, to reallocate time to the private provision of patient care and away from the provision of patient care in the public sector and away from non-patient-care professional activities. On net, the predicted impact on total hours of work is ambiguous—if the income effect dominates, total physician work hours would fall; if the substitution effect dominates, total physician work hours would increase, but the analysis predicts unambiguously that among the hours worked the share of hours devoted to direct patient care in the private practice would increase, the share devoted to direct patient care in the public sector, and non-patient-care professional activities would decrease. But because of the ambiguous effect on total hours of work, the amount of physician time spent providing patient care could increase, decrease, or remain the same.

We have no direct evidence specifically documenting the impact of parallel private finance on physician labour supply and the associated supply of physician services. We do, however, have evidence regarding how physician labour and service supply responds to changing fees, on the impact of payment on the allocation of physician effort across professional activities, and on the allocation of time and effort across the public and private sectors in systems that allow dual practice. Studies of the total number of hours worked by physicians find that, in general, it is not highly responsive to modest changes in earnings, with some studies showing small positive responses (higher wages cause physicians to work more) and others small negative ones (higher wages cause physicians to work fewer hours).[30] The evidence regarding their allocation of time across the public and private sectors is more limited but indicates that increases in wages in one leads physicians to allocate more time to that sector for which the wage increased while holding total hours of work constant.[31] Within Canada, higher expedited fees offered by some provincial workers' compensation boards have led physicians to allocate work effort toward workers' compensation cases, though we

---

30   Thomas F Crossley, Jeremiah Hurley & Sung-Hee Jeon, "Physician Labour Supply in Canada: A Cohort Analysis" (2008) 18 Health Econ 437; Sung-Hee Jeon & Jeremiah Hurley, "Physician Resource Planning in Canada: The Need for a Stronger Behavioural Foundation" (2010) 36:3 Can Pub Pol'y 359; Leif Andreassen, Maria Laura Di Tommaso & Steinar Strøm, "Do Medical Doctors Respond to Economic Incentives?" (2013) 32:2 J Health Econ 392; Guyonne Kalb et al, "What Factors Affect Physicians' Labour Supply: Comparing Structural Choice and Reduced-Form Approaches" (2017) 27 Health Econ 749.

31   Erik Magnus Sæther, "Physicians' Labour Supply: The Wage Impact on Hours of Practice Combinations" (2005) 19:4 Labour 673; Terence C Cheng, Guyonne Kalb & Anthony Scott, "Public, Private or Both? Analyzing Factors Influencing the Labour Supply of Medical Specialists" (2018) 51:2 Can J Econ 659.

do not know what impact this may have had on time spent treating patients in the public system.[32]

We have more limited evidence regarding how the allocation of effort across different professional activities responds to financial incentives, but a study from Quebec found that a policy that increased wages for some professional activities and decreased them for others caused hospital-based specialist to reallocate work effort, decreasing hours of work spent seeing patients by 2.6 per cent and increasing time spent on teaching and administrative duties (tasks not previously remunerated) by 7.9 per cent.[33]

The evidence available, therefore, suggests that the expansion of a parallel private system and higher earnings opportunities for physicians would have little or no effect on the total hours worked by physicians, would cause them to reallocate effort from the public to the private sector, and may cause some to reallocate effort from non-patient care to patient care. Overall, it would be expected to decrease labour supplied to patient care in the public sector.

In recent years, concern has emerged about underemployment of certain types of specialist physicians in Canada, a situation with roots in an array of health-system, economic, social, and personal factors.[34] A particular concern among some surgical specialities has been the impact of limited access to operating room time and/or hospital beds in the public system. In such a situation, it is argued, physicians could undertake increased surgery in the private sector with no loss to the public system. To the extent that some physicians who desire to work more overall are truly sitting idle, this would represent untapped capacity that could be employed in the private sector with no loss to the public system. Often, however, the challenge is less that of no work or underemployment overall but of allocation of work effort across clinical activities within the public system; some surgical specialists spend less time doing surgery and

---

32   Jeremiah Hurley et al, "Parallel Payers and Preferred Access: How Canada's Workers' Compensation Boards Expedite Care for Injured and Ill Workers" (2008) 8:3 Healthcare Papers 6.

33   Etienne Dumont et al, "Physicians' Multitasking and Incentives: Empirical Evidence From a Natural Experiment" (2008) 27:6 J Health Econ 1436.

34   Danielle Frechette et al, *What's Really Behind Canada's Unemployed Specialists? Too Many, Too Few Doctors?* (Ottawa: Royal Colleges of Physicians and Surgeons of Canada, 2013).

more time on non-surgical clinical care than they desire.[35] In such a situation, unless increased private-sector surgery represented a net addition to work overall, it would come at the expense of clinical care in the public system. Unfortunately, we have limited data on the nature and extent of these issues within the Canadian system.

Regulatory Approaches

The ongoing *Cambie* case challenges multiple elements of the Canadian approach to the regulation of private finance—private insurance, extra-billing, and opted-in physicians' ability to charge patients directly—and its impact would be national in scope. If the prohibition against parallel private insurance is struck down, it would affect five provinces (British Columbia, Alberta, Manitoba, Ontario, Prince Edward Island) that currently prohibit parallel private insurance, and possibly pose a threat to Quebec's (newer) restrictive limits on such insurance passed in response to *Chaoulli*.[36] If the prohibition on extra-billing is struck down, this would affect the eight provinces (British Columbia, Alberta, Saskatchewan, Manitoba, Ontario, Quebec, Nova Scotia, Newfoundland and Labrador) that explicitly prohibit extra-billing. If the restrictions on billing patients directly are struck down, this would affect five other provinces (Manitoba, Ontario, Quebec, Nova Scotia, Newfoundland and Labrador) with similar provisions. And if the restrictions on the amount opted-out physicians can charge are struck down, this would affect four other provinces (Alberta, Manitoba, Ontario, Nova Scotia) with similar provisions. If fully successful, therefore, the Cambie case would strike down multiple elements for most

---

35   Geographic preferences can also play a role in this phenomenon. Some physicians prefer to be located in urban areas, even at the cost of a less desired mix of professional activities, while opportunities exist in more rural areas. Although beyond the scope of this analysis, an expanded private sector would likely be concentrated in urban areas, which could exacerbate the geographic maldistribution of physicians.

36   Colleen M Flood & Tom Archibald, "The Illegality of Private Health Care in Canada" (2001) 164:6 CMAJ 825; Gerard W Boychuk, "The Regulation of Private Health Funding and Insurance in Alberta under the Canada Health Act: A Comparative Cross-Provincial Perspective" (2008) 1:1 U Calgary SPS Research Papers, online: <https://www.policyschool.ca/publications/regulation-private-health-funding-and-insurance-alberta-under-canada-health-act-comparative/>.

provinces.[37] Note that, with the exception of Ontario since 2004, no province explicitly bans dual practice; rather, the inability to engage in dual practice follows from the combination of restrictions on physicians' billing practices and beneficiaries' ability to obtain public reimbursement if billed directly by a physician for a covered service. Although the details vary across provinces, with the exception of Newfoundland and Labrador, in each province these restrictions preclude dual practice.

While court decisions change the regulatory tools available, they do not directly change the fundamental policy goal, which to date has been to restrict the role of parallel private finance so as to limit adverse spillovers from the parallel private system to the public system. The present regulatory approaches in Canada makes sense if one believes that other regulatory tools do not sufficiently limit the negative spillovers associated with a parallel system, making a highly restrictive approach the only effective option. If one or more of the current regulations are struck down, provincial governments will have to consider alternative approaches in pursuit of the overall goal of minimizing the negative impact on equity and access.

Regulating Private Insurance

As emphasized earlier, a robust parallel private sector requires a functioning market for parallel private insurance. Short of prohibition, both demand- and supply-side policies can limit the prevalence of private insurance. Tax policy can play a central role on the demand side. First and foremost would be to ensure no tax subsidies support the purchase of parallel private insurance as tax policy currently subsidizes complementary private insurance at the federal level and in all provinces except Quebec. The tax subsidy arises because the value of employer-provided private insurance is not included as a taxable benefit for an employee. The value of this tax expenditure was estimated to be $2.6 billion in 2015 for the federal government alone.[38] Unless the tax regulation is changed, the subsidy would also apply to employer-provided parallel private insurance, which has been the fastest growing component of

---

37   Flood & Archibald, *supra* note 36; Boychuk, *supra* note 36.
38   Department of Finance Canada, *Report on Federal Tax Expenditures: Concepts, Estimate, and Evaluations* (Ottawa: Government of Canada, 2018).

parallel insurance markets internationally.[39] Fully eliminating any subsidy would require action at both the federal and provincial levels. Tax policy, however, could go further than eliminating the subsidy; governments could tax the purchase of parallel private insurance (and ideally this could be coordinated between the federal and provincial governments, though this complicates matters). From an economic perspective, parallel private insurance imposes negative financial externalities on the public system, making the market-determined level of consumption of private insurance higher than the socially optimal level.[40] A standard economic regulatory response in such situations is to reduce consumption by imposing a tax on the good or service. The impact of the tax on purchases of parallel private insurance would depend on the size of the tax, but the evidence regarding the effects of the current tax subsidy on the demand for employer-provided private complementary insurance suggests that the impact could be substantial. A comparison of the demand for private insurance in Quebec (no provincial subsidy) with the demand in other provinces (all with subsidies) estimates that removal of the provincial tax subsidy in Quebec reduced demand by 20 per cent.[41] As a further advantage, the tax revenue could be used to counteract some of the negative financial spillovers of private insurance on the public system; the revenue could be used, for instance, to maintain the real value of public funding in the face of higher input prices caused by competition with the private sector for inputs. However, I am not aware of any country that has implemented such a tax, though private health insurance in the United Kingdom is subject to a 12 per cent "insurance premium tax" that applies to insurance premiums in general (i.e., it is not specific to health insurance).[42]

The growth of parallel private insurance could also be inhibited through regulation of permissible benefit packages. Following the *Chaoulli* decision that struck down Quebec's ban on private insurance,

---

39   Sagan & Thomson, *supra* note 1.

40   Glied, *supra* note 21.

41   Stabile, *supra* note 21; Amy Finklestein, "The Effect of Tax Subsidies to Employer-Provided Supplementary Health Insurance: Evidence From Canada" (2002) 84:3 J Pub Econ 305.

42   HM Revenue & Customs, "Guidance: Insurance Premium Tax Rates" (2017), online: <https://www.gov.uk/government/publications/rates-and-allowances-insurance-premium-tax/insurance-premium-tax-rates >.

for instance, the government's response (Bill 33) allowed for parallel private insurance but only for a very small number of procedures with long wait times.[43] To date, no insurer has offered a policy for sale. Somewhat paradoxically, the opposite approach—requiring a minimum basket of services that goes beyond the types of simple elective procedures that are the staple of the parallel private insurance industry—might also make offering insurance unattractive to insurance companies, effectively stifling the development of the market. Finally, regulations that prohibit discrimination on the basis of age or health status, and pre-existing conditions in particular, can be justified on grounds of equity and access but may similarly make entering the market financially unattractive for an insurer. The precise mix of policies would need to be determined, but the broader point is that regulation of benefit packages and terms of sale offers a possible regulatory approach to influence the size of the private insurance market and the nature of the services covered.

Extra-Billing

Should the courts strike down existing prohibitions on extra-billing, a number of regulatory options could limit is growth. New Brunswick and Nova Scotia do not prohibit extra-billing but curb its practice by denying public coverage to patients who obtain services from physicians who extra-bill.[44] A province could also prohibit private insurance coverage for the amount of extra-billing charged by physicians. Finally, while Australia allows extra-billing, it provides incentives for general practitioners to accept the public fee as payment in full (a practice known as bulk billing), which most general practitioners do and private insurance is not permitted to cover extra-billing charges.[45]

Dual Practice

Dual practice—which I take to include both physician dual practice and the practice of publicly funded hospitals providing care to both private-pay and publicly funded patients—presents a greater challenge. The latter has been a particular focus of regulation

---

43   Bill 33, *An Act to amend the Act respecting health services and social services and other legislative provisions*, 2nd Sess, 37th Leg, Quebec, 2006 (assented to 13 December 2006).

44   Flood, *supra* note 36; Boychuk, *supra* note 36.

45   Healy, Sharman & Lokuge, *supra* note 19.

internationally intended to ensure that public hospitals do not give priority to private-pay patients and that public dollars do not subsidize private-pay patients. Public hospitals have incentive to prioritize private patients because such patients bring additional revenue outside the public funding stream. Attempts to prevent prioritization of private patients often amount to little more than prohibiting such practices in principle, but with weak monitoring and enforcement, making the prohibition relatively ineffective. For example, although Australian regulations prohibit giving priority to private patients, in practice public hospitals do give priority to private-pay patients over public patients.[46]

The simplest and most effective approach to addressing both of these problems is to prohibit publicly funded facilities from treating private patients—but given public-sector fiscal constraints, the temptation is to allow this on the argument that such private revenue could subsidize public provision. An alternative option would be to require public facilities to charge a high price—unequivocally above the cost of care—to ensure that the public system does not subsidize private patients, and for the provincial government to then claw back that portion of the price above the cost to the facility. Such a scheme would ensure no subsidy to private patients, thwart the facility's incentive to prioritize private patients, and retain the incremental revenue for the general public funding stream rather than having all of it stay with the facility providing the care.

Regulating physician dual practice is more difficult, and options will depend importantly on what, if any, of current regulations are declared unconstitutional. Regulation of dual practice internationally generally takes a few basic forms, restricting the amount of private-sector activity allowable, providing incentives to devote time to the public rather than private sector, and structuring the work context to be able to monitor private provision.[47] Limitations generally

---

46   Meliyanni Johar, "Are Waiting List Prioritization Guidelines Being Followed in Australia?" (2014) 34:8 Med Decision Making 976; Meliyanni Johar, Glen Stewart Jones & Elizabeth Savage, "Emergency Admissions and Elective Surgery Wait Times" (2013) 22 Health Econ 749; Amir Shmueli & Elizabeth Savage, "Private and Public Patients in Public Hospitals in Australia" (2014) 115 Health Pol'y 189.

47   García-Prado & González, *supra* note 22; Karolina Z Socha & Mickael Bech, "Physician Dual Practice: A Review of Literature" (2011) 102:1 Health Pol'y 1; Paula González & Inés Macho-Stadler, "A Theoretical Approach to Dual Practice Regulations in the Health Sector" (2013) 32:1 J Health Econ 66.

take the form of limiting the amount of income an opted-in physician can earn through private-sector work, limiting the proportion of time a physician can allocate to private-sector work, or limiting the quantity of procedures that can be provided through private-sector work. Incentives take the form of increasing compensation in the public sector or offering some other kinds of perks. Attempts to enhance monitoring suggest allowing physicians to do private practice in public facilities on the logic that it is easier to observe than if private-sector work is in a different setting. Two key problems arise for Canada in drawing lessons from others' experience. First, although there is little high-quality evidence, the general consensus is that, commonly, these regulatory policies are not effective, particularly due to problems of monitoring and enforcement. Second, the context for most regulatory discussion differs from Canada's in two important ways: many studies derive from settings in which the public sector pays a fixed salary to physician employees (e.g., salaried hospital consultants), and the extant literature focuses notably on low- and middle-income settings, which face challenges distinct from those of Canada. If the courts rule that prohibiting dual practice is unconstitutional, two options may be feasible and effective. The first, which is really just an extension of the principle underlying the current approach, is to use indirect regulatory tools to make private practice economically unattractive so that, while dual practice is allowed, few choose the option. A second option would be to use carrots; for example, offer inducements for opted-in physicians who commit to not engage in dual practice. These could be financial incentives—admittedly further stressing already-strained provincial public budgets—but it may be possible to devise other inducements that make public practice easier or more attractive, similar in spirit, for example, to Australia's use of bulk billing for physicians who choose not to extra-bill. Either way, this approach amounts to competing directly with the private sector for physician time and effort.

Discussion

To achieve its goal of limiting the role of parallel private finance while not prohibiting it outright, Canadian provinces have devised an effective, coordinated set of regulations across both the insurance and health-service sectors, and across the demand and supply sides of each. Canada is frequently portrayed as an outlier among peer countries in the extent to which it limits parallel private finance for its core medicare services, but even countries that permit a larger role for parallel private finance regulate such finance and its inter-action with the public system.[48] Indeed, as emphasized, protecting the public system while allowing a larger role for parallel private finance requires a more elaborate and robust regulatory regime to address the more numerous, nuanced, and complex ways the two systems interact. Should the courts strike down components of the provinces' current regulations, the need to develop a carefully constructed regulatory approach will become even more important, while the set of available tools becomes more limited and may not be politically feasible (for a discussion of the difficulties of achieving public medicare in the first place, and of the various interest groups opposed, see chapter 1).

Regulation in such a world is likely less effective than the current regulatory approach, but provincial governments will still, in theory, have options to limit both the size of the parallel private sector and the adverse impacts of parallel private finance on the public system. Central to this will be the more active use of tax pol-icy, more emphasis on the demand side, and a continued focus on a coordinated approach across both the insurance and service sectors with regulations that complement and mutually reinforce each other. At this time, there is limited good evidence on which to base such regulation, so governments will have to remain flexible, evaluate, and be willing to modify their approaches as they gain experience, assuming, of course, they have the political will to wish to maintain and improve publicly funded medicare.

Given the evolution of the health care sector, the opportunities and pressures for parallel finance will unquestionably expand even if the current regulations are upheld, making renewed attention to regulation, including possibly new elements, important. Both increased government contracting with private facilities for the pub-licly financed delivery of covered services and expanding markets for privately financed non-medically necessary services (e.g., cosmetic procedures) will attract new private capital to the health sector. The investors in these private facilities will seek to maximize their

---

48   Colleen M Flood & Amanda Haugan, "Is Canada Odd? A Comparison of European and Canadian Approaches to Choice and Regulation of the Public/Private Divide in Health Care" (2010) 5:3 Health Econ Pol'y & L 319.

return, and privately financed parallel delivery represents an obvi-ous opportunity. Further, if dual practice is allowed, these private facilities offer opportunities for physicians to provide private care without making large investments themselves, increasing the attrac-tiveness of the option. Regardless of the outcomes of the court cases, Canadian provinces must develop more sophisticated approaches to regulating private finance.

CHAPTER 4

Chaoulli v Quebec: Cause or Symptom of Quebec Health System Privatization?

Amélie Quesnel-Vallée, Rachel McKay, and Noushon Farmanara

Chaoulli v Quebec

In a much-publicized and contentious decision, the Supreme Court of Canada ruled in 2005 that Quebec's legal prohibition on the purchase of private insurance for publicly insured services contravened the *Quebec Charter of Human Rights and Freedoms, when the public system wait times are too long.*[1] Jacques Chaoulli, an orthopaedic surgeon, had a longstanding, strained relationship with the Quebec health care system. He had opted out of the public health insurance system but was unsuccessful in his attempts to obtain a license for providing privately financed home-delivered medical services and to operate an independent private hospital. In his challenge of Quebec's law banning private insurance, he was supported by George Zeliotis, a user of the health care system who claimed his quality of life had been compromised as a result of having to wait a year for hip-replacement surgery.[2] Notably, Chaoulli and Zeliotis' claims

We gratefully acknowledge funding from the McGill Observatory on Health and Social Services Reforms, research assistance from Arisha Khan and Hugo Tartaglia, and comments from the participants at the *Is Two-Tier Care the Future? Private Finance in Canadian Medicare* Conference, 6–7 April 2018. Amélie Quesnel-Vallée was supported in this work by the Canada Research Chair on Policies and Health Inequalities.

1   *Chaoulli v Quebec (Attorney General)*, 2005 SCC 35 [*Chaoulli*].
2   *Ibid.*

were not initially joint but they merged their mutual interests after both had unsuccessful attempts with their individual challenges.[3] As discussed in chapter 2, the applicants' challenge relied on both the *Canadian Charter of Rights and Freedoms*[4] and the *Quebec Charter of Human Rights & Freedoms*,[5] but it was only in the latter that the Supreme Court reached a majority conclusion. With respect to the *Canadian Charter*, the court was divided (a 3–3 ruling with one abstention). Therefore, the ruling's influence was largely applicable only in Quebec (although its normative potential as harbinger of future *Charter* challenges was significant).

As others discuss in this volume, the forthcoming challenge in *Cambie*[6] relies on the *Canadian Charter*, and, if successful, will have national implications given the similarities of laws across Canada protective of public medicare. Further, *Cambie* is a much broader challenge than *Chaoulli*, tackling not only the ban on private health insurance, but also provisions related to extra-billing bans, user-fee bans, tariff limits, and dual-practice bans. The implications, therefore, are much broader in terms of potential impact.

In this chapter, we describe the Quebec government's response to *Chaoulli*, explore the extent of privatization of health care in Quebec, and discuss the extent of the evidence showing a relationship between privatization growth and the *Chaoulli* ruling. The introduction of Bill 33 by the Quebec government on the heels of *Chaoulli* raised several concerns about the potential for expansion, and runaway, of the private market,[7] while the then health minister (Philippe Couillard) downplayed its potential impact, pronouncing: "En réponse au jugement rendu par la Cour suprême du Canada, le gouvernement entend agir avec grande prudence et ne permettre qu'une ouverture très limitée à l'assurance privée."[8]

---

3   Christopher P Manfredi and Antonia Maioni, "*Chaoulli v Québec*: The Last Line of Defence for Citizens" in *Health Care and the Charter: Legal Mobilization and Policy Change in Canada* (Vancouver: University of British Columbia Press, 2018).

4   *Canadian Charter of Rights and Freedoms*, Part I of the *Constitution Act, 1982*, being Schedule B to the *Canada Act 1982* (UK), 1982, c 11 [*Charter*].

5   *Charter of Human Rights and Freedoms*, CQLR, 2016, c C-12 [Quebec *Charter*].

6   *Cambie Surgeries v British Columbia (Medical Services Commission)*, (2015) Vancouver S090663 [*Cambie*].

7   Marie-Claude Prémont, "Clearing the Path for Private Health Markets in Post-Chaoulli Quebec" (2008) Health LJ 237.

8   National Assembly of Québec, Committee on Social Affairs, *Consultations Particulières Sur Le Projet de Loi No 33 — Loi Modifiant La Loi Sur Les Services*

In this chapter, we look at the consequences of Bill 33 twelve years after its 2006 implementation. First, we will present the government's response to the *Chaoulli* decision, Bill 33, and demonstrate that the elements of the bill that were of greatest concern—namely, that there would be a surge growth of duplicative private insurance and of private medical clinics—did not manifest as problems. Having said that, Quebec is arguably home to one of the most dynamic private health markets in the country, and thus, as we will discuss, *Chaoulli* may have had an impact outside the scope of Bill 33. In the second section of this chapter, we turn to review some of the critical "hot spots" of privatization in Quebec that could have been exacerbated by *Chaoulli*. We find evidence to show that privatization *was already under way* before this decision, sometimes decades prior. This is true of private diagnostic services, which are reimbursable by private insurance; of physicians opting out of the public system; and of user fees. We then conclude with a contrast of the policy instruments targeted respectively by *Chaoulli* and *Cambie*, and draw hypotheses regarding future responses in Quebec considering the trends observed to this day. Through these examples, we demonstrate that *Chaoulli* was not so much the cause as much as a symptom of rampant privatization of the Quebec system. This would lead us to expect that a decision in favour of *Cambie* would find fertile ground in Quebec.

The Government's Response

One year after the *Chaoulli* ruling, the Quebec government enacted Bill 33, *An Act to amend the Act respecting health services and social services and other legislative provisions*. This legislation did allow for the purchase of private insurance, but only for three procedures (hip, knee, and cataract surgeries). However, it also provided that procedures for which private insurance would be allowed would be determined by regulation, thereby facilitating the subsequent expansion of such. The list of such procedures was indeed subsequently amended in 2008 to include some cosmetic surgeries performed with anaesthesia, and, when provided under general or regional anaesthesia, included some forms of breast, cosmetic, orthopedic, upper

---

de Santé et Les Services Sociaux et d'autres Dispositions Législatives, 39, No 45 (12 September 2006).

respiratory tract, vascular and lymphatic, digestive, gynecological, nervous system, eye, ear, and cutaneous surgeries, and breast biopsies.[9] While the government's white paper, which preceded the bill and outlined the intended response, proposed clear guidelines for wait times guarantees, no such standard was present in Bill 33, and any designation of "how long would be too long" was ultimately left up to the health minister's discretion.[10] In addition, the bill provided a legal framework for the establishment of (private) specialized medical clinics to perform the above-mentioned surgical procedures, also allowing public hospitals to contract out procedures listed in the regulations to these private clinics when the public system could not meet its wait time objectives. Finally, Bill 33 effectively maintained a seal between public and private practice. First, it maintained the prohibition against public-private dual practice, which prevents physicians from billing both privately and publicly for the same medically necessary acts that are publicly insured. In addition, it included a new provision prohibiting physicians from the public and the private sectors from working under the same roof. In effect, this meant that physicians staffing the private medical clinics had to entirely opt out from receiving any remuneration from the Quebec public insurance plan (RAMQ).

The introduction of Bill 33 was contentious. While the Quebec government asserted that it was a necessary response to a Supreme Court of Canada ruling, commentators claimed that other options were possible. Many indeed argued that the government could (and indeed, should) have invoked the notwithstanding clause (s. 33) of the *Canadian Charter* to maintain the prohibition against private insurance, declaring that it applies despite section 52[11] of the Quebec *Charter*.[12] An in-depth review of stakeholder input during

---

9   *Regulation Respecting the Specialized Medical Treatments Provided in a Specialized Medical Centre*, CQLR c S-4.2, r 25.

10   "Guaranteeing Access: Meeting the Challenges of Equity, Efficiency and Quality" (2006), online (PDF): *Government of Québec* <https://www.bibliotheque.assnat.qc.ca/DepotNumerique_v2/AffichageFichier.aspx?idf=101908>.

11   Section 52 of the Quebec *Charter* states: "No provision of any Act, even subsequent to the Charter, may derogate from sections 1 to 38, except so far as provided by those sections, unless such Act expressly states that it applies despite the Charter."

12   Jean-Francois Gaudreault-Desbiens & Charles-Maxime Panaccio, "Chaoulli and Québec's Charter of Human Rights and Freedoms," in Colleen M Flood, Kent Roach & Lorne Sossin, eds, *Access to Care, Access to Justice: The Legal Debate over*

the bill's review process indicates that very little changed between its introduction and final assent, despite vocal reservations from interest groups; for instance, the Confédération des organismes de personnes handicapées du Québec,[13] the Fédérations des infirmières et infirmiers du Québec,[14] and the Confédération des syndicats nationaux[15] all expressed concern during the consultations over the extension of private health care provided for in the bill; the Fédération des médecins omnipraticiens du Québec (FMOQ)[16] and the Fédération des médecins résidents du Québec (FMRQ),[17] while generally agreeing with the government's objectives to reduce wait times, also questioned the necessity of further gains in the private sector. However, despite the concerns raised by stakeholders

Private Health Insurance in Canada (Toronto: University of Toronto Press, 2005) at 32.

13 La Confédération des Organismes de Personnes Handicapées du Québec, "Avis de La Confédération des Organismes de Personnes Handicapées Du Québec (COPHAN) Présenté à La Commission Des Affaires Sociales Sur Le Projet de Loi 33: Loi Modifiant La Loi Sur Les Services de Santé et Les Services Sociaux et d'autres Dispositions Législatives" (October 2006), online (PDF): <http://www.assnat.qc.ca/Media/Process.aspx?MediaId=ANQ. Vigie.Bll.DocumentGenerique_2613&process=Original&token=Zy-MoxNwUn8ikQ+TRKYwPCjWrKwg+vIv9rjij7p3xLGTZDmLVSmJLoqe/vG7/YWzz>.

14 Fédération des infirmières et infirmiers du Québec, "Mémoire: Des Cliniques Publiques Financées Publiquement" (12 September 2006), online (PDF): <www.assnat.qc.ca/Media/Process.aspx?MediaId=ANQ. Vigie.Bll.DocumentGenerique_6711&process=Original&token=Zy-MoxNwUn8ikQ+TRKYwPCjWrKwg+vIv9rjij7p3xLGTZDmLVSmJLoqe/vG7/YWzz>.

15 Confédération des syndicats nationaux, "Commentaires de La Confédération Des Syndicats Nationaux Sur Le Projet de Loi No 33: Loi Modifiant La Loi Sur Les Services de Santé et Les Services Sociaux et Autres Dispositions Législatives" (7 September 2006), online (PDF): <www.assnat.qc.ca/Media/Process.aspx?MediaId=ANQ.Vigie.Bll.DocumentGenerique_2633&process=Original&token=-ZyMoxNwUn8ikQ+TRKYwPCjWrKwg+vIv9rjij7p3xLGTZDmLVSmJLoqe/vG7/YWzz>.

16 Fédération des médecins omnipraticiens du Québec, "Mémoire de La Fédération Des Médecins Omnipraticiens Du Québec à La Commission Des Affaires Sociales" (13 September 2006), online (PDF): <www.assnat.qc.ca/Media/Process.aspx?MediaId=ANQ.Vigie.Bll.DocumentGenerique_2691&process=Original&token=ZyMoxNwUn8ikQ+TRKYwPCjWrKwg+vIv9rjij7p3xLGTZDmLVSmJLoqe/vG7/YWzz>.

17 Fédération des médecins résidents du Québec, "Mémoire de La FMRQ Déposé Dans Le Cadre Des Travaux de La Commission Des Affaires Sociales" (5 September, 2006), online (PDF): <http://www.assnat.qc.ca/Media/Process.aspx?MediaId=ANQ.Vigie.Bll.DocumentGenerique_2693&process=Default&token=Zy-MoxNwUn8ikQ+TRKYwPCjWrKwg+vIv9rjij7p3xLGTZDmLVSmJLoqe/vG7/YWzz>.

during the consultative process, the final bill contained no major amendments.[18] Accordingly, the government appeared to be politically compliant with the goal of private market expansion. Finally, while the bill was introduced as a response to long wait times, it did not include any legislated wait time guarantees.

Consequences of Bill 33

Thirteen years later, what is the legacy of Bill 33 in Quebec? We will examine the three most prominent elements of this legislation; namely, the provisions allowing specialized medical centres (i.e., private medical clinics performing surgical procedures) to contract with the public sector, duplicative private health insurance for specific procedures, and wait times targets. The first two were highly contentious elements that were thought to pave the way for increased privatization of the system, while the third could be a positive development for the public system, helping it to address the problem of wait times that justified the legal challenge in the first instance.

Specialized medical centres and duplicative private health insurance

In 2015, there were thirty-nine specialized medical centres in Quebec.[19] Of these, most centres offer plastic and cosmetic surgeries,[20] with only a minority delivering medically necessary (also publicly insured) services. Contracts between private clinics and public hospitals were similarly extremely rare, from a height of three in 2011 down to one in 2015.[21] In turn, duplicative private health insurance did not develop at all in Quebec with regard to the list of approved

---

18   "Stages in the consideration of the Bill" (2018), online: *National Assembly of Quebec* <http://www.assnat.qc.ca/en/travaux-parlementaires/projets-loi/projet-loi-33-37-2.html>.

19   "L'étude des crédits 2015–2016 — Réponses aux questions particulières — Opposition Officielle — Volume 1" (5 May 2015), online (PDF): *Ministère de la Santé et des Services Sociaux* <www.assnat.qc.ca/Media/Process.aspx?MediaId=ANQ.Vigie.Bll.DocumentGenerique_104227&process=Original&token=ZyMoxNwUn8ikQ+TRKYwPCjWrKwg+vIv9rjij7p3xLGTZDmLVSmJLoqe/vG7/YWzz>.

20   Yanick Labrie, "The Public Health Care Monopoly on Trial: The Legal Challenges Aiming to Change Canada's Health Care Policies" (November 2015), online (PDF): *Montreal Economic Institute* <www.iedm.org/sites/default/files/pub_files/cahier0515_en.pdf>.

21   However, we were not able to document whether this agreement is still in operation.

services. In sum, the impact of Bill 33 per se on private health care in Quebec through two of the most prominent instruments appears to have been quite limited.

Wait times

One of the most prominent issues in the *Chaoulli* decision, and the Bill 33 response, was that of wait times: perhaps the most salient issue at the heart of private versus public health care debates. Prior to 2005, wait list issues were already on the government radar; the 2004 Health Accord, a ten-year framework that identified Federal priorities for provincial and territorial health systems funding provided through the Canada Health Transfer, emphasized the importance of reducing wait times across Canada,[22] including the development of a $5.5 billion Wait Times Reduction Fund.[23] With the principle of asymmetry in Canadian federalism, Quebec was permitted to develop its own wait times reduction strategy under the agreement rather than subscribe to the federal priorities, although it was acknowledged that the priorities were similar.[24] Quebec's initial focus was on improving timely access for tertiary cardiology and radio-oncology.[25] At that time, cataract and joint-replacement surgery were also determined to be priorities, but a system to manage wait lists in these areas was not yet in place.

By December 2005, the Quebec government had committed to assess current wait lists and endeavour to move patients more quickly. Part of the government's response to the *Chaoulli* decision was to guarantee access to these services at a public facility within six months. Notably, this guarantee was not written into the Bill 33 legislation but was enacted as an administrative target. Should the

---

22 "A 10-Year Plan to Strengthen Health Care" (2004), online (PDF): *Canadian Intergovernmental Conference Secretariat* <www.scics.gc.ca/CMFiles/800042005_e1JXB-342011-6611.pdf>.

23 Sonya Norris, "The Wait Times Issue and the Patient Wait Times Guarantee" in *Current Publications: Health* (Ottawa: Parliament of Canada, October 2009).

24 Health Canada, "Asymetrical Federalism That Respects Quebec's Jurisdiction" (9 May 2006), online: *Government of Canada* <www.canada.ca/en/health-canada/services/health-care-system/health-care-system-delivery/federal-provincial-territorial-collaboration/first-ministers-meeting-year-plan-2004/asymetrical-federalism-respects-quebec-jurisdiction.html>.

25 "Bilan des progrès accomplis à l'égard de l'entente bilatérale intervenue à l'issue de la rencontre fédérale-provinciale-territoriale des premiers ministres sur la santé de septembre 2004" (2005), online (PDF): *Ministère de la santé et services sociaux Québec* <publications.msss.gouv.qc.ca/msss/fichiers/2005/05-720-01F.pdf>.

facility not be able to attain the service within the guaranteed time, it was required to offer the patient another solution by facilitating (and paying for) the procedure in a private facility (a "specialized medical clinic"). Some have argued that this strategy opened the door to increased privatization by explicitly regulating private clinics.[26]

Data allowing a systematic assessment of the impact of this private insurance provision on wait times are scarce. Having said that, there is clear evidence that increasing duplicate private insurance does not alleviate public wait lists.[27] In Quebec, the market for this duplicate health insurance did not develop substantially in the wake of Bill 33, and there has been limited uptake by consumers, likely due to the restricted scope of the products and the parallel efforts to impose wait time guarantees for the same services in the public sector (e.g., cataract, knee, and hip surgeries).[28]

What we can document is that, as of 2017, Quebec's public waits outperformed the Canadian average for the services targeted with the legislation. Eighty-three per cent of hip-replacement surgeries were completed within the benchmark of 182 days (fig. 4.1).[29] Similarly, for knee-replacement surgery, 80 per cent of (public) surgeries achieved the benchmark (fig. 4.2). For cataract surgeries, the benchmark is 112 days; 85 per cent of procedures in Quebec reached this benchmark, surpassed only by Newfoundland and Labrador, with 87 per cent (fig. 4.3).[30]

It is relevant to consider whether Quebec's relatively high performance on these metrics is due to the expansion of the private market for these services. However, we lack data on the performance of private clinics, both in terms of volume and wait times. One of the typical arguments made in favour of allowing two-tier care is

---

26   Prémont, *supra* note 8.

27   Carolyn DeCoster et al, "Waiting Times for Surgical Procedures," (1999) 37:6 Med Care 187; Stephen Duckett, "Private Care and Public Waiting" (2005) 29:1 Austl Health Rev 87; Carolyn Hughes Tuohy, Colleen M Flood & Mark Stabile, "How Does Private Finance Affect Public Health Care Systems? Marshaling the Evidence from OECD Nations" (2004) J Health Pol Pol'y & L 359.

28   "No One Wants Quebec's Limited Private Health Insurance," *CBC News* (30 March 2009), online: <http://www.cbc.ca/news/canada/montreal/no-one-wants-quebec-s-limited-private-health-insurance-1.853098>; Marco Laverdière, "Les Suites de l'Arrêt *Chaoulli* et les Engagements Internationaux du Canada en Matière de Protection des Droits Fondamentaux" (2007) 38 RDUS 1.

29   Canadian Institute for Health Information, "Wait Times" (2017), online: <http://waittimes.cihi.ca/>.

30   *Ibid.*

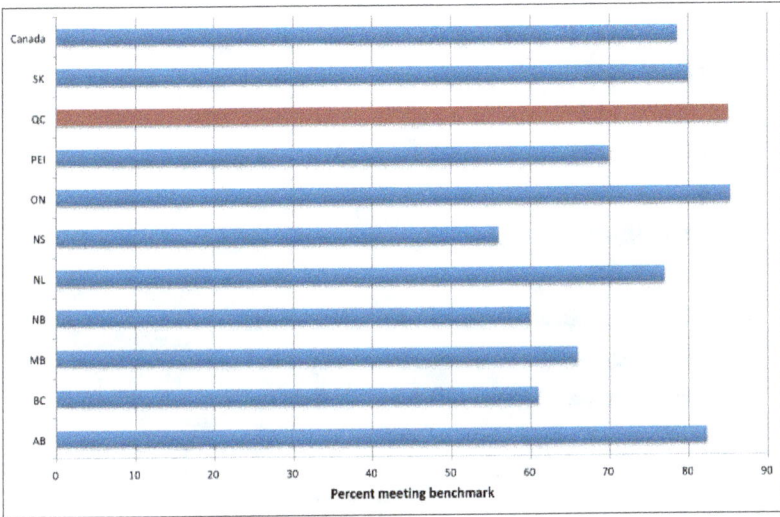

Figure 4.1 Hip-replacement surgeries: Percentage of surgeries meeting benchmark for waiting times in 2016, by province.
Source: Canadian Institute for Health Information, "Benchmarks for treatment and wait time trending across Canada" (2019), online: <http://waittimes.cihi.ca/>.

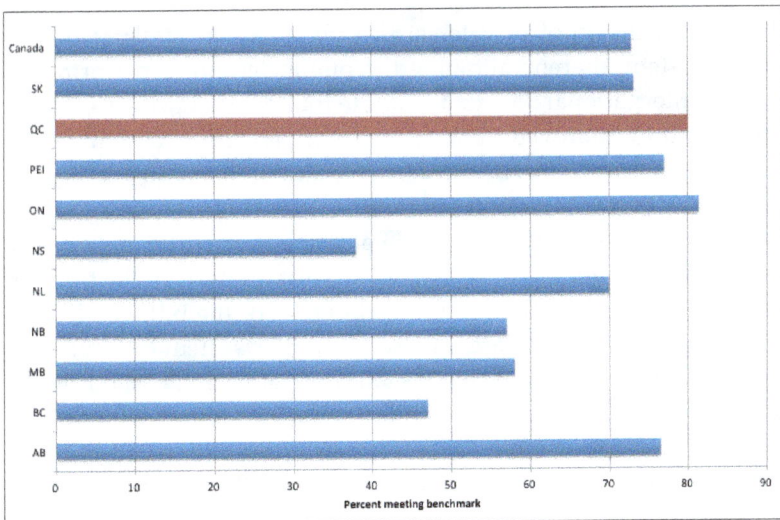

Figure 4.2 Knee-replacement surgeries: Percentage of surgeries meeting benchmark for waiting times in 2016, by province.
Source: Canadian Institute for Health Information, "Benchmarks for treatment and wait time trending across Canada" (2019), online: <http://waittimes.cihi.ca/>.

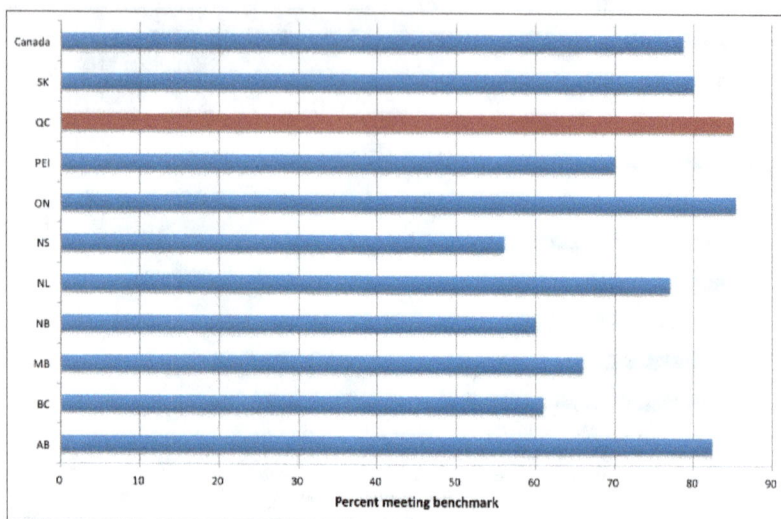

Figure 4.3. Cataract surgeries: Percentage of surgeries meeting benchmark for waiting times in 2016, by province.
Source: Canadian Institute for Health Information, "Benchmarks for treatment and wait time trending across Canada" (2019), online: <http://waittimes.cihi.ca/>.

that an expansion of private services will reduce pressure on the public system, thereby allowing the public system to perform better. But international data demonstrate that parallel private systems rarely lead to improved public-sector performance,[31] and, in fact, a Canadian natural experiment showed that public-private dual practice increased wait times in the public sector.[32] Furthermore, we do not have comparable time-series data dating back sufficiently before the implementation of Bill 33 to allow a clear analysis of the trend in wait times—and the potential causal impact of the bill. Finally, the provisions in Bill 33 put pressure on the public system to attain wait time standards or else assume the administrative and cost burden of accommodating patients in a parallel sector. This alone could explain a potential improvement in performance. Finally, in addition to revoking the prohibition on private insurance, Bill 33 also mandated centralized wait list mechanisms for specialized services within each hospital centre and required increased monitoring of the amount of time patients were spending on wait lists. In our view, it is highly

---

31   Duckett, *supra* note 28; Tuohy, *supra* note 28.
32   DeCoster, *supra* note 28.

likely that these provisions did far more to improve wait times than the few specialized medical centres operating in Quebec.

Hot Spots of Health Care Privatization in Quebec

Diagnostic Imaging

With regard to the privatization debate and the growth of private services, one area in which Quebec has been widely publicized has been in the growth of private diagnostic-imaging clinics.[33] According to Canadian Institute for Health Information (CIHI) statistics on select medical-imaging equipment in Canada (fig. 4.4), there has been a steady growth in the availability of MRI and CT scanners in free-standing facilities in Quebec over the past twenty years.[34] Based on the data collected in the CIHI survey, free-standing facilities reported private health insurance, out-of-pocket payments, and other private insurance as their primary source of operating revenue.[35] While some have argued that the *Chaoulli* decision acted as a catalyst for the introduction of duplicative private health insurance and the growth of private health markets,[36] we demonstrate in this section that the provision of private insurance for services such as diagnostic imaging in Quebec *precedes Chaoulli*, and is rooted in legislative and regulatory amendments throughout the 1980s and 1990s.

In December 1981, the Quebec government passed Bill 27, *An Act to amend various legislation in the field of health and social services*.[37] Among other changes, the bill allowed the government greater authority in publicly delisting certain medical services, notably on the basis of location. Previously, governments could only determine the *type* of services that could be included or excluded from the

---

33   Wendy Glauser, "Private Clinics Continue Explosive Growth" (2011) 183:8 CMAJ 437.

34   Canadian Institute for Health Information, "Medical Imaging in Canada, 2007," (Ottawa: Canadian Institute for Health Information, 2008), online: <https://secure.cihi.ca/free_products/MIT_2007_e.pdf>; Canadian Institute for Health Information, "Medical Imaging in Canada, 2012" (2013), online (PDF): <https://www.cihi.ca/en/mit_summary_2012_en.pdf>.

35   Gilles Fortin, Jennifer Zelmer & Kira Leeb, "More Scans, More Scanners" (2005) 8 Healthcare Q 28.

36   Prémont, *supra* note 8.

37   *An Act to Amend Various Legislation in the Field of Health and Social Services*, SQ 1981, c 22.

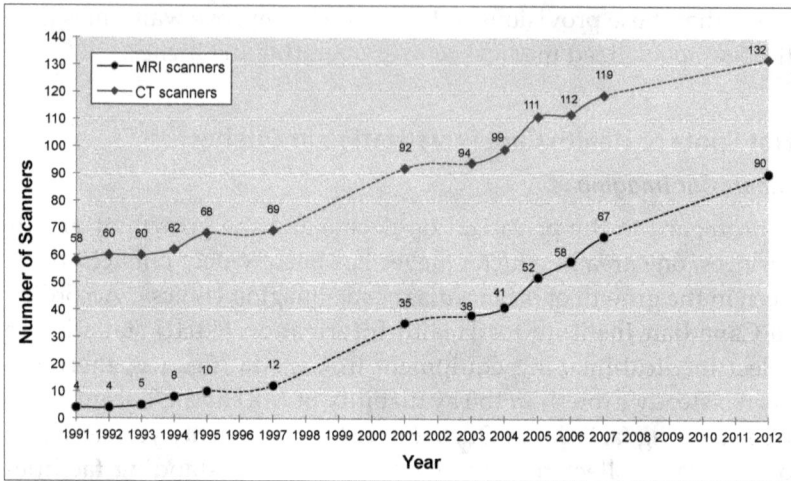

Figure 4.4. Number of MRI and CT scanners in free-standing facilities, Quebec, 1991–2012.
Source: Canadian Institute for Health Information, "Medical Imaging in Canada 2007" (2007), online (PDF): <https://secure.cihi.ca/free_products/MIT_2007_e.pdf>.

public basket, and how often they could be delivered.[38] These reforms were applied in 1982 to delist mammograms, thermography, and ultrasonography from public coverage when services were delivered *outside of a hospital*. CT scans and MRIs were subsequently delisted in 1988 and 1989, respectively. The delisting of diagnostic tests in out-of-hospital settings took place in a period of economic strain brought on by a national recession, from 1981 to 1982, and cutbacks in federal transfers for health following the replacement of the Canada Assistance Plan by the Established Programs Financing in 1977.[39] Given the economic context in which the changes were brought about, and the explicit goal of Bill 27 to "rationalize the provision of health ... and social services by health establishments," it seems that cost containment was the primary goal of the reform by effectively throttling back the supply of diagnostic services.[40]

It is important to note that this experience was not unique to Quebec. A review by Vandna Bhatia of the policy shifts in the

38   Amélie Quesnel-Vallée, "Delisting Medical Imaging in Private Settings from Public Coverage in Québec" (2013) 1:1 Health Reform Observer 1.
39   *Ibid.*
40   *Ibid* at 2.

funding and delivery of health care in Canada argued that the 1980s and 1990s signified a shift in debates on medicare to defining "core" services based on what was "prudently reasonable" for governments.[41] She argues that it was policy shifts such as these that laid the legal foundation for a duplicative private health system to deliver for-profit imaging services outside of the public system. Quebec has largely maintained the ban on duplicate private health insurance for services under the public basket (except for select procedures as prescribed in Bill 33 and later changes to the regulation). However, it is important to note that by delisting diagnostic-imaging services such as CT and MRI by location, the purchase of private health insurance for these services was no longer duplicative but, rather, supplementary. Therefore, the prohibition on duplicative private health insurance (and other tenets of the *Canada Health Act*[42] such as extra-billing, user fees, and dual practice) arguably did not now apply to these diagnostic services delivered in out-of-hospital settings in Quebec.[43]

Emergence of a private health insurance market?

Despite this permissive legal provision, Quebec has not evidenced an explosive growth of private markets at the expense of public diagnostic-imaging services. Undoubtedly, there has been a marked growth in MRI and CT scanners in free-standing facilities since the early 1990s (fig. 4.4). However, in comparing the proportion of private MRI and CT scanners relative to public scanners (fig. 4.5), we see that it has remained relatively stable over the last decade. Thus, the number of private machines appears to be increasing at the same pace as public scanners over this period. Although the data are incomplete (there were no data collected between 2008 and 2011), we do not suspect substantial deviations from this trend. With regard to the emergence of a private health insurance market for diagnostic-imaging services in Quebec, the data are limited, though there is

---

41 Vandna Bhatia, "Social Rights, Civil Rights, and Health Reform in Canada" (2010) 23:1 *Governance* 37.

42 *Canada Health Act*, RSC 1985, c C-6.

43 Colleen M Flood & Bryan Thomas, "Blurring of the Public/Private Divide: The Canadian Chapter" (2010) 17:3 Eur J Health L 257.

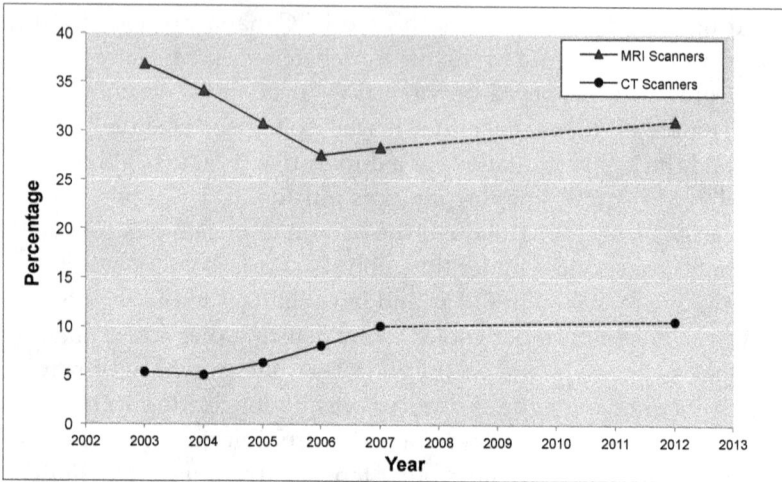

Figure 4.5. Proportion of MRI and CT scanners in free-standing facilities, 2003–2012.
Source: Canadian Institute for Health Information, "Medical Imaging in Canada 2007" (2007), online (PDF): <https://secure.cihi.ca/free_products/MIT_2007_e.pdf>.

evidence of the existence of both individual and group markets for private insurance for imaging services.[44]

Post-Chaoulli: Relisting of services?

Delisting has not been a unidirectional process in Quebec, as some relisting has or may be about to occur. First, at the end of the 1990s, dangerously long wait lists for breast-cancer screening in public hospitals led the government to relist mammograms performed out of hospital; however, this relisting was not extended to all private clinics, and only applied to governmentally approved designated screening centres (centres de dépistage désignés).[45]

More recently, in December 2016, the health minister announced that ultrasound services carried out in private radiol-

---

44   SunLife Financial, "Plan Comparison," online: <https://www.sunlife.ca/slfas/ Health/Personal+health+insurance/ PHI/Plan+comparison?vgnLocale=en_CA>; Quebec Blue Cross, "Compare Our Plans," online: <https://qc.bluecross.ca/ health-insurance/health-insurance-101/compare-our-plans>.

45   Minh-Nguyet Nguyen et al, "Quebec Breast Cancer Screening Program: A Study of the Perceptions of Physicians in Laval, Que," (2009) 55:6 Can Fam Physician 614.

ogy clinics would be covered under the public plan.[46] However, it is noteworthy that the public coverage extends only to ultrasounds performed or evaluated by radiologists,[47] while ultrasounds performed by another provider (i.e., a technician in radiology) are not publicly covered and may still be eligible for reimbursement under a private insurance plan. Similarly, as of 26 January 2017, optical tomography services (excluding retinal imaging) provided by ophthalmologists within private clinics are also covered under the Quebec public health care plan.[48] The Ministry of Health and Social Services (Ministère de la Santé et des Services sociaux) reported that it will extend coverage to include CT scans and MRIs in the future, although these services currently remain delisted outside of hospital settings.[49]

However, the announcement and implementation of these changes were met with considerable resistance from specialists in Quebec, notably the Fédération des médecins spécialistes du Québec (FMSQ) and the Association des radiologistes du Québec (ARQ). These specialist organizations claimed that private clinics would lack the human resources and financial capacity to immediately meet the demand for services by the public.[50] Several media reports have documented claims of appointment cancellations by private clinics, seemingly due to the lingering uncertainty of how much specialists in these settings will be reimbursed.[51]

This negative response from physicians suggests that the relisting did not arise from their leadership but rather from the Quebec government, and under conditions that they do not deem favourable. Furthermore, much as the relisting of mammograms in 1998 occurred

46   "Ultrasounds in Private Clinics Now Covered Under Medicare," *Montreal Gazette* (29 December 2016), online: <http://montrealgazette.com/news/local-news/ultrasounds-in-private-clinics-now-covered-under-medicare>.

47   Gouvernement du Québec, (2016) GOQ II, 50.

48   "Quebec to Foot the Bill for Ultrasounds in Private Clinics," *CBC News* (6 July 2016), online: <https://www.cbc.ca/news/canada/montreal/quebec-health-care-ultrasounds-covered-2016-1.3667513>.

49   *Ibid.*

50   "Ultrasounds in Private Clinics Now Covered Under Medicare," *Montreal Gazette* (29 December 2016), online: <https://montrealgazette.com/news/local-news/ultrasounds-in-private-clinics-now-covered-under-medicare>.

51   Catherine Solyom, "Private Clinics Turning Away Patients for Ultrasounds," *Montreal Gazette* (10 January 2017), online: <http://montrealgazette.com/news/private-clinics-turning-away-patients-for-ultrasounds>.

in reaction to a crisis, this latest wave of relisting by the Quebec government is plausibly occurring in reaction to (or anticipation of) increasing pressure from the federal government to cut down on user fees and threats of clawbacks of the Canada Health Transfer.[52] More generally, this physician resistance to relisting services illustrates that past private health-sector expansion could set off an institutional path dependency, which risks impeding future broadening of public programs.[53] Under this framework, not only physicians but also patients who are able to access and afford private services may be resistant to these changes, making privatization all the more challenging to overturn.[54]

Physicians Withdrawing From the Public System

Physicians in Quebec can choose between three statuses vis-à-vis the public insurance one-payer system: participating, non-participating, and opted out. Most physicians in Quebec are *participating* in the public system, whereby they agree to bill the government directly for medically insured services rendered, and are remunerated at the tariffs set by the province. These physicians must also abide by the regulation that they cannot directly bill patients for services deemed "medically necessary" (i.e., publicly covered under the law). Few physicians elect to be *non-participating* in the public system, as this status entails that they bill patients directly, but at the tariffs that are set out by the province. Patients receiving medically necessary services from these physicians bear the onus of subsequently applying to the ministry for full reimbursement of costs. Finally, a small but growing proportion of physicians have *opted out* of the public system altogether, beyond the scope of the provincial *Act respecting health and social services*. As such, they bill patients directly for all services rendered and at rates set at their discretion, usually higher than the tariffs set out by the province. These physicians are not allowed to bill the public system for any

---

52   Benjamin Shingler & Jonathan Montpetit, "Ottawa Threatens to Cut Quebec's Health Payments over User Fees," *CBC News* (19 September 2016), online: <http://www.cbc.ca/news/canada/montreal/quebec-gaetan-barrette-user-fees-philpott-1.3768799>.

53   Bhatia, *supra* note 42.

54   Daniel Béland & Jacob S Hacker, "Ideas, Private Institutions and American Welfare State 'Exceptionalism': The Case of Health and Old-Age Insurance, 1915–1965" (2004) 13:1 Int J Soc Welfare 42.

service rendered, and they cannot practice in the same location as participating physicians. However, while physicians are not permitted to practice in both the public and private systems at the same time, moving between is relatively easy: the opt-out requests take effect thirty days after submission of the required form to the RAMQ, and opting back into the system only requires eight days.[55] Patients who receive services from these physicians must pay at the point of service and are not eligible for any reimbursement from either public or private insurance.

The RAMQ publishes a list of prevalent non-participating and opted-out physicians, updated monthly. These lists provide the physician name, name of the clinic if applicable, health region, specialty, and the start date of this status. Using these data, we reconstructed annual flows of physicians opting out from the system who were still opted out as of December 2017. It is important to note that these data are likely an underestimate, as we are not able to reconstruct a full history of movement in and out of the public system. Given the ease of movement between the participating and opted-out statuses noted above, there may have been past spikes in opting out that have since abated as physicians reassumed participating status, and the current state of RAMQ data does not render this movement.

Bill 33 could have influenced the number of physicians opting out through its provision allowing for the establishment of specialized medical centres (private surgical clinics), which were then permitted under the *Act respecting health and social services*[56] to provide services otherwise publicly insured on a private-purchase basis (with another provision allowing for private health insurance reimbursement for these particular services), and, most notably, to be contracted by public hospitals to provide these services. Given the nature of these services, we would expect to see an impact on specialists but not family physicians. To examine the association of Bill 33 on opting-out behaviour, we present in figures 4.6 and 4.7 the number of family physicians and specialists who have opted out.

Looking at the year 2006 in figures 4.6–4.8, we see that the number of physicians opting out (and were still opted out as of

---

55 *Regulation Respecting the Application of the Health Insurance Act,* CQLR c A-29, r 5, s 29; Héloïse Archambault, "Des spécialistes font le va-et-vient entre les deux systèmes" *Journal de Montréal* (8 February 2017), online: <http://www.journaldemontreal.com/2017/02/08/des-specialistes-font-le-va-et-vient-entre-les-deux-systemes>.

56 *Act respecting health services and social services,* CQLR c S-4.2.

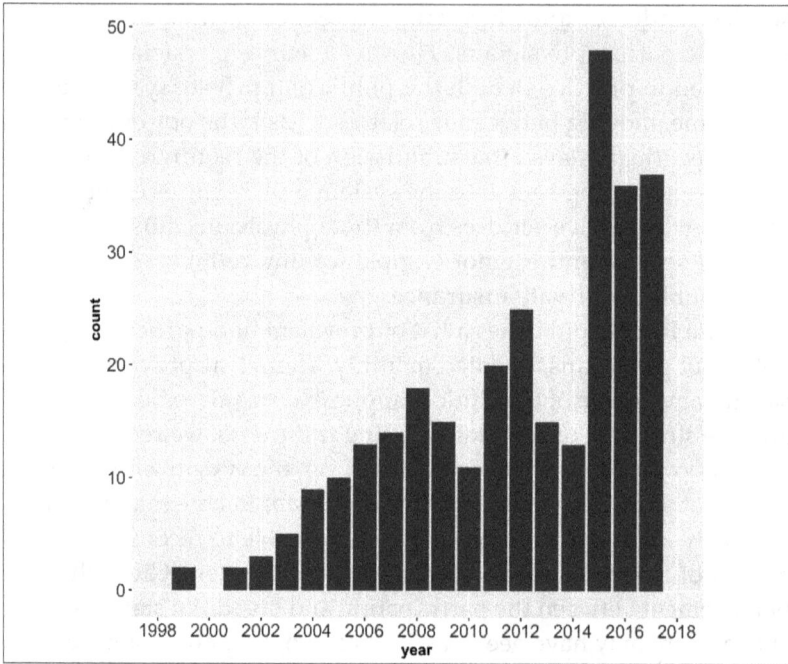

Figure 4.6. Number of family physicians opted out of the public insurance system as of December 2017, by year of exit.
Source: Régie de l'Assurance Maladie Québec, "Number of Family Physicians Opted Out of the Public Insurance System as of December 2017" (December 2017), online (PDF): <http://www.ramq.gouv.qc.ca/SiteCollectionDocuments/professionnels/facturation/desengages.pdf>.

December 2017) did not radically increase after the bill was passed. Instead, the onset of the trend appears to predate this decision. Figure 4.6 indeed suggests that among family physicians, the data show a generally linear, gradual progression since 2001. According to the Collège des médecins du Québec, there were 9,976 family physicians actively practicing in the province at the end of 2017, of whom our data show 296 are opted-out physicians (3 per cent). As shown in figure 4.7, among specialists, there are much fewer opted-out physicians, with a non-discernable pattern over the period, aside from a remarkable peak in 2017. Data disaggregated by specialty in figures 4.9 and 4.10 which indicate that the bulk of the 2001–2015 opt-out physicians were among plastic surgeons and dermatologists, ostensibly for the elective cosmetic-procedures market. Similar to family physicians, though, the cumulative trend shown in figure 4.8 indicates a gradual, linear progression (with the exception of 2017, skewing

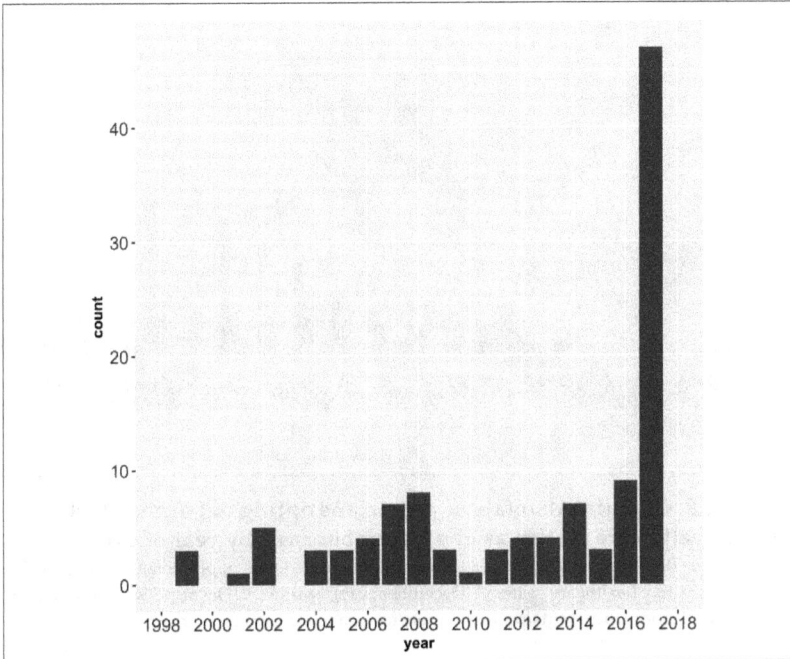

Figure 4.7. Number of medical specialists opted out of the public insurance system as of December 2017, by year of exit.
Source: Régie de l'Assurance Maladie Québec, "Number of Medical Specialists Opted Out of the Public Insurance System as of December 2017" (December 2017), online (PDF): <http://www.ramq.gouv.qc.ca/SiteCollectionDocuments/professionnels/facturation/desengages.pdf>.

the data upward). There are currently 13,650 specialists practicing in Quebec, of whom 117 are opted-out physicians (0.86 per cent).

Figure 4.6 shows a 2015 peak among family physicians, which can likely be attributed to the passing of a highly contentious bill that imposed practice quotas (Bill 20), on the heels of a massive reform of the governance of the primary-care system.[57] In turn, the 2017 peak among specialists is likely associated with protests over the formal prohibition of user fees that was implemented by the Quebec government in early 2017. Indeed, the data disaggregated by specialty, shown in figures 4.9 and 4.10, indicates that the bulk of the opt outs

---

57   Bill 10, *An Act to modify the organization and governance of the health and social services network, in particular by abolishing the regional agencies*, 1st Sess, 41st Leg, Quebec, 2014; Amélie Quesnel-Vallée & Renée Carter, "Improving Accessibility to Services and Increasing Efficiency Through Merger and Centralization in Québec" (2018) 6:1 Health Reform Observer 1.

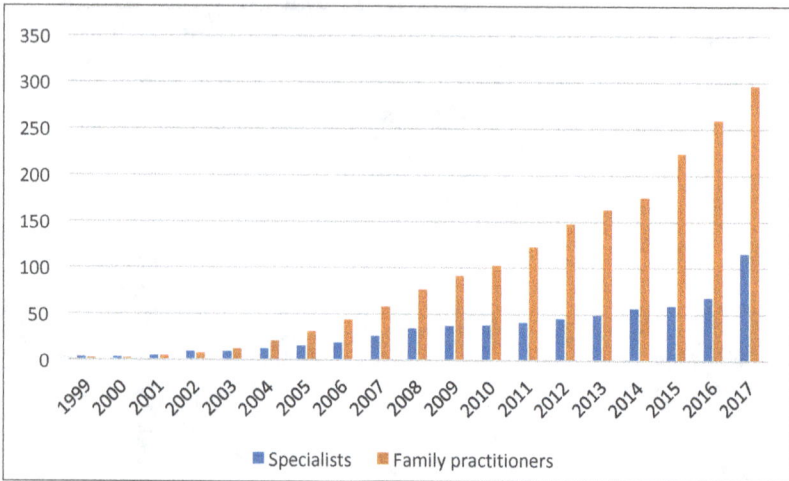

Figure 4.8. Cumulative totals of physicians opting out of the Quebec public health care system as of 7 December 2017, by year of exit.
Source: Régie de l'Assurance Maladie Québec, "Cumulative totals of physicians opting out of the Quebec public healthcare system" (December 2017), online (PDF): <http://www.ramq.gouv.qc.ca/SiteCollectionDocuments/professionnels/facturation/desengages.pdf>.

occurred among gastroenterologists, urologists, radiologists, and ophthalmologists, who were highly affected by this decision. The Quebec government's decision to reign in user charges followed acrimonious exchanges with the federal government on the prevalence of user fees in Quebec, in contravention of *Canada Health Act* requirements. One of the important sources of user fees came from participating specialists working outside hospitals—that is, in private clinics—who collected fees from the RAMQ for publicly insured services, while also charging users a fee to (arguably) cover the practice overhead. With the prohibition of user fees, some specialists have deemed this business model not viable, and have opted out of the system to charge patients for the entirety of the service.

In sum, based on this indicator of physician status in the program, it does not appear that the *Chaoulli* decision had a lasting effect on physicians opting out of the program. Instead, the steady growth of family physicians opting out began in 2001, and has continued relatively unabated since then. In contrast, recent peaks suggest both family and specialist physicians are opting out in protest over governmental actions they disagree with. However, we are not entirely able to rule out that there may have been a larger group of

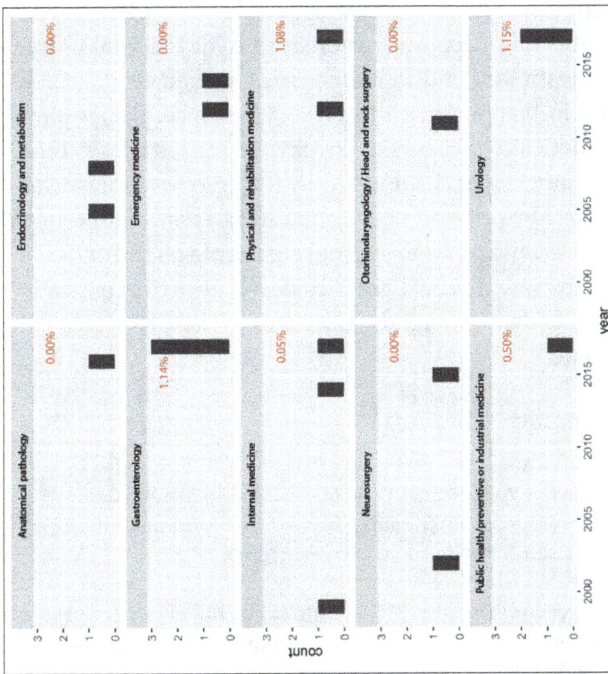

Figure 4.10. Number of specialists withdrawing per year.
Note: Percentages in red refer to the percentage of the practicing specialist population in that year.
Source: Régie de l'Assurance Maladie Québec, "Number of Medical Specialists Opting Out of RAMQ by Year" (7 December 2017), online (PDF): <http://www.ramq.gouv.qc.ca/SiteCollectionDocuments/professionnels/facturation/desengages.pdf>.

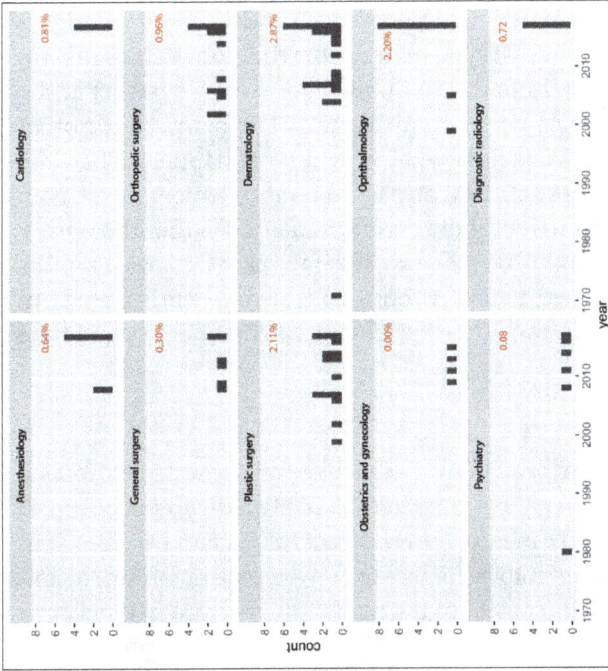

Figure 4.9. Number of Specialists withdrawing per year.
Note: Percentages in red refer to the percentage of the practicing specialist population in that year.
Source: Régie de l'Assurance Maladie Québec, "Number of Medical Specialists Opting Out of RAMQ by Year" (December 2017), online (PDF): <http://www.ramq.gouv.qc.ca/SiteCollectionDocuments/professionnels/facturation/desengages.pdf>.

physicians who have opted out in 2005–2006 and would have subsequently rejoined the public system. Indeed, while physicians are not permitted to practice in both the public and private systems at the same time, moving between is relatively easy. Furthermore, the other counterfactual that we lack is what would have happened had the government not passed Bill 33, or passed a more lenient law. Given the movements we currently observe, it is plausible that the opting out of specialists might have begun several years ago. Meanwhile, looking into the future, whether those who have recently opted out in protest will remain out of the system for extended periods of time remains to be seen.

User Fees

User fees have been prevalent in Quebec for some time, despite being prohibited in the *Canada Health Act* for "medically necessary" hospital services and "medically required" physician services.[58] In fact, they were written into agreements between the government and physician unions at the outset of the medicare program in Quebec in 1970 but were meant to be restricted to a few outpatient procedures, charged to patients only exceptionally, and only if they involved small amounts of money.[59] In practice, the Quebec ombudsman has found that the number of procedures increased over the years, that the practice was widespread, and that amounts charged could reach several hundreds of dollars per procedure.[60] For instance, clinics have often charged an amount to patients to cover costs of eye drops, IUD insertion, and instruments and medication for colonoscopies,[61] as well as to cover general overhead costs, including rent, equipment, and staffing. The shift toward treating more patients as outpatients that began in the 1990s saw medical practice performing increasingly advanced services outside of hospitals. User fees generally increased in step with this trend.

---

58   *Canada Health Act, supra* note 43.

59   Le Protecteur du citoyen, "Avis Sur Les Frais Accessoires En Matière de Santé et de Services Sociaux" (1 October 2015), online (PDF): <https://protecteurducitoyen. qc.ca/sites/default/files/pdf/2015-10-01_avis-frais-accessoires.pdf>.

60   *Ibid.*

61   Loreen Pindera & Benjamin Shingler, "What Can You Be Billed for? A Guide to Québec's Ban on Medical User Fees," *CBC News* (26 January 2017), online: <www. cbc.ca/news/canada/montreal/gaetan-barrette-user-fees-abolition-1.3951648>.

Bill 33 may have sent a signal of governmental leniency toward the imposition of user charges in out-of-hospital settings and, indeed, in 2011, following a series of investigative journalism reports uncovering significant infractions in the use of user fees, the RAMQ established an investigative team. Nine investigation reports have been published on the RAMQ website, six of which represent unique investigations after 2011.[62]

Four of the six reports pertained to health "plans" in which prospective patients were required to pay annual membership fees to access a clinic's physicians (some of whom were participating in

---

62　Régie de l'assurance maladie du Québec, "Enquêtes de la Régie de l'assurance maladie du Québec sur des coopératives de santé" (28 September 2011), online (PDF): *Régie de l'assurance maladie du Québec* <http://www.ramq.gouv.qc.ca/ SiteCollectionDocuments/citoyens/fr/rapports/rappenq-coop-fr.pdf> [Régie de l'assurance maladie du Québec, "Coopératives de Santé"]; Régie de l'assurance maladie du Québec, "Enquête de la Régie de l'assurance maladie du Québec sur le centre de chirurgie et de médecine Rockland inc." (16 February 2012), online (PDF): *Régie de l'assurance maladie du Québec* <http://www.ramq. gouv.qc.ca/SiteCollectionDocuments/citoyens/fr/rapports/rappenq-rockland-fr. pdf> [Régie de l'assurance maladie du Québec, "Chirurgie et de médecine Rockland inc."]; Régie de l'assurance maladie du Québec, "Enquête de la Régie de l'assurance maladie du Québec sur la Clinique Globale Santé Express de Blainville" (22 March 2012), online (PDF): *Régie de l'assurance maladie du Québec* <http://www.ramq.gouv.qc.ca/SiteCollectionDocuments/citoyens/fr/rapports/ rappenq-clinique-blainville-fr.pdf> [Régie de l'assurance maladie du Québec, "Clinique Globale Santé Express de Blainville"]; Régie de l'assurance maladie du Québec, "Enquête de la Régie de l'assurance maladie du Québec sur la Clinique chirurgicale de Laval," (22 March 2012), online (PDF): *Régie de l'assurance maladie du Québec* <http://www.ramq.gouv.qc.ca/SiteCollectionDocuments/citoyens/ fr/rapports/rappenq-clinique-laval-fr.pdf> [Régie de l'assurance maladie du Québec, "Clinique chirurgicale de Laval"]; Régie de l'assurance maladie du Québec, "Enquête de la Régie de l'assurance maladie du Québec sur la clinique médicale Plexo Médiclub" (17 January 2013), online (PDF): *Régie de l'assurance maladie du Québec* <http://www.ramq.gouv.qc.ca/SiteCollectionDocuments/ citoyens/fr/rapports/rappenq-clinique-medicale-plexo-mediclub-jan-2013-fr. pdf> [Régie de l'assurance maladie du Québec, "Plexo Médiclub"]; Régie de l'assurance maladie du Québec, "Enquête de la Régie de l'assurance maladie du Québec sur le Service de concierge pédiatrique Medisys 123" (28 February 2013), online (PDF): *Régie de l'assurance maladie du Québec* <http://www.ramq.gouv.qc.ca/ SiteCollectionDocuments/citoyens/fr/rapports/rappenq-medisys-faits-saillants- fev-2013-fr.pdf> [Régie de l'assurance maladie du Québec, "Pédiatrique Medisys 123"].

the RAMQ).[63] These were found to be not in accordance with the law in a few respects—they typically required payment in advance of service provision, payment or membership was required before access to a physician would be granted, and, in some cases, the fees were considered accessory costs (i.e., costs related to covered services for which the professional is billing the government, which are prohibited under the *Canada Health Act*). One of those reports found that a clinic had sufficiently changed its business plan following a change in ownership such that the law was no longer contravened.[64] One report assessed fees charged to insured persons for insured services and found that some practices were not in accordance with the law.[65] Finally, the last report uncovered a situation that appears to still be in practice to this day.[66] This pertains to the use of the third-party payer provision in contravention of the law. The *Health Insurance Act*[67] contains a provision allowing for third-party payment for insured health services, which permits, notably, the province's workplace compensation board, athletics organizations, or employers, for instance, to pay privately for services for their members. The rationale was that it is more cost effective to ensure the promptest return to work possible for wage earners unable to work because of an accident or a disabling condition than to have them wait for public services while on a disability pension. The physicians performing the insured services may be participating in the public system, but in these cases their services are paid directly by the organization and not reimbursed by RAMQ. However, this provision does not allow for patients to pay for services, whether directly or indirectly, through a third party. Yet, the RAMQ investigation in 2012 found that the Clinique chirurgicale de Laval had allowed patients to pay for an insured service indirectly through a third party, and the clinic

63   Régie de l'assurance maladie du Québec, "Coopératives de Santé," *supra* note 63; Régie de l'assurance maladie du Québec, "Clinique Globale Santé Express de Blainville," *supra* note 63; Régie de l'assurance maladie du Québec, "Plexo Médiclub," *supra* note 63; Régie de l'assurance maladie du Québec, "Pédiatrique Medisys 123," *supra* note 63.

64   Régie de l'assurance maladie du Québec, "Clinique Globale Santé Express de Blainville," *supra* note 63.

65   Régie de l'assurance maladie du Québec, "Chirurgie et de Médecine Rockland Inc," *supra* note 63.

66   Régie de l'assurance maladie du Québec, "Clinique chirurgicale de Laval," *supra* note 63.

67   *Health Insurance Act*, CQLR c A-29.

had to reimburse the patients.[68] Despite this precedent, reports suggest other clinics have recommended this provision as a loophole to encourage patients to pay indirectly for services as recently as 2017.[69]

Following public discontent about the widely varying nature of these user charges, in November 2015, Bill 20 was passed,[70] which, among other things, included an amendment to regulate user fees. However, as mentioned earlier, the *Canada Health Act* explicitly prohibits the charging of user fees for medically insured services. In September 2016, the federal government thus sent Quebec a letter threatening to clawback transfer payments if user fees were not banned, and, in response, on 26 January 2017, user fees were legally banned in Quebec.[71] This regulation was reinforced through a law to increase the powers of RAMQ to recover fees deemed to be user fees or extra-billing from the physicians who charged them, which had been passed in the National Assembly seven weeks earlier.[72]

A community group has been maintaining a registry of complaints about user charges.[73] The conclusions from their 2017 report suggest that while user charges have decreased since implementation of the regulation, administrative fees—which are allowed—have increased. The implication is that clinics may have shifted invoicing from one category to another to offset the lost revenue.[74]

---

68 Régie de l'assurance maladie du Québec, "Clinique chirurgicale de Laval," *supra* note 63.

69 Salimah Shivji, "Quebec Doctors Use Loophole to Sidestep New Law Banning Extra Fees," *CBC News* (24 January 2017), online: <http://www.cbc.ca/news/canada/montreal/rockland-md-loophole-user-fees-1.3950216>.

70 *Act to promote access to family medicine and specialized medicine services and to amend various legislative provisions relating to assisted procreation*, CQLR 2015, c A-2.2.

71 *Règlement abolissant les frais accessoires liés à la dispensation des services assurés et régissant les frais de transport des échantillons biologiques*, CQLR c A-29, r 7.1.

72 "Projet de loi no 92: Loi visant à accroître les pouvoirs de la Régie de l'assurance maladie du Québec, à encadrer les pratiques commerciales en matière de médicaments ainsi qu'à protéger l'accès aux services d'interruption volontaire de grossesse (titre modifié)" (2016), online: *Assemblée nationale du Québec* <www.assnat.qc.ca/fr/travaux-parlementaires/projets-loi/projet-loi-92-41-1.html>.

73 Clinique Communautaire de Pointe-Saint-Charles, "Registre de Surveillance Des Frais Accessoires: Analyse Préliminaire Des Données Quantitatives" (November 2017), online (PDF): <https://ccpsc.qc.ca/sites/ccpsc.qc.ca/files/donn%C3%A9espreliminaires%20R.surveillance.pdf>.

74 Amélie Daoust-Boisvert, "Près de 300 remboursements de frais accessoires en santé depuis un an," *Le Devoir* (12 February 2018), online: <https://www.ledevoir.com/societe/sante/519932/frais-accessoires-un-an-et-des-rembourse-

Anticipated Response to *Cambie v British Columbia*

In the preceding two sections, we have shown that the Quebec government's response to *Chaoulli*, Bill 33, did not in and of itself directly contribute to further privatization of the health system, at least insofar as its two principal policy instruments of (private) specialized medical clinics and a very limited role for duplicative private health insurance are concerned. However, it is still true that Quebec is now home to a dynamic private health market, and to better understand this phenomenon we examined three "hot spots" of this market, namely private diagnostic imaging and insurance for these services, physicians opting out of the system, and user fees. Taken together, these hot spots are indicative of underlying trends that predated the *Chaoulli* decision—trends which have not abated since then; far from it.

So why did the *Chaoulli* decision have so little impact, and what might we gather from this experience for Quebec looking toward a future where *Cambie* is successful in liberalizing some or all of the laws under challenge?

Policy Instruments at Stake

Flood and Archibald[75] provided a framework for understanding the legal hurdles against the development of a private market in provincial health systems. In table 4.1, we present the policy instruments they outlined in the article, for British Columbia, Quebec pre- and post-Bill 33, and as to whether they were or are targeted by the *Chaoulli* or *Cambie* case, respectively. We highlight in red the instruments acting as a barrier against privatization, and in green those that are more permissive (or in the absence of which we could expect greater development of private health care). Beyond the fact that *Cambie* is directed at the *Canadian Charter*, which would increase its jurisdictional reach relative to *Chaoulli*, a clear picture emerges

---

ments>; Catherine Crépeau, "Les frais administratifs remplacent les frais accessoires," *Protégez-Vous* (5 April 2018), online: <www.protegez-vous.ca/nouvelles/ sante-et-alimentation/les-frais-administratifs-remplacent-les-frais-accessoires>; "Quebec Doctors Still Charging Administrative Fees, Watchdog Group Says," *CBC News* (21 January 2018), online: <www.cbc.ca/news/canada/montreal/ quebec-doctor-fees-pointe-st-charles-1.4497324>.

75   Colleen M Flood & Tom Archibald, "The Illegality of Private Health Care in Canada" (2001) 164:6 CMAJ 825.

from this table to the effect that the *Cambie* decision would have far more profound implications by targeting essentially the whole range of policy instruments at hand.

Table 4.1. Provincial regulation of privately financed hospital and physician services

Red indicates the instruments acting as a barrier against privatization, and green those that are more permissive.

Policy issue	BC	QC, pre-Bill 33	QC, post-Bill 33	Targeted by *Chaoulli*	Targeted by *Cambie*
Opting out of public insurance plan					
Can physicians opt out of the public plan?	Y	Y	Y		
Can opted-in physicians bill patients directly?	N	N	N		
Extra-billing measures					
Direct prohibition: Is there an explicit ban on extra-billing for opted-in physicians?	Y	Y	Y		X
Can opted-out physicians bill any amount?	Y	Y	Y		
Status disincentive: Is public-sector coverage denied for patients receiving insured services from opted-out physicians?	Y	Y	Y		?
Private insurance for publicly insured services					
Are contracts of private insurance for publicly insured services prohibited?	Y	Y	N*	X	X
Can private insurance pay for all or part of opted-out physician's fees?	N	N	Y*	X	X
* Restricted to services listed in the regulation.					

Source: Adapted from Colleen M Flood & Tom Archibald, "The Illegality of Private Health Care in Canada" (2001) 164:6 CMAJ 825.

Fertile Ground in Quebec

Beyond the hot spots presented above, other elements of the Quebec health system suggest that liberalization of the legislation limiting the purview of the private sector could be met with support from the business sector, as well as from certain segments of the physician population.

The first potential zone of support comes from the business sector. In Quebec, physician incorporation played out at two levels: at the level of the individual physician, in which case the primary benefit of incorporation is a reduction in personal taxes; and at the level of the medical clinic, which allows for broader ownership beyond physicians. A review of the Supreme Court decision in the *Chaoulli* case, and its potential impact on privatization of health care in Quebec, points out that the provisions in Bill 33 allow for greater involvement of investors (up to 50 per cent of shares of a special-ized medical centre can be owned or managed by investors) than a subsequent regulation on physician incorporation, which requires that "all voting shares of a medical practice [be] the property of a physician and all managing directors [must be] physicians as well."[76] The review goes on to warn: "The incorporation of physicians and the development of investor-owned health facilities introduce major pressures for the commercialization and transformation of medical practice."[77]

The second potential seed for private growth in Quebec that we see has to do with a small but vocal minority of physicians who would welcome greater liberalization of their practice conditions with regard to the ban on public-private practice. In recent years, the FMSQ—the specialist-physicians' union—launched a legal chal-lenge arguing that the provisions from Bill 33 that prevented partic-ipating and non-participating physicians from practicing together in specialized medical clinics infringed on the right to freedom of association guaranteed by both the Quebec and Canadian charters. The Quebec Superior Court ruled in 2015 that this right was not infringed, a decision that was subsequently upheld by the Quebec Court of Appeal in 2017.[78]

Along with the hot spots, these two areas offer fertile grounds for a liberalization of the legislation preventing the development of private health care in Quebec. As we have shown, the policy instru-ments that were modified following *Chaoulli*[79] resulted in relatively

---

76   Prémont, *supra* note 8.

77   *Ibid* at 247.

78   *Fédération des médecins spécialistes du Québec v Bolduc*, 2017 QCCA 860.

79   *Chaoulli, supra* note 2.

benign changes, and the hot spots that we pointed to had roots that predated this decision, which persist to this day. This is what leads us to argue that *Chaoulli* was more a symptom than a cause of the private expansion in Quebec, and why we would expect that commercial interests are poised to act promptly and decisively following any decision in favour of *Cambie*.

CHAPTER 5

Experiences with Two-Tier Home Care in Canada: A Focus on Inequalities in Home Care Use by Income in Ontario

Sara Allin, David Rudoler, Danielle Dawson, and Jonathan Mullen

As we debate the future of two-tier care for physician and hospital services, we do not have to look abroad for lessons of the impact of two-tier care. Within Canada, home care is an example of a system where blended public-private financing has always been permissible. Over the past decade, home care use has increased both in Canada and in other high-income countries, largely due to efforts to shift care out of institutions and into the community.

Home care services fall outside the protections of the *Canada Health Act*.[1] Therefore, there is no requirement for services to be delivered on a uniform basis; nor do they need to be publicly administered, portable across the provinces, accessible without financial barriers, and provided on a universal basis. In contrast to "medically necessary" physician and hospital services for which private pay options are curtailed by regulation, individuals seeking home care can choose among a wide variety of private pay options.[2] Moreover,

---

1   RSC 1985, c C-6.
2   Cloutier-Fisher & Alun E Joseph, "Long-term care restructuring in rural Ontario: retrieving community service user and provider narratives" (2000) 50:7–8 Soc Sci Med 1037–1045; Tavia Grant, "Private home care fills big service gap for seniors," *Globe and Mail* (14 April 2011), online: <https://www.theglobeandmail. com/report-on-business/private-home-care-fills-big-service-gap-for-seniors/article576860/>; A Paul Williams et al, *Integrating Long-Term Care into a Community-Based Continuum* (Montreal: Institute for Research on Public Policy, 2016), online: <hsprn.ca/uploads/files/IRPP_2016.pdf>.

while residency is the only requirement for eligibility for hospital and physician services, access to home care services in Canada is determined in each province and territory on the basis of a formal and generally standardized needs assessment.[3] Over time, the provinces and territories have implemented systems of publicly funded home care to provide some social protection for their residents. Yet little attention has been paid to the potential interaction between the public and private home care sectors.

In light of the ongoing court challenge to the regulatory restrictions on private finance for physician and hospital services (e.g., the restrictions on dual practice, extra-billing, price regulation) in *Cambie*,[4] this chapter takes a closer look at the evidence regarding the functioning of Canada's two-tiered home care sector. In the home care sector, the lack of constraints on the development of a two-tiered system allows for the private sector to offer home care services that can compete with, or top up, publicly funded services. One of the concerns with respect to two-tier systems is the potential to draw health professionals away from the public system to the more profitable private pay sector. Another concern, which is the focus of this study, is how two-tier systems impact persons with lower socio-economic status, and, specifically, whether they contribute to inequalities in access to and quality of care among seniors. The objective of this chapter is twofold: to describe the trends over time in the use of publicly and privately funded home care, and to estimate the association between income and home care use among older people in Ontario. The focus of this study is on Ontario, since home care funding and delivery varies across provinces/territories, and Ontario is the only province with available data on both public and private home care use.

In what follows, we first define key terms and, in the second section, describe Ontario's home care sector in order to shed light on the ways in which the publicly and privately funded home care systems interact. We explain eligibility criteria, assessment processes, and trends in funding and supply. In the third section, we describe the methods and data used to examine the receipt of public and

---

3   Income, or means, is not an eligibility criterion in any province; however, in some provinces (e.g., British Columbia, Saskatchewan, Nova Scotia), there are copayments for publicly funded home care services that vary depending on level of income.

4   *Cambie Surgeries v Medical Services Commission of British Columbia*, Statement of Claim, No S-090663 (Supreme Court of British Columbia).

private home care in Ontario, and, in the fourth section, we summarize the results of our empirical analysis. Our results suggest there are regressive impacts in relying upon private finance for home care under Ontario's current two-tier system. We find that people with higher income are more likely to use private home care and this primarily tops up the publicly funded home care services they receive. In conclusion, we map out questions remaining for future research as well as provide insights into the potential impact of allowing two-tier care.

1.1 Defining Home Care:
Care or Support Offered to Older People in their Homes

Home care includes a broad range of health or support services for people with "acute, chronic, palliative, or rehabilitative health care needs" in their homes.[5] These services are delivered by both regulated and unregulated professionals, and paid and unpaid caregivers (e.g., family members, volunteers, friends). Services cover a wide range of health and nursing care, help with activities of daily living, mobility, self-care, and emotional support services. Home care includes short-term care, such as short-term "post-acute" care in the home following a hospital discharge. It also includes long-term care to support clients with chronic needs. Consistent with the literature[6] and Ontario regulations pertaining to home care,[7] we distinguish between home health care services, delivered by health care professionals such as nurses and physiotherapists, and home support and "homemaking" services, delivered mostly by personal-support workers (PSWs) and unpaid caregivers. However, given the nature of the survey question (described in section 2) we are not able to distinguish between short-term care, which is more likely to be professional or nursing services,

---

5   Canadian Home Care Association, Canadian Nurses Association & The College of Family Physicians of Canada, *Better Home Care in Canada: A National Action Plan* (2016), online: <https://www.cna-aiic.ca/-/media/cna/page-content/pdf-en/better-home-care-in-canada_a-national-action-plan-copy.pdf> at 1.

6   Audrey Laporte, Ruth Croxford & Peter C Coyte, "Can a publicly funded home care system successfully allocate service based on perceived need rather than socioeconomic status? A Canadian experience" (2006) 15:2 Health Soc Care Community 108–119; Gustavo Mery, Walter P Wodchis & Audrey Laporte, "The determinants of the propensity to receive publicly funded home care services for the elderly in Canada: A panel two-stage residual inclusion approach" (2016) 6:1 Health Econ Rev 8.

7   *Home Care and Community Services Act, 1994*, SO 1994, c 26.

and long-term care, which tends to include more home support and homemaking services.[8]

In this chapter, we focus on formal or paid home care for older people—individuals aged sixty-five years and older—living in the community. Older people living at home represent the majority of home care users in Ontario.[9] While the definition of a home can be broad, and often includes group homes and retirement communities, it generally excludes long-term care facilities or similar institutions. The focus on paid care misses the important role unpaid care by family, friends, and neighbours plays in supporting older people in their homes. The literature suggests that, in Ontario, the majority of at-home caregiving is delivered by this informal sector. Studies estimate that 70–90 per cent of home care services are delivered by informal caregivers,[10] with approximately seven hours of informal support for every two hours of professional care.[11]

1.2 Organization of Home Care in Ontario: Evolution of a Two-Tier System

Ontario's publicly funded long-term care sector is comprised of two main components integrated by an access point since the mid-1990s. One component is institutional or facility-based care, inclusive of long-term hospital stays and most nursing homes. The other component, and our focus, is the community-based services, including home care. Professional home care providers include, but are not limited to, registered nurses (RNs), registered practical nurses (RPNs), PSWs, occupational therapists (OTs), and physiotherapists (PTs). Entitlement to publicly funded home care services is determined by the relevant Local Health Integration Network (LHIN)—regional bodies charged

---

8   Laporte, *supra* note 6.

9   Ontario, Office of the Auditor General of Ontario, 2015 *Annual Report*, Section 3.01 CCACs—Community Care Access Centres—Home Care Program (Toronto: Queen's Printer for Ontario 2015).

10   Vivian W Leong et al, "The Magnitude, Share and Determinants of Private Costs Incurred by Clients (and Their Caregivers) of In-home Publicly" (2007) 3:1 Healthc Pol'y 141–159; Clare McNeil & Jack Hunter, *The Generation Strain: Collective Solutions to Care in an Aging Society* (London: Institute for Public Policy Research, 2014), online: https://www.ippr.org/files/publications/pdf/genera-tion-strain_Apr2014.pdf; Mery *supra* note 6; Allie Peckham, A Paul Williams & Sheila Neysmith, "Balancing Formal and Informal Care for Older Persons: How Case Managers Respond" (2014) 33:2 Can J Aging 123–136.

11   Williams, *supra* note 2.

with coordinating public health care services within a defined geo-graphical area.[12]

Prior to the 1990s, the long-term care model was considered to be disjointed, with little integration between health, social, and community services.[13] In the early 1990s, Ontario's rate of insti-tutionalized seniors was 25 per cent higher than the Canadian average, signalling a need for the provincial government to refocus its attention on the policy and funding surrounding the care of its older population.[14] The *Home Care and Community Services Act, 1994,* formalized eligibility and entitlement requirements to reduce the number of institutionalized seniors and divert them to home care where possible. With minor adjustments, this legislation still exists in largely the same form, and continues to guide eligibility for home care.[15]

Over the previous decade the structures and funding of home care remained largely intact. Although government spending on home care doubled between 2003 and 2013,[16] even with significant reform efforts such as the provincial government's Aging at Home Strategy,[17] spending on home care as a proportion of total health-sys-tem spending has represented a relatively stable 4–5 per cent of overall provincial health spending over the past decade.[18] In other words, the public-spending increases seen in home care were not proportionately greater than in other sectors (e.g., physicians, drugs, institutions), nor has there been a change to the balance of home and institutional long-term care in spite of some efforts to do so.[19]

---

12   In 2019, the Ontario government introduced new legislation allowing for the consolidation of the LHINs along with other agencies into one provincial agency (Ontario Health); though, to date, these changes have not been implemented, and home care assessment and delivery has not changed.

13   Howard Litwin & Ernie Lightman, "The Development of Community Care Policy for the Elderly: A Comparative Perspective" (1996) 26:4 Int J Health Serv 691–708.

14   *Ibid.*

15   *Supra* note 7.

16   Ontario, Minister of Finance, *2018 Ontario Budget: A Plan for Care and Opportunity* (Toronto: Queen's Printer for Ontario, 2018), online: <budget.ontario.ca/2018/budget2018-en.pdf>.

17   Allie Peckham et al, "Community- Based Reform Efforts: The Case of the Aging at Home Strategy" (2018) 14:1 Healthc Pol'y 30–43.

18   *Supra* note 9.

19   *Supra* note 19.

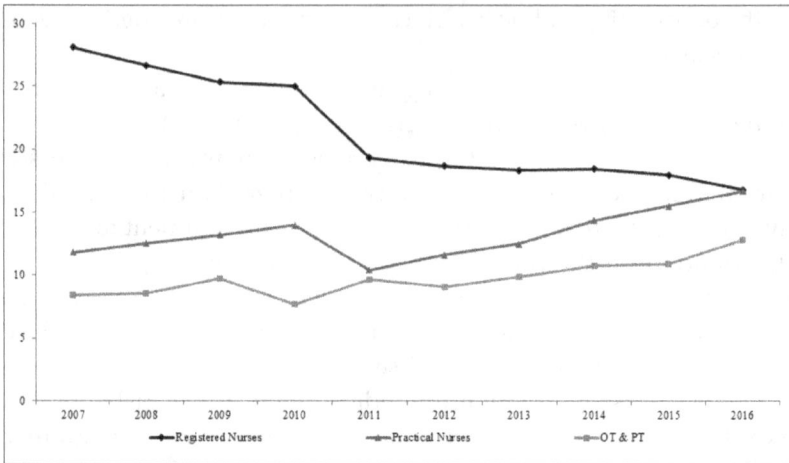

Figure 5.1. Head counts of home care workforce in Ontario, per 100,000 population (CIHI data).

Yet there is some sign that the traditional roles of service providers are changing. For example, figure 5.1 illustrates the trend over time in the registered professionals working in home care (for which there are data available), showing a slight decline in the role of RNs over the past decade, and only a slight increase in the role of practical nurses. With fewer RNs performing home care service roles, their duties are being assumed by PSWs, often without formalized training.[20] The role of PSWs is expanding to include tasks such as assistance with medications, wound care, complex lifts and transfers, catheterization, and feeding pumps.[21] Broadly, these trends in the home care workforce are suggestive of an effort to contain costs by shifting away from higher paid professionals.

As in most other high-income countries, access to home care services in Ontario is needs-based.[22] Using a standardized assessment tool called the Resident Assessment Instrument-Home Care (RAI-HC), eligibility for home care is determined on a case-by-case

---

20   Margaret Saari et al, "The evolving role of the personal support worker in home care in Ontario, Canada" (2017) 26:2 Health Soc Care Community 240–249.

21   *Ibid.*

22   Francesca Colombo et al, *Help Wanted? Providing and Paying for Long-Term Care* (OECD Publishing, 2011), online: <www.oecd.org/els/health-systems/help-wanted.htm>.

basis by a client-case manager within the LHIN.[23] The RAI-HC entails a face-to-face interview that includes a set of clinical-assessment protocols that identify potential negative outcomes and serves as the basis for the development of a home care service plan.[24] The role of the case manager is to ensure the appropriate services are provided within a timely manner to the clients most in need.[25] Once a client is determined to be long-stay, or in need of at least sixty uninterrupted days of services, the general target has been to complete the RAI-HC within seven to fourteen days.[26]

In response to evidence of regional variations in eligibility and care packages received for similar levels of assessed need,[27] the previous Liberal government implemented a levels of care framework in 2016.[28] This framework allows for clients with similar levels of functional need to receive similar hours of publicly funded support services per month, regardless of which part of the province they live. It remains to be seen whether this approach will reduce the variations in access and eligibility across the province that have characterized home care in Ontario since its inception. The uncertainty that clients face, and the case-by-case determination of eligibility, gives rise to situations where clients may not be deemed eligible and may thus be forced to rely on unpaid care, or privately paid services. Another key feature of the Ontario home care system is the presence of a service maximum, which we discuss further below. Placing a limit on the receipt of publicly funded services may generate demand for an active private sector.

Unlike most OECD countries that have an element of client contributions (e.g., copayments), in Ontario there are no fees for publicly

---

23 *Supra* note 7.

24 Amanda M Mofina & Dawn M Guthrie, "A comparison of home care quality indicator rates in two Canadian provinces" (2014) 14 BMC Health Serv Res 37.

25 Ontario, Office of the Auditor General of Ontario, 2010 *Annual Report*, Section 3.04 Home Care Services (Toronto: Queen's Printer for Ontario 2010).

26 *Supra* note 9.

27 *Ibid.*

28 Dipti Purbhoo & Irfan Dhalla,"Thriving at Home: A Levels of Care Framework to Improve the Quality and Consistency of Home and Community Care for Ontarians" (Presentation delivered at the HSSOntario Achieving Excellence Together Conference, Toronto, 15 June 2017), online: <https://hssontario.ca/Who/Conference/Documents/2017-Conference-Presentations/TA04_Levels_of_Care_Expert_Panel_Report.pdf>.

funded in-home health and support services.[29] On the other hand, Ontario is one of only three jurisdictions (along with Slovenia and South Korea) that employs a "service maximum" design to contain costs.[30] In Ontario, the maximum home care services a client is able to receive is 120 hours in the first thirty days of service, and ninety hours in any subsequent thirty-day period.[31] Occasionally, the LHIN may determine extraordinary circumstances which justify the provision of additional support hours on a client-by-client basis.[32] Such circumstances might include palliative-care cases or individuals awaiting placement into a long-term care facility.[33] In most cases where the service maximum has been reached, clients must go without the care they need, look to family members or friends, or, if they are able, pay privately.[34]

Notably, despite being a two-tier system, there are significant wait times for the publicly funded home care sector, and this is another factor fuelling demand for private alternatives. In the 2010, the auditor general of Ontario reviewed Ontario's home care programming, and made recommendations to reduce lengthy wait times and strengthen efforts toward timely service;[35] however, at the time of the 2015 audit, there was no evidence of progress.[36] As seen in acute care settings (e.g., specialist services, surgical procedures), wait lists may be a key stimulus for a two-tier sector but causation is much in dispute. For example, it is possible that the existence of a two-tier system actually lengthens wait times in the public sector by undermining political support for further public investments to meet needs and/or drawing away professional labour from the public to private spheres.[37]

---

29   *Supra* note 24; Tim Muir, *Measuring social protection for long-term care* (Paris: OECD Publishing, 2017), online: <oecd-ilibrary.org/social-issues-migration-health/measuring-social-protection-for-long-term-care_a411500a-en>.

30   Muir, *ibid.*

31   *Supra* note 7.

32   *Ibid.*

33   *Supra* note 9.

34   Williams *supra* note 3.

35   *Supra* note 9; *supra* note 14.

36   *Supra* note 14.

37   Jeremiah Hurley & Malcolm Johnson, *A Review Regarding Parallel Systems of Public and Private Finance* (Hamilton: Centre for Health Economics and Policy Analysis, 2014), online: <chepa.org/docs/documents/14-2.pdf>.

To our knowledge, there has been little attention paid to the nature and extent of the privately funded home care sector in Ontario. The limited evidence that does exist has focused on estimating the costs associated with informal caregiving, not the formal, paid sector.[38] The current study examines the impact of the two-tier system of financing home care on persons with lower socio-economic status, by estimating the associations between income and home care use among the full population of community-dwelling seniors in Ontario.

2. Methods and Data

2.1 Conceptual Framework

Our conceptual framework is based on Kemper's model of demand for home care.[39] Kemper suggests that the quantity of formal and informal home care demanded is related to five factors: the need for care, price, income, availability of family support, and individual tastes. This framework suggests that, on average, the demand for formal home care services will increase with need and income, and decrease with price and the availability of family supports.

It is important to note that Kemper's model was developed for the US context, where public insurance programs cover a small proportion of home care services.[40] In the Ontario context, where there are dual publicly and privately financed home care sectors, we expect the role of income to be different across these two sectors. We expect income to be negatively associated with the use of public home care services; in other words, we assume that higher-income clients, who have greater ability to pay out of pocket (and may have access to private insurance),[41] are more likely to use private instead

---

38   Denise N Guerriere et al, "Costs and determinants of privately financed home-based health care in Ontario, Canada" (2007) 16:2 Health Soc Care Community 126–136.

39   Peter Kemper, "The Use of Formal and Informal Home Care by the Disabled Elderly" (1992) 27:4 Health Serv Res 421–451.

40   *Ibid.*

41   The private insurance market in long-term care is very small and private health insurance is held by less than 1 per cent of Canadians. This limited take-up of private insurance may relate to insufficient information on the extent of public coverage of long-term care, and the high price of the insurance relative to its value due to market failure. Michel Grignon & Nicole F Bernier, *Financing Long-Term Care in Canada* (Montreal: IRPP, 2012) at 9.

of public home care services.[42] Another question is whether high income individuals are likely to top up public services with additional privately financed home care. Ontario's two-tier system of home care financing enables clients to pay privately for services to bypass queues for public home care services, expedite their treatment plan, and/or to supplement their publicly funded home care.[43] As in Ontario, where there is no income test on access to home care services, we may see an income gradient as wealthier persons are able to pay a higher price to top up publicly funded services with private services.

Early studies have employed similar approaches for modelling the demand for formal home care services.[44] Following these examples, we estimate the relationship between income and use of formal home care services, while controlling for other determinants of formal home care use.

2.2 Data

This study relied on Canadian Community Health Survey (CCHS) data, analyzed at the Toronto Region Statistics Canada Research Data Centre, at the University of Toronto. The CCHS is a nationally representative cross-sectional survey of persons aged twelve and older.[45] The survey captures data from all thirteen provinces and territories, and information on diseases and health conditions, health status, health care services, lifestyle and social conditions, and mental health and well-being.

The CCHS data is collected on two-year cycles, but an annual microdata file is available. The cross-sectional surveys can be pooled to examine specific populations or rare events, conditions, and characteristics. For this study, we pooled annual cross-sections from 2007 to 2014 for Ontario. Ontario was the only province to capture the home care component of the survey, which was optional content, in

---

42   Correspondingly, we expect the impact of income to be positively associated with the use of private services.

43   Williams *supra* note 3.

44   Mery *supra* note 6; Helen Stoddart et al, "What determines the use of home care services by elderly people?" (2002) 10:5 Health Soc Care Community 348–360; Courtney Harold Van Houtven & Edward C Norton, "Informal care and health care use of older adults" (2004) 23:6 J Health Econ 1159–1180.

45   The survey does not include full-time members of the Canadian Forces or institutionalized populations.

all of the study years. We excluded all CCHS participants in Ontario who were under the age of sixty-five, or who had missing values for home care service use, self-assessed health, or limitations with activities of daily living (ADLs). The result was a total sample of about 40,000 respondents over the study period.

2.3 Explaining our Variables and Empirical Strategy

This study attempts to identify the relationship between older Ontarians' income and their use of home care (both public and private), controlling for other variables such as health status and access to family supports. All variables for this study were derived from the CCHS data. Our outcome variables focused on home care use and included use of public and private home care, and access to informal care. We also differentiated between in-home health care (e.g., nursing and rehabilitation services) and in-home support (e.g., homemaking) services.

We included explanatory and control variables to account for the different elements of the conceptual framework (above). Our key explanatory variable was income (specifically, household income quintile). Control variables included measures of need (self-reported health status, self-reported limitations with ADLs, and self-reported unmet home care needs) and access to family supports (marital status, whether persons lived alone, and whether they had access to informal care). We also included other socio-demographic variables, which may have had an influence on home care use, including age, sex (male or female), and whether clients lived in an urban community. Detailed descriptions of these variables are included in table 5.1.

Table 5.1. Variable definitions

Variable Name	Description
Any home care	Respondent reported any home care use in the previous year.
Public home care	Respondent received any home care services in the past twelve months, with the cost being entirely or partially covered by government?
Private home care	Respondent received any home care services in the past twelve months, with the cost not being covered by government, and care was provided by a "nurse from a private agency," a "homemaker or other support services from a private agency," or a "physiotherapist from a private agency."

Variable Name	Description
Private + public home care	Respondent reported receiving both public and private home care in the previous year.
Home health care	Defined as any (public or private) home care service use in the previous year delivered by a nurse or other health care service provider (e.g., physiotherapy occupational therapy, speech therapy, nutrition counselling), or that provided support with medical equipment or supplies.
Home support	Defined as any (public or private) home care service use in the previous year that provided support with personal care (e.g., bathing, foot care), housework, meal preparation or delivery, shopping, or caregiver respite. Also includes any services reported as "other."
Receipt of unpaid/ informal care	Respondent reported having access to home care services delivered by a neighbour or a friend, a family member or spouse, or a volunteer.
Age	Age in years.
Fair/poor self-assessed health	Respondent reported having self-perceived poor or fair health (versus good, very good, or excellent health).
Household income quintile	Categorical variable that ranges from 1 = first quintile, to 5 = fifth quintile. The variable is based on the derived variable "incdrca" in the CCHS. This is an indicator of household income distribution. Missing values are coded as = 9.
Live alone	Respondent reported living alone. Derived from the "dhhdlvg" derived variable in the CCHS.
Married	Respondent reported being married or living common law.
One or more activities of daily living (ADL) limitations	Respondent reported requiring help with one or more of the following tasks: preparing meals, getting to appointments/ running errands, housework, personal care, moving about inside the house, and/or personal finances.
Self-reported unmet need	Respondent answers yes to the question "During the past 12 months, was there ever a time when you felt that you needed home care services but you didn't receive them."
Sex	Respondent reported being female.
Urban	Respondent lives in "urban core" community. Urban areas are defined as those with a density of four hundred or more persons per square kilometre.

Source: Canada, Health Canada, *Canadian Community Health Survey*, (National Survey), 2007–2014.

We used the CCHS data to describe home care use and the relationship between home care use and income.[46]

3. Results

Figure 5.2 shows the trends for self-reported public and private home care use (excluding informal care) in Ontario over the study period (2007 to 2014). Self-reported public home care use trended downward, from 10.0 per cent of the sixty-five and older population in 2007 to 7.3 per cent in 2014. In contrast, private home care use showed a slight trend upward, from 1.7 per cent of the population sixty-five and older to 2.6 per cent in 2014. The proportion of the population sixty-five

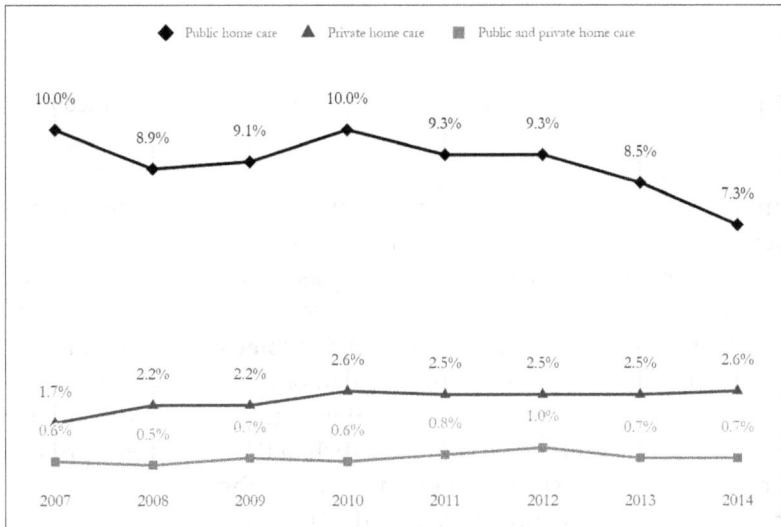

Figure 5.2. Trends of home care use in Ontario, 2007–2014.

---

46   Multivariate regression analyses of the probability of accessing public and private home care services were estimated using a multinomial logit (MNL) model. The MNL model is used for the estimation of the selection of unordered categories. Respondents could choose to use public, private, or public and private home care services. We estimated this model using the *mlogit* command in Stata 15. Hypothesis tests and confidence intervals were generated using heteroskedasticity robust standard errors. In addition, all descriptive statistics and regressions were weighted using CCHS survey weights. Canada, Statistics Canada, *Canadian Community Health Survey (CCHS): Household weights documentation*, (Statistics Canada, 2010), online: <www23.statcan.gc.ca/imdb-bmdi/pub/document/3226_D57_T9_V1-eng.htm>.

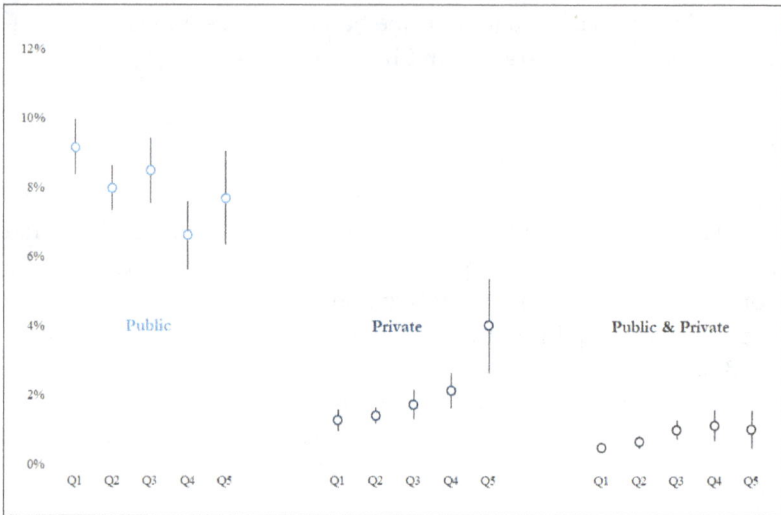

Figure 5.3. Predictive margins of home care use by household income quintile.

and older reporting use of a mix of public and private home care services was constant over the study period.

The results of the regression analysis are presented in table 5.2 and reported graphically in figure 5.3. We only report the results for the relationship between household income and home care use (full results are provided in table 5.3). In our figures, we report the likelihood of receiving home care (after controlling statistically for health status and other variables) for each of the five income groups, or quintiles: the first income group includes the 20 per cent of the population with the lowest income; the fifth income group includes the 20 per cent of the population with the highest income.[47] In 2016 in the Ontario population, the lowest income quintile had an average income, after taxes, of $18,600; the highest had an average income of $103,200.[48]

---

47   The results for income are reported as predictive margins. To calculate predictive margins we set each observation in our sample to each of the income quintiles holding all other covariates constant. The predictive margins on each income level can be interpreted as the probability of home care use if the entire sample had that level of income.

48   Financial Accountability Office of Ontario 2019. *Income in Ontario: Growth, Distribution and Mobility,* online: <https://www.fao-on.org/en/Blog/Publications/income-report-2019>.

Table 5.2. Effect of household income on home care use in the previous 12 months

		Any home care											
		No home care			Public			Private			Private + Public		
		Marg.	95% CI		Marg.	95% CI		Marg.	95% CI		Marg.	95% CI	
Household income quintile	1	.891	.882	.899	.092	.084	.100	.013	.010	.016	.005	.004	.006
	2	.900	.893	.907	.080	.073	.086	.014	.012	.016	.007	.005	.008
	3	.888	.878	.898	.085	.076	.094	.017	.013	.022	.010	.007	.013
	4	.901	.890	.912	.066	.056	.076	.021	.016	.026	.011	.007	.016
	5	.873	.856	.890	.077	.063	.090	.040	.026	.054	.010	.005	.016
Missing		.901	.890	.913	.077	.067	.087	.016	.011	.022	.006	.003	.008

		Home health care											
		No home care			Public			Private			Private + Public		
		Marg.	95% CI		Marg.	95% CI		Marg.	95% CI		Marg.	95% CI	
Household income quintile	1	.942	.934	.949	.044	.037	.050	.013	.008	.017	.002	.001	.003
	2	.940	.934	.945	.045	.040	.051	.011	.009	.014	.004	.002	.005
	3	.932	.923	.940	.046	.040	.052	.015	.010	.020	.007	.004	.010
	4	.935	.926	.945	.045	.036	.054	.013	.009	.017	.007	.004	.010
	5	.921	.907	.935	.053	.041	.065	.018	.009	.027	.007	.003	.011
Missing		.938	.928	.948	.045	.036	.053	.014	.008	.020	.003	.001	.006

		Home support											
		No home care			Public			Private			Private + Public		
		Marg.	95% CI		Marg.	95% CI		Marg.	95% CI		Marg.	95% CI	
Household income quintile	1	.917	.910	.924	.064	.058	.070	.014	.010	.019	.005	.003	.007
	2	.931	.925	.936	.049	.044	.054	.014	.012	.017	.006	.004	.008
	3	.920	.911	.929	.054	.046	.062	.018	.014	.021	.008	.005	.012
	4	.934	.924	.943	.037	.030	.044	.021	.016	.027	.008	.005	.012
	5	.917	.902	.931	.044	.032	.055	.034	.023	.046	.006	.002	.010
Missing		.932	.923	.941	.048	.041	.055	.017	.011	.023	.003	.002	.005

Notes: 95% confidence intervals calculated using heteroskedasticity robust standard errors.
Table abbreviations: "Marg." = Predictive margins; "95% CI" = 95% confidence interval.
Source: based on the research and analysis of the authors.

Table 5.3. Multinomial logit estimator results for home care use in the previous 12 months (base = no home care use)

	65+ years of age								
	Public			Private			Private + Public		
	RRR	95% CI		RRR	95% CI		RRR	95% CI	
Household income quintile (base = 1)									v
2	0.847	0.724	0.991	1.082	0.789	1.484	1.304	0.871	1.952
3	0.943	0.783	1.136	1.406	0.951	2.079	2.116	1.405	3.186
4	0.702	0.562	0.877	1.659	1.128	2.440	2.263	1.341	3.819
5	0.903	0.701	1.162	3.541	2.184	5.741	2.361	1.240	4.495
Missing	0.811	0.665	0.990	1.246	0.816	1.903	1.099	0.613	1.968
Age	1.061	1.052	1.070	1.093	1.073	1.113	1.097	1.075	1.119
Female	0.838	0.743	0.946	1.516	1.134	2.026	1.390	0.992	1.948
Married	0.963	0.792	1.170	1.740	1.248	2.425	1.867	1.177	2.961
Live alone	1.499	1.235	1.821	3.376	2.459	4.636	3.367	2.210	5.129
Urban	0.706	0.629	0.792	1.021	0.823	1.267	0.627	0.464	0.848
Fair-poor self-assessed health	2.036	1.794	2.312	1.349	1.024	1.778	1.786	1.304	2.445
One or more ADL limitations	4.598	4.017	5.263	6.131	4.564	8.236	11.129	7.163	17.293
Access to informal care	2.006	1.705	2.361	1.329	0.992	1.781	2.002	1.439	2.785
Self-reported unmet need	1.469	1.182	1.827	1.787	1.154	2.767	3.832	2.671	5.497
Year (base = 2007)									
2008	0.903	0.725	1.125	1.539	0.955	2.479	0.931	0.488	1.778
2009	0.916	0.733	1.145	1.307	0.868	1.970	1.192	0.656	2.165
2010	0.967	0.783	1.195	1.559	0.966	2.517	1.036	0.560	1.918
2011	0.896	0.713	1.125	1.451	0.953	2.208	1.337	0.751	2.380
2012	0.874	0.689	1.107	1.284	0.824	2.003	1.668	0.974	2.857
2013	0.824	0.651	1.043	1.577	1.010	2.460	1.138	0.671	1.928
2014	0.704	0.563	0.880	1.682	1.070	2.644	1.162	0.658	2.051

Notes: Heteroskedasticty robust standard errors were used to calculate confidence intervals. Table abbreviations: "RRR" = Relative risk ratio; "95% CI" = 95% confidence interval; "ADL" = Activities of daily living.

Table 5.3 (continued). Multinomial logit estimator results for home care use in the previous 12 months (base = no home care use)

	75+ years of age								
	Public			*Private*			*Private + Public*		
	RRR	*95% CI*		*RRR*	*95% CI*		*RRR*	*95% CI*	
Household income quintile (base = 1)									
2	0.855	0.713	1.025	1.041	0.721	1.503	1.244	0.777	1.990
3	0.986	0.783	1.242	1.538	0.970	2.441	2.086	1.301	3.346
4	0.683	0.520	0.896	1.380	0.865	2.200	2.236	1.213	4.123
5	0.920	0.660	1.284	3.072	1.731	5.452	2.170	1.044	4.511
Missing	0.864	0.680	1.097	1.217	0.747	1.981	1.327	0.703	2.504
Age	1.082	1.067	1.098	1.108	1.081	1.137	1.101	1.066	1.137
Female	0.827	0.713	0.960	1.518	1.087	2.119	1.315	0.892	1.939
Married	1.022	0.798	1.308	1.882	1.289	2.748	1.858	1.107	3.120
Live alone	1.486	1.173	1.883	3.418	2.364	4.941	3.105	1.960	4.918
Urban	0.785	0.683	0.901	0.979	0.766	1.249	0.678	0.480	0.960
Fair-poor self-assessed health	2.006	1.733	2.322	1.285	0.927	1.783	1.675	1.159	2.419
One or more ADL limitations	4.113	3.490	4.846	4.646	3.441	6.274	10.094	6.102	16.697
Access to informal care	1.842	1.531	2.217	1.176	0.843	1.640	1.725	1.184	2.514
Self-reported unmet need	1.390	1.087	1.777	1.672	0.962	2.903	3.805	2.506	5.777
Year (base = 2007)									
2008	0.884	0.665	1.175	1.587	0.910	2.767	0.949	0.448	2.011
2009	0.919	0.684	1.234	1.184	0.739	1.896	0.932	0.483	1.797
2010	0.886	0.677	1.160	1.221	0.735	2.030	0.829	0.407	1.688
2011	0.873	0.653	1.167	1.269	0.781	2.062	1.425	0.739	2.751
2012	0.846	0.625	1.147	1.175	0.696	1.985	1.611	0.874	2.972
2013	0.809	0.604	1.084	1.421	0.844	2.392	1.184	0.654	2.145
2014	0.737	0.551	0.986	1.643	0.957	2.820	1.146	0.597	2.202

Notes: Heteroskedasticty robust standard errors were used to calculate confidence intervals. Table abbreviations: "RRR" = Relative risk ratio; "95% CI" = 95% confidence interval; "ADL" = Activities of daily living.
Source: based on the research and analysis of the authors.

Our results suggest that the receipt of any (public or private) home care is fairly constant across all income quintiles, holding all else constant (health status, access to family supports). However, the patterns of use by income were different when we examined public and private home care separately. The predicted proportion of the sample that used no home care ranged from 87.3 per cent in the fifth quintile to 90.1 per cent in the fourth. Individuals in the lowest income group were more likely to use public home care than individuals in the higher income groups; the predicted proportion of the sample that used public home care services was 9.2 per cent in the first income quintile (the poorest) and 7.7 per cent in the fifth quintile (the wealthiest). However, this effect differs for in-home health and support services. For home health, the effect is constant across income levels while home support decreases with increasing income (see figs. 5.4 and 5.5 for a graphical depiction of these relationships).

On the other hand, those with higher income were more likely to use private home care services. The predicted proportion of the sample that used private home care was 1.3 per cent in the first income quintile, and 4.0 per cent in the fifth. This positive relationship remained when the results were separated by in-home health and support services, although the relationship was much stronger for in-home support services.

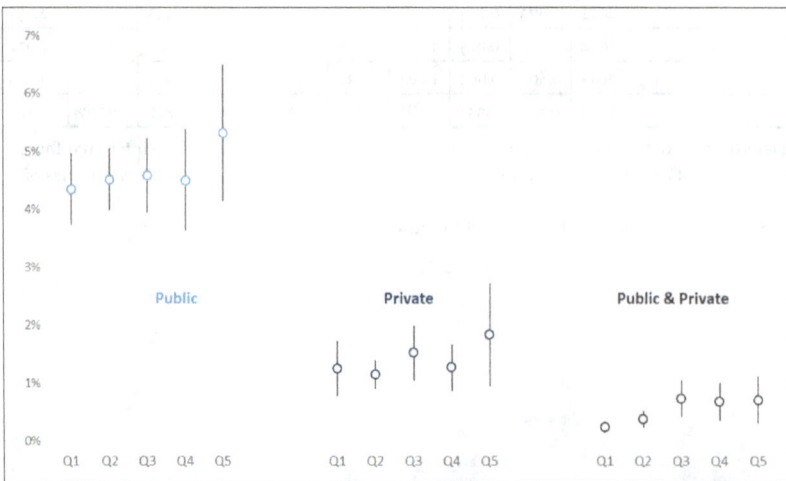

Figure 5.4. Predictive margins of home health care use by household income quintile.

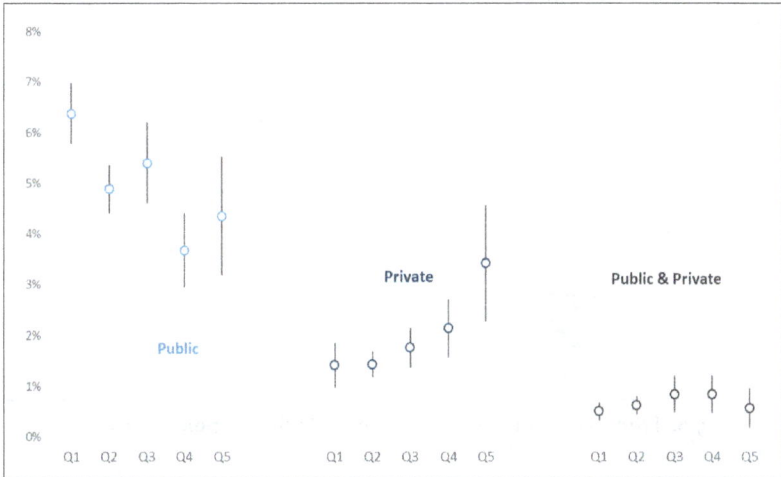

Figure 5.5. Predictive margins of home support use by household income quintile.

Those with higher incomes were also slightly more likely to use a combination of public and private home care. We predicted that 0.05 per cent of the lowest income quintile would use both public and private home care services, while 1.0 per cent of those in the highest would use both services in the previous year. When we separated our analysis by in-home health and support services, only in-home health care consistently increased with income.

4. Conclusion

To our knowledge, this is the first study to examine the receipt of both publicly funded and private-pay home care services in any Canadian province for the whole population of seniors living in community. Over the past decade, there appears to have been a slight decrease in the proportion of seniors who reported having received publicly funded home care services (including both in-home health and in-home support services), while at the same time the proportion of seniors reporting that they pay privately for such care has increased. The nature of the private market appears to be both to top up publicly funded care and to substitute for these services. In both cases, the private market is still relatively small: our results suggest that, in 2015, less than 3 per cent of seniors in Ontario had reported they exclusively used private in-home health or support services, and

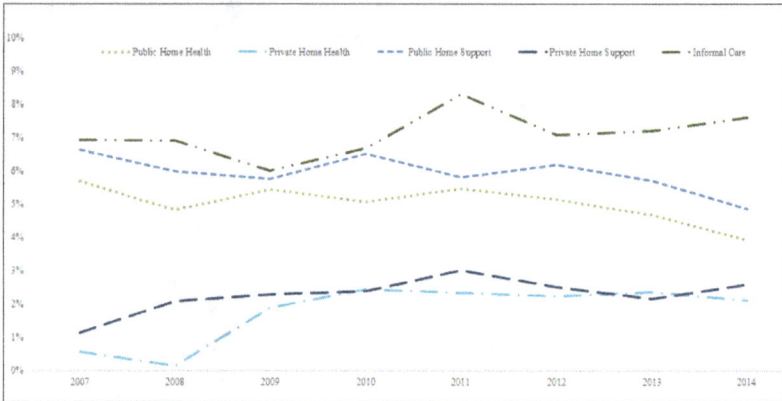

Figure 5.6. Trends of Home Care Use in Ontario for Seniors 65+

less than 1 per cent reported using both. This is not surprising given the limited use of private health insurance for home care, such that people are paying out of pocket for the care they need at a time in their lives when incomes are generally reduced.

We also find evidence that a small proportion of low-income seniors are topping up public in-home health care services with private ones. It is possible that some low-income seniors with unmet needs are seeking additional support, and paying out of pocket to meet these needs. We could not observe the motivation for this decision, but we would expect the financial impact of having to pay out of pocket to have more serious implications for low-income seniors than seniors in higher income brackets.

Overall, the study draws attention to the two-tier nature of home care in Ontario, which has largely gone unnoticed in the debates about two-tier health care in Canada. Another strength of the study is that it exploits rich data over a period of ten years to estimate the size and nature of the private-pay market for home care, and in particular the role of income as a factor in predicting home care use in the different sectors, and separately by health and support services. The analysis was able to control for possible variations in health status across income levels, given that the survey includes questions about general health as well as limitations in activities of daily living. The results of the analysis of income effects largely support our hypotheses: on average, with higher income, public home care use decreases and private home care use increases. We also expected to see a positive association between income and the use of both public and private services, where older people with greater ability to pay would be more willing and able to top up the publicly funded services to meet their health and other needs. There was a slightly positive association with income, but surprisingly there is some evidence of topping up even among the older people in the lowest income quintiles.

There are several limitations that are worth pointing out, many owing to the nature of the CCHS as the only source of information on the use of both publicly and privately funded home care in Canada. First, we are unable to measure the intensity of service use, as modelled in earlier studies of the public system.[49] We rely on estimating the likelihood/propensity of a visit over a period of a year; this offers a crude estimate of the size of the private-pay market for home care. Second, we cannot observe the impact of receiving home care on seniors' health and well-being, or the extent to which access to home care can prevent or delay admission to institutional care. Furthermore, while we can observe unmet need for home care as reported by seniors in this survey, we cannot determine whether unmet need preceded the receipt of home care (and whether those services met their needs), or unmet need persisted upon receipt of home care (and whether the services they received were inadequate).

Future research is needed to begin to examine some of these unanswered questions. This could be done by exploiting linked data sets or by designing new surveys with more detailed questions on motivations for the types of home services being used. For instance, studies could investigate why seniors are paying out of pocket for home care, even when they have very little income. What impact does this have on their ability to purchase other needed goods or services? As noted by Muir, even if we are able to measure the amount people are paying privately for their home care services, we do not know whether these payments are significantly affecting their well-being (especially for those with little disposable income).[50] We also do not yet know the extent to which the design of the publicly funded system and its service maxima are having the unintended effect of forcing lower-income seniors with more complex needs to institutions, while those with similar needs but with the ability to pay privately for additional home care services are able to stay in their homes.

---

49   Laporte, *supra* note 6.
50   Muir, *supra* note 30.

Our results suggest there are regressive impacts in relying upon private finance for home care, undermining equitable access to care. From the perspective of the ongoing *Cambie* litigation, challenging various laws protective of public medicare for hospital and physician services, the experience with home care in Ontario suggests that, at a minimum, further privatization is likely to exacerbate inequality. Having said this, the analogy is somewhat complicated because the market for home care includes not only public and private payment but also informal delivery. Further, there is no prohibition on private health insurance for home care or long-term care and yet very little of it is supplied or purchased, and, thus, it seems the private insurance market for home and long-term care differs from the market for hospital and physician services. Further, we don't yet understand, and further research is required on, (i) the extent, if any, to which privately financed home care draws away needed labour from the publicly funded sector; and (ii) the extent, if any, to which public support for further public spending is diminished because of a second, private-tier option.

CHAPTER 6

Self-Regulation as a Means of Regulating Privately Financed Medicare: What Can We Learn from the Fertility Sector?

Vanessa Gruben

The *Cambie* case, where the plaintiffs are seeking to overturn key sections of the *Medicare Protection Act*, could have a profound impact on Canada's universal health care system and encourage the growth of a second tier of privately financed health care in Canada.[1] As the possibility of greater privately financed health services looms large, this chapter asks what lessons can be learned from the regulation of the fertility sector—one of the few private for-profit health care sectors in Canada that is primarily paid for by private finance (private insurance and out-of-pocket payments) and delivered by for-profit facilities. This chapter examines how the professionals who provide fertility care, as well as the facilities where these services are provided, are regulated, and compares how the regulation of these services differ from publicly funded health care services.[2] This analysis demonstrates that, for the most part, two principal regulatory tools govern this sector: self-regulation (which is a form of internal regulation) through

---

I would like to thank Alexandra Herzig Cuperfain and Karen Chow for their excellent research assistance. All errors, however, are my own.

1   *Cambie Surgeries v Medical Services Commission of British Columbia* (28 January 2009), Vancouver, British Columbia S-090663 (statement of claim).

2   For the purpose of this chapter, I focus on the professionals and clinics that offer in vitro fertilization, intracytoplasmic sperm injection, intrauterine insemination, and oocyte cryopreservation (whether for medical or non-medical reasons).

physicians' regulatory colleges, and clinical-practice guidelines (CPGs). External regulation by government plays a relatively minor role. Indeed, in Canada, despite the risks associated with various fertility procedures like in vitro fertilization (IVF), provincial governments have only sought to directly regulate the fertility sector where they have extended public funding to assisted reproduction, as occurred in Quebec.[3]

Fertility services are, for the most part, delivered in private for-profit clinics in Canada.[4] Currently, there are thirty-six clinics offering fertility services across Canada; almost half located in Ontario.[5] These clinics offer a number of privately financed services, such as IVF, intracytoplasmic sperm injection (ICSI), as well as sperm and egg freezing. IVF is the most common service that patients pay for out of pocket and, as such, provides a good indication of the marked increase in demand for fertility services. In 2010, there were twenty-eight clinics reporting 18,454 cycles of IVF.[6] By 2017, the number of cycles of IVF performed by Canadian clinics had soared to 32,359.[7] That is an increase of 75 per cent over seven years. Although most fertility services are paid for out of pocket, there has been some limited public coverage for IVF in Quebec[8] and Ontario.[9] Public funding for IVF has been spurred in

---

3   Esme Kamphius, "Are we overusing IVF?" (2014) 348 British Medical J 15.

4   There are a few exceptions, such as the Mount Sinai Fertility Centre in Toronto.

5   Here is a breakdown from 2018: British Columbia (5), Alberta (2), Saskatchewan (2), Manitoba (1), Ontario (23; notably, there is one centre that has four offices, which have been counted as individual clinics in the total), Quebec (8), New Brunswick (1), and Nova Scotia (1).

6   Joanne Gunby, "Assisted reproductive technologies (ART) in Canada: 2010 results from the Canadian ART Register," online: *Canadian Fertility and Andrology Society* <cfas.ca/_Library/_documents/CARTR_2010.pdf>.

7   "Canadian Assisted Reproductive Technologies Register Plus (CARTR Plus)" (Report Presented at the 64th Annual Meeting of the Canadian Fertility and Andrology Society, Montreal, 13–15 September 2018), online: *Canadian Fertility and Andrology Society* <https://cfas.ca/_Library/cartr_annual_reports/CFAS-CARTR-Plus-presentation-Sept-2018-FINAL-for-CFAS-website.pdf>.

8   François Bissonnette et al, "Working to eliminate multiple pregnancies: a success story in Québec" (2011) 23 Repro BioMed Online 500.

9   Ontario introduced a funding program for IVF treatments in January 2016. Under the program, the province funds one IVF cycle per eligible patient per lifetime. One funded cycle of IVF includes the egg retrieval (as multiple eggs may be retrieved) and single-embryo transfer for the resulting embryos. There are some exclusions: women who are over the age of forty-three, and women

large part by the high incidence of multiple births (twins or triplets) resulting from the transfer of more than one embryo per IVF cycle (multiple-embryo transfer). Patients who pay privately often opt for multiple-embryo transfer as they assume it will increase the chance of pregnancy. As discussed in greater detail below, there are significant health risks for women carrying a multiple pregnancy and increased negative health outcomes for twins and triplets.[10] These poor health outcomes for pregnant women and the resulting children result in significant costs for the public health care system. To reduce these costs, provincial governments tied public funding of IVF to a single-embryo transfer policy. Studies have demonstrated that such an approach is cost effective.[11] This aspect of the program has been a success—multiple births drop dramatically under a mandatory single-embryo transfer policy.[12] Importantly, no such restriction has been imposed on individuals who are paying out of pocket for IVF, although the risks are the same.

An analysis of the legal frameworks governing the private for-profit fertility sector demonstrates that although internal regulation plays an important role, it is an insufficient regulatory tool to protect and promote patient health and safety. CPGs are generally less effective at bringing about change than external standards. Patients have fewer options for bringing complaints about providers and facilities, and these processes offer less effective remedies; and data collection, which is a key tool for promoting patient safety, is less rigorous. By contrast, the statutory frameworks that govern publicly funded services offer a range of more rigorous regulatory tools, such as enforceable clinical standards, various external oversight mechanisms, and mandatory data collection

---

who wish to freeze their eggs for non-medical reasons (also known as social egg freezing): Ontario Ministry of Health and Long-Term Care, "Ontario's Fertility Program," online: <www.health.gov.on.ca>. Notably, there is a program cap of 5,000 cycles per year. See also Tamas Gotz & Claire Jones, "Prioritization of Patients for Publicly Funded IVF in Ontario: A Survey of Fertility Centres" (2017) 39:3 JOGC 138.

10   Jocelynn L Cook et al, "Assisted Reproductive Technology-Related Multiple Births: Canada in an International Context" (2011) 33: 2 J Obstetrics & Gynaecology Canada 159.

11   Bissonnette, *supra* note 9. See also W Ombelet, "The Twin Epidemic in Infertility Care—Why do we Persist in Transferring Too Many Embryos?" (2016) 8:4 Facts Views Vis Obgyn 189.

12   Bissonnette, *supra* note 9.

and disclosure. In doing so, government regulation plays a critical role in ensuring patients receive safe, high-quality care. Thus, the story of how the fertility sector is regulated in Canada serves as a cautionary tale should a second tier of privately financed health care take hold in Canada.

In section 1, I offer a brief introduction to the different forms of health care regulation. In section 2, I describe the regulation of the fertility sector in Quebec, Ontario, British Columbia, and Alberta since they are home to the majority of fertility clinics and offer the majority of fertility procedures in Canada.[13] Self-regulation and CPGs are the primary tools for regulating the fertility sector, although there is greater government regulation where fertility services are funded by government. In section 3, I examine three examples to illustrate how self-regulation in the fertility sector has fallen short, as concerns single-embryo transfer, complaints about care, and health-data collection. These examples illustrate that the regulation of the private for-profit fertility sector, which occurs primarily through self-regulation and CPGs, is less rigorous and effective than external regulations, especially provincial legal frameworks governing publicly funded health care services. This analysis also indicates that governments appear to be more reluctant to regulate health care services that they do not fund directly, and failure to do so may put patients at greater risk. In my view, the provincial governments should not leave regulation primarily to health care professionals but should take an active role in regulating all health care services, regardless of who is funding those services. To be clear, I do not support the claim in *Cambie*, nor do I support increasing privately financed health care in Canada. However, if Canada is to make a turn toward more privately financed medical services, provincial governments must carefully consider how to regulate this sector to ensure the quality of these services. Anything less may jeopardize the health and safety of Canadian patients.

---

13   "IVF Clinics" (last visited 4 October 2019), online: *Canadian Fertility & Andrology Society* <https://cfas.ca/ivf-clinics.html>. There are thirty-eight IVF clinics in Quebec, Ontario, British Columbia, and Alberta.

Health Care Regulation

A range of regulatory tools governing health care professionals and institutions may be employed to promote safe, high-quality, patient-centred health care.[14] As Judith Healy explains, regulation is

> about steering and channeling as well as enforcement, and may be undertaken by state or non-state actors, whether external or internal to the field being regulated. Regulators steer through the use of supports (rewards) and sanctions (punishments).[15]

Generally speaking, health care regulation focuses on two domains: health care professionals and health care facilities or institutions.[16] Health care professionals include members of the health professions, such as physicians, nurses, physiotherapists, and others. By contrast, health care institutions are the facilities where health care is provided, such as hospitals and clinics. Health care institutions are, however, becoming increasingly diverse.[17] In this section, I offer a brief description of how each of these domains are subject to different forms of internal and external regulation.

Internal Regulation

Internal regulation, regulation which flows from members of the health profession, may take different forms, and commonly includes

---

14   There are two modes of regulation: "input" regulation, which includes measures that control who can practice a particular profession and includes licensure, certification, and registration; and "output" regulation, which is more reactive and includes professional discipline, civil liability, and accountability mechanisms such as the Canadian Institute for Health Information: Amy Zarzeczny, "The Role of Regulation In Health Care—Professional and Institutional Oversight" in Joanna Erdman, Vanessa Gruben & Erin Nelson, eds, *Canadian Health Law and Policy*, 5th ed (Toronto: LexisNexis, 2017) at 161. This chapter focuses on output regulation.

15   Judith Healy, "Regulating the Health Professions: Protecting Professionals or Protecting Patients?" in Stephanie D Short & Fiona McDonald, eds, *Health Workforce Governance: Improved Access, Good Regulatory Practice, Safer Patients* (Burlington, VT: Ashgate, 2012) 205 at 205.

16   Peter D Jacobson, "Regulating Health Care: From Self-Regulation to Self-Regulation?" (2001) 26:5 J Health Pol Pol'y & L 1165 at 1166. See generally Zarzeczny, *supra* note 15.

17   See generally John J Morris & Cynthia D Clarke, *Law for Canadian Health Care Administrators*, 2nd ed (Markham, ON: LexisNexis, 2011).

self-regulation and the issuance of CPGs by medical associations and professionals.[18]

In Canada, self-regulation plays an important role in both the public and private health care domains. Self-regulation, where the state confers on health care professionals the authority to regulate members of their own profession, is an important regulatory mechanism for all forms of health care. [19] Physicians, whether they practice in the publicly funded system or provide privately financed health care services, are subject to the regulatory oversight of their respective regulatory colleges. The overarching purpose of self-regulation is to promote patient health and safety, and, in many provinces, to ensure that professionals are regulated and coordinated in the public interest.[20] To achieve this objective, the regulatory colleges exercise a number of functions, including licensing members, setting practice standards, establishing practice guidelines, providing training and continuing education to members, and remediating or disciplining members who do not meet the standards of the profession.[21]

---

18   Fleur Beaupert et al, "Regulating Healthcare Complaints: A Literature Review" 27:6 (2014) Intl J Health Care Quality Assurance 505.

19   Tracey Epps, "Regulation of Health Care Professionals" in Jocelyn Downie, Timothy Caulfield & Colleen M Flood, eds, *Canadian Health Law and Policy*, 4th ed (Toronto: Lexis Nexis, 2011) 75 at 83. See generally Margot Priest, "The Privatization of Regulation: Five Models of Self-Regulation" (1997–1998) 29:2 Ottawa L Rev 233; Tracey L Adams, "Regulating Professions in Canada: Interprovincial Differences Across Five Provinces" (2009) 43:3 J Can Stud 194; Donald M Berwick, "Postgraduate Education of Physicians: Professional Self-regulation and External Accountability" (2015) 313:18 J American Medical Assoc 1803.

20   Glenn Regehr & Kevin Eva, "Self-assessment, Self-direction, and the Self-regulating Professional" (2006) 449 Clinical Orthopaedics and Related Research 34; Roger Collier, "Professionalism: The Privilege and Burden of Self-regulation" (2012) 184:14 CMAJ 1559. For example, in Ontario, the *Regulated Health Professions Act, 1991*, SO 1991, c 18, s 3 provides that "[i]t is the duty of the Minister to ensure that the health professions are regulated and co-ordinated in the public interests."

21   David Orentlicher, "The Role of Professional Self-Regulation" in Timothy S Jost, ed, *Regulation of the Healthcare Professions* (Chicago: Health Administration Press, 1997) 129 at 130; Sylvia R Cruess & Richard L Cruess, "The Medical Profession and Self-Regulation: A Current Challenge" (2005) 7 Ethics J of the American Medical Assoc at 1.

The right and obligation of self-regulation can be traced back to the nineteenth century and is rooted in the social contract.[22] As Cruess and Cruess explain: "In return for a physician's commitment to altruistic service, a guarantee of professional competence, the demonstration of morality and integrity in their activities, and their agreement to address issues of social concern, society grants to both individual physicians and the profession considerable autonomy in practice, status in the community, financial rewards, and the privilege of self-regulation."[23]

Several justifications are invoked in support of professional self-regulation. First, self-regulation reflects the strong need for professional autonomy.[24] Second, professionals have the expertise and technical knowledge needed to set standards for medical practice, and to determine whether those standards have been met.[25] Advocates of professional regulation maintain that these standards will be more readily accepted by professionals and the public where they are developed by experts, as opposed to external bodies who do not have the same level of expertise.[26] Third, self-regulation is said to avoid the politicization of medical standards and keeps those standards independent from political processes.[27] Finally, some argue that professionals should be permitted to resolve problems within the profession through self-regulatory mechanisms before resorting to external processes because it is more efficient to do so.[28]

But self-regulation gives rise to several important concerns. Many relate to the oversight and complaints functions—the processes that ensure that professionals meet the standards established by the colleges.[29] These concerns include that complaints must generally be brought by patients;[30] there is no compensation for patient

---

22 Mary Dixon-Woods, Karen Yeung & Charles L Bosk, "Why is UK Medicine no Longer a Self-regulating Professional? The Role of Scandals Involving 'Bad Apple' Doctors" (2011) 73:10 Social Science & Medicine 1452.

23 Cruess, *supra* note 22 at 1.

24 Orentlicher, *supra* note 22 at 130.

25 *Ibid* at 131.

26 *Ibid* at 131–132; Berwick, *supra* note 20.

27 Orentlicher, *supra* note 22 at 132. He refers to the government's decision to delay the implementation on fetal-tissue transplantation based on political ideologies.

28 *Ibid* at 132–133.

29 Zarzeczny, *supra* note 15 at 172.

30 In certain provinces, colleges can initiate inspections of physicians; e.g., in Ontario, *Regulated Health Professions Act*, *supra* note 21 s 75.

complainants; the complaints processes may not be well known to patients, and may be difficult to navigate; the remedial dispositions or penalties are often considered to be inappropriate or not sufficiently severe; and, the colleges do not provide enough information to the public about professionals who have received an educational or remedial disposition.[31] Further, the regulatory colleges tend to be quite slow in introducing and implementing policy changes.[32] As a result, there is a perception that dispositions are too lenient and professionals are favouring or protecting their own members.[33] Further undermining the public confidence in self-regulation are high-profile media reports of "bad apples," health care professionals who have engaged in egregious misconduct or whose care falls well below the standard of care.[34] These concerns may lead the public to believe that self-regulation is about protecting professionals rather than patients.

The fertility sector increasingly relies on a second form of internal regulation: CPGs. The Canadian Fertility and Andrology Society (CFAS), the professional society that represents fertility practitioners and other allied professionals, is responsible for creating CPGs for Canadian fertility clinicians.[35] Clinical guidelines are intended to promote high-quality, consistent, evidence-based practice.[36] There

---

31   Cruess, *supra* note 22 at 1; Colleen Flood & Bryan Thomas, "Regulatory Failure: The Case of the Private-for-Profit IVF Sector" in Trudo Lemmens et al, eds, *Regulating Creation: The Law, Ethics and Policy of Assisted Human Reproduction* (Toronto: UTP, 2017) 359 at 369. For criticisms about self-regulation, see generally Fiona McDonald, "Challenging the Regulatory Trinity: Global Trends in Health Professional Regulation" in Fiona McDonald & Stephanie D Short, eds, *Health Workforce Governance: Improved Access, Good Regulatory Practice, Safer Patients* (London: Routledge, 2012) 97.

32   Flood, Thomas & Harrison-Wilson observed that it took several years for the College of Physicians and Surgeons to implement reforms that would provide more rigorous oversight of cosmetic-surgery clinics following the death of Krista Stryland, who died after suffering complications from a liposuction procedure: Colleen Flood, Bryan Thomas & Leigh Harrison-Wilson, "Cosmetic Surgery Regulation and Regulation Enforcement in Ontario" (2010) 36 Queen's L J 31.

33   Cruess, *supra* note 22 at 1.

34   Dixon-Woods, *supra* note 23 at 1452.

35   For a description of the CFAS, see Canadian Fertility & Andrology Society, online: <https://cfas.ca>.

36   Dylan Kozlick, "Clinical Practice Guidelines and the Legal Standard of Care: Warnings, Predictions, and Interdisciplinary Encounters" (2011) 19 Health LJ 125 at 131. CPGs may be used by a court in establishing the standard of care

is, however, some question about whether CPGs do indeed achieve this goal. First, a CPG may reflect biased views, where members have relationships with industry or institutional affiliations that raise a conflict of interest.[37] There are also concerns about the extent to which health care professionals follow CPGs. Some argue that developing and disseminating CPGs does not, on its own, change physician behaviour.[38] Since they are not binding per se, physicians may disregard these guidelines because they do not agree with them or because of external factors, such as lack of time for implementation.[39]

External Regulation

External authorities, such as governments or private organizations, play a critical role in the regulation of health professionals and facilities. Indeed, as Beaupart notes, external regulation of health care professionals by provincial governments is on the rise.[40] In Canada, one of the most important sources of external regulation is the provincial government. Each province has passed legislation governing various aspects of health care, such as legislation governing public hospitals or non-hospital facilities.[41] For example, under Ontario's *Public Hospitals Act*, the minister of health may appoint an inspector to conduct a review of a hospital, which may include an audit of all or part of the accounts, records, and other affairs of the hospital.[42] Among the act's enforcement provisions is the minister's power to

---

owed to the patient. This is one of the four elements that must be established in order to succeed in a negligence claim: Bernard Dickens, "Medical Negligence" in Jocelyn Downie, Timothy Caulfield & Colleen M Flood, eds, *Canadian Health Law and Policy*, 4th ed (Toronto: Lexis Nexis, 2011) 83 at 117.

37 Indeed, most recently, it was revealed that the opioid guidelines endorsed by Health Canada were drafted by a group of experts who had multiple conflicts of interest with industry: Kelly Crowe, "Opioid conflict-of-interest controversy reveals extent of big pharma's ties to doctors," *CBC News* (19 May 2017) online: <https://www.cbc.ca/news/health/opioid-pain-philpott-mcmaster-university-purdue-pharma-drug-industry-conflict-1.4121956>.

38 Orentlicher, *supra* note 22 at 138.

39 Brent Graham, "Clinical Practice Guidelines: What Are They and How Should They Be Disseminated?" (2014) 30:3 Hand Clinics 361 at 362–363.

40 Fleur Beaupart et al, "Regulating Healthcare Complaints: A Literature Review" (2014) 27:6 Intl J Health Care 505.

41 John J Morris & Cynthia D Clarke, *Law for Canadian Health Care Administrators*, 2nd ed (Markham, ON: LexisNexis, 2011) at 2.

42 *Public Hospitals Act*, RSO 1990, c P40, s 18.

suspend or the lieutenant-governor's power to revoke a hospital's approval where it is in the public interest.[43]

In addition, private organizations may play a regulatory role; for example, by accrediting professionals or facilities. Accreditation may have different meanings but is generally understood to be a process whereby an independent body issues a certificate indicating that a facility has met certain predetermined standards.[44] For example, Accreditation Canada is a private not-for-profit organization that develops accredited standards and programs for community and home care, health facilities, residential care, and others.[45] As such, accreditation is, in many respects, the privatization of regulation. Although it is beyond the scope of this chapter, Accreditation Canada has sought to fill some of the regulatory gaps in the delivery of fertility services in Canada by establishing three standards relevant to assisted reproduction, including clinical services, laboratory services, and work with third-party donors.[46]

Regulating the Fertility Sector in Canada

Both the funding and regulation of fertility services varies across Canada. While an exhaustive analysis is beyond the scope of this chapter, a brief look at the regulatory frameworks in Quebec, Ontario, Alberta, and British Columbia reveals two trends: first, that self-regulation and CPGs play a significant role in the regulation of the fertility sector, and second, provincial governments seek to more closely regulate the fertility sector when public funding is offered. For example, in Quebec there is extensive government regulation of assisted reproduction, although the Collège des médecins du

---

43   *Ibid*, at s 4(5).

44   Ontario, Health Quality Ontario, *Building an Integrated System for Quality Oversight in Ontario's Non-Hospital Medical Clinics* (Ontario: Health Quality Ontario, 2016) at 24.

45   See, e.g., Accreditation Canada, "About Accreditation Canada," online: <https://accreditation.ca/about/>.

46   Accreditation Canada, "Assisted Reproductive Technology (ART) Standards for Laboratory Services," online: <https://store.accreditation.ca/products/assisted-reproductive-technology-art-standards-for-laboratory-services>. While accreditation provides patients with an assurance that a clinic has met the requisite standards, there are some concerns about the effectiveness of accreditation as a regulatory tool, including that, since it is voluntary, a clinic that may be in breach of one of the standards may opt not to be accredited.

Québec (CMQ) continues to play a significant role in the regulation of the fertility sector. By contrast, in Ontario, Alberta, and British Columbia, the regulation of the fertility sector falls primarily to the regulatory colleges.

National Standards: The Canadian Fertility and Andrology Society

The regulation of fertility clinics in Canada falls primarily to the provinces, but some national standards do apply. Although the federal government had established a comprehensive regulatory framework, including a licensing and inspection scheme, to govern the fertility sector in the *Assisted Human Reproduction Act* in 2004, these provisions were declared unconstitutional by the Supreme Court of Canada in *Reference re Assisted Human Reproduction Act* in 2010.[47] The impugned provisions were subsequently repealed by Parliament in 2012.[48] As a result, the federal government's regulatory role vis-à-vis fertility clinics is quite limited.[49] While regulation of the health professionals and the clinics themselves now clearly falls largely to the provinces, most provincial governments, with the exception of Quebec, have not stepped in to fill the regulatory void left by the Supreme Court's decision.

In light of the relatively minimal role of the federal government, most national clinical standards are set by the CFAS.[50] The CFAS is a not-for-profit organization representing reproductive specialists, scientists, and allied health professionals in Canada.[51] The CFAS has

---

47   *Reference re Assisted Human Reproduction Act*, 2010 SCC 61, [2010] 3 SCR 457. The former provisions of the *AHRA* established a licensing and inspection regime: Glenn Rivard & Judy Hunter, *The Law of Assisted Human Reproduction* (Markham, ON: LexisNexis, 2005) at 187–200.

48   The federal government repealed the impugned provisions in 2012: *Jobs, Growth and Long-Term Prosperity Act*, SC 2012, c 19, s 713.

49   Section 10 of the *AHRA* was introduced in 2012 and its purpose is to reduce the health and safety risks arising from the use of third-party sperm and ova. Health Canada recently promulgated regulations under section 10, which were not in force at the time of writing: Safety of Sperm and Ova Regulations: SOR/2019–2192. These regulations impose certain requirements on fertility clinics and other entities in the fertility industry vis-à-vis the importation, storage, and transport of third-party gametes and embryos.

50   One exception is section 8, which sets out the requirements for consent to the reproductive use of a human embryo: *Assisted Human Reproduction Act*, SC 2004, c 2, s 8.

51   Canadian Fertility & Andrology Society, "About," Canadian Fertility & Andrology Society, online:

set a number of CPGs that establish national best practices for the fertility sector, including third-party reproduction, fertility preservation
in reproductive-age women who are facing gonadotoxic treatments,
the management of ovarian hyperstimulation syndrome, and the
number of embryos transferred.[52] The CFAS is also responsible for
the collection and disclosure of information about fertility services in
Canada. The Canadian Assisted Reproductive Technologies Register,
also known as CARTR Plus, has been collecting and reporting aggregate data on assisted-reproduction procedures, such as the number
of IVF cycles and their outcome (e.g., pregnancy and multiple birth
rate) in Canada since 2001.[53]

Quebec

In Canada, fertility services have been most rigorously regulated
in Quebec since 2010 and the advent of public funding for IVF services. Fertility services such as IVF, ICSI, and others are offered in
both hospital-based clinics as well as private clinics, both of which
are subject to provincial regulation.[54] In 2010, Quebec's provincial
legislature introduced a detailed provincial regulatory framework

---

<https://cfas.ca/about-cfas/>.

52   Canadian Fertility & Andrology Society, "CFAS Clinical Practice
      Guidelines," Canadian Fertility & Andrology Society, online: <https://cfas.ca/
      clinical-practice-guidelines/>.

53   While CARTR publishes aggregate data to the general public, "the CARTR
      outcome-improvement committee has confidential access to clinic-specific data,
      permitting them to identify and offer help to clinics whose results fall below
      the national standard." Bissonnette, *supra* note 9 at 501.

54   "There are three public, hospital-based centers for assisted reproduction in
      Québec, located at the McGill University Health Centre (CUSM), the Centre
      hospitalier de l'Université de Montréal (CHUM), and the Centre hospitalier
      universitaire Sainte-Justine. There are currently six centers for assisted repro-
      duction in private facilities: the Clinique Procréa in Montréal and Québec City,
      the Clinique Ovo in Montréal, the Montreal Fertility Center, the OriginElle
      Fertility Clinic, and the Fertylis center in Laval. These are private centers under
      agreement (hereinafter private centers). There are also four regional public
      centers designated to provide some ART services closer to home to Quebecers
      living outside major urban centers: Centre de santé et de services sociaux (CSSS)
      de Chicoutimi, Centre hospitalier régional de Trois-Rivières, Centre hospitalier
      universitaire de Sherbrooke (CHUS), and Centre hospitalier universitaire de
      Québec (CHUQ)." Commissaire à la santé et au bien-être Québec, "Summary
      Advisory on Assisted Reproduction in Québec," (June 2014) online: <https://
      www.csbe.gouv.qc.ca/fileadmin/www/2014/Procreation_assistee/CSBE_PA_
      SummaryAdvisory_2014.pdf> at 13.

concurrently with its decision to include assisted reproduction as an insured service.[55] Although the funding program was dismantled at the end of 2015, the regulatory framework has largely remained in place. It would, of course, seem odd if the same services funded by the public system were in fact more lightly regulated if privately financed, given concerns that private for-profit provision may have incentives to skim on quality and safety in pursuit of the profit motive, discussed in more detail below. But that is indeed the Canadian approach now, outside of Quebec.

Quebec's *Act respecting clinical and research activities relating to assisted procreation (APA)* is thus an example of direct regulation referenced in part 1 above, and establishes a licensing regime for fertility clinics and practitioners "in order to ensure high-quality, safe, and ethical practices."[56] Under the *APA*, all assisted-reproduction procedures must be carried out in a licensed facility.[57] The *APA* imposes a range of requirements on clinics, including providing an annual report to the minister.[58]

While the provincial government is responsible for licensing,[59] inspection, and oversight,[60] it is the CMQ that sets the applicable clinical standards,[61] with a couple of notable exceptions. First, the *APA* requires physicians to ensure that the treatment chosen for a patient not pose a serious risk to the health of the person or the resulting child, and must document this in the patient record.[62] Further, the

---

55   The provincial government expanded the provincial health plan to fund up to three cycles of IVF with ovarian stimulation or up to six cycles of natural or modified natural cycle IVF either in hospital-based facilities or private facilities: *Act respecting clinical and research activities relating to assisted procreation*, CQLR c A-5.01, the *Regulation respecting clinical activities related to assisted procreation*, c A-4.01, r 1, and the *Regulation to amend the Regulation respecting the application of the Health Insurance Act*. For a discussion of the scheme, see Stefanie Carsley, "Funding In Vitro Fertilization: Exploring the Health and Justice Implications of Quebec's Policy" (2012) 20:3 Health L Rev 15; and Bissonnette, *supra* note 54 at 501.

56   *Act, supra* note 56 at s 1.

57   *Ibid*, ss 6 and 7.

58   *Ibid*, at Chapter III, Division I, s 14.

59   *Ibid*, at Chapter II, Division II, ss 15–22.

60   *Ibid*, at Chapter IV, ss 25–35.

61   *Ibid*, s 10.

62   *Ibid*, s 10.1.

APA mandates, with limited exceptions, that only one embryo may be transferred in an IVF cycle (referred to as single-embryo transfer).[63]

Although Quebec's regulatory scheme for IVF is quite rigorous, a number of regulatory gaps remain. As Flood and Thomas highlight, there does not seem to be a regular inspection mechanism in place to enforce the *APA*; the conditions or suspensions of licenses is at the discretion of the CMQ, and is, therefore, a matter of self-regulation, and the penalties for breaching the act "pale in comparison to the high prices charged for IVF services and the potential for profits."[64]

Ontario

In Ontario, greater regulation of the fertility sector followed the government's decision to introduce a funding program for assisted reproduction in December 2015. As discussed, the provincial government currently funds one stimulated cycle of IVF for every Ontarian.[65] Ontario has more than twenty private for-profit fertility clinics, which offer both publicly and privately funded fertility services.[66] Fertility services are also offered in one public hospital in Ontario, Mount Sinai in Toronto, and as such this clinic falls under the regulatory umbrella of public hospitals.

---

63   *Ibid*, s 10.3. The *Act* provides: "In the course of an *in vitro* fertilization activity, only one embryo may be transferred into a woman. However, taking into account the quality of embryos, a physician may decide to transfer two embryos if the woman is thirty-seven years of age or over. The reasons for the decision must be entered into the woman's medical record." The *Act* also imposes age restrictions on who may access publicly funded IVF. There is some debate about whether this rationale is justified based on the evidence which is beyond the scope of this chapter. For a discussion about the legitimacy of these policies, see Flood & Thomas, *supra* note 32 at 376–377.

64   Flood & Thomas, *supra* note 32 at 372–373.

65   The Ontario government funds one stimulated cycle of IVF, which includes one at a time transfer for all viable embryos for every Ontarian. Women must be under the age of forty-three. Women who act as a surrogate are eligible for an additional stimulated cycle of IVF. The *Act* also imposes age restrictions on who may access publicly funded IVF. Government of Ontario, "Get fertility treatments" (9 May 2017), Government of Ontario, online: <https://www.ontario.ca/page/get-fertility-treatments>. There is some debate about whether this rationale is justified based on the evidence, which is beyond the scope of this chapter. For a discussion about the legitimacy of these policies, see Flood & Thomas, *supra* note 32 at 376–377.

66   Canadian Fertility & Andrology Society, "IVF Clinics," online: *CFAS* <cfas.ca/ivf-clinics.html>.

The most notable regulatory change that accompanied public funding was a single-embryo transfer requirement: all publicly funded cycles require one-at-a-time embryo transfers, with limited exceptions.[67] Notably, the province has not placed a restriction on IVF cycles that patients pay for out of pocket. For privately funded cycles, it is up to the treating physician to follow the CFAS's CPG on multiple-embryo transfers. Since there is no hard and fast rule, there is more discretion here for physicians to transfer multiple embryos.[68]

The Ontario government also called for a regulatory framework tailored to fertility services following the introduction of the funding program. This enhanced regulatory model will, however, continue to fall within the jurisdiction of the College of Physicians and Surgeons of Ontario (CPSO) through the Out-of-Hospitals Premises Inspection Program (OHPIP). The OHPIP is a program mandated by the province but designed and administered by the CPSO.[69] OHPIP establishes standards for premises where procedures are performed using anesthesia where the premises do not fall under another provincial regulatory oversight scheme.[70] These other regulatory schemes include the *Public Hospitals Act*,[71] the *Excellent Care for All Act (ECFAA)*,[72] and the *Independent Health Facilities Act*[73]—the latter provides a licensing and oversight framework for facilities that offer diagnostic facilities that are funded by the Ministry of Health, and ambulatory-care facilities that provide surgical, therapeutic, and diagnostic procedures, such as dialysis and plastic surgery.[74]

---

67   Government of Ontario, *supra* note 66.

68   Joint SOGC-CFAS Clinical Practice Guideline, "Elective Single Embryo Transfer Following In Vitro Fertilization" (2010) 241 J Obstetrics & Gynaecology Canada 363, online: <https://www.jogc.com/article/S1701-2163(16)34482-6/pdf>.

69   *Medicine Act, 1991*, SO 1991, c 30.

70   *Ibid*.

71   *Public Hospitals Act*, RSO 1990, c P 40.

72   *Excellent Care for All Act, 2010*, SO 2010, c 14. The *Act* applies to public hospitals in Ontario and requires hospitals to, among others things, establish quality committees that report on quality-related issues, create annual quality-improvement plans and make these available to the public, and establish a patient-relations process to address and improve the patient experience.

73   *Independent Health Facilities Act*, RSO 1990, c I 3. The *IHFA* program is administered by the Ministry of Health and Long-Term Care but the minister may request more frequent inspections of IHFs and IHFs are posted on the ministry website: Ontario, *supra* note 45 at 14.

74   Flood & Thomas, *supra* note 32.

Although fertility clinics are subject to OHPIP, its requirements are ill-suited to fertility clinics and practitioners delivering IVF, IUI, and ICSI, as well as gamete and embryo retrieval and storage, as the guidelines do not establish standards for these specialized procedures.[75]

Following the introduction of the public funding program, the Ontario government asked the CPSO to develop and implement a quality and inspection framework to specifically govern fertility services.[76] The proposed standards for fertility services apply to IVF, IUI, and fertility preservation for medical purposes (all of which are fully or partially funded services).[77] Notably, the standards do not apply to fertility preservation for non-medical purposes, or social egg freezing (e.g., where a woman freezes her eggs for later reproductive use).[78] It is unclear why this is the case as the health and safety risks for women are similar, regardless of the reason for oocyte preservation. Perhaps it is because the government does not consider social egg freezing to be a health service, although it begs the question why this would matter given the associated health risks.

The proposed OHPIP for fertility-services premises sets detailed standards for fertility services in Ontario.[79] The program contains comprehensive standards on a range of aspects of fertility practice, including the handling of human gametes and transfer of cryopreserved human cells and tissues for assisted reproduction;[80] physical

75   *Ibid.* Indeed, as the Health Quality Ontario panel explained: "OHP oversight enforcement is limited to particular procedures. Facilities failing to receive a pass rating could continue to perform procedures that do not require anaesthesia or sedation even if the cause of the failed inspection may affect the facility as a whole (e.g., substandard infection control practices)." Ontario, *supra* note 45 at 27.

76   The CPSO released a draft of the standards that would apply to fertility-services premises in September 2016: The College of Physicians & Surgeons of Ontario, *Applying the Out-of-Hospital Premises Inspection Program (OHPIP) Standards in Fertility Services Premises*, CPSO, 2016, online: <http://policyconsult.cpso.on.ca/wp-content/uploads/2016/11/Fertility-Services-Draft-Companion-OHPIP.pdf>.

77   The revised standards will amend section 44 of O Reg 114/94, Part XI.

78   O Reg 114/94, *ibid*, s 44(1)(b.1) includes (i) in vitro fertilization, (ii) intra uterine insemination; (iii) fertility preservation for medical purposes.

79   CPSO Draft Standards, *supra* note 77 at iii. The standards are broadly divided into two parts, IVF units and ovulation induction/intracervical insemination/intrauterine insemination units, to reflect the types of services offered by fertility-services premises.

80   *Ibid* at 2, 2.2.6.1.5ff.

standards for fertility premises (e.g., layout for the IVF laboratory and the procedure room);[81] nurse and laboratory staff qualifications;[82] clinical standards (e.g., taking a focused history and physical examination before the procedure[83] and including certain documents in the medical record);[84] and verification processes to ensure patients receive the correct gametes or embryos.[85] Further, OHPIP establishes "essential outcome measures" for monitoring quality of care, including reporting information regarding access (e.g., patient criteria for acceptance consultation, wait times for first appointments, and first fertility treatments), patient population (e.g., age and reason for treatment), and fertility preservation.[86] However, there is no requirement to submit this information to CARTR Plus or to any federal or provincial agency, nor is there any requirement to disclose it to the public.[87]

The proposed OHPIP for fertility-services premises is a significant improvement to the current regulation of Ontario's fertility sector. By creating a regime tailored to fertility services it better promotes the health and safety of fertility patients. Yet there are important gaps. Its principal weakness is that the standards are set and enforced by a self-regulatory body.[88]

While the Ontario fertility sector currently falls outside of provincial oversight, it appears that this may change with the new *Oversight of Health Facilities and Devices Act (OHFDA), 2017*.[89] Following recommendations by Health Quality Ontario, the province's health-quality watchdog, the *OHFDA* will establish a single legislative framework to govern independent health facilities and non-hospital medical clinics that provide privately financed care (known as "community health facilities").[90] In other words, the same regulatory framework would apply to both publicly and privately financed care. The proposed integrated framework will establish a licensing and inspections process, as well as a complaints and

81   *Ibid* at 4–5, 4.1 and 4.2ff.

82   *Ibid* at 9, 5.6ff.

83   *Ibid* at 12, 6.2ff.

84   *Ibid* at 11, 6.1ff.

85   *Ibid* at 14–15, 6.4–6.6ff.

86   *Ibid* at 21–22.

87   *Ibid* at 20, 8.1ff.

88   *Public Hospitals Act, supra* note 72.

89   *Oversight of Health Facilities and Devices Act, 2017*, SO 2017, c 25, Schedule 9.

90   Health Quality Ontario, *supra* note 45.

independent review process, together with a mechanism for disclosing this information.[91] The act is not yet in force and the regulations are not yet available, but the *OHFDA* may well provide a consistent, comprehensive, and transparent regulatory framework for both publicly and privately financed health care services, which may well serve as a model for the better regulation of privately financed care. Unfortunately, it appears that these important regulatory changes have been shelved, likely as a result of a change in government and the introduction of legislation that will overhaul the delivery of health care services in Ontario.[92]

Alberta

The College of Physicians and Surgeons of Alberta (CPSA) is responsible for the regulation of non-hospital surgical facilities, regardless of whether they provide insured or uninsured services. In Alberta, most assisted-reproduction services are uninsured and are offered in one of two private for-profit fertility clinics.[93] Although there are some important differences between the regulation of insured and uninsured services in non-hospital surgical facilities, the regulation of Alberta's fertility clinics that offer IVF and other assisted reproduction, an uninsured service, is quite similar to the regulation of facilities that provide insured services.

In Alberta, the *Health Care Protection Act* (*HCPA*) establishes the regulatory frameworks for facilities that provide insured surgical

---

91   See *supra* note 90. The definition of "community health facilities" includes (a) a place or collection of places where one or more services prescribed in regulations made by the minister are provided, and includes any part of such a place; and (b) a place or collection of places in regulations made by the minister. The *OHFDA* creates a licensing process for CHFs under the oversight of an "executive officer" (EO) appointed by cabinet (s 2). The EO has the discretion to decide whether to issue a license and to impose conditions on the license (ss 5–7); the OHFDA requires CHFS to have a complaints process to receive and respond to complaints from patients & services providers (s 35), an incident-review process (s 36), and a disclosure-of-information process (s 37–38). The regulation will designate inspecting bodies for CHFs (s 40) and inspections will be carried out by inspectors. Inspectors and the EO can impose compliance orders (s 54), cessation orders (s 55), and administrative monetary penalties (s 58). All orders made by the EO must be made public (s 67).

92   *The People's Health Care Act*, SO 2019, c 5.

93   At present, Alberta has only two clinics: see www.cfas.ca.

services and facilities that provide uninsured surgical services.[94] The *HCPA* establishes a number of standards common to both facilities. The CPSA is primarily responsible for the oversight of all non-hospital surgical facilities. All facilities must be accredited by the CPSA before they can be designated as such by Alberta's minister of health.[95] Also common to both is that "significant mishaps" or "reportable incidents" must be reported to the CPSA and the health authority.[96] Similarly, the CPSA has established a common set of standards that apply to all non-hospital surgical facilities, including standards for personnel, patient care, infection prevention and control, and others.[97] The CPSA also establishes a process for granting privileges to members to practice in non-hospital surgical facilities.[98] Notably, clinics must also meet many of the same standards as public hospitals, including reporting of incidents, physician qualifications, and compliance with medical staff bylaws.[99]

However, a couple of important differences exist. First, public reporting of the facilities' performance differs. The non-hospital surgical facilities that provide insured services must enter into agreements with regional health authorities, which in turn require annual performance reports from the facility, which must be made public.[100] A similar requirement for an annual performance report does not appear to exist for public hospitals under Alberta's *Hospital Act.*[101] The second difference is the disclosure of health data. A range of data about insured surgical services for outpatient services must be disclosed to the provincial reporting authority and for inpatient services to the Canadian Institute of Health Information (CIHI).[102] Yet, there is no equivalent requirement to report data about

---

94   *Health Care Protection Act*, RSA 2000, c H-1. For non-hospital surgical facilities providing insured services see s 11(1)(b) and for uninsured services see s 15(2).

95   *Ibid*, ss 11, 15 and 21.

96   *Health Care Protection Regulation*, AR 208/2000 at s 17.

97   College of Physicians and Surgeons of Alberta, *Non-Hospital Surgical Facility: Standards & Guidelines*, CPSA, March 2016 v 23, online: <http://cpsa.ca/wp-content/uploads/2015/03/NHSF_Standards.pdf>.

98   *Ibid*.

99   Health Quality Ontario, *supra* note 45 at 17.

100   CPSA, *supra* note 98 at s 16.

101   *Hospitals Act*, RSA 2000, c H2. See also, *Operation of Approved Hospitals Regulation*, A/R 247/1990.

102   *Ibid*, at s 15(2).

uninsured services to any provincial authority or federal agency, which is discussed in greater detail below.[103]

Notably, the CPSA has established a set of standards specific to assisted reproductive technologies.[104] Unlike the proposed OHPIP for fertility premises, these standards are quite brief: they establish specific qualifications for medical directors, physicians, and assisting personnel who provide fertility services; and requirements for information that must be included in a patient's medical record. In addition, the CPSA standard requires clinics to submit data about fertility services to CARTR Plus and the college.[105]

In my view, Alberta's integrated regulatory framework for surgical facilities, whether publicly or privately financed, is the right approach. Regulatory frameworks should not differ solely on the basis of who is paying for the health care service. But Alberta's system suffers from two important problems: much of the regime falls to a self-regulating body, and there is insufficient data reporting and disclosure for privately financed clinics.

British Columbia

Like Ontario and Alberta, the College of Physicians and Surgeons of British Columbia (CPSBC) is primarily responsible for the regulation of private for-profit facilities and professionals who work in these facilities. In British Columbia, IVF is an uninsured service and is delivered in private for-profit clinics.[106] The CPSBC, pursuant to college bylaws under BC's *Health Professions Act*, has established a framework for the accreditation for private non-hospital medical and surgical facilities: the Non-Hospital Medical and Surgical Facilities Accreditation Program (NHMSFAP).[107]

The NHMSFAP establishes a number of standards and an accreditation program for private non-hospital facilities and health care professionals working in those facilities. For example, the CPSBC

---

103 See Part C, Regulatory Gaps, c. Health information: Evaluating and improving health systems and outcomes.

104 College of Physicians and Surgeons of Alberta, *Assisted Reproductive Technology: Standards & Guidelines*, CPSA, May 2017, v 2, online: <http://www.cpsa.ca/wp-content/uploads/2017/11/Assisted-Reproductive-Technology-Standards-and-Guidelines.pdf>.

105 *Ibid.*

106 See IVF Clinics, *supra* note 14.

107 *Health Professions Act*, RSBC 1996, c 183, s 25.5(1)(e).

has established a policy for patient-safety incidents, reporting to the NHMSFAP's committee.[108] Importantly, the medical director of a facility must notify the committee within twenty-four hours of becoming aware of a patient-safety incident or a death that occurred within twenty-eight days of a facility procedure.[109] The CPSBC also sets a number of standards that clinics must meet to be accredited.[110] The standards address a range of elements including physical standards, patient care, medical record keeping, and facility governance.[111]

The CPSBC also establishes an appointment process for medical staff[112] who work in non-hospital medical and surgical facilities. The NHMSFAP authorizes the medical director of the facility to approve applications from medical staff for appointment and reappointment to non-hospital medical surgical facilities.[113] It also establishes a series of standards, rules, policies, and guidelines respecting the skills and training necessary for the appointment of medical staff.[114]

Although there is a list of accredited non-hospital medical and surgical facilities available on the CPSBC website, there is no other information provided to the public about the facility, such as when they were accredited. Thus, while there are provisions that require reporting of patient safety incidents or death, it does not appear that this information is made available to the public. This information would likely be of interest to patients choosing between surgical facilities.

---

108 College of Physicians and Surgeons of British Columbia—Non-Hospital Medical and Surgical Facilities Accreditation Program, *Bylaw Policy: Patient Safety Incidents Reporting*, CPSBC, 2018, online: <https://www.cpsbc.ca/files/pdf/NHMSFAP-BP-Patient-Safety-Incidents-Reporting.pdf>.

109 The NHMSF requires that each clinic have a medical director: *Ibid.*

110 College of Physicians and Surgeons of British Columbia—Non-Hospital Medical and Surgical Facilities Accreditation Program, *Bylaw Policy: Terms of Accreditation*, CPSBC, 2017, online: <https://www.cpsbc.ca/files/pdf/NHMSFAP-BP-Terms-of-Accreditation.pdf>.

111 For a list of the various standards, see College of Physicians and Surgeons of British Columbia, "Standards" CPSBC, online: <https://www.cpsbc.ca/programs/nhmsfap/standards>.

112 Medical staff includes physicians and allied health care professionals.

113 College of Physicians and Surgeons of British Columbia—Non-Hospital Medical and Surgical Facilities Accreditation Program, *Bylaw Policy: Appointment of Medical Staff to Facilities*, CPSBC, 2018, online: <https://www.cpsbc.ca/files/pdf/NHMSFAP-BP-Appointment-of-Medical-Staff.pdf>.

114 *Ibid.*

In summary, in most provinces, self-regulated bodies are the principal regulators of the fertility sector. As described, the colleges have, to varying degrees, introduced a number of tools—such as setting basic clinical standards, requiring critical-incident reporting, and introducing a process for physician privileges—that promote patient health and safety. But because these regulatory frameworks are set and enforced by a self-regulating body, they are subject to a range of criticisms described above, including that these processes and decisions are not sufficiently transparent, and that, because they are administered and overseen by members of the profession, they are inherently self-interested and are not well suited to protecting patient health. As such, greater external oversight is needed, whether through an integrated system such as that proposed in Ontario or a specific/separate regulatory framework created, implemented, and enforced by government, like certain aspects of Quebec's approach.

Fertility Services: The Regulatory Gaps

While internal regulation is an important form of regulation, it is insufficient to protect and promote patient health and safety. There are general concerns about the safety and quality of care in the private for-profit health care sector. Although there is no Canadian study comparing the delivery of IVF services in publicly funded as opposed to privately funded clinics, there are studies from other sectors that compare quality and safety in private for-profit facilities and public not-for-profit facilities. For example, Devereaux et al found that private for-profit hospitals and facilities are associated with an increased risk of death when compared to their not-for-profit counterparts.[115] The authors explain that the difference in quality of care may be explained by various cost-cutting practices, such as staffing or duration of procedures. More recently, there are reports of observational evidence which demonstrate that publicly funded care in *for-profit* long-term care facilities is inferior to publicly funded

---

115 PJ Devereaux et al, "A Systematic Review and Meta-Analysis of Studies Comparing Mortality Rates of Private For-Profit and Private Not-for-Profit Hospitals" (2002) 166:11 CMAJ 1399 at 1400. See also PJ Devereaux et al, "Comparison of Mortality between Private For-Profit and Private Not-for-Profit Hemodialysis Centres: A Systematic Review and Meta-analysis" (2002) 288:19 JAMA 2449.

care in *not-for-profit* long-term care facilities.[116] However, there is not unanimous consent on this question. Flood and Thomas note there is disagreement between scholars regarding the connection between profit status and quality of care.[117] In addition to quality and safety concerns in the for-profit sector, there are concerns about potential conflicts of interests. Although a detailed examination of these concerns in the fertility sector is beyond our scope here, they have been highlighted by Flood and Thomas[118] and others.[119]

Below, I focus on three examples that illustrate how regulation of the privately financed fertility sector is less rigorous and effective than government regulation of publicly funded health care. First, although CPGs have had some impact on physician practice, they have not proven to be nearly as effective as legislative mandates in Quebec and Ontario. The legal rule in Quebec mandating single-embryo transfer had a swift and profound impact on clinical practice. By contrast, the CPG recommending single-embryo transfer has resulted in fewer multiple births, but the change in practice has been much more gradual. Second, there are fewer complaints processes available for patients who receive privately financed health care services, and the college complaints and investigation process suffers from several shortcomings. Third, although the CFAS has taken steps to collect and disclose some aggregate data about assisted reproduction in Canada, information collection and disclosure for privately financed care is less rigorous than for publicly funded care. Of course, there are other regulatory challenges unique to this sector, such as the

---

116 See Lisa A. Ronald, "Observational Evidence of For-Profit Delivery and Inferior Nursing Home Care: When Is There Enough Evidence for Policy Change" (2016) 13(4) PLoS Med e1001995.

117 Flood & Thomas, *supra* note 32 at 364 citing to Mark B McClellan & Douglas O Staiger, "Comparing Hospital Quality at For-Profit and Not-for-Profit Hospitals" in David M Cutler, ed, *The Changing Hospital Industry: Comparing For-Profit and Not-for-profit Institutions* (Chicago: University of Chicago Press, 2000) 93.

118 Flood & Thomas, *supra* note 32 at 366 and 371.

119 For example, a recent study in Denmark demonstrated that while meniscal procedures increased in both public and private sectors in Denmark between 2000 and 2011, the incidence of meniscal procedures was "particularly conspicuous in the private sector" as its proportion increased in private clinics from 1 per cent to 32 per cent: Kristoffer Borbjerg Hare et al, "Large regional differences in incidence of arthroscopic meniscal procedures in the public and private sector in Denmark" (2015) BMJ Open e006659.

concerns about conflicts of interest and advertising highlighted by
Flood and Thomas, but these are beyond the scope of this chapter.[120]

Enforcing Clinical Standards: Single-Embryo Transfer Policies

Clinical-practice guidelines appear to be less effective than legal rules
mandating clinical care. There is some debate about the efficacy of
CPGs and the extent to which they impact clinical practice has been
questioned.[121] The relative inefficacy of CPGs as compared to a legal
mandate is well illustrated by single-embryo transfer policies.

Single-embryo transfer policies are intended to address the
disproportionately high rates of multiple pregnancies resulting from
IVF. Multiple pregnancies increase the health risks for pregnant
women, including an increase in cardiac complications, preeclampsia,
gestational diabetes, postpartum hemorrhage, and the possibility
of a surgical intervention such as a hysterectomy.[122] Multiple pregnancies also increase the chance of poor outcomes for the resulting
children, including preterm birth, which is associated with a number
of adverse outcomes such as lung and eye disorders, and the possibility of neurodevelopmental conditions such as cerebral palsy.[123]
Traditionally, multiple embryos were transferred during a cycle of
IVF in order to maximize the chance of pregnancy. Where patients
are paying out of pocket, patients may choose to transfer more than
one embryo in the hopes that they will become pregnant and will
not have to pay for additional cycles.[124] Clinics may also have an
incentive to transfer more than one embryo to boost their success
rates.[125] As discussed at the outset, this has prompted some governments to fund IVF and, in exchange for public funding, impose a
single-embryo transfer requirement, which ultimately reduces the
costs associated with multiple pregnancies and births in the public
system.[126] Prior to regulatory efforts, Canada had one of the high-

---

120   Flood & Thomas, *supra* note 32 at 367.
121   See above, section 1.
122   Jocelyn L Cook et al, *supra* note 11 at 159.
123   *Ibid.*
124   Bissonnette, *supra* note 9 at 501.
125   *Ibid.*
126   Jason G Bromer et al, "Preterm Deliveries that Result from Multiple Pregnancies
      Associated with Assisted Reproductive Technologies in the USA: A Cost
      Analysis" (2011) 23:3 Current Opinions in Obstetrics & Gynecology 168; Patricia
      Fauque et al, "Cumulative results including obstetrical and neonatal outcome
      of fresh and frozen-thawed cycles in elective single versus double fresh embryo

est multiple-birth rates resulting from assisted reproduction in the world.[127]

In 2010, the Society of Obstetrics and Gynaecology of Canada (SOGC) and the CFAS, recognizing the health risks with multiple-embryo transfer, introduced a joint CPG that recommended single-embryo transfer in the majority of IVF cycles.[128] This followed the Quebec government's decision to require single-embryo transfer for publicly funded cycles, described above. The SOGC/CFAS's CPG on single-embryo transfer has had a gradual, but notable, impact on multiple births resulting from assisted reproduction. In 2010, CARTR reported that the multiple birth rate was 23.8 per cent of all assisted-reproduction cycles.[129] In 2016, the multiple pregnancy rate had decreased to 9.7 per cent of all assisted-reproduction cycles.[130] By contrast, the legislated limit in Quebec had an immediate and profound impact on multiple pregnancy rates. In 2009, the year prior to the introduction of the IVF-funding program, the multiple pregnancy rate in Quebec was 25.6 per cent. Six months after the introduction of the program, the multiple pregnancy rate plummeted to 3.7 per cent.[131] Although it increased slightly, it remained relatively low, at 6.9 per cent.[132]

At the time of writing, we do not yet know the impact of the single-embryo transfer requirement in most publicly funded cycles of IVF in Ontario. It is likely that there will be a drop in Ontario's

---

transfers" (2010) 94:3 Fertility & Sterility 927; Jan Gerris, "Single-embryo Transfer Versus Multiple-embryo Transfer" (2009) 18 Reproductive BioMedicine Online (Supplementary 2) 63; Abha Maheshwari, Siriol Griffiths & Siladitya Bhattacharya, "Global Variations in the Uptake of Single Embryo Transfer" (2011) 17:1 Human Reproduction Update 107; Bissonnette, *supra* note 9 at 501.

127 Jocelyn L Cook et al, *supra* note 11 at 165.

128 Jason K Min, Ed Hughes & David Young, "Joint SOGC-CFAS Clinical Practice Guideline: Elective Single Embryo Transfer Following In Vitro Fertilization" (2010) 32 J Obstetrics & Gynaecology Canada 363.

129 Canadian Fertility & Andrology Society, "CARTR Annual Report—2010," Canadian Fertility and Andrology Society, online: <https://cfas.ca/_Library/_documents/CARTR_2010.pdf>.

130 Canadian Fertility & Andrology Society, "CARTR Annual Report—CARTR Plus 2016 Report—Powerpoint Presentation," Canadian Fertility & Andrology Society, online: <https://cfas.ca/_Library/cartr_annual_reports/CFAS-CARTR-Plus-presentation-Sept-2017-for-CFAS-website.pdf>.

131 Bissonnette, *supra* note 9 at 504.

132 M P Vélez et al, "Universal Coverage of IVF pays off" (2014) 29:6 Human Reproduction 1313 at 1316.

multiple-birth rate. But will the drop be as pronounced as in Quebec? Because single-embryo transfer is only required in publicly funded cycles, it is difficult to predict the impact on the multiple-birth rate overall. Will physicians and patients adopt the same clinical practice for privately funded cycles? If not, it may also spur the provincial government to take regulatory action. How will the provincial government justify allowing a practice it considers unsafe for women and children to continue solely because it is paid for out of pocket? If there is a disparity between clinical practice in publicly and privately funded cycles, it is imperative that the provincial government addresses it. If not, it may send a message that the government is willing to tolerate greater health risks in the context of privately financed care.

Complaints Processes: The College's Complaint Investigating Authority as the Only Resort

Another significant difference between the regulation of publicly and privately financed care is the extent to which patients have access to processes and procedures for raising concerns about the conduct of a health professional or an incident at a health facility. Generally, there are more opportunities for patients to complain about publicly funded as opposed to privately funded health care services. As discussed, complaints processes are critical to ensure that clinical standards are being met and that patients receive high-quality health care.[133] Complaints or disciplinary processes are "key elements" of self-regulation, as they ensure that health care professionals meet the standards set by the profession.[134] However, these processes are often lacking—in most cases they are patient-initiated, they may fail to adequately address the unsatisfactory practice of a member, they do not make enough information available to the public,[135] they are often ill-equipped to make systemic remedies, and they tend to

---

133   Tom W Reader, Alex Gillespie & Jane Roberts "Patient Complaints in Healthcare Systems: A Systemic Review and Coding Taxonomy" (2014) 23:8 British Medical J Quality & Safety 678.

134   Zarzecnzy, *supra* note 15 at 165. See also Epps, *supra* note 20 at 81–82.

135   Julie Maciura & Lonny J Rosen, "A New Era of Transparency in Health Care Regulation" (Paper delivered at the OBA's Institute—Health Law Update: Privacy, Transparency & Class Action, 4 February 2016) (Toronto: OBA Continuing Professional Development, 2016) 1.

address the conduct of professionals rather than facilities. Two cases illustrate the shortcomings of the college's complaints process.

In *Applicant v AA*, the applicant brought a complaint to the CPSO against her obstetrician, A.A., who provided her fertility care and treatment.[136] The applicant underwent IVF with an egg donor, L.T., who was located in Washington state in the United States.[137] The applicant paid between $8,000 and $10,000 in fees to the donor. The applicant brought a number of complaints against the physician, including that he prescribed medication to the egg donor, L.T., who resided outside of the jurisdiction in which he was licensed without first examining her to determine whether she was an appropriate candidate to be an egg donor; and he provided the applicant with a copy of L.T.'s confidential medical record at the conclusion of her care and treatment, thereby breaching her privacy. The CPSO's inquiries, complaints, and reports committee investigated the complaint and decided to require A.A. to attend at the college to be cautioned in person,[138] and to take a continuing-education or remedial program that would include a preceptorship and reassessment. In its decision, the committee noted that the powerful medications prescribed to L.T. were associated with a significant risk of dangerous complications. Nevertheless, the committee did not decide to refer the patient's complaint to the discipline committee, which can issue more severe sanctions.[139] Nor did the college choose to carry out an inspection of the physician's clinic.[140]

Despite the severity of the case, the public does not know this physician's identity. Because this case was commenced prior to 1 January 2015, neither the caution nor the educational order appears on the physician's public record on the physician's registry.[141] Therefore, potential patients have no way of identifying this

136 *Applicant v. A.A.*, 2016 CanLII 30077, File # 14-CRV-0386, online: (ON HPARB) <https://www.canlii.org/en/on/onhparb/doc/2016/2016canlii30077/2016canlii30077. html?searchUrlHash=AAAAAQALImVnZyBkb25vciIAAAAAAQ&resultIndex=1>.

137 *Ibid* at para 7.

138 A caution is ordered when the committee has a significant concern about conduct or practice that can have a direct impact on patient care, safety, or the public interest: *Regulated Health Professions Act*, *supra* note 21 Schedule 2, s 10.

139 *Ibid*, Schedule 2, s 36.

140 *Ibid*, Schedule 2, s 75.

141 Cases commenced after 1 January 2015, cautions, specified continuing education or remedial program, and undertakings will appear on the CPSO public

physician, and, as such, cannot choose not to see him.[142] Although the CPSO has sought to increase transparency of its decisions since January 2015, important information is still not disclosed to the public, including when a physician has entered into a voluntary remedial agreement with the CPSO, or when the committee states its expectation of a physician.[143]

A second case further illustrates the limitations of the college's complaints process and its failure to adequately address a member's misconduct. Norman Barwin was a fertility doctor who practiced in Ontario until his retirement in August 2014. Dr. Barwin was disciplined by the CPSO in 2013 (discipline decision) and is the defendant in a class-action lawsuit.[144] Both the discipline decision and the class-action lawsuit arise from Dr. Barwin's use of sperm other than the sperm chosen by his patients and their partners for the purposes of artificial insemination. In many cases, the evidence indicates that Dr. Barwin used his own sperm rather than that of the intended parent or anonymous donor. The agreed statement of facts from the discipline decision reveals that Dr. Barwin engaged in a long-standing pattern of misconduct beginning in the mid-1980s and had been the subject of numerous patient complaints. The college notified Dr. Barwin of an error he had made in his insemination of a patient (Patient E) in the mid- to late 1990s. Patient E, following the birth of her child in 1995, had discovered that her child was not conceived with the donor sperm she had instructed Dr. Barwin to use. This error did not appear on Dr. Barwin's public record.

Three similar complaints followed: Patient A, following DNA testing of her child in 2007, discovered that she had been inseminated with sperm other than the donor sperm she had instructed

---

register: The College of Physicians and Surgeons of Ontario, "Transparency of Physician-Specific Information," CPSO, online: <https://www.cpso.on.ca/>.

142 The only reason there is any public information about this case is because the applicant asked the Health Professions Appeal and Review Board to review the CPSO's decision.

143 In 2012, the six health-professional colleges (medicine, nursing, dentistry, optometry, pharmacy, and physiotherapy) formed a working group on transparency called the Advisory Group for Excellence, which has resulted in greater information sharing on college websites. However, important information remains private: CPSO, *supra* note 142.

144 *Re Barwin*, [2013] OCPSD No 5 (Ontario College of Physicians and Surgeons Discipline Committee) and *Dixon, Dixon and Dixon v Barwin*, Statement of Claim, File No 16-70454CP (Ontario Superior Court of Justice).

Dr. Barwin to use in 2003; Patient C, who was acting as a surrogate for her sister (Patient B), discovered in 2008 that the resulting child (born in 2007) was not biologically related to the intended father; and Patient D discovered in 2011 that her child, who was born in 1986, was not conceived with her husband's sperm (which he had frozen prior to cancer treatments in 1984).[145] The discipline committee accepted an order proposed jointly by Dr. Barwin and counsel for the college and found that Dr. Barwin had engaged in professional misconduct, suspended him for two months, and issued a public reprimand and a costs order of $3,650.

In 2016, eleven plaintiffs launched a class action against Dr. Barwin, alleging he engaged in similar misconduct, namely using sperm other than that chosen by the plaintiffs for the purpose of artificial insemination.[146] Shortly thereafter, the CPSO announced that it would launch a third investigation into Dr. Barwin's conduct.[147] As one former patient stated: "This is the third time the college has investigated. Why did they not take his license away? Why didn't they test the children back then to see how widespread this was? As far as I am concerned, they should be investigating themselves."[148]

It was not until 25 June 2019 that the CPSO revoked Dr. Barwin's licence in response to his serious misconduct.[149]

Not only is Dr. Barwin's conduct deeply troubling, the CPSO's failure to adequately address Dr. Barwin's long-standing misconduct is also concerning and illustrates a number of shortcomings of the college's complaints process. First, the complaints process is slow and lacks transparency. Despite numerous complaints of a similar nature, beginning in 2007 and 2008, the discipline committee did not issue a decision until 2013. During this five-year

---

145 *Re Barwin, ibid* at para 5.

146 *Dixon, supra* note 145 at paras 25 and 27. The representative plaintiff in the class action was born in 1990 and refers to another woman born in 1991, both of whom were conceived at Dr. Barwin's clinic and who discovered in 2015 and 2016, respectively, that they were conceived using his sperm.

147 Elizabeth Payne, "College of Physicians Investigating Former Fertility Doctor Norman Barwin—Again," *Ottawa Citizen* (18 June 2018), online: <https://ottawacitizen.com/news/local-news/college-of-physicians-investigating-former-fertility-doctor-norman-barwin-again>.

148 *Ibid.*

149 *Ontario (College of Physicians and Surgeons of Ontario) v Barwin*, 2019 ONCPSD 39.

period, many patients continued to be treated by Dr. Barwin and were unknowingly put at risk of harm or were subject to his acts of misconduct.

Second, the CPSO's initial investigation appears to have been deficient. If the allegations in the class action are proven, the college failed to identify a number of additional cases of misconduct. Because there is little public information available about the nature of the investigation, it is difficult to identify what steps the college took in investigating these complaints. But the discipline committee's brief reasons seem to indicate that the committee was focused on investigating Dr. Barwin's role in these individual complaints rather than engaging in a wider investigation into the storage and use of sperm in the clinic. A number of systemic failures appear to have facilitated Dr. Barwin's misconduct, including a lack of clinic policies and procedures regarding patient and donor record keeping, and the identification, preservation, and storage of sperm.[150] A broader investigation of the clinic may have uncovered systemic problems such as Dr. Barwin's failure to put much-needed policies and procedures in place at his fertility clinic, and may have exposed additional cases of misconduct. The current investigatory process appears to be ill-equipped to deal with systemic or facility-level problems, because the committee relies heavily on an *ex post* response of patients initiating complaints, and its mandate under the *RHPA* is to investigate a professional rather than the facility.

Third, the finding and penalty in this case, a two-month suspension, strike many as woefully inadequate. The discipline committee accepted an agreement between Dr. Barwin and counsel for the college, whereby Dr. Barwin admitted to committing an act of professional misconduct and counsel for the college withdrew a second allegation of professional misconduct, as well as an allegation of incompetence.[151] Such a weak finding and penalty in the face of this egregious conduct leaves the impression that the college is focused on protecting its members rather than patients and the public.

It is impossible to say whether Dr. Barwin's misconduct would have been uncovered earlier or would not have happened at all if fertility services were delivered in a public hospital or if they were publicly funded and subject to the applicable provincial frameworks.

---

150 *Dixon, supra* note 145 at para 43.
151 *Re Barwin, supra* note 145 at para 4.

However, the additional safeguards in place at public hospitals as a result of the *Public Hospitals Act*,[152] and at health care organizations that receive public funding which are subject to the *ECFAA*,[153] may well have reduced the likelihood of harm to patients. These safeguards include detailed requirements for patient record keeping,[154] as well as internal supervisory mechanisms over physicians in hospital[155] and broader quality committee processes in health care organizations that receive public funding.[156]

Another safeguard for patients receiving publicly funded care is access to additional processes for raising concerns and filing complaints about health professionals and facilities. Two examples of external quality-of-care processes established by the government and administered by independent third-party agencies are facility-based patient-relations processes,[157] and ombudspersons or quality review boards.[158]

Ontario has created two additional processes for patients who receive publicly funded care in health care organizations pursuant to the 2010 *ECFAA*.[159] First, the *ECFAA* requires health care

---

152 *Public Hospitals Act, supra* note 72.

153 *Excellent Care for All Act, 2010*, SO 2010, c 14.

154 *Hospital Management*, RRO 1990, Reg 965, s 19.

155 For example, in Ontario there are processes for an officer of the medical staff who becomes aware that if, in his or her opinion, a serious problem exists in the diagnosis, care, or treatment of a patient, the officer shall forthwith discuss the condition, diagnosis, care, and treatment of the patient with the attending physician, and may relieve the attending physician of his duties with respect to the physician and advise the medical advisory committee of the problem with the attending physician: *Supra* note 72, s 34. Further, physicians are supervised by the medical advisory committee, which determines hospital privileges and which are empowered to revoke or suspend privileges where appropriate: *Ibid*, ss 35–36.

156 *Excellent Care for All Act, supra* note 153 s 4. Notably, the *ECFAA* only applies to health care organizations that are public hospitals or receive public funding: *Ibid*, s 1.

157 In Ontario, see *ECFAA, supra* note 153 s 6 requires all health care organizations to have a patient relations process and make information about that process available to the public.

158 In Ontario, see *ibid*, s 13.1.

159 *Ibid*, s 1. The *ECFAA* applies to "health care organizations" and "health sector organizations," which include public hospitals as well as organizations that receive public funding and does not include complains regarding privately financed care.

organizations to have a patient-relations process.[160] These processes allow patients or caregivers to bring complaints directly to the health care organization. Second, the *ECFAA* creates a "patient ombudsman" in order to improve quality of health care and to promote the health of patients.[161] The patient ombudsman is charged with undertaking an investigation either as a result of a patient complaint or on her own initiative.[162] The patient ombudsman must report to the minister of health, the LHIN, and the public on her activities and recommendations.[163] Although there have been calls for greater independence and more robust powers, the patient ombudsman is an important avenue for redress for patients receiving publicly funded health care.[164]

Similarly, patients in British Columbia may bring a "care quality complaint" to one of British Columbia's Patient Care Quality Review Boards.[165] These complaints may not duplicate the complaints investigation authority of the professional bodies, but they do provide patients with an opportunity to complain about the quality of publicly funded health care services.[166] Like Ontario's patient ombudsman, a patient-care quality review board is restricted to making recommendations.

The complaints and investigation processes available through self-regulated bodies play an important role in determining whether health care professionals meet clinical standards and in addressing conduct that does not. However, the current gaps in the process may put patients' health at risk. Although these concerns exist for both publicly and privately funded care, they are almost

---

160 *Ibid*, s 6.

161 *Ibid*, s 13.1.

162 *Ibid*, s 13.1(2). David Watts & David Solomon, "Day-to-Day Operations of Hospitals and Other Health Institutions: The Impact of Recent Legislative Amendments and Regulatory College Initiatives" (Paper delivered at the OBA's Institute—Health Law Update: Privacy, Transparency & Class Action, 4 February 2016) (Toronto: OBA Continuing Professional Development, 2016) 1 at 2.

163 *Excellent Care for All Act, supra* note 153, s 13.5.

164 Watts & Solomon, *supra* note 162 at 1.

165 *Patient Care Quality Review Boards Act*, SBC 2008, c 35.

166 These review boards will not consider complaints regarding health care services that are paid for entirely by the patient or the patient and a private insurer; British Columbia—Patient Care Quality Review Boards, "Frequently Asked Questions"; British Columbia—Patient Care Quality Review Boards, online: <https://www.patientcarequalityreviewboard.ca/faqs.html#Q1>.

certainly less acute where self-regulation is buttressed by external oversight mechanisms. Although patient-relations processes and independent review bodies are intended to complement rather than replace self-regulation, they effectively shore up the college's complaints process and offer additional oversight of professionals and facilities.

Health Information: Evaluating and Improving Health Systems and Outcomes

Finally, there are important differences in terms of the collection and disclosure of publicly funded and privately financed health care information. Health information is also essential to measure population health, to evaluate and improve health systems, and to engage in evidence-based decision making.[167] As Collier notes, data is critical for physicians to offer high-quality, consistent health care as it ensures they provide appropriate care to patients.[168] Publicly available health information is also critical for patients to make informed health care decisions. While there is a robust legislative framework for data collection, use, and disclosure of publicly funded health care services, the collection and disclosure of information about privately financed services like fertility services has fallen to health care professionals and their regulatory bodies. Data collection for Quebec and Ontario's publicly funded IVF services improved following public funding but, unfortunately, still falls short.

All provincial governments have legislation requiring the collection of certain health information from patients and authorizing the disclosure of non-identifying information in certain circumstances.[169] This legislation applies to publicly funded health care services—the province has comprehensive information because

---

167 Gregory P Marchildon, *Health Systems in Transition*, 2nd ed (Toronto: World Health Organization, 2013) at 124.

168 Collier, *supra* note 21.

169 For example, in Ontario, the minister and the general manager may directly or indirectly collect, use, and disclose personal information for purposes related to the administration of this *Act*, the *Commitment to the Future of Medicare Act, 2004*, SO 2004, c 5, the *Independent Health Facilities Act, supra* note 74 or *Health Insurance Act*, RSO 1990, c H 6. As described above, in Alberta, although many common standards apply to non-hospital surgical facilities, the information-disclosure requirements apply only to facilities offering insured services.

it pays for the health care service. Robust pan-Canadian data on publicly funded health care services also exists. CIHI, an agency created through a federal, provincial, and territorial partnership, is responsible for the collection and disclosure of pan-Canadian health data and information, and is generally considered to be one of the world's "premier national health information repositories."[170] Notably, CIHI primarily receives data from the provincial and territorial health care insurance plans, and as such its pan-Canadian databases generally contain information on publicly funded health services.[171]

By contrast, the CFAS is primarily responsible for information collection and disclosure of information regarding fertility services in Canada. As mentioned above, the CFAS, through the initiative of the medical directors of the fertility clinics, is responsible for collecting and disclosing information for assisted-reproduction services through CARTR Plus.[172] Fertility clinics may disclose a range of information about assisted-reproduction services, including patient information and history, details about the type and number of IVF cycles undertaken, the number of embryos transferred per IVF cycle, the use of donor eggs, the number of gestational surrogacies, and live-birth rates to CARTR Plus.[173] The CFAS also publishes an annual report that provides aggregate data from the CARTR Plus database.[174]

CARTR Plus offers important information about assisted-reproduction services in Canada; but it is not nearly as robust as data collection about publicly funded health care. First, disclosure is voluntary. While most fertility clinics disclose information to CARTR Plus, it is not mandatory, and therefore clinics may opt out

---

170 Marchildon, *supra* note 167 at 124.

171 For a list of CIHI's data holdings, see www.cihi.ca/en/access-data-and-reports/ make-a-data-request/data-holdings.

172 The federal government had established a national registry for the information collection, use, and disclosure system in the *Assisted Human Reproduction Act, supra* note 51 ss 14–18. These provisions were declared unconstitutional by the Supreme Court of Canada in 2010: *Reference re Assisted Human Reproduction Act, supra* note 48.

173 Born Ontario, "Data Elements in CARTR Plus through BORN Ontario—April 2013" on file with author.

174 The CFAS annual reports are available at Canadian Fertility & Andrology Society, "CARTR Annual Report," Canadian Fertility & Andrology Society, online: <https://cfas.ca/cartr-annual-reports/>.

of disclosure without penalty.[175] Only the CPSA requires clinics to disclose information to CARTR Plus.[176] Second, there appears to be no process for the data disclosed to CARTR Plus to be verified and, as a result, there may be some question about its reliability. Third, while the CFAS discloses some aggregated data to the public, clinic-specific data is generally not available. As Dr. François Bissonette explains, the clinic-specific data is available to the CARTR outcome-improvement committee in order for them "to identify and offer help to clinics whose results fall below the national standard."[177] It is troubling that clinic-level data is not made available to patients, as one would expect that this information would be relevant to patients when deciding which fertility clinic to attend. Further, the directors of the fertility clinics have taken the position that they own the data and, as such, will only consider requests for more detailed data on a case-by-case basis, and, in most cases, charge a fee for disclosure.

Both the Quebec and Ontario governments have taken steps to improve information collection for publicly funded fertility services, but a number of gaps remain. In Quebec, the ministère de la Santé et des Services sociaux set up an information registry for assisted reproduction, but it has been criticized for failing to meet international standards, failing to accurately calculate success rates, and being limited in scope.[178] Work is underway to improve data collection and monitoring of assisted reproduction, but there is little information about the progress of this initiative.[179]

In Ontario, it appears the provincial government is collecting information about publicly funded fertility services, although it is unclear how the government plans to disclose this information.[180] OHPIP for fertility-service premises has proposed better data collection for all fertility services regardless of who pays. In particular,

---

175 For example, in 2012, thirty-two of the thirty-three clinics participated in CARTR: Joanne Gunby, "Assisted Reproductive Technologies (ART) in Canada: 2012 Results from the Canadian ART Register," Canadian Fertility & Andrology Society, online: <https://cfas.ca/public-affairs/canadian-art-register/report-2012/>.

176 CPSA, *supra* note 105.

177 Bissonnette, *supra* note 9.

178 Summary Advisory, *supra* note 55 at 35.

179 *Ibid* at 36.

180 One scholar has obtained this information through a freedom-of-information request.

it proposes that fertility-service premises provide the CARTR Plus patient data to an assessor who is reviewing the premises. However, there is no requirement to disclose information to CARTR Plus or a provincial registry, as in Quebec.

Conclusion: What Lessons can be Learned?

The regulation of the fertility sector in Canada offers important lessons about the steps governments should take to regulate privately financed care, which may become more of a necessity if the *Cambie* litigation is successful in striking down laws protective of public medicare. First, while self-regulation plays an important role, external regulation of health care professionals and facilities is necessary to promote patient health and safety. However, as evidenced by the privately financed fertility sector, the present Canadian approach is to leave the privately financed sector lightly regulated via self-regulating bodies and CPGs. This has resulted in regulatory gaps in terms of clinical standards, complaints, and investigation processes, and with information collection and disclosure.

There are a number of legislative frameworks that buttress self-regulation, such as additional complaints processes and rigorous data-collection frameworks; but these are only applicable to health care services that are publicly funded. The fertility sector demonstrates that health law and policy-makers should be wary of leaving privately financed health care services to self-regulation and the enormous challenges, both in terms of access as well as quality and safety, that will arise if greater privatization is permitted.

Second, provincial governments appear reluctant to directly regulate privately financed fertility services. The Quebec and Ontario governments only took steps to regulate the fertility sector more tightly after it decided to fund these services. While greater external oversight of the fertility sector is laudable, it has led to a concerning practice in Ontario, where the government has different clinical standards and oversight for the same clinical practices, in this case single-embryo transfer, depending who is paying for the service. This may leave the impression that governments are willing to tolerate higher risks for patients who are receiving privately financed health care services.

Finally, provincial governments should take steps to regulate all health care, regardless of who pays. To reiterate, I do not support increasing privately financed health care in Canada. However, should this come to pass, governments must address the quality of privately financed services and the safety of patients who received these services. Governments should strive to introduce integrated frameworks that establish the same set of regulations for both publicly and privately financed care, such as that occurs for certain standards in Alberta and as proposed in Ontario's *Oversight Act*.[181] In my view, this is the best way to ensure that the overall objective of health care regulation, to ensure patients receive safe, high-quality health care, is met.

181 *The People's Health Care Act, 2019,* SO 2019, c 5-Bill 74.

PART II
IS CANADA ODD? LOOKING AT THE REGULATION OF PUBLIC/PRIVATE MIX OF HEALTH CARE IN OTHER COUNTRIES

CHAPTER 7

The Politics
of Market-Oriented Reforms:
Lessons from the
United Kingdom, the United States,
and the Netherlands

Carolyn Hughes Tuohy

In the three "millennial" decades surrounding the turn of the twenty-first century (from the mid-1980s to the mid-2010s), a wave of enthusiasm for "market-oriented" reforms to public services swept across many advanced nations. In the health care arena, these reforms took a variety of forms. For example, some replaced or augmented hierarchically integrated arrangements with contractual and, in some cases, competitive arrangements, either within the public sector or between public and private entities, or both. Others created new, publicly managed markets for private insurance. In the process, such reforms re-drew the boundaries between public and private sectors, creating openings for entrepreneurs to bring private capital to bear in new modes of operation. They did so, however, in very different ways, with different implications for the political and economics of the system, and different equity consequences.

Private capital can provide a base of influence in the health care arena in two principal ways: either through the ownership of the production of health care services and goods (the delivery side), or through the purchase of health care services and goods (the demand side). In each respect, the political and economic power of private capital will depend on how ownership and control of that capital is structured. On the delivery side, private ownership of health care providers can take for-profit, proprietary or not-for-profit ownership forms. On the demand side, private purchasers of health care may draw on their own individual capital or upon pools of capital controlled by private insurance funds, which may in turn be under for-profit or not-for-profit ownership. On both delivery and demand sides, private capital may be subject to public regulation of varying degrees of stringency. All of these roles for private capital in some way involve those who control it in making fundamental decisions about the allocation of health care: who gets what, when, where, and how.

As systems of public health insurance were established in the twentieth century, they restricted the role of private capital in different ways, by establishing public ownership and employment of health care providers, and by purchasing health services and goods with public funds. From an equity perspective, the most fundamental shift was the supplanting of private finance by public funding on the demand side by entitling some or all citizens to health care at public expense. To the extent that private ownership of health care facilities continued, it could affect what the state paid for health care, but public funding meant that the distribution of access was taken out of private hands in all or part. No advanced democracy, however, has a purely public system, and tensions between public and private objectives continue to exist in different ways in different systems.

The English, Dutch, and American reforms reviewed in this chapter all attempted to use mechanisms modelled on a competitive market to improve the functioning of their health care systems: to increase efficiency, to expand access, or both. However, each had different implications for the role of private capital. In England, the reforms were largely internal to the public system, although they did create more opportunities for privately capitalized providers on the delivery side. The Dutch reforms focused on the demand side, drawing public and private insurers under a common regulatory and financial structure largely controlled by the state. In the United States, a new, heavily regulated, and publicly subsidized market segment for private insurance was created in the form of state-based insurance "exchanges."

The effects of these reforms were correspondingly different but they have at least one trait in common: they show that features inherent to the politics of health care led governments to limit opportunities for profit while buffering private entities against financial risk. As a result, increases in the weight of private capital were marginal, and the typical results were to reinforce the clustering of privately capitalized providers of health care in niche areas, to increase the degree of concentration among private providers or insurers or both, and in some cases to generate complex corporate structures that greatly complicated lines of accountability. The principal effect of all of these changes, however, was to increase the regulatory role of the state, not to diminish state influence.

In Canada, such developments have been very limited in scope, although provincial governments have experimented in various ways with contracting between public payers and privately owned and operated providers. Although these experiments have been controversial, a far more heated debate surrounds proposals for allowing for the development of a purely private tier parallel to the public system, similar to a long-standing feature of the British system, which was only marginally affected by market-oriented reforms. The remedy sought by *Cambie* in British Columbia, a case discussed throughout this book, could bring Canada closer to this parallel-tier model, and I will therefore review that experience briefly later.[1] On balance, this comparative experience suggests that even if the applicants in *Cambie* are successful in striking down some or all of the laws tamping down a role for private capital, other kinds of regulatory structures will emerge in their place to rebalance public and private interests.

Reforms in Three Nations: A Brief Summary

The founding models of the health care state in Britain, the Netherlands, and the United States closely represented three "ideal types"; the national health service, social insurance, and residual models, respectively. The British National Health Service (NHS) was established in 1948 as a tax-financed, hierarchical system that owned and operated hospitals and employed physicians—either on salary, in the case of hospital-based specialists, or under capitation contracts, in the case of formally independent general practitioners. (This contrasts with Canada's "single-payer system," in which the state pays for physician and hospital services that are provided by privately constituted not-for-profit hospitals and proprietary physician practices.) Alongside this universal public system, a small private system has

---

1   The discussion in this chapter draws heavily on the much more extensive presentation in C H Tuohy, *Remaking Policy: Scale, Pace and Political Strategy in Health Care Reform* (Toronto: University of Toronto Press, 2018).

historically operated in parallel. Before and after the internal market reforms, health care services continued to be provided on a purely private basis as an alternative to NHS-funded services, paid for by private insurance or out of pocket by individuals.[2] The reforms did little to change that purely private market. Nonetheless, because the parallel model is often cited in the contemporary debate in Canada, I will review it in some detail later here.

From the mid-twentieth century to the late 1990s, the Netherlands system corresponded to a classic social-insurance model for the population in the lower two-thirds of the income distribution, complemented by voluntary private insurance for those in the upper third. Social insurance was provided through "sickness funds," pooling compulsory contributions from employers and workers. In the 1960s, the system was further undergirded by a tax-financed universal program for long-term and chronic care. The US "residual" model assumed that the principal source of coverage would be employer-based private insurance (publicly subsidized through the non-taxation of health benefits), supplemented by public coverage for certain groups outside the workforce, notably the elderly and disabled (under the US Medicare programs adopted in 1965) and the federal-state Medicaid program for certain low-income categories (adopted at the same time).

In each of these nations, the founding model of the health care state was transformed in the past three decades. Table 7.1 summarizes the changes. In Britain, internal market reforms brought in by the Conservative government in 1990 split the NHS hierarchy into separate "purchaser" (demand) and "provider" (delivery) components that were to negotiate contracts for services. These changes were absorbed and mediated by established networks, and appropriated and reshaped by a successor Labour government after 1997. Among other things, the Labour party established a "Foundation Trust" model, giving NHS hospitals yet greater independence in matters of finance and governance, and sought to increase the potential for patients to choose among providers of publicly funded services. The Conservative–Liberal Democrat Coalition government established after the 2010 election took the internal market concept

---

2   As part of the founding bargain with specialist physicians (known as consultants), NHS hospitals could also offer services to privately paying patients in so-called pay beds.

even further on the demand side by delegating the bulk of the NHS purchasing budget to consortia of general practices. These statutory organizations, known as Clinical Commissioning Groups (CCGs), drew general practices together on a regional basis for the purpose of purchasing hospital and community services, while leaving the provision of primary care in the hands of the practices themselves.

Table 7.1. Shifts in health care policy frameworks in the United Kingdom, the Netherlands, the United States, and Canada, 1987–2017

Country	Founding Model (as of the 1980s)	Post-Reform Model (as of 2017)
United Kingdom	*National Health Service* services provided through unified regional state hierarchy	*Internal market* purchaser/provider split formal distancing of the state
Netherlands	*Social insurance* sickness funds plus private insurance	*Mandatory insurance, comprehensive model* comprehensive regulation of universal mandatory insurance
United States	*Residual* tax-subsidized employer-based private insurance as norm plus public programs for the elderly and poor	*Mandatory insurance, complementary model* universal mandatory* insurance employer-based private insurance as norm, plus public programs for the elderly and poor, plus managed competition and subsidies in individual and small-group markets
Canada	*Single-payer plus mixed market* single-payer for physician and hospital services; mixed market for all other services	*Single-payer plus mixed market* single-payer for physician and hospital services; some changes in organization and remuneration increased cross-provincial variation in mixed market; some changes in eligibility, especially with respect to drugs

*In December 2017, the tax penalty enforcing the mandate was repealed as part of tax-reform legislation passed on party-line votes by a Republican-controlled Congress, and signed by the Republican president. The mandate itself remains in effect but is the subject of continuing litigation and is unenforced.

Source: C H Tuohy, *Remaking Policy: Scale, Pace and Political Strategy in Health Care Reform* (Toronto: University of Toronto Press, 2018).

Most of these reforms were effectively internal to the public system, aimed at structuring relationships among purchasers and providers along market lines without changing the principles of tax-based funding and universal first-dollar (or rather first-pound) coverage. Initially, for example, hospitals were established as NHS Trusts with greater financial independence, subsequently expanded by the Labour government based on a "Foundation after Trust" model. Trusts were allowed to borrow within regulated limits, and Foundation Trusts were not required to balance year-over-year, and were allowed to retain surpluses. The original internal market reforms also included a fundholding model, whereby GPs could opt to hold publicly financed budgets for the purchase of a range of hospital and community services for their patients. Though fund-holding was formally abolished by the Labour government elected in 1997, the involvement of GPs in purchasing decisions continued under various guises. More significantly, fundholding had spurred GPs into an ongoing political engagement that shaped the CCG model embraced by the Coalition government after 2010.

Although primarily focused on the public sector, the British reforms did include some openings for private capital on the delivery side—that is, for providing publicly financed services, especially as the reforms were extended under successive governments, as will be discussed below.

In the Netherlands, reforms begun in the late 1980s and rolled out over the next two decades, which transformed a system that had been bifurcated between compulsory social insurance for those in the lower two-thirds of the income distribution and voluntary private insurance for the wealthiest third. The new system was a universal regime of compulsory insurance, financed on a roughly fifty-fifty basis by community-rated premiums[3] charged by insurers and income-scaled contributions collected by the state (effectively taxes) and distributed to insurers according to the risk profile of their enrolled populations. Although all insurers were formally con-stituted under legislation governing private corporations, and one of the largest insurers is part of a large for-profit corporate entity,

---

3   Income-scaled subsidies were also provided for the payment of these premiums.

the strong public role in regulation and finance renders this unique model effectively "public."[4]

The United States moved toward its own unique "complementary" model of universal coverage, aimed at those who fell into the gaps in an existing system grounded in employer-based coverage and "residual" government programs for the elderly and some lower-income groups. The principal targets of the reforms introduced under the *Affordable Care Act* of 2010 were twofold.[5] First, they enlarged the "residual" role of the state by expanding the established Medicaid program to cover essentially all below certain income limits. Second, they developed a new infrastructure aimed at ensuring coverage for those served neither by employer-based plans nor by government programs, through a combination of mandates, fines, and subsidies, and new health insurance "exchanges" in each state to regulate and subsidize the individual and small-group market in which private insurers would compete on terms defined by federal and state regulators. Most importantly, insurers participating in the state-based health insurance exchanges were required to cover a defined comprehensive package of benefits at "community rates" that could vary across individuals only by broad age and tobacco-use categories.

Public and Private Objectives

To the extent that market-oriented reforms opened up opportunities for private capital in health care, on either the delivery or the payment side, they imported private-sector objectives into the sphere of the public sector and opened up opportunities for entrepreneurs. In some key respects, those private objectives were in tension with fundamental public-sector objectives of equity and stability, and the need to respond to those tensions drove public policy toward increased regulation of private actors. Understanding these dynamics requires attention to two definitive aspects of entrepreneurial activity: risk-taking and profit-making. Entrepreneurship implies that actors have both the autonomy and the incentive to take risk. Entrepreneurs need sufficient freedom from established institutional

---

4   For example, the OECD treats all spending for the basic compulsory coverage
    package, whether by insurers or the state, as public spending.

5   *Patient Protection and Affordable Care Act*, Pub L No 111-148, 124 Stat 119 [*Affordable
    Care Act*].

constraints such that they can pursue independent courses of action. They must also expect to appropriate the gains of their activity. In each of these respects, however, certain inherent characteristics of public-policy environments, including health care, are ill-suited to entrepreneurial behaviour.

Risk

Almost all public-policy frameworks are heavily conditioned by political imperatives to promote (or be seen to promote) values of probity, stewardship, and equity. The high-risk/high-potential-profit model of the private sector fits ill with these norms.[6] The potential for failure is an inherent aspect of entrepreneurialism in the private sector; only through failures of less successful enterprises can resources be freed up for reinvestment in more successful enterprises. But as the British economist Peter Smith has provocatively commented, it takes a "brave state" to allow organizations delivering public services to fail.[7]

Market-oriented reforms are predicated in part on the assumption that if those who make decisions about the allocation of resources are required to bear the risk of the costs of those decisions, the resulting allocation will be more efficient than if the costs are spread across the tax base.[8] But if the costs of failure will also be borne by the *clients* of those decision makers, questions of equity might arise. These questions are exacerbated in an arena such as health care, where the very public programs at issue were established in the first instance to socialize risk.

Governments accordingly have a number of motivations to buffer entrepreneurs against risk under market-oriented reforms. Some are technical considerations: it might take time to develop the necessary regulatory infrastructure to underpin risk-bearing. Some are political pressures: buffering might be necessary to dampen opposition from entrepreneurs accustomed to operating in an environment of socialized risk. It also might be necessary to protect clients against the possibility that requiring insurers or providers to bear new risks will cause them to fail, exit the market, attempt to shed high-risk and high-cost individuals, or compromise the quality of their offerings, leading to a

---

6   Charles Edwards et al. "Public Entrepreneurship: Rhetoric, Reality, and Context" (2002) 25 Intl J Public Administration 1539.

7   Personal communication, 19 September 2012.

8   See, C Cheng, I Ioannis & D Sokol, eds, *Competition and the State* (Redwood City, CA: Stanford University Press, 2014) 62–63.

reduction in the quality and availability of necessary insurance or care in at least some localities or market segments. As governments have attempted to encourage entrepreneurialism in areas such as health care, where they are not willing to tolerate the social costs of failure, they have become embroiled in the inherent contradiction of simultaneously expanding and circumscribing the potential for risk taking.

We have observed risk-buffering mechanisms of various types in each case of market-oriented reform reviewed here. Some were aimed at limiting the exposure of various entities to risk as a matter of ongoing design. For example, contracts with "independent sector treatment centres (ISTCs)" under the Labour government were for given volumes of service, at a premium above standard NHS rates, whether or not those services were actually chosen by patients. Other mechanisms were transitional—as, for example, the gradual increase over twenty years in the risk exposure of insurers in the Netherlands after, as an early step, regional monopolies for social insurers were abolished in 1992. Between 1993 and 2015, retrospective payments from the centre designed to buffer insurers were gradually reduced, raising the proportion of revenue for which insurers were at risk from 3 per cent to 100 per cent. The Dutch process began in a context in which both social insurers and regulators were entering a new world of risk, although the buffering period was arguably far longer than necessary to allow for the development of a risk-adjustment mechanism.

In the United States, private insurers participating in the exchanges created under the *Affordable Care Act* faced unfamiliar risks because the new customer base was "a less educated, racially diverse population that is more likely to cycle on and off government support"[9] than that to which private insurers were accustomed. Transitional risk-buffering mechanisms for insurers were accordingly adopted, although they were designed to be in effect over only three years, from 2014 through 2016—a much shorter period than in the Dutch case.

---

9   PWC Research Institute, "Health Insurance Exchanges: Long Options, Short on Time" (2012), online: *PricewaterhouseCoopers* <www.pwc.com/us/en/health-indus-tries/health-insurance-exchanges/assets/pwc-health-insurance-exchanges-im-pact-and-options.pdf>.

Profit

Allowing private actors to profit financially from public mandates and/or public investment attracts the criticism that it privatizes gains while socializing costs. Accordingly, policy frameworks that offer platforms for entrepreneurs to deliver public services include regulations aimed not only at cushioning failure but also at limiting profit. For example, the US *Affordable Care Act* established regulatory limits on the scope for profit for private insurers, not only within the new state-based regulated exchanges but even outside those exchanges, by establishing permissible "medical loss ratios." It required insurers in the individual and small-group market to spend at least 80 per cent of premium revenue on medical benefits, which conversely meant that no more than 20 per cent could go to administrative costs (including executive compensation) and profits. (The limit in the large-group market was 85 per cent.) But such regulations can be counterproductive: they can render the arena unattractive to private investors outside certain niche areas; they can drive entrepreneurs to adopt convoluted strategies to preserve areas of profit; and they can fail to achieve the very public objectives of innovation that prompted their adoption in the first place.

Nonetheless, there were a number of reasons for some private actors to take up these opportunities. First, they saw a platform within the public sector as an opportunity to establish a clientele to which they could market other lines of service or insurance, such as supplementary coverage for health care services not covered by public plans or even non-health insurance, such as property and casualty insurance. Second, they saw such opportunities as a way to expand market share, making them more attractive to investors, and/ or increasing their bargaining power in negotiating with providers to build networks and establish rates of payment.

The Role of Private Capital under British, Dutch, and American Health Care Reforms

Britain

Although the internal market reforms of the 1990s, discussed above, had little impact on private insurers, they did open up opportunities on the *delivery* side for privately constituted and capitalized entities to provide NHS services under contract with public purchasers. (Only one entity, Bupa, is both an insurer and a health care provider.)

Until 2000, NHS purchase of care from such private providers was infinitesimally small, amounting to less than 1 per cent of the total NHS budget. From 2000 onward, the Labour government began to experiment in marginal ways to involve non-NHS entities in the provision of NHS-funded services, initially to deal with long wait times for NHS providers and later to expand patient choice. In 2005, the NHS began to contract centrally with privately owned specialty clinics as ISTCs, as discussed above, and, in 2008, the government began to allow patients to choose to receive a range of elective services[10] from "any willing provider" approved for the provision of NHS-funded services. A requirement of the contracts was that the availability of providers in the public sector could not be reduced—that is, the clinics could not "poach" providers from the public sector.[11] As well as proprietary and for-profit firms, qualified private sector providers included "social enterprises" owned by employees and/or beneficiaries, most of them spun off from public sector organizations.

These initiatives had a substantial impact within the small private sector. The share of income for private hospital facilities derived from public sources increased from 14 per cent in 2005 to 25 per cent in 2010.[12] NHS spending on secondary care commissioned from ISTCs and other private sector providers increased by 150 per cent from 2006/07 and 2011/12.[13] But this represented a marginal change from the perspective of the much larger public sector. Total funding awarded to private sector providers amounted to about 6 per cent of total NHS spending in 2014, and the chief executive of NHS England indicated that he did not expect that proportion to increase

---

10   Under both central and local contracts, the principal services commissioned from private providers were hip and knee replacements. The proportion of those services purchased by the NHS from private-sector providers increased from about 4 per cent to about 19 per cent between 2006/07 and 2011/12. S Arora et al, *Public payment and private provision* (London: Nuffield Trust and Institute for Fiscal Studies, 2013) 12.

11   S Turner et al, "Innovation and the English National Health Service: A qualitative study of the independent sector treatment centre programme" (2011) 73 Social Science & Medicine 522 at 524.

12   LaingBuisson, "Hospitals Competing for a Static Private Healthcare Pot" (2012), online: <www.laingbuisson.co.uk/MediaCentre/PressReleases/LaingsReviewPressRelease201112.aspx>.

13   S Arora et al, *Public payment and private provision* (London: Nuffield Trust and Institute for Fiscal Studies, 2013) 12.

substantially.[14] Using Department of Health data, the British Medical Association estimated the proportion to be 7.7 per cent in 2016/2017.[15]

One high-profile exception to the focus of private sector providers on niche areas nonetheless drew wide attention. Circle Health, a hybrid entity with a complex and opaque corporate structure comprising for-profit and not-for-profit elements, took over, under contract with the NHS, the operation of a failing NHS hospital. After a promising start,[16] Circle Health struggled to eliminate the hospital's operating deficit, and after receiving a starkly negative assessment of its clinical services from the quality regulator, the Care Quality Commission (CQC), Circle Health chose to exit its contract.[17]

The experience of Circle Health sheds light on the inherent tensions in involving for-profit entities in the provision of publicly funded services. The broad regulatory architecture and operational culture of NHS hospitals presented a complex and largely unfamiliar environment for equity investors. The hospital sector offered the potential for neither growth nor profitability in the relevant term. Although Circle's complex structure guaranteed a stream of interest payments to its for-profit arm, it required "patient capital" (i.e., investors willing to wait for returns in the longer term) if it were to turn around a failing entity. Private investors had little appetite for seeing through such a process, especially given the increased level of central NHS oversight that had been triggered by several instances of failures in the quality of care in publicly financed NHS hospitals.

Recently, the NHS leadership has moved to re-integrate purchasing and provision functions through administrative action, without legislative change, as signaled with the emphasis on integrated-care models in the strategic document *Five Year Forward View*

---

14   D Campbell, "Private firms on course to net £9bn of NHS contracts" *The Guardian* (19 November 2014), online: <www.theguardian.com/society/2014/nov/19/private-firms-nhs-contracts-circle-healthcare-bupa-virgin-care-care-uk>; G Iacobucci, "A Third of NHA Contracts Awarded since Health Act Have Gone to Private Sector, BMJ Investigation Shows" (2014) 349 BMJ g7606. >

15   British Medical Association, *Privatisation and independent sector provision in the NHS* (London: BMA, 2018) at 2.

16   UK, The King's Fund, *The UK private health market* (London: King's Fund, 2014), online: *The King's Fund* <www.kingsfund.org.uk/sites/default/files/media/commission-appendix-uk-private-health-market.pdf>.

17   UK, HC Committee of Public Accounts, *An update on Hinchingbrooke Health Care NHS Trust*, 2014/15–46.

issued by the then-new NHS Chief Executive in 2014. In subsequent implementation documents, the NHS has suggested several types of integrated care systems, giving rise to some concerns that these entities could provide vehicles for a greater role for private providers in networks spanning NHS and non-NHS providers. A leading authority on the NHS, however, discounted these allegations, among other things evoking the cautionary tale of Circle Health to point out that that "there are limited opportunities to generate profits from NHS contracts."[18]

Netherlands

In the Netherlands, because the reform legislation that came into effect in 2006 was the culmination of a twenty-year process, both health insurers and government regulators had had a long time to prepare for the new world of compulsory comprehensive coverage. The first phases of the reforms applied only to the social (public) insurers, abolishing their regional monopolies and allowing them to compete nationally. This further drove a concentration of the insurance industry through mergers and acquisitions (many involving both public and private insurers) that was already underway in the 1980s, and resulted in a market dominated largely by not-for-profit firms with regional bases but national presences. The move to a common platform in 2006 consolidated this concentration: by 2014, there were in total nine "business groups" comprising twenty-six insurance firms. The four largest firms accounted for more than 90 per cent of all health insurance coverage.[19]

Three of those firms were not-for-profit; the fourth (Achmea) was structured as a mutual insurer, nested within a complex and continually evolving for-profit corporate entity.[20] Notwithstanding their private status, insurers drew half of their revenue for the basic insurance package through the public treasury in the form of centrally collected and risk-adjusted compulsory premium payments.

---

18   C Ham, "Making sense of integrated care systems, integrated care partnerships and accountable care organisations in the NHS in England" (London: King's Fund, 2018), online (blog): <https://www.kingsfund.org.uk/publications/making-sense-integrated-care-systems>.

19   M Kroneman et al, "The Netherlands: Health System Review 2016" 18(2) Health Systems in Transition 1 at 33.

20   C H Tuohy, *Remaking Policy: Scale, Pace and Political Strategy in Health Care Reform* (Toronto: University of Toronto Press, 2018) 469–470.

In this context, strong norms existed regarding moderation in profit-making. Insurers are free to set their own flat-rate premiums, but in setting the compulsory income-scaled premiums, public authorities make an assumption about the level of the additional flat-rate premium that insurers will charge to generate the remainder of their premium revenue. The Dutch Authority for Consumers and Markets reports that "health insurers are expected not to make a lot of profit, even though profit-making is a core element of the free-market principle. Policymakers seek to influence this dilemma by making statements about 'desirable' behavior by health insurers when setting the [compulsory] premiums … and, at the same time, the Minister incorporates such calls in the nominal premium calculation."[21] As for the insurers themselves, the one insurer that is part of a for-profit undertaking takes pains to present itself as socially responsible, declaring that it aims at "ensuring long-term services for [our] customers," and abjures a focus on " short-term shareholder profit" in favour of "a socially responsible and accepted return on our health insurance activities."[22]

In practice, the profit margins of Dutch health insurers were below those of other insurance lines. In fact, insurers on average lost money covering the basic package in the first two years of the new compulsory regime but edged into the profitable range thereafter.[23] Even taking all of their costs and revenues into account (including those related to supplementary health insurance and investments), health-insurer profits averaged 5 per cent as a share of gross premiums in 2012, lower than any other single line of insurance,[24] even though there is some evidence that, in the post-reform period, health insurers chose to seek profit over pursuit of market share in order to add to their solvency buffers—a matter of importance for both for-profit and not-for-profit entities.[25]

---

21   Netherlands Authority for Consumers and Markets, Monitor Financial Sector, *Competition in the Dutch health insurance market* (Interim report) (The Hague: Netherlands Authority for Consumers and Markets, 2016) 14–15.

22   Netherlands, Achmea, *Achmea Annual Report 2013* (Zeist, Netherlands: Achmea, 2014) 6, 16.

23   Netherlands Authority for Consumers and Markets, *supra* note 21 at 24.

24   J A Bikker & A Popescu, "Efficiency and competition in the Dutch non-life insurance industry: Effects of the 2006 health care reform" (25 September 2014) De Nederlandsche Bank Working Paper No 438, online: *Social Science Research Network* < https://ssrn.com/abstract=2501932>.

25   Netherlands Authority for Consumers and Markets, *supra* note 21.

The Dutch reforms also deregulated prices for a range of hospital services (known as "Segment B" services) beginning in 2005. Some of these services were also offered by day-surgery clinics, which, unlike hospitals, could be constituted on a for-profit basis. The number of such clinics grew rapidly after a policy change allowing for "independent treatment centres" in the late 1990s. As in England, however, these clinics functioned in niche areas and offered relatively uncomplicated, high-volume elective procedures such as surgery for cataracts and varicose veins. They accounted for a tiny portion, estimated in 2013 at about 2.3 per cent, of all specialist medical care.[26] In contrast to England, where ISTCs were paid a premium above the fee for hospitals, Dutch clinics provided care on average about 20 per cent more cheaply than hospitals—although, without adjusting for case mix, it is impossible to know whether this difference resulted from greater efficiency or less complicated cases.[27]

The 2006 reforms retained the long-standing ban on for-profit hospitals. The political climate nonetheless created uncertainty as to how long the for-profit ban would remain in place, and gave private entrepreneurs the incentive to establish footholds, gambling that the regulations would be loosened further.[28] Meanwhile, hospital-capital financing provided another route of entry for private capital, especially after a change in the hospital-financing formula allowed capital costs to be included in the pricing of services. Prior to 2008, hospital-capital projects required central approval, and funding was guaranteed either through loan guarantees or incremental additions to hospital budgets over long amortization periods. After 2008, these

---

26 F T Schut & M Varkevisser, "The Netherlands" in L Siciliani, M Borowitz & V Moran, eds, *Waiting Time Policies in the Health Sector: What Works?* (Paris: OECD, 2013) 185, online: *OECDiLibrary* <https://doi.org/10.1787/9789264179080-13-en>.

27 W Schäfer et al, "The Netherlands: Health System Review" 12(1) Health Systems in Transition 1 at 178.

28 Z Bouddiouan, "Redefining the Boundaries in Health Care: Hospitals and Public and Private Equity Investors." (Master's thesis, Erasmus University, 2008) [unpublished]; J van der Zwart, H de Jonge & T van der Voordt, "Private Investment in Hospitals: A Comparison of Three Healthcare Systems and Possible Implications for Real Estate Strategies" (Paper delivered at 3 TU Research Day on Innovation in Design and Management of Health Care Facilities and Healthy Environments, Rotterdam, 2009) 4, online: *ResearchGate* <www.researchgate.net/publication/49690684/download>.

guarantees were progressively withdrawn,[29] providing yet another reason for hospitals to seek increased scale in order to reassure potential private investors.

United States

As in the Netherlands but on a much more limited scale, private insurers in the United States were drawn into a scheme of regulated and subsidized insurance through public agencies—in this case, the state-based exchanges. Even before the reforms, insurers that focused on business under contract with governmental insurance programs (primarily Medicare and Medicaid) generally had lower profit margins than those that focused on the commercial sector.[30] The *Affordable Care Act* established further regulatory limits on the scope for profit, not only within the exchanges but across the board, by establishing permissible medical-loss ratios. As noted earlier, it required insurers in the individual and small-group market to spend at least 80 per cent of premium revenue on medical benefits, which conversely meant that no more than 20 per cent could go to administrative costs (including executive compensation) and profits. (The limit in the large-group market was 85 per cent.)

In the event, as in the Netherlands, private insurers struggled to make any profit in the exchanges in the early years of the reforms.[31] These low returns were somewhat offset by the temporary risk-buffer payments noted above. And by 2017, despite the uncertainty created by Republican attempts to repeal and/or undermine the reforms, profitability had improved considerably[32]— but continued to come in well below the margins typical in other areas of the financial

---

29   W Schäfer et al, "The Netherlands: Health System Review" (2016) 12(1) Health Systems in Transition 1 at 120.

30   D Donahue, "Profit Margins Converge for Top Health Plans" (1 November 2013) Healthcare Business Strategy Monthly Brief, online: *Mark Farrah Associates* <www.markfarrah.com/uploaded/mfa-briefs/profit-margins-converge-for-top-health-plans.pdf>.

31   C Cox, A Semanskee & Larry Levitt, "Individual Insurance Market Performance in 2017" (Issue Brief, Kaiser Family Foundation, May 2018), online: *Kaiser Family Foundation* <www.kff.org/health-reform/issue-brief/individual-insurance-market-performance-in-2017/>.

32   *Ibid*; Farrah Associates, "Improved Profit Margins for Leading Blue Cross & Blue Shield Plans in Third Quarter 2017" (2018), online: *Mark Farrah Associates* <www.markfarrah.com/healthcare-businessstrategy/Improved-Profit-Margins-for-Leading-Blue-Cross-and-Blue-Shield-Plans-in-Third-Quarter-2017.aspx>.

sector. This experience led to a considerable shakeout of the exchange marketplaces, with a number of insurers exiting the exchanges.[33] Thus, again, as in the Netherlands although not to the same degree, the individual insurance market in particular regions became much more concentrated. Many large insurers who had exited the exchanges, however, continued to offer managed-care plans under contract with the expanded Medicaid program, which were, on balance, profitable.[34]

Regulatory Implications of Market-Type Reforms

A common feature[35] of attempts by governments to use market-type mechanisms to achieve public purposes, in health care and other arenas, is that these reforms entail an elaboration of the regulatory presence of the state, as governments anticipate and react to the ways in which private-sector objectives could subvert public objectives. For example, where providers offered both publicly and privately financed products, there is the danger that the latter could become de facto screens for access to the former. Such might occur if supplementary insurance for services more likely to be attractive to relatively healthy populations were packaged with basic public insurance in marketing as a way for insurers to effectively cream off the market. On the health care delivery side, private payment for certain enhancements to publicly funded services, such as higher-quality lens for cataract surgery, might become a condition for faster access to the procedure. The public component of the practice or facility could become a guaranteed platform for providers to offer additional care privately. These risks are in addition to those that derive from the more traditional existence of private systems in parallel to the public system: the risk that care in the public sector will suffer if providers are drawn away into private practice, or the risk that private treatment will impose costs on the public sector if

33   US, Department of Health and Human Services, *Health Plan Choice and Premiums in the 2017 Health Insurance Marketplace* (ASPE Research Brief, October 2016).

34   US, Council of Economic Advisers, *The Profitability of Health Insurance Companies* (Washington, DC: Office of the President of the United States, 2018).

35   Steven Vogel, "Why Freer Markets Need More Rules" in Mark K. Landry, Martin A. Levin & Martin Shapiro, eds, *Creating Competitive Markets: The Politics of Regulatory Reform* (Washington, DC: Brookings Institution, 2007) at 25–42.

complications occurring in niche-based practices revert to the broadly based public sector for remedy.

In each of the three countries reviewed here, market-oriented reforms were accompanied by a growth and reconfiguration of regulatory bodies. Although their principal focus was on the regulation of the insurance and delivery of the comprehensive basic package of services to which universal (or near-universal) access was to be ensured, the effect was also to increase regulatory oversight of private insurers and providers across the board.

England

From the beginning of the internal market reforms in the 1990s to the present, central regulatory agencies were continually reconfigured along three intersecting lines of regulation. One was primarily economic, focused on the financial health of providers, the price of services, and the efficiency of local delivery in local catchment areas (the latter focus blurred by unresolved tensions between contradictory desires for strategic planning and provider competition). The principal economic regulator was Monitor, established in 2004 as with a mandate to oversee Foundation Trusts, later extended to all providers of NHS services, including those in the private sector. A second line concerned quality of care, including wait times for care, and cycled through emphases on the establishment and monitoring of centrally determined targets on the one hand or self-monitoring and reporting on the other. The CQC, established in 2009, was the successor to a previous string of quality and safety regulators. In 2010, the mandate of the CQC was extended to all providers of care, public and private. The CQC launched a comprehensive regime of regulation for the private sector in 2014 and issued its first report in 2018. A third line of oversight related to the purchasing or commissioning of service, driven by concerns about access to and integration of various types of treatment and care. This line rested with the central executive of the NHS, established as an agency (NHS England) separate from the Department of Health in 2013. The marbling of responsibilities among these various agencies and the Department of Health for matters of quality, price, financial integrity, capacity, and integration of service presented ongoing challenges, and drove various reorganizations over time. In ongoing attempts to manage these intersections, a number of agencies were consolidated, and, in 2018, a further consolidation was announced that effectively established a regionally tiered hierarchy of regulators that integrated their operations while remaining statutorily separate agencies. In short, market-style reform in England generated a plethora of regulatory bodies and regulation, leading to recent attempts at rationalization.

Netherlands

In the Netherlands, a somewhat similar multi-pronged, complex, and shifting regulatory structure was developed as part of the twenty-year transition from the bifurcated social/private-insurance model to one of universal regulated insurance. From 1995, the quality and safety regulation of providers rested largely with a Healthcare Inspectorate, formed from the merger of three pre-existing sectoral inspectorates. A 2000 reorganization reconfigured the regulatory structure for social insurers, creating new agencies. Then with the establishment of the universal regime in 2006, all insurers were drawn under a powerful new regulatory body, the Dutch Healthcare Authority (NZa), building upon and further streamlining the structural changes of the previous decade by consolidating the tariff-regulation function and the financial and governance oversight of all insurers. The mandate of the NZa also explicitly included the promotion of conditions for effective competition, including policing risk-selection activity. A separate Healthcare Insurance Board (later reorganized to become the National Health Care Institute) continued to administer the central fund for the compulsory insurance package, including the risk-adjusted allocations to all insurers, and also played an increasingly important advisory role in the regulatory process for determining the content of the compulsory package.[36] As in England, then, the adoption of market-type reforms in the Netherlands generated an elaboration and ongoing reconfiguration of the regulatory supra-structure.

United States

Although the American reforms focussed largely on the individual and small-group market, and otherwise left the existing system of employer-based coverage essentially alone, the *Affordable Care Act* did contain provisions addressed to all private health insurers regardless of their clientele. Notably, it banned underwriting practices such as the denial or withdrawal of coverage based on

---

36 JK Helderman, et al, *Dike-Reeve of the Health Care Polder* (Nijmegen, Netherlands: Radboud University, Institute for Management Research, 2014).

pre-existing conditions, and the establishment of annual or lifetime caps on benefits, which had previously been variously constrained under the terms of some employer plans and under regulations in a number of states. As noted above, it also required insurers to spend a specified proportion (which varied across markets) of their premium revenue on benefits. The more consequential requirements for mandatory enrollment, community rating of premiums, and limits on copayments that were placed on insurers who wished to qualify for participation in the state-based exchanges have been noted above. The point to be made here is that these regulations also related to off-exchange activity. Significantly, insurers participating in the exchanges also had to respect these requirements *even for plans offered off the exchanges*. And all insurers were required to offer the basic mandatory package of benefits, and to cover at least 60 per cent of actuarial costs,[37] *whether or not they offered plans through an exchange*. (Insurers participating in the exchanges were also required to offer a range of plans, covering 80–85 per cent of actuarial costs.) Each insurer was also required to maintain a single state-wide risk pool for all its plans, and thus to cross-subsidize among its own policyholders.

In an unintended development, the *Affordable Care Act* reforms also boosted the activity of a number of private web-based entities that had been developing over a decade to assist consumers in online searches for appropriate coverage. At first, because of restrictions on web-based brokers administering federal subsidies, a cumbersome "double redirect" process of ping-ponging the applicant between the broker's site and the federal site was employed. Finally, in May 2017, the Department of Health and Human Services announced a new "proxy direct enrollment pathway," to be available for certain enrollments beginning in 2018, through which consumers would be able to complete the full process, including application for subsidy, through web brokers under agreements with federally facilitated exchanges or state-based exchanges, provided that the web brokers complied with a set of regulatory conditions.[38]

---

37   At this level, insurees could expect to have to cover 40 per cent of their health care expenses through deductibles and copayments. This was the requirement for the least expensive plans offered on the exchanges.

38   T Jost, "CMS to Expand Direct Enrollment on HealthCare.gov" (17 May 2017), online (blog): *Health Affairs* <https://www.healthaffairs.org/do/10.1377/hblog20170517.060181/full/>.

Thus were private web brokers, as well as insurers themselves, drawn into the public regulatory orbit.

The Private Market in Britain

As noted above, a purely private market (on both delivery and demand sides) has existed in Britain in parallel to the public system from the beginning of the NHS. Although this sector was little affected by the internal reforms with which I am concerned here, it merits some attention because of its relevance to the current Canadian debate. An excellent overview can be found in a report by the Kings Fund,[39] a health think tank, and a few points can be summarized. The small private market is heavily focused on elective surgery; it is estimated that only about 3 per cent of GP visits, as compared to about 13 per cent of elective surgery, take place on a private basis.[40] The private hospital market is dominated by a few large chains, with the seven largest accounting for about 75 per cent of the market. This degree of concentration, considerably higher in London, has drawn attention from the UK's Competition and Markets Authority, which, in 2011, launched an investigation that led initially to two large firms being ordered to divest themselves of certain hospitals. The ruling was successfully appealed by the firms, and the final result was a regime in which hospitals were required to publicly report information on their prices and other data.[41]

Only a small minority of the British population takes out private insurance: having risen sharply in the 1980s, the proportion has remained in the 10–12 per cent range over the past two and a half decades, although the content of those policies varies widely.[42] Private insurance accounted for only about 3.3 per cent of total health

---

39   UK, The King's Fund, *The UK private health market* (London: King's Fund, 2014), online: *The King's Fund*, <www.kingsfund.org.uk/sites/default/files/media/commission-appendix-uk-private-health-market.pdf>.

40   *Ibid* at 3–4.

41   UK, Competition and Markets Authority, *Private healthcare market investigation* (London: Competition and Markets Authority, 2017), online: www.gov.uk/cma-cases/private-healthcare-market-investigation.

42   T Foubister et al, *Private Medical Insurance in the United Kingdom* (Copenhagen: European Observatory on Health Systems and Policies, 2006) 40, 55; UK, The King's Fund, *The UK private health market* (London: King's Fund, 2014) 3, online: <www.kingsfund.org.uk/sites/default/files/media/commission-appendix-uk-private-health-market.pdf>; LaingBuisson, "Hospitals Competing for a Static

expenditure in the United Kingdom in 2016.[43] The balance between
employer-based and individually purchased coverage shifted over
time, as employer-based coverage rose from roughly half of the
total in the 1980s to about 82 per cent in 2011.[44] Coverage rates are
highest in the forty to sixty-four age group and lowest for those
over sixty-five.[45] The industry is concentrated in a few large firms:
the largest two insurers accounted for an estimated 62.5 per cent of
coverage in 2003, and the largest four accounted for 78 per cent.[46]
Given their niche focus, relatively healthy enrolled population, and
industry concentration, the large private health insurers in England
are generally more profitable than the more comprehensive private
insurers in the United States.[47] Unlike the case in many other nations,
including the United States, Canada, and Australia, there is no tax
subsidy in Britain for employer-based insurance; on the contrary,
such coverage is not only taxed as income but is also subject to an
additional tax on insurance premiums.[48]

Although, as noted, the reforms discussed here were not aimed
at this private sector,[49] they did nonetheless have some impact on
private-sector firms. First, private providers were regulated at the
interface between public and private sectors; for example, they were
subject to central economic regulation (aimed at ensuring the financial stability of providers) if they provided any services under contract with the NHS. Other controls were embedded in these contracts,

Private Healthcare Pot." (2017), online: <www.laingbuisson.co.uk/MediaCentre/
PressReleases/LaingsReviewPressRelease201112.aspx>.

43   UK, Office for National Statistics, *UK Health Accounts: 2016 Statistical bulletin*
(2018), online: <www.ons.gov.uk/peoplepopulationandcommunity/
healthandsocialcare/healthcaresystem/bulletins/ukhealthaccounts/2016#
financing-of-healthcare>.

44   UK, The King's Fund, *The UK private health market* (London: King's Fund, 2014)
2, online: <www.kingsfund.org.uk/sites/default/files/media/commission-appen-
dix-uk-private-health-market.pdf>.

45   T Foubister et al, *Private Medical Insurance in the United Kingdom* (Copenhagen:
European Observatory on Health Systems and Policies, 2006) 50–51.

46   *Ibid* at 61.

47   *Ibid* at 71.

48   *Supra* note 44 at 5.

49   The Thatcher government in the late 1980s briefly considered a proposal to
radically reform the system of health care financing around a voucher model
built on a much larger role for private finance, before rejecting that option in
favour of the internal market reforms aimed at public-sector purchasers and
providers.

such as the "anti-poaching" provision noted above.[50] Specialist physicians working in both public and private sectors were required by their contract to spend a specified number of hours in the public sector. But even in their purely private activities, privately owned and operated facilities were drawn under the ambit of the quality regulator that was a product of the reforms (the CQC) and held to the same standards as NHS providers *whether or not they were offering NHS-funded services.* Because the remedy sought in the *Cambie* case would bring Canada closer to the British parallel-sector model, it is worth noting that actual experience in Britain suggests that effecting that remedy would not likely achieve the freedom of action expected by the plaintiffs, especially if they spanned the public-private boundary by offering services on both a publicly and a privately paid basis.

Summary—and Implications for Canada

There are lessons in this review of experience of market-oriented reforms for both government policy-makers and private actors. The first concerns the unexpected and unintended consequences of reform, especially for those who might have expected a diminution of the role of government. The effect of all of the reforms discussed was increasingly to draw private providers, insurers, and brokers under the regulatory umbrella of the state, and to increase the overall weight of social control of individual behaviour.[51] This phenomenon more generally has led scholars to speak of the emergence of "regulatory capitalism"[52] or the "post-regulatory state."[53] The nugget of this insight is the recognition of the increasing *interconnectedness* of forms of social control as governments seek to act through what has been called "meta-regulation": stimulating, steering, guaranteeing, and auditing private mechanisms of market governance and professional self-regulation.[54]

---

50   See note 11.

51   Tuohy, *supra* note 1 at 561–62.

52   D Levi-Faur, "The Global Diffusion of Regulatory Capitalism" (2005) 598 Annals of the American Academy of Political and Social Science at 12.

53   C Scott, "Regulation in the Age of Governance: The Rise of the Post Regulatory State" in J Jordana & D Levi-Faur, eds, *The Politics of Regulation: Institutions and Regulatory Reforms for the Age of Governance*, (Cheltenham, UK: Edward Elgar, 2004).

54   *Ibid* at 664.

A second lesson concerns unanticipated developments among privately capitalized providers and insurers of health care themselves. Where reforms were deliberately aimed at universalizing or substantially expanding coverage by regulating private insurers and subsidizing their clientele (as in the Netherlands and the United States), the incentives facing private-sector entrepreneurs as they sought to take advantage of public mandates drove a further concentration of the insurance industry, especially in regional markets. Because regulatory constraints limited the potential for profit, insurers and providers sought to increase profits by expanding their customer/patient base—both to realize economies of scale and to buttress their positions in negotiating contracts in which the currency was "enrolled lives" and catchment areas. In both the Netherlands and the United States, this dynamic propelled a series of mergers on both the demand and, to a somewhat lesser extent, the delivery sides of the market. A corollary development was an increasing complexity of structures of accountability. In some cases, this complexity of the regulatory structure was mirrored in the corporate structures of the regulatees themselves, as they sought to limit the reach of regulators and, especially, the application of strictures against profit-making. In both the Netherlands and the United Kingdom, private firms such as Achmea and Circle Health were part of intricate ownership structures that allowed for-profit parent companies to benefit from the business of the not-for-profit that held public mandates or contracts.

A third lesson is not new but is reinforced by experience under the reforms. The presence of universal public coverage for a comprehensive range of services (as in Britain and the Netherlands) means that private providers are likely to focus on niche areas of provision. This has long been the lesson of the parallel private market in the United Kingdom, and those niche focuses were reflected under public contracting with private providers (with the rule-proving exception of a failed private contract to run an NHS hospital). In the Netherlands, public contracts with private clinics as part of the reforms also displayed this niche-based phenomenon.

None of these reforms shrank the fiscal presence of the state in the health care sector.[55] The public share of total health expen-

---

55   This observation seems to hold for market-oriented reforms in the welfare state more generally; see, e.g., F Castles, *The Future of the Welfare State Crisis Myths and Crisis Realities* (Oxford: Oxford University Press, 2004).

diture, and the share of health care spending in public budgets, grew in the Netherlands and the United States from 1985 to 2012, while remaining relatively constant in the United Kingdom.[56] But while market reforms did not diminish the influence of the state in fiscal terms, the organizing principles underlying state influence did change. The state's legitimate functional role was increasingly understood to be one of regulation and contracting, rather than direct management, even where, as in the Netherlands and United States, the scope of public authority expanded. Ironically, only in Canada, where market-oriented reforms in the physician and hospital sectors were explicitly resisted, did the fiscal share of the state contract, as the design of the single-payer system failed to keep pace with technological change. Even so, the public share continued to dominate, shrinking from 76 per cent to 70 per cent from the 1970s to the 1990s.

So, what can we expect in Canada? Should there be an opening to a greater role for private clinics, either in contracting with the public sector or on a purely private basis? Experience in other nations suggests that the material effect would likely be marginal and confined to niche areas, and would be constrained by new forms of regulation. Concerns have been raised that accustomation to a greater role for private finance could undermine political support for the public system. Evidence of such an effect in other nations is mixed,[57] and it has not been studied in the Canadian context, where the principle of coverage on "uniform terms and conditions" is a key component of a health care system that has come to be emblematic of "Canadian values."

---

56   Tuohy, *supra* note 1 at 548, 559–61.

57   Tuohy and colleagues find limited evidence that an *increase* in the private share of finance was likely to fuel public demand for increased public spending in eleven nations, not including Canada. C H Tuohy, C M Flood & M Stabile, "How Does Private Finance Affect Public Health Care Systems? Marshalling the Evidence from OECD Nations." (2004) 29 J Health Pol Pol'y & L 359 at 388. Burlacu and Immergut, however, find that individuals who switched from public to private insurance, or who took out supplementary private insurance coverage in Germany, became *less* supportive of the public system. D Burlacu & E M Immergut, "Welfare State Institutions and Welfare State Attitudes: Using Privatization to Gain Causal Leverage on the Problem of Attitude Formation" (Paper prepared for presentation at the 114th APSA Annual Meeting, Boston, 30 August–2 September 2018).

Private capital can play a role in systems of universal coverage, within well-considered policy frameworks. The evidence presented in this chapter has suggested both the opportunities and the challenges inherent in developing such frameworks. Canadian policy-makers have so far avoided these questions, allowing the scope of public coverage to shrink de facto. That may no longer be a tenable stance.

CHAPTER 8

The Public-Private Mix in Health Care: Reflections on the Interplay between Social and Private Insurance in Germany

Achim Schmid and Lorraine Frisina Doetter

As Canadian courts consider *Charter* challenges to restrictions on private finance in health care, they will look to the experiences of other countries to attempt to gage the prospective impact of allowing a greater role for the private sector. In this chapter, we explore the interplay between Germany's public *social health insurance* (SHI) scheme, and its *substitutive private health insurance* (SPHI) scheme. In contrast to the predominantly tax-financed, single-payer system found in Canada, the German health care system is an SHI system.[1] Historically rooted in the Bismarckian welfare state and legally enshrined in *Sozialgesetzbuch V* (*SGB V*; the German social code, vol. 5), the German system—even in its current form, over a hundred years later—is said to represent a prototypical social-insurance

---

1   The SHI system is characterized by self-regulation of collective actors representing sickness funds and providers. The system is mainly financed by social-insurance contributions and includes a mandate to insure, as well as a definition of contribution rates irrespective of the individual's health risk. Providers of health services are typically private actors contracted by sickness funds. Hence, the dominant actors in the regulation and financing of the health care system are rather societal than state actors, while market actors prevail as providers. See Katharina Böhm et al, "Five Types of OECD Healthcare Systems: Empirical Results of a Deductive Classification" (2013) 113:3 Health Pol'y 258. See also Claus Wendt, Lorraine Frisina & Heinz Rothgang, "Healthcare System Types: A Conceptual Framework for Comparison" (2009) 43:1 Soc Pol'y & Admin 70

system.[2] It covers the overwhelming share of the population through what are currently 109 "sickness funds" (Krankenkassen).[3] Still, despite the predominance of this scheme, Germany stands out among OECD countries in its incorporation of SPHI[4] for around 11 per cent of the population.[5] Indeed, since the convergence of SHI and SPHI in the Netherlands in 2006, Germany is the only OECD country where a substantial share of the population is given the opportunity to opt out of compulsory SHI into the SPHI market.[6] Germany also has a role for "supplementary private insurance," but again its role is different from that called for in the *Cambie* claim, being primarily for the purposes of covering services not covered in the SHI scheme; for example, copayments for dental service.

The German system represents an insurance dualism that collectively achieves near to full coverage of the population. While it may be described as two-tier, a critical insight is that German SPHI is a fundamentally different type of private insurance than the applicants in *Cambie* are pursuing. In the former, it is only available as an option if one is in a high-income bracket or a member of certain professional groups, and, critically, one cannot then rely on the SHI (public) plan at all. Moreover, if one opts out of the SHI scheme (the public scheme), one must then buy SPHI. Both in *Chaoulli* and in *Cambie*, in Canada, the applicants sought/seek a form of private health insurance where everyone maintains public insurance coverage but wherein one may use private health insurance to pay for faster access. Thus Canadian courts, in examining the respective performances of the German and Canadian systems, need to understand the fundamentally different roles private health insurance can serve across different countries, and ensure that any lessons or insights from other countries are carefully calibrated to the Canadian context.

---

2   Wendt, *supra* note 1.
3   GKV-Spitzenverband, *Kennzahlen der gesetzlichen Krankenversicherung* (Berlin: GKV-Spitzenverband, 2019).
4   Basic regulations for private insurance can be found in the German *Insurance Contract Act* (VVG).
5   "Der Datenservice der PKV" (2018), online: *PKV-Verband, Verband der privaten Krankenversicherung* www.pkv-zahlenportal.de/werte/2007/2017/12 [*PKV-Verband*].
6   Francesca Colombo & Nicole Tapay, "Private Health Insurance in OECD Countries: The Benefits and Costs for Individuals and Health Systems" (2004) OECD Health Working Papers; Ralf Götze, *Ende der Dualität? Krankenversicherungsreformen in Deutschland und den Niederlanden* (Frankfurt: Campus Verlag, 2016).

We would note at the outset that notwithstanding its success and remarkable longevity, the German version of a two-tiered health care system has not been immune to criticism or reform, especially since 2003, when proposals to merge both systems (into the so-called citizens insurance scheme) first entered the political agenda.[7] Calls for reform have been grounded in a concern for *equity* in financing and access, particularly as regards advantages enjoyed by the privately insured, such as shorter wait times and access to chiefs of staff within hospitals. Moreover, given that SPHI is a funded rather than a pay-as-you-go scheme, low interest rates have led to financial difficulties within the private system that support a case for convergence.[8]

In what follows, we do not specifically address the viability of the citizens' insurance model but do explore the strength of the claims made in its name. We ask what evidence can be found concerning the effects of Germany's mixed system of SHI and SPHI on patients and providers in Germany? We begin by offering an overview of the basic features and organization of both insurance schemes, particularly with a view to the regulatory frameworks surrounding matters of *coverage, financing,* and the *provision of services,* including timely access to care. We also address the regulatory incentives in place concerning the remuneration of doctors and the obligation to treat patients. In a final section, we reflect on lessons to be learned from Germany regarding the ongoing interplay between SHI and SPHI, as well as the consequences for equity, quality, and financial sustainability.

---

7   Wissenschaftlicher Dienst des Deutschen Bundestags, *Argumente für und gegen eine "Bürgerversicherung"* (Berlin: Deutscher Bundestag, 2018); Jochen Pimpertz, "Bürgerversicherung—kein Heilmittel gegen grundlegende Fehlsteuerungen. Argumente zur Orientierung in einer komplexen Reformdiskussion" (2013), online: *Köln: Institut der deutschen Wirtschaft* <www.iwkoeln.de/studien/iw-policy-papers/beitrag/jochen-pimpertz-buergerversicherung-kein-heilmittel-gegen-grundlegende-fehlsteuerungen-123776.html>; Heinz Rothgang et al, *The State and Healthcare: Comparing OECD Countries* (Basingstoke, UK: Palgrave Macmillan, 2010).

8   Stefan Greß & Markus Lüngen, "Die Einführung einer Bürgerversicherung: Überwindung des ineffizienten Systemwettbewerbs zwischen GKV und PKV" (2017) 71:3 Gesundheits- und Sozialpolitik 68; Hartmut Reiners, "Nebelkerzen und alte Kamellen: Der Streit um die Bürgerversicherung" (2017), online: *Makroskop* <makroskop.eu/2017/12/nebelkerzen-und-alte-kamellen-der-streit-um-die-buergerversicherung/>.

Population Coverage under the Umbrella of
Social and Private Insurances

The introduction of the *Health Insurance Act* of 1883 is generally regarded as the birth of the German SHI system, although the law had built upon earlier professional insurance schemes.[9] While in its early years SHI covered only 10 per cent of the population, mainly in the form of sick pay, it expanded gradually in terms of coverage and scope of benefits.[10] The main steps toward expanding coverage were the inclusion of workers in agriculture and forestry (1911), pensioners (1941), farmers (1972), the disabled (1975), students in higher education (1975), and artists (1983).[11] Nowadays, SHI provides coverage for some 87 per cent of the population, including compulsory insurance for all wage earners with incomes up to a ceiling set by the federal government (discussed below) and those claiming unemployment benefits.[12]

Those not covered by the SHI mandate include civil servants[13] and the self-employed, who are the major clients of SPHI. Alongside these two groups, employees with regular wages above €59,400 per year (approximately $89,000 Canadian), as of 2018, can *fully* opt out of SHI and choose to purchase SPHI.[14] It is required that those who

---

9   Götze, *supra* note 6 at 72.

10 Reinhard Busse et al, "Statutory health insurance in Germany: a health system shaped by 135 years of solidarity, self-governance, and competition" (2017) 390:10097 The Lancet 882.

11 Jens Alber, "Bundesrepublik Deutschland" in Jens Alber & Brigitte Bernardi-Schenkluhn, eds, *Westeuropäische Gesundheitssysteme im Vergleich* (Frankfurt: Campus, 1992) 31.

12 For details, see s 5 SGB V.

13 As defined by the Federal Ministry of the Interior, the term "civil servant" refers to public employees "who stand in a relationship of service and loyalty defined by public law (art 33 (4) GG)," who are "intended to guarantee sound administration based on expertise, professional ability and loyal fulfilment of duties, and ensure that essential tasks are carried out without interruption." See Germany, Federal Ministry of the Interior, *The federal public service. An attractive and modern employer* (Berlin: Federal Ministry of the Interior, 2014) at 34. Civil servants typically take positions involving the exercise of sovereign authority: public administration, police forces, fire brigades, judges, professors, school-teachers, etc., as well as postal and telecommunication services before these were privatized. Alongside civil servants, there are public employees working on the basis of a contract under private law and, therefore, subject to the same regulations as employees in the private sector.

14 "Beitragsbemessungsgrenzen steigen 2018" (2018), online: *Bundesregierung* <www.bundesregierung.de/breg-de/aktuelles/beitragsbemessungsgrenzen-steigen-2018-452362 >.

do opt out must buy private health insurance and, further, that such plans meet minimum coverage conditions, preventing the possibility of under-insurance (what our Australian colleagues in chapter 10 refer to as "junk" policies) among the young and healthy. Thus, SPHI benefits must include reimbursement for outpatient and inpatient services, while copayments and deductibles must be limited to €5,000 per year.[15] Although all German citizens must now purchase either SHI or SPHI, applications for SPHI contracts can be declined (in which case the person must enroll under the SHI plan). Pre-existing conditions can be excluded, and risk-rating based on health status and age are allowed.[16] It is worth noting that the birth of German SPHI is generally dated to 1924, when the number of health insurance policies started to soar.[17] At this time, hyperinflation following the First World War had consumed the savings of the middle class, rendering out-of-pocket payments for health services unfeasible, making private health insurance an attractive option for large parts of the population excluded from the then-modest SHI scheme. Another milestone in the history of private health insurance in Germany was the introduction of the aforementioned upper-income threshold, at which employees no longer qualified for SHI. The income ceiling, however, now refers to an *option* to leave social insurance, rather than an obligation. This has been the subject of enormous political contest between the Christian Democrats and the Free Democratic Party on the one side and the Social Democratic Party on the other, as well as by the different health insurance lobby groups. Switching between SHI and SPHI has become increasingly difficult over time. Most

---

15 Klaus Jacobs, "Wettbewerb im dualen Krankenversicherungssystem in Deutschland. Fiktion und Realität" in Klaus Jacobs & Sabine Schulze, eds, *Die Krankenversicherung der Zukunft* (Berlin: KomPart Verlag, 2013) 47.

16 There are two exceptions to this rule. First, applications for newborn (or adopted) children of people already within SPHI plans must be accepted without individual risk adjustment of premiums. Second, since 2009, SPHI companies are obliged to provide a common basic tariff for all residents who are exempt from SHI and who had no private insurance contract by the end of 2008. Those with private insurance contracts before 2009 were allowed to opt into the basic tariff by the end of June 2009. Since then, it can only be taken up at age fifty-five or older, or, as a recipient of welfare benefits.

17 David Klingenberger, *Die Friedensgrenze zwischen gesetzlicher und privater Krankenversicherung: ökonomische und metaökonomische Kriterien einer optimierten Aufgabenabgrenzung zwischen Sozial- und Individualversicherung* (Regensburg: Transfer-Verlag, 2001) at 34.

significantly, since the *Statutory Health Insurance Reform Act* of 2000, those aged fifty-five and older have virtually no ability to switch back to the statutory SHI scheme;[18] this is to prevent free-riding upon the social scheme once one's health deteriorates in old age. Hence, choosing SPHI in Germany can be a decision for life.[19]

Table 8.1. Health care coverage in Germany

	Million	Percentage
Total population	82.8	100
Statutory health insurance (SHI)	72.3	87.3
Compulsory insurance	49.9	60.3
Voluntary insurance	6.0	7.3
Co-insured dependents (compulsory and voluntary)	16.3	19.7
Substitutive private health insurance (SPHI)	8.8	10.9
Supplementary private insurance	19.5	23.7

Source: Data on Federal Ministry of Health: KM 6-Statistik, online: *Gesundheitsberichterstattung des Bundes* <www.gbe-bund.de/>; number of private insurees extracted from *PKV-Verband, supra* note 5. Total population to calculate the percentages is based on the German census. See "Schätzung für 2018: Bevölkerungszahl auf 83,0 Millionen gestiegen" (2018), online: *Statistisches Bundesamt* <www.destatis.de/DE/Themen/Gesellschaft-Umwelt/Bevoelkerung/Bevoelkerungsstand/_inhalt.html>.

As one can see from table 8.1, most people are covered by SHI, compulsorily (about 60 per cent of the population), as voluntary members (7.3 per cent), or co-insured dependents (about 20 per cent). Nearly 11 per cent of the population are covered by SPHI as the primary scheme.[20] As of 2017, about half of all persons with SPHI are active or retired civil servants who qualify for state grants, covering

---

18   Reinhard Busse & Miriam Blümel "Germany: Health System Review" (2014) 16:2 Health Systems in Transition 138.

19   Jacobs, *supra* note 15.

20   As opposed to other health care systems featuring a strong role for private insurance as the primary scheme (e.g., the United States), employer-based group insurance has no part. Those with SPHI choose individual health plans with a defined scope of benefits. The employer only supports the insured by paying a share of the premium. The latter is limited to the maximum employer's share payable to SHI contributions. By contrast, there are employer-based health-insurance funds within the SHI system. They follow the same rules as other SHI funds. Access to those funds may be restricted to the employees of the company running the fund. Moreover, employers are involved in the self-regulatory committees of SHI, where they aim to control cost increases.

50 per cent (70 per cent for the retired) of health care costs, including costs for dependents (70–80 per cent).[21] Those without a state grant (some 4.4 million private insurees) mainly include the self-employed and salaried employees who have opted out of SHI.

As it is neither a unique nor central feature of the German two-tiered system, *supplementary* private insurance is not the focus of the present study. However, it may be worth noting that more than a fifth of the population—that is, nearly 27 per cent of SHI beneficiaries—have purchased supplementary insurance. The lion's share of insurance policies is aimed at additional dental-care benefits, but supplemental plans also exist for select outpatient and inpatient services not included in SHI. These typically refer to added amenities (e.g., private versus shared hospital rooms), as opposed to quicker access to care. In theory, the combination of SHI-reimbursement tariffs[22] and supplementary private insurance can be used to jump queues and access higher-quality GP and specialist care. However, this approach is rarely taken.[23] People with an income to purchase such health plans instead opt out of SHI and into SPHI.

Financing across the Two Tiers

In 2017, the OECD estimated total current spending on health at nearly €368 billion and approximately 11.3 per cent of GDP, which is comparable to other high-spending nations such as France (11.5 per cent) and Switzerland (12.3 per cent), though considerably less than the United States (17.2 per cent). At the same time, Canada spent only 10.4 per cent of GDP on health, according to OECD figures. Health care in Germany is mainly financed by social insurance (70.3 per cent), that is, SHI, and, to a minor extent, social long-term care, pension, and accident insurance. SHI contribution rates are determined by the government and currently amount to 14.6 per cent of earned

---

21   *PKV-Verband, supra* note 5.

22   Reimbursement tariffs (s 13 *SGB V* and s 53 at para 4 *SGB V*) deviate from benefits in kind usually provided by SHI. Patients are charged according to the medical fee schedule similar to patients with SPHI. Their statutory sickness fund will reimburse the costs at the level spent for benefits in-kind minus a lump sum for extra administration costs and minus any rebates negotiated between the SHI fund and providers. Those with SHI who choose the reimbursement option can contract supplementary insurance to cover the extra costs.

23   Stefan Greß et al, "Kostenerstattung in der Gesetzlichen Krankenversicherung" (2011) Hochschule Fulda Working Paper No 01.

income up to an annual income ceiling of €53,100, divided equally between employees and employers. Private insurance financing amounted to 8.8 per cent of health expenditure, including SPHI and supplementary health insurance. Further, German households contributed 12.4 per cent of total health expenditure as out-of-pocket (OOP) spending, somewhat less than OOP spending in Canada (14.8 per cent).[24]

An important aspect not captured by OECD financing statistics on Germany is the role played by transfers from federal tax revenues to statutory health and pension funds—a topic which Fiona McDonald and Stephen Duckett also explore in their analysis of the Australian system in chapter 10. In Germany, the federal government subsidizes SHI funds to compensate for expenditures on areas perceived as more of a societal responsibility, such as the free co-insurance of children. Subsidies to the SHI health care fund (€14 billion) and statutory pension insurance (about €737 million) added up to around 4.2 per cent of total spending on health care in 2016.[25] Moreover, contributions to SHI, as well as the core part of SPHI premiums, are exempt from income taxes. By contrast, payments for supplementary insurance, sick pay, and SPHI for services falling outside the scope of social-insurance benefits are not tax deductible.[26] Further, there are tax reductions for providers of health care services. Public inpatient health care and nursing facilities are exempt from local business tax. For private facilities, tax exemptions kick in if they provide at least 40 per cent of their services for SHI schemes. Curative treatments and health care provided in hospitals accredited by federal states are also exempt from value-added tax.

Private health insurance premiums are regulated and may be risk-adjusted according to the age of the applicant, the design of the

---

24   All figures extracted from "OECD Health Statistics 2018" (2019), online: *OECD* <stats.oecd.org/> [OECD]. Figures refer to 2017 or the latest available year.

25   "Current Health Expenditure in millions of Euro (year, provider, function, financing agent)" (2018), online: *Gesundheitsberichterstattung des Bundes* <www.gbe-bund.de/>; "Einnahmen und Ausgaben der gesetzlichen Rentenversicherung (Geschäfts- und Rechnungsergebnisse der gesetzlichen Rentenversicherung)" (2018), online: *Gesundheitsberichterstattung des Bundes* <www.gbe-bund.de/>.

26   Theresa Grün, "Die Absetzbarkeit von Vorsorgeaufwendungen nach dem Bürgerentlastungsgesetz Krankenversicherung" (2009) Deutsches Steuerrecht 1457.

benefit package (range of services, deductibles), and health status at the point of underwriting. Due to a European Court of Justice decision,[27] gender differences may not influence premium calculation.[28] In contrast to SHI, family members are not automatically included under SPHI and must negotiate separate contracts of insurance. Employees holding SPHI[29] can claim a grant from their employer of 50 per cent of the premium but this cannot exceed the highest contribution paid for SHI.

The SPHI sector is also regulated to prevent the offering of low initial premiums to lure subscribers in, only to see rapid increases subsequently, or to prevent insurers from pricing subscribers out of the market as they age. Premiums for new entrants may not differ from premiums for those already insured if both share equal conditions, and SPHI must accrue reserves to cushion premium increases in old age.

Provision of Care and Definition of Benefits

Inpatient and Outpatient Providers

Among OECD countries, the German health care system stands out for its quantity of hospital beds per capita. By way of comparison, curative acute-care beds in Germany amounted to 6.1 per 1,000 of population in 2016, whereas the OECD average was nearly 40 per cent lower, at 3.7 beds per 1,000 people,[30] and by the same measure in Canada the average was only 2.0 beds. Nearly half of all beds are public, while a third are owned by charitable organizations, and about 18 per cent are owned by private for-profit companies, having grown from only 4 per cent in the early 1990s.[31] The advisory council of the health care system estimates that 95 per cent of the population can reach a hospital by car within twenty minutes.[32] Similarly,

---

27   01.03.2011—case C-236/09

28   Helge Sodan & Jörg Adam, *Handbuch des Krankenversicherungsrechts* (München: Beck, 2014).

29   Civil servants cannot claim support for premiums since they already receive state grants to meet at least half of their health costs.

30   OECD, *supra* note 24.

31   "Krankenhausstatistik. Grunddaten der Krankenhäuser und Vorsorge- oder Rehabilitationseinrichtungen" (2018), online: *Statistisches Bundesamt* <www.destatis.de/DE/Themen/Gesellschaft-Umwelt/Gesundheit/Krankenhaeuser/_inhalt.html> [*Statistisches Bundesamt*].

32   Sachverständigenrat zur Begutachtung der Entwicklung im Gesundheitswesen SVR Gesundheit, *Gutachten 2014 des Sachverständigenrates zur Begutachtung der*

Germany maintains 4.2 practicing physicians per 1,000 of population, outnumbered only by Austria (5.1), Lithuania (4.5), Norway (4.5), and Switzerland (4.3), while being considerably higher than those in Canada (2.6), the United States (2.6), and the United Kingdom (2.8). Approximately 78 per cent of practicing physicians are specialists, somewhat above the OECD average (68.8 per cent), as specialists are not only concentrated in hospitals but are often situated in outpatient practices. Contrary to physician density, the number of practicing nurses is low by international standards. The OECD counts only 3.25 nurses per 1,000 of population for Germany, whereas the OECD average is 8.9, almost three times higher.[33]

Irrespective of ownership structure, most hospitals offer services to patients insured in the SHI and SPHI alike. In 2016, only 343 of 1,607 German hospitals[34] exclusively served SPHI patients or those paying out of pocket, and these tend to be small hospitals, representing only 2 per cent of beds.[35] With respect to the outpatient sector, the German Medical Association registered around 154,400 practicing physicians (i.e., about 1.8 per 1,000 of population) in 2017.[36] Only about 7,000 physicians (4.6 per cent) opt to provide services exclusively to private patients, underscoring the predominance of SHI over SPHI. With nearly 90 per cent of the population covered by SHI, physicians would be remiss to ignore this market. This said, SHI physicians are free to offer services to SPHI patients.

In terms of what providers are obliged to offer SHI versus SPHI patients, different benefit rules apply. While the scope of health care benefits for SHI is listed in *SGB V*, detailed benefits are regularly negotiated in light of medical-technological progress. By contrast, SPHI benefits packages are defined by private insurance companies that are then chosen by insurees within regulations set by law.

Entwicklung im Gesundheitswesen: Bedarfsgerechte Versorgung. Perspektiven für ländliche Regionen und ausgewählte Leistungsbereiche (Berlin: Deutscher Bundestag, 2014) [*SVR Gesundheit*].

33   *Ibid.*

34   Note that this does not include psychiatric clinics.

35   *Statistisches Bundesamt, supra* note 31.

36   "Montgomery: Es ist höchste Zeit, den Ärztemangel ernsthaft zu bekämpfen Bundesärztekammer" (2018), online: *Bundesaerztekammer* <www.bundesaerzte-kammer.de/ueber-uns/aerztestatistik/aerztestatistik-2017/>.

Definition of SHI Benefit Package

In contrast to the protections of the *Canada Health Act*,[37] which is limited to hospital and physician services, German SHI benefits include prevention and health-screening measures, outpatient health care, some dental care, dental prostheses, pharmaceuticals, physiotherapy rehabilitation, orthopedic and prosthetic devices, hospital care, and rehabilitative care. According to section 12 of *SGB V*, benefits must be adequate, appropriate, and cost-effective. The details are regulated by the Federal Joint Committee,[38] Germany's highest decision-making body in health care issues, which may decide to exclude services from the basket of services insured by SHI if they fail to satisfy metrics for clinical effectiveness, medical necessity, cost-effectiveness, or pharmaceuticals if they are inexpedient or if more cost-effective alternatives exist.[39]

Each sickness fund can augment the benefit catalogue for its members. The general categories of benefits which may be expanded are defined in *SGB V*. They include preventive and rehabilitative care, care by midwives, in vitro fertilization, dental services (excluding dental prostheses), non-prescription drugs, remedies, home care, home help for the ill, and services by non-medical or alternative-care practitioners (sec. 11 at para 6, *SGB V*). Variations in the benefit catalogue are often designed to attract groups with low health risks, yet, thus far, discretionary benefits remain marginal. Expenditures related to the augmentation of SHI core plans amount to only €337.8 million, compared to total expenditures of €202 billion.[40]

---

37   *Canada Health Act*, RSC 1985, c C-6.

38   The committee, known as the G-BA (Gemeinsamer Bundesausschuss), consists of thirteen members entitled to vote: an impartial chair and two impartial representatives proposed by the federal health ministry. Five members represent the sickness funds appointed by the National Association of Statutory Health Insurance Funds (GKV-Spitzenverband). Five members represent provider interests: the federal associations of SHI physicians (2), dentists (1), and the German Hospital Association (2). Further, accredited patient organizations and, depending on the topics under review, other stakeholders join the committee as advisors.

39   Katharina Böhm & Claudia Landwehr, "Strategic Institutional Design: Two Case Studies of Non-Majoritarian Agencies in Health Care Priority-Setting" (2015) 51:4 Gov & Opposition 632 at 650.

40   Bundesministerium für Gesundheit, *Gesetzliche Krankenversicherung* (Berlin: Bundesministerium für Gesundheit, 2016).

Definition of Benefits in SPHI

In 2009, concurrent with the introduction of a mandate to insure for all citizens (either SHI or SPHI), the *Insurance Contract Act* began to set a floor for the content of SPHI contracts. The benefit package must include reimbursement for comprehensive outpatient and inpatient health care, while copayments and deductibles are limited to maximum of €5,000 per year.[41] Beyond these regulations, benefits provided by SPHI insurance are a matter of individual contracts between the insurance company and the insured and, generally speaking, SPHI tends to be more comprehensive and provides remuneration at a more generous level than in the SHI scheme.

Regulating Providers of Health Care

Regulation in the German health care system is characterized by complex structures, but the main governing instruments are collective agreements between the sickness funds and provider associations, which govern the organization of health care delivery and the remuneration of providers. Concerning hospital services, collective agreements also include the Association of Private Health Insurers. Further, the German Medical Association (which all physicians must join) and the Associations of Statutory Health Insurance Physicians and Dentists have a mandate to improve professional education, guarantee professional ethics, and supervise professional practice.

In what follows, we describe the conditions set within this regulatory landscape for the main providers of health care services; namely, outpatient and inpatient physicians. We focus especially on the differences in provider remuneration between the two insurance tiers, as well as the regulatory incentives in place for private practice and the limits on private billing.

Remuneration and Regulatory Incentives in the Outpatient Sector

Physicians in the outpatient sector are usually self-employed. About 95 per cent own a license issued by the regional association of SHI physicians and offer services under a collective contract funded by SHI. At the same time, they deliver health care for close to 11 per cent of the population that are privately insured. As in Canada, physicians are free to offer services not included in the benefit package of the

---

41   Jacobs, *supra* note 15 at 50.

SHI and financed OOP or through supplementary private insurance. Hence, public and private domains are not separated on the delivery side. As mentioned earlier, about 5 per cent of physicians are not part of SHI and work on a private basis only. The remuneration of outpatient practice under SPHI differs substantially from SHI rules. Private billing is based on the medical-fee schedule decreed by the government as a result of negotiations between the German Medical Association and SPHI carriers. A similar fee schedule is in place for dental services. Physicians can bill up to 3.5 times the base rate of services depending on their time and effort, for which SPHI guarantees coverage. Around 85 per cent of physician services are billed by a factor of 2.3 times the base rates.[42] Since the schedule is outdated, physicians can create their own fees for new and innovative treatments not addressed in the fee schedule. The SPHI funds will reimburse all medically required physician services without any volume limits. By contrast, remuneration within SHI involves a combination of flat rates and fee-for-service remuneration based on a Uniform Value Scale up to a maximum volume.[43] A series of studies have found that remuneration for similar services in the outpatient sector paid by SPHI is, on average, 2.25 to 3.9 times higher than SHI payments.[44]

Special rules apply to the social tariffs that SPHI carriers are required to offer for the elderly who can no longer afford their health plan (standard tariff) and SPHI insured who become dependent on welfare benefits (basic tariff; see n16 above), and for those patients,

42 Frank Niehaus, *Ein Vergleich der ärztlichen Vergütung nach GOÄ und EBM* (2009) Wissenschaftliches Institut der PKV Discussion Paper No 7 at 16.

43 The remuneration of outpatient physicians for SHI services is a complex multilevel procedure. First, based on earlier expenditures the federal representatives of SHI funds and SHI physicians negotiate orientation values for prices and morbidity-oriented volumes, which are, in a second step, translated into regional prices and volumes by the regional bodies of the negotiation partners. The associations of SHI physicians are responsible for allocating the volumes to the different groups of physicians. About 70 per cent of outpatient physician services are remunerated according to this procedure and subject to volume limits. Physician services beyond these limits will be remunerated with a reduced price or not paid at all. The remaining 30 per cent of services (e.g., outpatient surgery, vaccination, prevention, or specific cancer treatment) are remunerated according to the negotiated prices without limits. See Busse & Blümel, *supra* note 18 at 268.

44 Niehaus, *supra* note 42 at 30.

physicians are not permitted to bill more than 1.8 times (standard tariff) and 1.2 times (basic tariff) the base rate. Reduced rates also apply for technical services and laboratory work.[45]

In 2015, the average physician practice received 70.4 per cent of total revenue from SHI and 26.3 per cent from private practice.[46] Private sources included private insurance (mainly SPHI, while supplementary insurance is only a relevant source for dental service), as well as OOP spending by SHI patients for extra services. Revenue from private practice increased by 4.1 per cent between 2003 and 2015.[47] Revenue from private practice also varies by specialty. The average general practice earns only 17.5 per cent through private billing, while the average private share for specialist practice such as radiology or orthopedics can increase to around 45 per cent. The income of dentists is composed almost evenly of SHI and private sources, reflecting the stronger role of cost sharing in this sector.[48] Data also show that the higher the revenue per practice, the more the income derives from private practice.[49]

Since the different remuneration schemes generate incentives that favour private billing by physicians, regulations are necessary to protect SHI patients. Among the responsibilities of SHI physicians, for example, is an obligation to be present for consultation at least twenty hours per week. The regional associations of SHI physicians (known as Kassenärztliche Vereinigungen, or KVs) have a mandate to guarantee state of the art, timely outpatient care. In agreement with the associations of sickness funds, KVs are responsible for needs- and demand-based planning according to the decrees of the Federal Joint Committee. Benchmarks for physician density are set for each district, and specific groups of physicians qualified by types of regions. In the case of oversupply, licenses for the respective district are restricted. Responses to undersupply mainly include

---

45   PKV-Verband, Sozialtarife in der PKV (Köln: PKV-Verband, 2009).

46   "Unternehmen und Arbeitsstätten. Kostenstruktur bei Arzt- und Zahnarztpraxen sowie Praxen von psychologischen Psychotherapeuten" (2015), online: *Statistisches Bundesamt* <www.destatis.de/DE/Themen/ Branchen-Unternehmen/Dienstleistungen/Publikationen/Downloads- Dienstleistungen-Kostenstruktur/kostenstruktur-aerzte-2020161159004.pdf?__ blob=publicationFile&v=3> at 13.

47   *Ibid* at 15.

48   *Ibid* at 16.

49   *Ibid* at 32.

economic incentives, such as subsidies or loans, for taking over an existing practice or investment costs.[50] A new decree for needs- and demand-based planning initiated with the *Statutory Health Insurance Care Structures Act* of 2012 allows for the adjustment of benchmarks in response to regional demographic and morbidity characteristics.[51] The associations of SHI physicians and dentists are also responsible for guaranteeing service provision for those in SPHI who are entitled to pay basic or standard tariffs (i.e., the elderly or welfare recipients who cannot switch to SHI).

Of crucial importance in the protection of those within the SHI scheme is the prohibition of extra-billing for SHI services, as defined in the collective agreement between SHI doctors and the sickness funds.[52] By the same token, it is unlawful to bill SHI patients for shorter waiting times. There are, however, media reports about such practices, and consumer-protection advocates criticize weak control mechanisms by KVs.[53] Although there are specific regulations preventing SHI physicians from pushing patients to private care when they are entitled to care under the SHI scheme,[54] examples of abuse can be found. One reported example, found in the 20 March 2014, issue of a physicians' journal, involved an eye specialist who offered swift access to private consultation for SHI patients, instead of regular waiting times of several months.[55] Professional sanctions include a reprimand, fines, or the temporal/permanent revocation of the license to treat SHI patients.

If the KV fails to guarantee service provision for SHI, the responsibility falls on sickness funds, who are then allowed to contract physicians selectively, authorize hospital doctors to provide outpatient practice, or obligate physicians to serve SHI. As an

---

50   Michael Simon, *Das Gesundheitssystem in Deutschland. Eine Einführung in Struktur und Funktionsweise* (Bern: Hans Huber, 2010) at 196.

51   *SVR Gesundheit, supra* note 32 at 444.

52   "Bundesmantelvertrag—Ärzte" (2019), online: *Kassenärztliche Bundesvereinigung* <www.kbv.de/media/sp/BMV_Aerzte.pdf>.

53   Anette Dowideit & Anja Ettel, "So kaufen sich Kassenpatienten einen Privat-Termin" (2016), online: *Die Welt* <www.welt.de/152760917>.

54   The respective rules can be found in s 128 paragraph 5a *SGB V* and s 18 paragraph 8 of the collective agreement BMV-Ä.

55   Ärzte Zeitung, "Disziplinarverfahren gegen Cottbuser Ärztin" (2014), online: Ärzte Zeitung <www.aerztezeitung.de/praxis_wirtschaft/vertragsarztrecht/article/857363/verdachtsfall-termin-geld-disziplinarverfahren-cottbuser-aerztin.html>.

example, some dentists refused to treat SHI patients and cancelled their SHI license to protest against the *Statutory Health Insurance Modernization Act* of 2004.[56] The dentists who participated in the collective action were banned for six years and could not participate in the SHI system. The *Social Court* of Stuttgart of First Instance confirmed disciplinary measures by the regional KV in response to the striking SHI physicians[57] but granted permission for a direct appeal at the Federal Constitutional Court, where the issue is still under review.[58]

Remuneration and Regulatory Incentives in the Inpatient Sector

The core regulatory framework for the provision of hospital care can be found in the *Hospital Financing Act*. The federal states are responsible for guaranteeing needs-based health care delivery in hospitals. This translates to a key role in the infrastructural development and accreditation of hospitals. The federal states bear the investment costs of accredited hospitals while operating costs are financed by patients and their insurance. At the same time, accredited hospitals have a mandate to provide specific, pre-defined services, as well as a license to provide services for members of SHI. The sickness funds, however, are responsible for contracting with hospitals directly and negotiating individual budgets.[59] Hospital plans are mostly developed according to current use, while the estimation of future needs based around general demographic developments rather than detailed medical needs.[60]

Running costs for hospital services are mainly financed in line with a diagnosis-related groups (DRG) system, that is, fixed prices for defined groups of diagnoses, which share similar expected costs.[61] Hospitals receive additional funding for patients whose medical condition force much longer stays than to be expected from their diagnosis. They receive less for discharging patients too early,

---

56   See BSG, Federal Social Court decision, 17.06.2009: B 6 KA 16/08 R, online: <https://openjur.de/u/169475.html>.

57   Social Court Stuttgart AZ.: S 4 KA 3147/13

58   Ärzte Zeitung, "Streikrecht für Vertragsärzte: Karlsruhe ist jetzt am Zug" (2017), online: Ärzte Zeitung <www.aerztezeitung.de/politik_gesellschaft/berufspolitik/article/942007/streikrecht-vertragsaerzte-karlsruhe-jetzt-zug.html>.

59   Simon, *supra* note 50 at 262.

60   *SVR Gesundheit, supra* note 32.

61   Simon, *supra* note 50.

thereby causing medical problems. Moreover, there are extra funds for innovative treatments and several activities not adequately covered through the DRG system.[62] In terms of two-tier care, at this stage there is no difference between SHI and private insurance. However, hospitals can generate additional revenue through providing amenities such as private rooms and other related amenities. Moreover, private patients can choose treatment by more experienced doctors and selected specialists—generally, chief-of-staff physicians entitled to issue a private invoice. Such services are billed according to the medical-fee schedule discussed earlier. Here, physicians and hospitals profit from private patients, and this can motivate preferential treatment of the privately insured.[63]

Generally, and in contrast to Canada, hospital doctors are primarily salaried employees. However, in recent years, hospitals have increasingly made use of independent physicians who are contracted to provide fee-based services.[64] Meanwhile, chiefs of staff have a standard salary, which they can augment by treating private patients on a fee-for-service basis. Recently defined standard contracts issued and recommended by the German Hospital Association place new emphasis on activity-based wage-components rather than the right to bill patients.[65] Still, the mode of remunerating chief-of-staff physicians tends to incentivize the treatment of privately insured patients.[66]

Effects of German Two-Tiered System on Patient Access to Services

Generally, the German health care system scores well in terms of access to family doctors and specialists, and is considered "one of

62 *Ibid* at 298; "Zu- und Abschläge" (2016), online: *GKV-Spitzenverband* <www.gkv-spitzenverband.de/krankenversicherung/krankenhaeuser/krankenhaeuser_abrechnung/zu_abschlaege/zu_abschlaege.jsp>.

63 Christoph Schwierz et al, "Discrimination in waiting times by insurance type and financial soundness of German acute care hospitals" (2011) 12:5 Eur J of Health Economics 405.

64 Kassenärztliche Bundesvereinigung & Bundesärztekammer, *Honorarärztliche Tätigkeit in Deutschland* (Berlin: Kassenärztliche Bundesvereinigung und Bundesärztekammer, 2011).

65 Kienbaum, *Vergütungsreport: Ärzte, Führungskräfte und Spezialisten in Krankenhäusern* (Köln: Kienbaum, 2016).

66 Busse & Blümel, *supra* note 18.

the consumer-friendliest health systems in Europe."[67] Reibling[68] classifies Germany as having a health care system with a very high provider density, with few constraints on patient access to providers. Neither cost sharing nor gate-keeping instruments establish access restrictions. In what follows, we first examine the role of financial barriers, as well as the timeliness and quality of care specific to the two-tiers. We then proceed, in a final section, to reflect on the fairness and the sustainability of the German health care system in light of its effects on providers and patients, as well as with a view to future challenges. We conclude by offering some tentative lessons to be learned from the German case for other health care systems.

Financial Barriers

Copayments in SHI make up for only a small share of OOP spending. They mainly arise in the case of prescribed pharmaceuticals for which the patient pays 10 per cent of the price, but a minimum of €5 and maximum of €10 per prescription. Drugs for which the sickness fund of the insured has negotiated rebates are free of charge. For hospital stays, preventive spa, or rehabilitative inpatient care, patients are charged €10 per day for up to twenty-eight days per year. Inpatient stay for childbirth is free of charge. Total SHI copayments may not exceed 2 per cent of income or 1 per cent of income for people with chronic disease.

OOP spending amounted to €43.5 billion in 2016, and expenditures on over-the-counter remedies accounted for 37.2 per cent of that, since non-prescription drugs have been broadly excluded from the SHI benefit package since 2004. Medical services of physicians and dentists accounted for roughly another third of OOP spending (32.5 per cent), and mainly refer to services not included in the SHI benefit package. Only a minor share of OOP spending (3.4 per cent) was spent in hospitals.[69] Surveys by the Commonwealth Fund show that relatively few people had problems accessing health care due to financial barriers in Germany. Combining different indicators of cost-related access problems, Germany was ranked fourth among

---

67   *Ibid* at 266.

68   Nadine Reibling, "Healthcare systems in Europe: towards an incorporation of patient access" (2010) 20:1 J Eur Social Pol'y 5.

69   "Co-payments of private households in the Statutory Health Insurance" (2018), online Gesundheitsberichterstattung des Bundes <www.gbe-bund.de>.

eleven high-spending OECD countries in terms of easy access.[70] Still, the study finds that between 7 per cent and 21 per cent of survey respondents encountered problems with paying medical bills. There is no information about the insurance status of these people. Cost sharing in private insurance is defined by the individual contract and may vary within the limits of the insurance contract act, that is, the maximum deductible of €5,000 per year. The insurance contracts of civil servants are generally designed without any deductibles since the plans only insure the part of the health costs not covered by the government allowance for civil servants.[71] The German SOEP household survey shows that deductibles tend to increase with age.[72] Since premiums increase in old age, SPHI-insurees often choose higher deductibles in exchange for reduced monthly premiums. While private insurance is generally regarded as advantageous, it also causes problems for a growing share of the insured; namely, the self-employed and civil servants with low incomes, dependents of civil servants who lose entitlements for public subsidies after family breakup, and the elderly.[73] These groups have problems bearing the costs incurred due to premium increases, and have to accept higher deductibles or reduced benefits.

Timeliness and Quality of Care

Perhaps due to one of the largest hospital capacities in the OECD world, and also given a high number of practicing physicians, waiting periods for treatment are short and, therefore, are not high on the German political agenda.[74] Concerning the timeliness of care, Germany was also placed fourth among eleven nations by

---

70   Karen Davis et al, *Mirror, Mirror on the Wall. How the Performance of the US Health Care System Compares Internationally* (UK: The Commonwealth Fund, 2014).

71   Stefan Greß & Stefanie Heinemann, "Schwachstellen im Geschäftsmodell der privaten Krankenversicherung" in Klaus Jacobs & Sabine Schulze, eds, *Die Krankenversicherung der Zukunft* (Berlin: KomPart Verlag, 2013) 107.

72   The German SOEP (Socio-Economic Panel) household-survey results of 2001 pointed to average annual deductibles of €400 for the privately insured aged forty or younger, and €850 annually for those sixty years and over. More recent data on OOP spending related to deductibles for the privately insured is not available. See Markus Grabka, "Prämien in der PKV: deutlich stärkerer Anstieg als in der gesetzlichen Krankenversicherung" (2006) 73:46 Wochenbericht des DIW Berlin 653.

73   Jacobs, *supra* note 15 at 56.

74   Busse & Blümel, *supra* note 18 at 267.

the Commonwealth Fund. Thus, 72 per cent of respondents waited less than four weeks to see a specialist, and only 10 per cent had to wait longer than two months.[75] There is, however, some evidence of preferential treatment for patients with private insurance, which at times motivates reform discussions and media attention. Privately insured patients report fewer problems with wait times.[76] According to Busse and Blümel,[77] there are shorter wait times and more consultation time given to those covered by SPHI. The difference in wait times ranges between an average of about two to three days to twenty-three days, and refer mainly to specialist appointments, not GP care.[78] Schwierz et al and Sauerland et al have tested hospitals to ascertain the effect of insurance status on waiting times.[79] One in three[80] or four[81] hospitals, respectively, actively asked for the insurance status of the test patient before offering a wait time for a disease category that was not an emergency but required early treatment. PHI holders had significantly shorter waiting times. In particular, hospitals with a superior financial performance (and probably with higher utilization rates) tended to engage more in this kind of discriminatory practice.[82] However, the magnitude of effects found was unlikely to bear detrimental consequences for the health of SHI patients. On average, longer waits of 2.5 days[83] and 1.6 days[84] were estimated. A study by the Bertelsmann Foundation, with 5,618 respondents, identified shorter wait times in primary care for patients covered by SPHI. The difference in average wait

---

75   Cathy Schoen et al, "Access, Affordability, And Insurance Complexity Are Often Worse In The United States Compared To Ten Other Countries" (2013) 32:12 Health Affairs 2205.

76   Klaus Zok, "GPV/PKV im Vergleich—die Wahrnehmung der Versicherten" in Klaus Jacobs & Sabine Schulze, eds, *Die Krankenversicherung der Zukunft* (Berlin: KomPart Verlag, 2013) 15.

77   Busse & Blümel, *supra* note 18 at 269.

78   *Ibid.*

79   Schwierz, *supra* note 63; Dirk Sauerland, Björn A Kuchinke & Ansgar Wübker, "Warten gesetzlich Versicherte länger? Zum Einfluss des Versichertenstatus auf den Zugang zu medizinischen Leistungen im stationären Sektor" (2009) 14:2 Gesundheitsökonomie und Qualitätsmanagement 86.

80   Schwierz, *supra* note 63;

81   Sauerland, Kuchinke & Ansgar, *supra* note 79.

82   Schwierz, *supra* note 63 at 413.

83   *Ibid.*

84   Sauerland, Kuchinke & Ansgar, *supra* note 79.

time was 3.3 days, compared to 4.0 days for those with SHI. Higher risks for excessive wait times, defined as ten days or more, were found for the elderly, as well as for those living in the eastern part of Germany.[85] These were attributed to a higher disease burden and larger areas with lower physician density in the east.[86]

As concerns other differences in access between the two tiers, it bears noting that physicians tend to prescribe fewer generics in favour of more patented and higher-priced pharmaceuticals for the privately insured.[87] Whether these differences actually contribute to health outcomes is not easy to measure. The risk profile of the privately insured differs from those within SHI. Members of SPHI are, on average, healthier, younger, and have higher socio-economic backgrounds.[88] A recent study indicates that superior health status among the SPHI population does not only result from a selection effect but is also related to access to better health services than those covered by SHI.[89] This said, there is also evidence for oversupply in SPHI.[90] That is, those covered by SPHI have more physician visits after first contact, indicating supplier-induced demand,[91] and they more frequently undergo unnecessary examinations.[92]

While Germany has high physician density on average, some problems arise due to regional disparities. The higher share of

---

85   Andres L Ramos, Falk Hoffmann & Ove Spreckelsen, "Waiting times in primary care depending on insurance scheme in Germany" (2018) 18:191 BMC Health Serv Res 18.

86   *Ibid.*

87   Dieter Ziegenhagen et al, "Arzneimittelversorgung von PKV-Versicherten im Vergleich zur GKV" (2004) 9:2 Gesundheitsökonomie und Qualitätsmanagement 108.

88   Dietmar Haun, "Quo vadis, GKV und PKV? Entwicklung der Erwerbs- und Einkommensstrukturen von Versicherten im dualen System" in Klaus Jacobs & Sabine Schulze, eds, *Die Krankenversicherung der Zukunft* (Berlin: KomPart Verlag, 2013) 75; Peter Kriwy & Andreas Mielck, "Versicherte in der Gesetzlichen Krankenversicherung (GKV) und der privaten Krankenversicherung (PKV): Unterschiede in Morbidität und Gesundheitsverhalten" (2006) 68:5 Das Gesundheitswesen 281.

89   Johannes Stauder & Tom Kossow, "Selektion oder bessere Leistungen. Warum sind Privatversicherte gesünder als gesetzlich Versicherte" (2016) 79:3 Das Gesundheitswesen.

90   Jacobs, *supra* note 15.

91   Hendrik Jürges, "Health Insurance Status and Physician Behavior in Germany" (2009) 129:2 Schmollers Jahrbuch 297.

92   Zok, *supra* note 76 at 23.

private patients in wealthy regions contributes to regional disparities.[93] Statistically, a 1 per cent higher share of SPHI coverage means
three SHI physicians more per 100,000 of population. The correla-
tion is stronger for specialists.[94] The concentration of physicians in
wealthy urban regions and shortages found in rural areas can also
be explained by the general attractiveness of the local labour market and cultural options. However, Vogt's[95] analysis of the regional
variation of office-based physicians shows that 14 per cent of the
variation in GP density, and between 2 per cent and 6 per cent of
specialist density, can be explained by the share of the population
with SPHI, when alternative motives are controlled for. Thus, the
insurance dualism intensifies regional disparities in supply for both
general practitioners and specialists.

Fairness, Sustainability, and Future Challenges for German Health Care

The German system, which fuses a large SHI system with a smaller
SPHI one, separates its population into the more affluent and typically
healthier (covered by SPHI) and the rest: the average income of those
covered by SPHI is more than double the average income of those in
SHI.[96] Hence, it is not surprising that many with the means to do so,
opt out of SHI in favour of SPHI. For those, SPHI premiums even tend
to be cheaper than the top contributions they would have to pay under
SHI, unless they are responsible for many dependents or bear adverse
health risks. Moreover, to attract enrollees, SPHI provides financial
incentives to health care providers (higher prices) for the preferential
treatment of the privately insured; although the effect of this is more
pronounced in community-based settings than in hospitals. Does
this kind of inequality have a negative effect on those within the
SHI? There is some limited evidence of such ill effects but it is not
determinative. Still, many on the political left criticize the opting out
of high incomes and "good risks" as a two-tier system.[97] The German

---

93   *SVR Gesundheit, supra* note 32 at para 441.

94   *Ibid.*

95   Verena Vogt, "The contribution of locational factors to regional variations in
      office-based physicians in Germany" (2016) 120:2 Health Pol'y 198.

96   Haun, *supra* note 88.

97   Karl Lauterbach, *Der Zweiklassenstaat. Wie die Privilegierten Deutschland ruinieren*
      (Berlin: Rohwolt, 2008).

Council of Economic Experts has also criticized the segmented insurance system for risk selection and misallocation of scarce resources.[98] The council has repeatedly suggested the integration of both schemes into a system where private insurance and SHI funds both offer a comprehensive basic health insurance, preferably financed through flat-rate contributions, and compete on a level playing field—much as is now the case in the Netherlands.[99]

Efforts toward integrating SHI and SPHI into one system have been and will be strongly opposed by SPHI stakeholders, and it would certainly evoke claims about its unconstitutionality.[100] Incremental change might however lead to convergence. The city state of Hamburg has reformed the allowance system for civil servants to provide for a free choice of SHI, and other states are likely to follow. At the same time, SPHI has, since 2012, sustained a net loss of insurees to SHI.[101] Demographic ageing, lower numbers of self-employed and civil servants, particularly high increases of premiums, and declining net interest rates for old-age provisions have challenged the SPHI model.[102] Moreover, shifting adverse risks to SHI has been made more difficult and recent reforms oblige private

---

98   Jacobs, *supra* note 15 at 67; Sachverständigenrat zur Begutachtung der gesamtwirtschaftlichen Entwicklung SVR Wirtschaft, *Erfolge im Ausland - Herausforderungen im Inland* (Köln: Bundesanzeiger Verlagsgesellschaft, 2004) [*SVR Wirtschaft, 2004*].

99   *SVR Witschaft, supra* note 98; Sachverständigenrat zur Begutachtung der gesamtwirtschaftlichen Entwicklung SVR Wirtschaft, *Die Finanzkrise meistern -- Wachstumskräfte stärken* (Köln: Bundesanzeiger Verlagsgesellschaft, 2008) [*SVR Wirtschaft, 2008*].

100   Constitutional claims are raised concerning the legislative competence of the federal government (art 74 of the German Constitution (GG)), the professional freedom of the private insurance funds (based on arts 12 and 14 GG), property rights of the insured (art 14 GG), and the right to include civil servants into social insurance (art 33 at para 5 GG). While claims concerning federal legislative competences and the inclusion of civil servants are unlikely to succeed, professional freedom and property rights can be constitutional obstacles to reform. The integration of SPHI into SHI would affect 75 per cent of the business volume of private health insurance. Further, property rights of about 200 billion active life reserves which belong to the insurance community rather than the individual insured cannot easily be integrated into SHI. At least, grandfathering clauses will apply to existing insurance contracts. See Wissenschaftlicher Dienst, *supra* note 7 at 10.

101   *Ibid.*

102   Greß & Heinemann, *supra* note 71 at 116.

insurance to provide social tariffs that are akin to conditions in SHI. Hence, the gradual integration of private insurance and SHI is likely to become an issue of future health reforms.

Lessons to be Learned from German "Two-Tier" Health Care

From one lens, the German health care system appears to be a showcase for at least a particular version of two-tier health care. The coexistence of SHI with a SPHI for part of the population provides many economic incentives for physicians and hospitals to privilege private patients. Indeed, evidence clearly points to shorter waiting times and more comprehensive medical treatment for those covered by SPHI. However, the vast majority of patients (and providers) are served and engaged by the SHI system. As concerns the effects of the two-tier system on providers, despite financial incentives generated by SPHI, physicians in Germany remain largely rooted in the SHI system. This is made possible through a combination of legal restrictions on physicians that secure their boundedness to the public system (e.g., minimum consultation hours per week), as well as by virtue of the vastly dominant size of the SHI market in relation to SPHI—a relation that is itself secured by regulations that allow for only limited possibilities for individuals to opt out of SHI and very restricted possibilities for those with SPHI to opt back into SHI when their income falls or their health deteriorates.

What can be made of all this complexity in design within the German system? Of the various lessons to be drawn from the German health care system, it bears emphasis, first and foremost, that its dualism does not owe to intelligent design but, rather, emerges from a historical evolution involving social risks incurred by industrialization, war, and economic depression, as well as ongoing political struggles among interest groups. That said, in its present form, the system has been rather successful at balancing the competing interests of employers, employees, unions, doctors, patients, etc., across the two tiers, suggesting that corporatist regulatory bodies are, at least in this context, quite effective at keeping the system afloat. The German experience therefore testifies to the possibility of allowing space for the private market within a predominantly social-insurance welfare-state universe. However, it is clear that the two can only coexist when regulation assures the pre-eminence and survival of the latter. It is, therefore, crucial for those countries looking to adopt a mixed-insurance system similar to that of Germany's that, in order for the advantages of SHI to come to the fore (e.g., timely and adequate access to care, expansive coverage, good hospital infrastructure, etc.), strong regulations must be in place to minimize access to SPHI, and also to control the effects of its incentives on providers; for example, regulation preventing extra-billing by SHI providers, regulation requiring SPHI carriers to carry the full risks of their insured population, and regulation requiring a certain amount of time and productivity devoted to SHI patients. Of course, this begs the question: In the absence of the particularities of German history, does such a two-tiered health care system even make sense given the high costs that regulation itself entails? This is a question, however, that can only be answered by future research.

CHAPTER 9

The Public-Private Mix in France: A Case for Two-Tier Health Care?

Zeynep Or and Aurélie Pierre

France has an employment-based statutory health insurance (SHI) system that guarantees universal access to a large basket of health care. While the SHI system imposes significant copayments, patients rely on a mix of public SHI and private complementary health insurance (CHI) schemes to defray these costs, leaving France with some of the lowest out-of-pocket expenditures in the OECD. Patients can choose from a mix of public and private providers without severe wait time problems, and the health status of the population ranks among the best in the world. At the same time, the French system is complex, with some apparent contradictions that raise concerns for solidarity, redistribution, and efficiency. Under pressure to curb growth in health expenditure without compromising equity of access and quality of care, the French funding model has been continuously fine-tuned. This chapter presents an overview of the key features of the hybrid public-private health care model in France, and assesses its advantages and principal weaknesses. By analyzing the French experience in regulating the system for sustaining its universal health care, we aim to provoke reflection about the role of private insurance and private suppliers in funding and providing health services. The chapter also discusses the extent to which the French system can be appropriately described as "two-tier." As we will see, although a hybrid public-private insurance system, the private tier is heavily regulated and its primary purpose is the covering of mandatory copayments imposed in the main public scheme. Moreover, through public subsidies and regulation, almost the entire population is covered by CHI. Nonetheless, there are some elements of a two-tier system. About 30 per cent of all the physicians and 50 per cent of specialists are able to extra-bill patients, allowing a measure of preferential access for those who have more generous CHI coverage or who are able to pay out of pocket. Also, despite the high density of doctors, there are profound inequalities in their distribution geographically. Therefore, CHI can be a means of faster access, especially to specialist care, in some areas.

1. Overview of the French Health System

The French health system is characterized by a hybrid public-private health insurance model, combining public and private insurance schemes that cover the entire population. The public scheme, a non-competitive statutory health insurance (SHI) model, covers 100 per cent of the resident population. It provides a comprehensive basket of care but requires cost sharing for all services, including doctor visits and hospitalizations. About 90 per cent of inpatient spending is covered by SHI, while this is about 65 per cent for outpatient physician visits and 70 per cent for medications. Prescriptions provided outside of hospital settings are reimbursed at 100 per cent, 65 per cent, or 15 per cent, depending on their therapeutic value. Therefore, about 95 per cent of the French population holds complementary private insurance, mostly for covering copayments. Patients have a large choice of public and private providers, wait times are not considered as a big problem, and the health status of the French population ranks among the best in the world.[1] There are three major principles—solidarity, liberalism, and pluralism—that define the values of the French health system and shape its organization and funding. Solidarity requires equal access to care by need and a financing system where the healthy and rich support the less wealthy and sick. This is assured via an obligatory, non-competitive statutory insurance scheme which provides standardized benefits. Liberalism means freedom for patients to choose their providers and for providers to choose their

---

1   OECD, *Health at a Glance 2017: OECD Indicators* (Paris: OECD, 2017) [OECD, 2017].

place and way of practice. Pluralism relates to health care delivery options, with a wide range of public and private providers and multiple supplementary private health insurance schemes. Despite a complex hybrid public-private funding system, France promotes equity in access to health care through a number of regulatory tools and policies. The equity principle has rooted ultimately in law and reinforced in all health plans as a strategic objective (article L. 1110-1 of the *Code de la santé publique*). Approximately 78 per cent of the total health care expenditure is funded by the SHI and 13 per cent is financed by private CHI schemes, making France's average out-of-pocket expenditures (around 9 per cent) among the lowest in the OECD.[2] Funding for the SHI comes mainly from income-based contributions from employers and employees, as well as, increasingly, through taxation. CHI is funded by individual insurance premiums, which are partly adjusted by the age of insured (as a proxy of health status), with subventions from the employers for wage and salary earners. Health care providers are also a mixture of public and private. The majority of the health care professionals are private contractors working on a fee-for-service basis. They usually contract with the SHI fund and respect the tariffs set at the national level. Private hospitals play an essential role in care provision, especially in providing surgery. About 55 per cent of all surgery and 25 per cent of obstetric care are provided by private for-profit hospitals. Private hospitals also contract with the SHI and are paid by regulated tariffs set at the national level.

This plurality in care provision and funding, together with a high degree of "liberty" for patients and providers, creates its own problems: the system is expensive, complex, and fragmented in its organization and funding. Ensuring equity in access to care between socio-economic groups and geographical regions is an ongoing struggle. Promoting a universal health system built on a mix of public and private funding and provision raises numerous challenges that have required continuous regulation of health care markets.

2   *Ibid.*

2. A Distinctive Hybrid Public-Private Health Insurance System

In France, the funding for health care comes from a mixture of public and private health insurance schemes reimbursing the same benefit package. Public health insurance covers a large range of services, but always leaves a part of the cost to patients. Hence, private health insurance is mostly a complementary health insurance in the sense that it typically covers the cost left to patients for services offered by the public health insurance. Different from other countries such as Australia and Ireland, private health insurance is not primarily used for getting faster access to some treatments or jumping public-sector queues since there are no apparent waiting lists in France, and waiting times are not considered a major problem as in other countries, such as in Australia and Canada.[3] CHI is not considered as a means to obtain higher-quality services, either, since public hospitals are rated highly and public insurance also covers services from private providers. Therefore, France stands out from other countries with similar public-private insurance schemes (such as Switzerland, Germany, South Korea) by the fact that private insurance mostly reimburses a portion of the cost of services that are included in the public insurance "benefit basket"[4]. The role of private insurance in reducing financial burden of care is essential since there is no cap on out-of-pocket expenditure of patients, as in some countries. This unique place of private health insurance is reflected in the high complementary insurance coverage in the general population (95 per cent) and, compared to similar countries, the high share of health care expenditure financed by private insurance.[5-6]

This two-layer insurance scheme allows the French population to have, on average, one of the lowest rates of out-of-pocket expenditures among OECD countries (about 9 per cent of health expenditure). Given that out-of-pocket payments are the least redistributive or the most unequal mechanism for financing health care, we can say that this second layer of private insurance, which is added to a mandatory

---

3   Patients are three times less likely to report forgone care because of long waits than the EU27 average. See Karine Chevreul et al, "France health system review" (2015) 17:3 Health Systems Transition 19.

4   The list of services, products, and drugs reimbursed by the SHI.

5   OECD 2017, *supra* note 1.

6   *Ibid*.

public protection (78 per cent of the total expenditure), reduces the direct costs of health care for households and contributes to equity in access.

However, public and private health insurances are based on different principles. Private CHI is by nature based on contractual freedom, financed mainly on the basis of risk (age) without considering ability to pay, variable in its guarantees, etc. Therefore, it is intrinsically less equal than public insurance and challenges the solidarity and equity goals of the social protection in France. In the following sections, we present the roles and functioning of public and private insurances and then discuss the challenges of such a hybrid system to attain equity and solidarity goals.

2.1 The First Tier: Universal Statutory Public Health Insurance

Since its creation in 1945, public health insurance in France has been based on two founding principles, namely, access to care depending on need, not income (the principle of horizontal equity), and solidarity between high- and low-income classes for financing the system (vertical equity). The principle of horizontal equity is reflected in compulsory and universal public insurance (i.e., SHI), resulting in solidarity between the healthy and the sick, the latter receiving care according to their medical needs and not according to their financial contribution to the system. The principle of vertical equity is reflected in the progressive nature of financial contributions to SHI, which are proportional to income with a higher contribution for wealthier individuals. Hence, the financing of SHI comes from a mix of income-based social contributions paid by employees and employers and, increasingly, from general taxation revenues.[7] Supplemental revenue is also sourced in specific taxes upon, for example, alcohol, cars, tobacco, and pharmaceutical companies. SHI is compulsory and universal for all individuals who work or reside regularly in France. It is provided under various insurance schemes, with automatic enrollment determined by employment status (wage

---

7   Since 1998, as a result of attempts to broaden the social-security system's financial base, employees' payroll contributions have been gradually replaced by a dedicated tax called the "general social contribution" (*contribution sociale généralisée*) based on total income rather than only on earned income, as was previously the case. See Helene Barroy et al, "Sustaining Universal Health Coverage In France: A Perpetual Challenge" (Discussion Paper, The World Bank, 2014), 91323 [World Bank, 2014].

earners, self-employed, farmers and agricultural employees, students, etc.). Individuals cannot choose their scheme or insurer, and cannot opt out. Thus, there are no competing health insurance markets for public health coverage in France. In 2000, universal medical coverage (Couverture maladie universelle de base, known since 2016 as *Protection universelle maladie*) was implemented in order to provide public health insurance to the 2 per cent of individuals who were not covered under any scheme given their employment status (e.g., those who have never worked). Three main SHI schemes cover about 97 per cent of the population. The largest one, known as the *Régime général*, insures wage and salary earners and their dependents, and covers about 85 per cent of the population. The two other schemes, covering self-employed (Régime social des indépendants) and farmers and agricultural employees (Mutualité sociale agricole), together cover about 12 per cent of the population[8]. In addition, sixteen small schemes cover specific professional categories (e.g., miners and clergy), representing 1 per cent of the population (see fig. 9.1). Since 2004, a federation of sickness funds (Union national des caisses d'assurance maladie; UNCAM) brings together the three

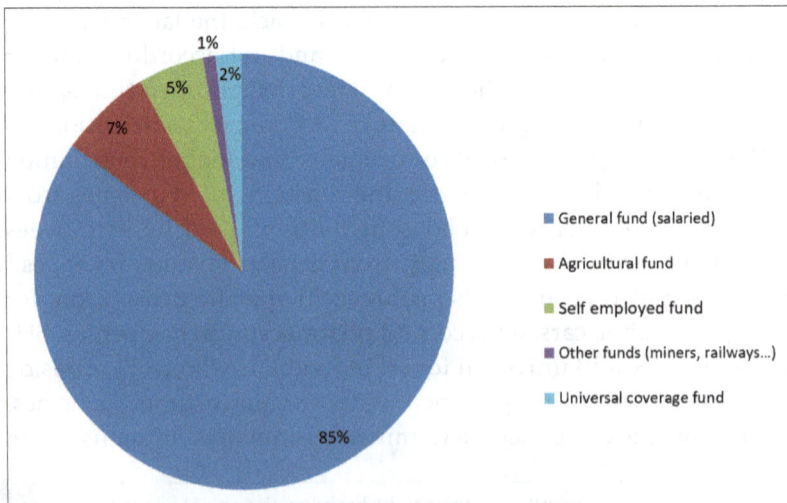

Figure 9.1. Statutory health insurance: Population coverage by affiliation, 2014
Source: World Bank, 2014, *supra* note 7 at 6.

---

8   Since 2019, the Régime social des indépendants" named now "La sécurité sociale des indépendants" is also managed by the *Régime général*.

major schemes at the national level, and is now the unique representative of all the insured in negotiations with the government and health care providers. The director of the UNCAM is nominated by the government and holds the ultimate decision-making power.[9]

Although there are several distinct insurers within the core SHI scheme, they have been gradually harmonized over time. Currently, all SHI insurers provide the same basket of services and goods. The standard benefit package under the SHI system covers a wide range of goods and services: inpatient hospital care (both in private and public hospitals), rehabilitation, home care, prescription drugs, physician visits, cost of transport, and all services and drugs prescribed by doctors, including care by paramedical professionals (nurses, physiotherapists, speech therapists, etc.). The SHI covers about 78 per cent of the total cost of the services and goods.[10] This goes up to 92 per cent for hospital care, 65 per cent for ambulatory treatments, and 45 per cent for drugs and medical goods, including optical and dental devices.[11] In general, patients are expected to pay the cost of ambulatory services at the point of service and then claim reimbursement from their insurance funds. The SHI reimbursements are based on predefined rates (negotiated tariffs) and are the same for all schemes.

Finally, there is also a fully state-funded scheme (*Aide médicale d'État*) which provides access to a standard benefit package for illegal immigrants. It is means-tested, and applicants must be resident for more than three months in the French territory. As of 2010, 227,705 people benefitted from the scheme.[12]

2.2 The Second Private Tier: Complementary Health Insurance

While the public SHI benefit package is comprehensive, it relies heavily on cost sharing for all of the services provided. People are therefore encouraged to enroll in private complementary health insurance (CHI) to limit costs that are not reimbursed by SHI. Patients' co-payments are defined as a percentage of regulated prices

---

9   The director of UNCAM negotiates multi-year contracts with the state defining the objectives and governing rules for the SHI.

10   France, Ministères des solidarités et de la santé, *Les dépenses de santé en 2017 — Résultats des comptes de la santé, 2018* (France: Panoramas de la DREES, 2018) [DREES, 2018].

11   *Ibid.*

12   World Bank, 2014, *supra* note 7.

and vary according to the type of care: from 10 per cent of regular fees for hospital care to 30 per cent for physician visits, and from 35 per cent to 85 per cent for (approved) prescription drugs, which are evaluated and listed in a public formulary.[13] In addition, there are a number of small deductibles concerning physician visits, paramedical procedures, drugs, and medical transport (see the list of deductibles in table 9.1). The deductibles generally are not reimbursed by the CHI,[14] but the total amount spent is capped (at a maximum of €50 per year for medications and €50 for consultations). Otherwise, there is no overall spending cap for out-of-pocket payments, and patients can face extra-billing from certain physicians (especially specialists) and for dental and optical devices, as we discuss in the next section.

Table 9.1. List of flat rate payments and deductibles

Types of services/goods	Flat rates	Limit
Flat-rate payments, not covered by CHI		
GP/specialist consultation	€1/visit	€50/year per person
Deductibles		
Drugs (prescriptions)	€0.5 /package	€50/year per person
Ancillary services	€0.5/procedure	
Medical transportation	€2/transport	
Usually covered by CHI		
Lab or radiography tests over €120	€24	none

Source: Isabelle Durand-Zaleski, "The French Health Care System," online: *The Commonwealth Fund* <international.commonwealthfund.org/countries/france/>.

As a result, about 95 per cent of the French population hold a CHI policy.[15] CHI policies can be purchased either through an

---

13   The reimbursement level by SHI is determined by the effectiveness of a given drug and the gravity of the disease treated: 100 per cent for rare, highly effective or expensive drugs (e.g., for cancer); 65 per cent, 35 per cent, or 15 per cent for diminishing therapeutic value, respectively. Drugs evaluated as ineffective are not reimbursed by the SHI.

14   The public insurance fund provides tax benefits to private insurers respecting these rules.

15   Nicolas Célant, Stéphanie Guillaume & Thierry Rochereau, "L'enquête santé européenne — Enquête santé et protection sociale (EHIS-ESPS) 2014" (September 2017), online (PDF): *L'Institut de recherche et documentation en économie de la santé (IRDES)* <https://www.irdes.fr/recherche/rapports/566-enquete-sante-europeenne-ehis-enquete-sante-et-protection-sociale-esps-2014.pdf>.

employer (i.e., collective contracts) for private-sector employees and their dependants or individually (i.e., an individual contract) for public-sector employees, self-employed individuals, and those unemployed. Collective CHI contracts, partly paid by the employer, have since 1979 been subsidized via tax and social contribution exemptions. CHI premiums vary depending on the age of the policyholder or on the average age of the pool of those insured for contracts obtained via an employer (where the premiums are uniform for all insured persons under the same contract). Those enrolled in individual CHI market—students, civil servants, the self-employed, unemployed, retired—are free to buy (or not) a CHI and choose their level of coverage. Except in the case of specific exemptions, subscription to collective CHI has been required by law for all private-sector employees since 2016.[16] Because of the bargaining power of employers and a high concentration of individuals with good health risks (e.g., younger, of working age), collective CHI contracts are more advantageous than individual ones in terms of guarantees and premiums. Thus, at equivalent coverage level, premiums for collective contracts are often lower than for individual contracts, even before the contribution made to the premium cost by the employer. Until 2016, about 60 per cent of CHI were individual contracts while 40 per cent were collective contracts. The rate of collective contracts is expected to reach to 50 per cent post the 2016 reform.[17]

Historically, CHI has focused on reimbursing *tickets modérateur*, i.e. copayments left to patients. CHI plans usually offer added coverage for medical goods and services that are poorly covered by the public scheme, especially for dental and optical devices. Some CHI plans *also cover* a part (or the totality) of extra-billing charges (*dépassement d'honoraires*) asked by some professionals. In general, collective contracts are more generous in reimbursing extra-billing charges,[18]

---

16   Carine Franc & Aurélie Pierre, "Restes à charge élevés: Profils d'assurés et persistance dans le temps." "Compulsory private complementary health insurance offered by employers in France: implications and current debate" (2015) 119:2 Health Pol'y 111.

17   Aurélie Pierre & Florence Jusot, "The likely effects of employer-mandated complementary health insurance on health coverage in France" (2017) 121:3 Health Pol'y 321.

18   France, Ministères des solidarités et de la santé, *La complémentaire santé: Acteurs, bénéficiaires, garanties, 2016* by Muriel Barlet, Magali Beffy & Denis Raynaud (France: Panoramas de la DREES, 2016); France, Ministères des solidarités et de

although recently these reimbursements have been regulated by the government in order to reduce the cost of extra-billing (see section 5). Some CHI contracts may also offer extended benefit coverage for goods and services that are not included in the SHI benefit basket (such as surgery for myopia) and/or provide access to private amenities (such as private hospital rooms).

The French CHI market is quite competitive. Around five hundred providers offer different kinds of CHI policies. Insurers can be gathered into three types.[19] First, *non-profit mutual insurance companies* (known as *mutuelles*), which have traditionally dominated the health insurance market and cover approximately 60 per cent of the insured, mostly by individual CHI contracts. Second, *non-profit provident institutions*, which are jointly managed by representatives of employers and employees and offer almost exclusively collective contracts; hence, they cover mainly working-age individuals (about 15 per cent of the population is insured via *provident institutions*). And last, *private for-profit insurance companies*, which introduced "health care" more recently in their insurance portfolio and now cover around 25 per cent of the CHI beneficiaries (mostly individual contracts). These three types of providers operate under distinct regulatory schemes.[20] However, differences between their premiums have diminished over time because of market competition.[21]

3. System Maintained by a Rich Mixture of Public-Private Providers

This hybrid health insurance model stimulates the diversity of health care providers in the system. With more than 3.4 physicians and 7.8 nurses per 1,000 population, France has relatively sufficient health human resources.[22] Access to specialist care in hospitals is relatively easier than in many OECD countries. Indeed, patients are not systematically asked for a referral from a general practitioner

---

la santé, *La complémentaire santé: Acteurs, bénéficiaires, garanties, 2019* by Muriel Barlet et al (France: Panoramas de la DREES, 2019).

19   *Ibid.*

20   *Mutuelles* are regulated by the *code de mutualité*, non-profit provident institutions are regulated by the social-security code, and private insurance companies by the commercial insurance code.

21   Barlet, Beffy & Raynaud, *supra* note 17.

22   OECD, 2017, *supra* note 1.

in order to visit a specialist despite recent reforms encouraging patients to use GPs as gatekeepers. Health care providers (health care professionals and hospitals), both public and private, contract with SHI funds, which act as a single payer, and generally respect the prices set via national negotiations. Therefore, one's treatment may be funded by the SHI public payer but delivered by a for-profit facility. Historically, health care in France is organized around four principles delineated by law: confidentiality of medical information, freedom of practice for physicians, patient's free choice of provider, and office-based fee-for-service practice in the ambulatory sector. Doctors are free to choose their place of practice while patients have free access to any physician or any facility, either public or private, with no limit on the number of doctors seen or the frequency of visits. However, some of these principles have been challenged with recent reforms in order to control escalating health care costs and chronic problems with unequal geographic distribution of doctor supply.[23]

Ambulatory care is mainly provided by private, self-employed health professionals (doctors, nurses, dentists, medical auxiliaries) working in their own individual practice or in health/medical centres and hospitals. Doctors working in the ambulatory sector, and those in private hospitals, negotiate with the SHI and are paid according to a national fee-for-service schedule. The official tariffs for reimbursement are set via a formal national negotiation process between the government, the union of SHI funds, the union of CHI schemes, and unions of health professionals. Doctors who agree to charge on the basis of the nationally negotiated fee (such doctors are known as "sector 1" contractors) in return get their social contributions (including pension) paid by the SHI fund. Some doctors and dentists are authorized by SHI to charge higher fees (i.e., "sector 2") based on their level and experience. Doctors working as sector 2 contractors are free to charge higher fees but must purchase their own pension and insurance coverage. The creation of sector 2 contractors in 1980 aimed to reduce the cost of social contributions for the SHI fund, but it did not have the expected impact

23   France, Cour des Comptes, *La médecine libérale de spécialité: Contenir la dynamique des dépenses, améliorer l'accès aux soins*, in Rapport sur l'application des lois de financement de la sécurité sociale (Paris: Cour des Comptes, 2017) [Cour des Comptes].

and the demand for the sector was much higher than predicted. Consequently, access to sector 2 has been limited since 1990; each year only 1,000 new doctors are allowed to work in sector 2. In 2012, about half of specialists and 85 per cent of generalists were working in sector 1, adhering to the national tariffs, but their distribution is uneven.[24] Membership in one sector or another is not an indicator of medical competence.

Extra-billing in France

Sector 1: The physician is required to bill in accordance with statutory tariffs set out in the national agreements with SHI insurers. Sector 1 doctors can only extra-bill above these amount in a few limited circumstances. In exchange for applying the statutory rates, sector 1 doctors get a part of their compulsory social contributions (including for pension) paid by SHI.

Sector 2: The physician is permitted to extra-bill any amount he or she wishes. The amount that is being extra-billed is not covered by SHI but may be covered by a CHI policy. Until 1990, physicians could choose which sector to join (1 or 2). The popularity of sector 2 led the government to restrict entry. Section 35.1 of the 2011 medical convention lists the type of physicians who are able to join sector 2:[25]

- former medical chiefs of clinics in universities,
- former hospital assistants,
- physicians or surgeons for the army,
- hospital practitioners appointed permanently, and
- part-time practitioners of hospitals with at least five years of experience.

The difference between sector 1 and sector 2 fees has been diminishing since 2012 with the creation of an observatory of tariffs by the SHI. In 2016, the average sector 2 fees for physicians was about 52 per cent higher than conventional tariffs, but there is a high degree of variation across regions, with over-billing rates varying between 10 per cent (for Cantal) and 115 per cent (for the Paris area). There are also strong variations across specialties, with gynecologists, rheumatologists, and psychiatrists asking on average 70 per cent to 100 per cent over the regulated tariff.[26]

---

24   France, Ministères des solidarités et de la santé, *Portrait des professionnels de santé, 2016* by Muriel Barlet & Claire Marbot (France: Panoramas de la DREES, 2016).

25   *Arrêté du 22 septembre 2011 portant approbation de la convention nationale des médecins généralistes et spécialistes*, JO, 11 July 2016.

26   L'assurance Maladie, "Dépassements d'honoraires des médecins: Une tendance à la baisse qui se confirme" (29 November 2017), online (PDF): *Ameli.fr pour les assurés* <http://www.ameli.fr/fileadmin/user_upload/documents/Observatoire_des_pratiques_tarifaires.pdf>.

Extra-billings in hospital settings

Approximately 40 per cent of hospital specialists are self-employed, working in private practice or private clinics, and an additional 13 per cent of specialists have mixed practices (seeing patients in their private offices and working shifts in hospitals). There is no regulation against extra-billing in a hospital setting (unless it is for a situation that requires urgent care). Until recently, there was little information on the extra fees charged in hospitals, but some reports have shown that extra-billing charges, although less frequent, can be up to four times higher than regulated prices in hospital settings.[27] In the past couple of years, the SHI (via the observatory of tariffs) has been following up more closely the physicians who are charging very high prices compared to the average. Also, a health directory which informs the general public on doctor fees in hospitals has been created now (annuairesante.ameli.fr). Patients can check the amount of extra fees asked by the specialists before choosing a hospital. According to the observatory of tariffs, different measures introduced by the SHI have been successful in containing extra fees in hospitals; the fees were (on average) about 45 per cent over the regulated fees in 2016, versus 80 per cent in 2005. But there is no direct information on actual out-of-pocket payments of patients at hospital.

Inpatient care is delivered by a large number of public, private for-profit, and non-profit hospitals. While the total number of hospital beds has decreased over the past decade, France still has 6.3 hospital beds per 1,000 inhabitants.[28] This is more than double the number of hospital beds per capita than in Canada (2.6 beds).[29] Patients can freely choose between public and private providers without needing a referral. Private hospitals also contract with the SHI fund and are paid by activity (measured by diagnostic-related groups, DRGs) based on regulated prices.

Public hospitals have the legal obligation of assuring continuity of care, which means providing twenty-four-hour emergency care, the obligation of non-discrimination (i.e., to accept any patient who seeks treatment), and to take part in activities related to national/regional public health priorities. They represent 60 per cent of all hospitals and 65 per cent of all acute inpatient beds. The private for-profit sector represents 25 per cent of all inpatient beds and is specialized mostly in elective surgery. The market share of private

---

27 "Dépassements d'honoraires: le "match" public — privé" (2014), online: *France Assos Santé* <https://www.france-assos-sante.org/2015/01/16/depassements-dhonoraires-le-match-public-prive/>.

28 OECD Health Statistics, "Hospital Beds" (2017), online: *OECD Data* <https://data.oecd.org/healtheqt/hospital-beds.htm> [OECD Health Statistics, 2017].

29 *Ibid.*

hospitals depends heavily on the type of hospital activity. About 55 per cent of all surgery and 25 per cent of obstetric care are provided by private for-profit hospitals. Their market share goes up to more than 80 per cent in some areas of elective ambulatory surgery, such as eye surgery (cataracts in particular), ear surgery, and endoscopies. However, certain complex care/procedures are provided almost exclusively by public hospitals; for example, in the case of stroke care, burn treatment, or surgery for multiple traumas. Finally, private not-for-profit hospitals are more specialized in medium- to long-term care; they represent about 8 per cent of acute-care activity. Three-quarters of these hospitals have a special agreement with the state, and they have the same engagement as public hospitals for providing "public services," such as continuous care. In return, they are eligible for public subsidies.

4. Measures for Avoiding a Two-Tier System

France's heavy reliance on CHI for coverage of copayments, together with a high degree of independence and choice for both providers and patients, has required several additional mechanisms to ensure equity of access to care and cost containment. First, given the importance of cost sharing, from its very inception the French system introduced protective mechanisms, initially to reduce the financial burden of care for patients suffering from long-term and costly illnesses, and later for those with very low incomes and, gradually, the entire population. Second, the prices of all health care services, drugs, and such are vigorously monitored and regulated in order to control the growth of health care costs. Third, since access to the private insurance market is inequitable, a mixture of regulatory measures and financial incentives is used for reducing the risk selection and dumping of patients by private insurers. Finally, CHI providers are given incentives to support public-sector objectives and policies for controlling the cost and quality of health care.

4.1 Exemptions for Chronic and Costly Illnesses

A long-term illness exemption scheme, called *Affection Longue Durée* (ALD), created at the inception of SHI in 1945, aims to reduce the financial burden of medical care for beneficiaries suffering from a list of long-term and costly chronic conditions. Initially introduced to cover four groups of diseases (cancer, tuberculosis, poliomyelitis, mental illness), the scheme was extended over time and now covers thirty-two groups of diseases. Irrespective of their income status, patients are exempted from the copayments (*tickets modérateurs*) concerning treatments associated with these conditions. Nevertheless, they still have to pay any fees linked to extra-billings and deductibles. About 90 per cent of the health care expenditure of ALD beneficiaries are funded by the SHI (compared to 61.5 per cent on average for the rest of the population).

In 2016, over ten million individuals were covered by the ALD scheme, representing about 17 per cent of SHI beneficiaries and accounting for roughly 60 per cent of health expenditures reimbursed by the SHI. The number of ALD beneficiaries has continuously increased in the last decade (10.4 billion in 2016 versus 8 billion in 2005). Expenditures linked to ALD recorded an average annual growth rate of 4.9 per cent over the period 2005–2010, versus 1.8 per cent for other health expenditures,[30] but the average share of public insurance in financing health expenditure has remained stable over the past fifteen years (around 77 per cent) because of improved management of the drug benefit basket and the introduction of deductibles for certain services in 2005.

4.2 Supporting Complementary Health Insurance for Low-Income Groups

Given the constraints on public resources for increasing SHI funding, public policy has primarily focused on supporting different population groups to purchase CHI. For decades, several measures have been introduced for extending CHI coverage, first to low-income populations, then to the entire population. Since January 2016, all employers are required to offer CHI contracts to their employees and pay at least 50 per cent of their premiums (as per the *Accord national interprofessionnel*, ANI).[31] Two specific schemes were introduced in 2000 and 2005, respectively, for supporting low-income

---

30   Paul Dourgnon, Zeynep Or & Christine Sorasith, "L'impact du dispositif des affections de longue durée (ALD) sur les inégalités de recours aux soins ambulatoires entre 1998 et 2008" (January 2013), online (PDF): *L'Institut de recherche et documentation en économie de la santé (IRDES)* <https://www.irdes.fr/Publications/Qes2013/Qes183.pdf>.

31   The reform also extended the portability of the private insurance for the unemployed up to twelve months after the end of their last job. See Franc & Pierre, *supra* note 15.

individuals to acquire CHI. The first, the universal complementary health coverage (*Couverture maladie universelle complémentaire*, CMU-C), a state-funded insurance scheme, allows people whose monthly income is effectively 20 per cent below the poverty line to benefit, free of charge, from a CHI contract. The CMU-C covers 100 per cent of negotiated prices of all drugs and services included in the benefit package of SHI (no copayment required). It further covers, albeit modestly, a number of dental and orthodontic treatments and eye glasses, which are poorly reimbursed by the SHI, like any other private CHI (e.g., €250 for a tooth crown, €500 for orthodontic treatment). Moreover, patients are exempted from upfront payments, and physicians are not allowed to extra-bill CMU-C patients. CMU-C covered approximately 5.5 million persons in 2017[32]. The second measure is public vouchers for buying CHI contracts (*Aide à la complémentaire santé*, or ACS). It aims to subsidize private CHI for low-income individuals who are not eligible for the CMU-C. The target population includes individuals with incomes up to 35 per cent above the CMU-C eligibility line in 2016. ACS provides cash support in the form of vouchers that can be only used to buy a CHI contract. Since 2013, the beneficiaries of ACS have also been exempted from extra-billing. By law,[33] physicians cannot deny care to a patient enrolled under CMU-C and ACS and cannot ask more than the negotiated tariffs. However, a few studies showed that some physicians, especially sector 2 specialists, nonetheless refuse appointments to CMU-C patients.[34]

Both these schemes are funded through specific taxes on private health insurance premiums (*taxe de solidarité additionnelle*; TSA), which amounted to €2 billion in 2012,[35] and, marginally, from taxes

---

32   Fonds CMU (2017), https://www.complementaire-sante-solidaire.gouv.fr/fichier-utilisateur/fichiers/2017_RA_VF.pdf

33   *Code de la sécurité sociale*, JO, 7 June 2019, s L162-1-14; *Code de la santé publique*, JO, 1 June 2019, art L1110-3.

34   Bénédicte Boisguérin, "Enquête auprès des bénéficiaires de la CMU — mars 2003" (2004) Ministère de L'emploi, du Travail et de la Cohésion Sociale & Ministère de la Santé et de la Protection Sociale Working Paper No 63; France, Ministères des solidarités et de la santé, *Analyse des attitudes de médecins et de dentistes à l'égard des patients bénéficiant de la Couverture Maladie Universelle — Une étude par testing dans six villes du Val-de-Marne* by Caroline Desprès & Michel Naiditch (France: DIES, 2006).

35   The additional solidarity tax is about 13 per cent for responsible contracts while it goes up to 20 per cent for other contracts.

on tobacco. In 2016, CMU-C and ACS schemes covered, respectively, 8 per cent and 1.9 per cent of the French population. However, the number of people eligible for these schemes are estimated to be higher: about 30 per cent of the individuals who are eligible to CMU-C and 60 per cent of those eligible to the ACS are not exercising their rights.[36] The national strategy against poverty presented by the government in September 2018 proposes, among other things, to merge these two schemes to simplify the system.

4.3 Price Regulations

The public-private mix in health care provision obliges the SHI fund to closely regulate prices of providers. In France, most of the health care providers are paid on a fee-for-service basis. Tariffs for physicians (whether they work in solo practice, groups practice, or a private hospital) are set nationally through a negotiation process between the insurance funds and different medical professions. Both public and private hospitals are paid under activity-based payment (using DRGs). Private hospitals also contract with the SHI and must respect regulated tariffs. Tariffs for private hospitals are usually lower than public ones (tariffs were first based on historical costs, but the gap has closed over time). Both sectors are regulated with the same price/volume control mechanism at the macro level to steer the activity growth by sector.[37] Prices of drugs included in the health insurance basket are also controlled rigorously, through structured negotiations with pharmaceutical companies and resellers to contain the overall cost of medications. Various common mechanisms, such as reference pricing, comparing prices in other countries, mandatory

---

36   "Fonds CMU — Rapport d'activité" (January 2010), online (PDF): *CMU* <https://www.complementaire-sante-solidaire.gouv.fr/fichier-utilisateur/fichiers/Rapport_activite_2009.pdf>; "Références - La lettre du Fonds de financement de la couverture maladie universelle" (January 2014), online (PDF): *CMU* <https://www.complementaire-sante-solidaire.gouv.fr/fichier-utilisateur/fichiers/ReferencesCMU54.pdf>; Sophie Guthmuller et al, "Comment expliquer le non-recours à l'Aide à l'acquisition d'une complémentaire santé ? Les résultats d'une enquête auprès de bénéficiaires potentiels à Lille en 2009" (February 2014), online (PDF): *L'Institut de recherche et documentation en économie de la santé (IRDES)* <https://www.irdes.fr/recherche/questions-d-economie-de-la-sante/195-comment-expliquer-le-non-recours-a-l-aide-a-l-acquisition-d-une-complementaire-sante.pdf>.

37   Zeynep Or, "Implementation of DRG Payment in France: Issues and recent developments" (2014) 117:2 Health Pol'y 146.

price discounts, volume-price regulation, and value-based pricing, have been used with some apparent success (see fig. 9.2).[38]

However, the presence of a sector 2, where physicians are not bound by nationally set tariffs, has required specific measures for controlling the prices in this sector.

- *Restrictions on extra-billings:* Section L162-1-14-1 of the social-security code and section 53 of the medical code of ethics requires that extra-billing be of a reasonable amount: "tact et mesure." However, until 2012, there was no regulatory or legislative definition of the term. This changed in 2012, when the Conseil national de l'ordre des médecins defined it as a fee exceeding three or four times the regulated prices.
- *Informing patients:* Section L1111-3 of the public health code requires physicians to inform their patients of all costs

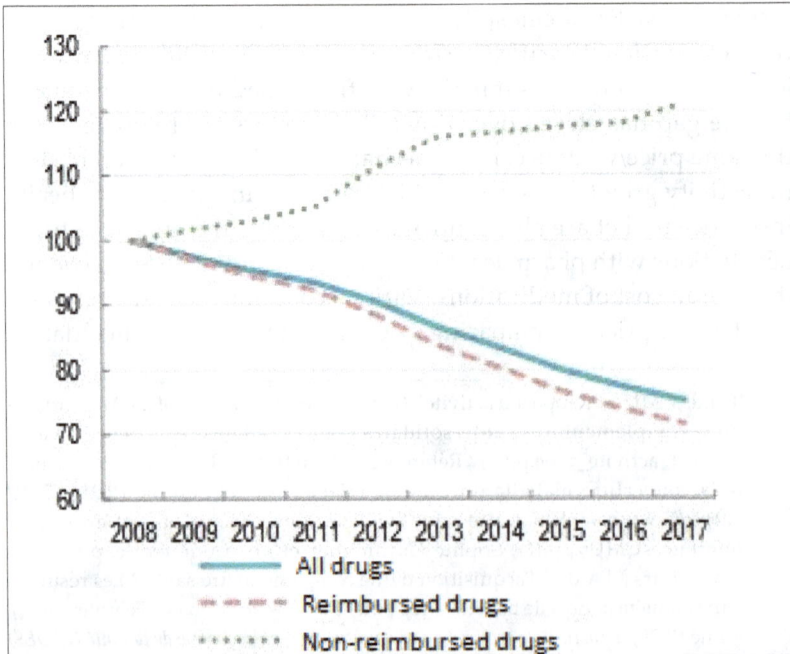

Figure 9.2. Trends in drug prices (2008=100).
Source: DREES, 2018, *supra* note 9.

---

38   DREES, 2018, *supra* note 9.

related to their visit: prices must be displayed inside medical practices and physicians must issue a receipt for any extra-billing exceeding €70 at the start of the appointment.[39] Nevertheless, this information is only available at the physician's practice. Patients cannot compare prices beforehand since there is no platform providing prices charged by sector 2 physicians.

- *Incentives to reduce extra-billings:* Since 2012, a voluntary contract (*Option pratique tarifaire maitrisée*) signed between SHI and sector 2 physicians encourage them to freeze their fees and not charge more than double the regulated tariffs. They are also asked to perform a share of their services at regulated SHI-tariff levels. In return, they receive a partial payment of social-security contributions usually reserved for sector 1 doctors (up to €4,300 per year on average).[40] In 2014, about 11,000 doctors had signed this contract.[41]

4.4 Regulation of CHI Market

The CHI market is, by definition, inequitable, since premiums increase according to an individual's risk levels (unhealthy and older individuals pay higher premiums). Moreover, private insurers are not required to pursue the system-wide efficiency and cost containment that is pursued by the public insurers/payers. Therefore, the CHI market in France is highly regulated, this is to foster public-sector objectives.[42] The primary objective is to limit the problems of access to insurance that may face high-risk individuals (e.g., low income, sick) in an unregulated market.[43] The second and increasingly

---

39 *Code de la santé publique*, JO, 1 June 2019, art L1111-3; France, Inspection générale des affaires sociales, *Evaluation de la place et du role des cliniques privées dans l'offre de soins* by Bartoli et al (France: 2012).

40 "L'exercice libéral de la médecine" (2017), online (PDF): *France Assos Santé, la voix des usagers* <https://www.france-assos-sante.org/publication_document/b-8-exercice-liberal-de-la-medecine-a-lhopital/>.

41 *Ibid.*

42 Michel Fromenteau, Vincent Ruol & Laurence Eslous, "Sélection des risques: où en est-on?" (2011) 31:2 Les Tribunes de la santé 63.

43 Thierry Lang et al, "Les inégalités sociales de santé: sortir de la fatalité" (December 2009), online (PDF): *Haut conseil de la santé publique* <hcsp.fr/Explore.cgi/avisrapportsdomaine?clefr=113>; Emmanuelle Cambois & Florence Jusot, "Ampleur, tendance et causes des inégalités sociales de santé et de mortalité en Europe: une revue des études comparatives" (2007) 2:3 Bulletin épidémiologique

prominent goal is to align CHI providers to support the SHI policies aimed at containing health care cost.

- *Tackling risk selection:* In an unregulated private insurance market, premiums go up with individual risk (and poorer health status), and for some health conditions, associated health expenditures can be, by definition, uninsurable.[44] Thus, as early as 1989, French authorities have required CHI providers to give a lifetime guarantee for anyone insured so that their premium cannot increase, upon renewal of a contract, above the premium offered to others in the same pool of insured for that contract (as part of the *loi Évin*). This law also aims to protect young pensioners, formerly covered by a collective contract, who may face increased insurance premiums in individual markets upon retirement. Moreover, in 2002, a tax reduction was applied to contracts in which the health status of the insured is not used as a variable of risk adjustment (selection) in defining the price. These contracts, called *contrats solidaires*, prohibit health questionnaires at the time the insurance is acquired.
- *Extending CHI coverage*: The expansion of CHI to a larger share of the population has been a constant objective among successive French governments for decades. Therefore, in addition to the specific schemes designed for low-income people (CMU-C and ACS), the French government has moved incrementally to ensure that all the workers have access to CHI coverage—first with tax incentives for private-sector employees and employers (since 1979), for the self-employed (since 1994), then by a mandate. Indeed, with the ANI, all private-sector employers must, as of 2016, offer CHI to all of their employees, and pay at least 50 per cent of their premium (they can choose to pay a higher share).[45] The idea is to secure and improve access to group CHI contracts known

---

hebdomadaire 10; Marcel Goldberg et al, "Les déterminants sociaux de la santé: apports récents de l'épidémiologie sociale et des sciences sociales de la santé" (2002) 20:4 Sciences sociales et santé 75.

44   Michael Rothschild & Joseph Stiglitz, "Equilibrium in competitive insurance markets: An essay on the economics of imperfect information" (1978) 90:4 J Econ 629.

45   *Loi relative à la sécurisation de l'emploi*, JO, 14 June 2013, art 1.

to be more advantageous than individual contracts because of risk pooling within employment groups. Moreover, in case of unemployment, individuals will benefit, free of costs, from the collective contract of their previous employer for up to twelve months. This agreement was introduced in response to the growing volatility in the labour market in order to protect the most precarious employees.[46] Also, employer-sponsored CHI contracts have to provide a higher minimum coverage concerning fees for dental and optical care (minimum of €100 for simple corrections, €150 for mixed, and €200 for complex corrections).

- *Controlling health-expenditure growth:* At the same time, SHI and successive governments have been constantly looking to regulate, legitimize, and enlarge the responsibility of the CHI scheme in controlling health expenditure. Copayments would, in theory, counter the problem of moral hazard— requiring patients to internalize some of the cost of care—but this effect is nullified when most of the population holds CHI-covering copayments. Therefore, while there is no restriction on what insurers are permitted to cover, in order to benefit from tax advantages and social contributions, CHI contracts have to respect certain conditions. These contracts, called *solidaires et responsables*, are designed to encourage responsible health care consumption. These contracts include various requirements designed to promote good medical practice. For example, they are not permitted to reimburse out-of-pocket payments imposed when patients visit an outpatient specialist directly (instead of using a GP as a gatekeeper) in order to support the voluntary gatekeeping reform introduced in 2004. Also, they cannot refund deductibles introduced in 2005 for controlling drug consumption, visits to health professionals, and for transportations.[47] In 2016, new constraints were introduced to limit differences in coverage levels between individual and collective contracts in order to reduce the impact of generous collective

---

46 Barlet, Beffy & Raynaud, *supra* note 18.

47 Monique Kerleau, Anne Fretel & Isabelle Hirtzlin, "Regulating Private Health Insurance in France: New Challenges for Employer-Based Complementary Health Insurance" (2009) Centre d'Economie de la Sorbonne Working Paper No 56.

contracts on health care prices. These contracts must now respect reimbursement ceilings for optical devices as well as extra-billings. These upper limits are intended to cap excess fees in sector 2, and also control prices of optical devices poorly regulated by the SHI. Today, almost all CHI contracts are defined as *solidaires et responsables*.[48]

5. Issues

5.1 Efficiency Concerns

Health is an important area of public spending in France. In 2017, health expenditure accounted for 11.5 per cent of the GDP, making it the third highest level of spending among the OECD countries. Despite the high contribution of CHI (compared to other countries), about 78 per cent of health expenditure is still paid publicly (see fig. 10.3).[49]

Therefore, in the past two decades, the rising cost of health care has been a major concern. While France has enjoyed relative success in controlling prices of health care services and pharmaceuticals through formal negotiations with health care providers and value-based pricing of drugs, low prices seem to have a limited impact on

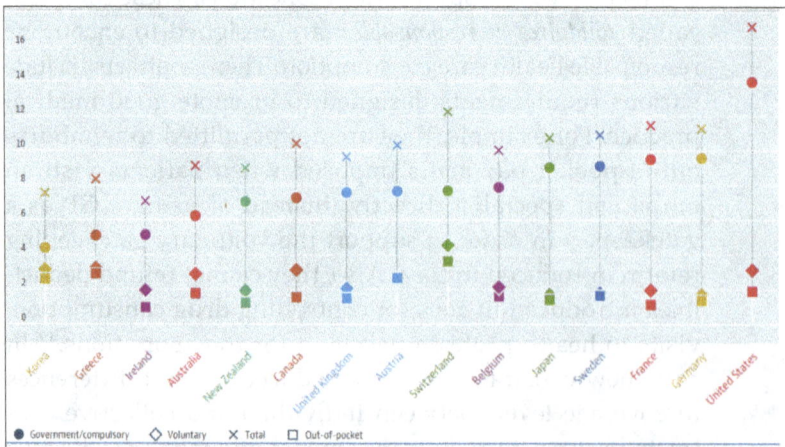

Figure 9.3. Health spending, percentage of GDP, 2017 (or latest available).
Source: OECD Health Statistics, 2017, *supra* note 28.

---

48   Barlet, Beffy & Raynaud, *supra* note 18; Barlet et al, *supra* note 18.
49   OECD Health Statistics, 2017, *supra* note 28.

health-expenditure growth. Health care providers tend to compensate for reduced revenues by increasing the volume of services they provide.[50] The lack of coordination between ambulatory, hospital, and social care has been recognized as a major drawback both in terms of cost control and quality of care. The fact that most providers work in solo practice—and with little collaboration between hospital, primary, and social care/services—means that patient care is fragmented and patients need to navigate a complicated system. Moreover, uncoordinated care, coupled with the high degree of independence and choice for both providers and patients, have been identified as key drivers of health care cost. Therefore, the latest reforms encourage group practice in primary care settings and testing alternative payment models for improving care provision and efficiency.

At the same time, the hybrid public-private insurance system, where private insurance complements and intersects with public funding for almost all types of care, generates a number of inefficiencies. The multiplicity of payers for the same basket of care does not always allow for an optimal use of resources: the generous coverage offered by some CHI contracts can be inflationary, and their reimbursement of copayments cancels the incentives initially sought to reduce moral hazard in the core public plan.[51]

Moreover, this combination of public-private insurance comes with a high management cost: France has the second highest administrative costs (6 per cent of the health spending) in the OECD, just after the United States, and almost half of this expenditure is related to CHI.[52]

5.2 Concerns for the Solidarity and Equity of the System

Despite the high share of public insurance in funding health expenditure, the important place of CHI in the financing of care will likely to induce social inequalities in health care coverage and, ultimately, in access to care. This is mostly due to the basic functioning of the

---

50   DREES, 2018, *supra* note 10.

51   Philippe Askenazy et al, "Pour un système de santé plus efficace" (2013) 8 Conseil d'Analyse Economique; Brigitte Dormont, Pierre-Yves Geoffard & Jean Tirole, "Refonder l'assurance maladie" (2014) 12 Conseil d'Analyse Économique; Pierre-Yves Geoffard, "L'AMO ne suffit plus à garantir un accès aux soins sans barrière financière" (2016) 49 Regards 157.

52   Thomas C Buchmueller & Agnes Couffinhal, "Private health insurance in France" (2004) OECD Health Working Paper No 12.

private insurance market, where premiums are based on individual risk without considering ability to pay, and guarantees (services covered) vary as a function of the bargaining power of payers. Despite the regulations limiting risk selection, CHI prices set on the basis of health risk (age) without considering ability to pay are less equitable. Thus, while only 5 per cent of the population lacked CHI in 2014, the rate was 16 per cent for the unemployed and 12 per cent for individuals in the lowest income quintile, despite the existence of CMU-C and ACS (see fig. 9.4).[53] The quality of coverage (in terms of services offered) also varies widely across contracts and across income groups. Since the premiums increase with the generosity of the CHI contract, it is more difficult for low-income groups to access a good CHI contract. Moreover, collective contracts, which are always more advantageous because of the employer's subsidy

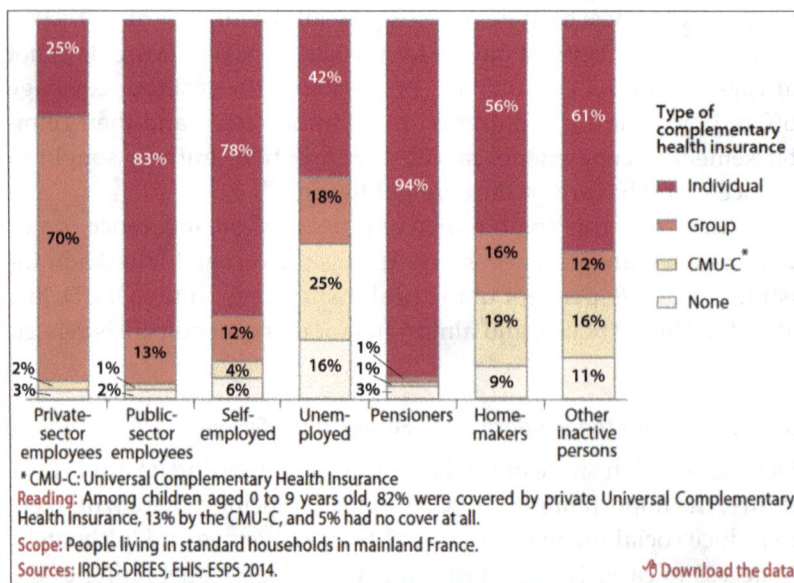

* CMU-C: Universal Complementary Health Insurance
Reading: Among children aged 0 to 9 years old, 82% were covered by private Universal Complementary Health Insurance, 13% by the CMU-C, and 5% had no cover at all.
Scope: People living in standard households in mainland France.
Sources: IRDES-DREES, EHIS-ESPS 2014.   ⬇ Download the data

Figure 9.4. Distribution of CHI coverage in 2014, by employment status.
Source: Marc Perronnin & Alexis Louvel, *supra* note 51.

53   Marc Perronnin & Alexis Louvel, "Complementary Health Insurance in 2014: 5 per cent Had no Cover and 12% of the Poorest 20% of Households Had no Cover" (January 2018), online (PDF): *L'Institut de recherche et documentation en économie de la santé (IRDES)* <https://www.irdes.fr/english/issues-in-health-economics/229-complementary-health-insurance-in-2014.pdf>.

to the premium and concentration of low risks, are not accessible for the most precarious and sickest individuals, who are outside of the labour market. As a result, good CHI contracts with better price and coverage are more often subscribed by the wealthier. Despite owning lower-quality CHI contracts, on average, individuals with lower income spend proportionally more of their income on private health insurance: up to 10 per cent of household income.[54]

Social inequalities in CHI coverage are particularly troubling given that the poorest individuals are often also the sickest.[55] Indeed, concentration of high out-of-pocket expenditures among those individuals with poor health status is a constant concern in France.[56] Although the reimbursement rates reflect the desire to better protect the sickest individuals (higher for hospital, lower for drugs), they do not cover all the financial risks associated with illness, which can be very high for some households. For example, in 2012, 1 per cent of the population paid an average of €4,971 per year for health care.[57] For certain benefits (especially dental care), which are only covered to a limited extent in the SHI package, out-of-pocket payments could be an important (especially for those who do not own CHI). However, studies show that out-of-pocket expenditure for health care covered in the SHI basket could also be a problem for patients with multiple, complex conditions, whether or not they benefit from the ALD scheme.[58] Individuals who have a chronic illness that are not enlisted for ALD can also face very high out-of-pocket payments.

---

54 Bidénam Kambia-Chopin et al, "Les contrats complémentaires individuels: quel poids dans le budget des ménages?" (April 2008), online (PDF): *L'Institut de recherche et documentation en économie de la santé (IRDES)* <www.irdes.fr/Publications/Rapports2008/rap1701.pdf>; France, Ministères des solidarités et de la santé, *Assurance maladie et complémentaires santé: Comment contribuent-elles à la solidarité entre hauts et bas revenus?* by Florence Jusot et al, (France: DREES, 2017).

55 Lang et al, *supra* note 43; Cambois & Jusot, *supra* note 41; Goldberg et al, *supra* note 43.

56 Pierre-Yves Geoffard & Grégoire de Lagasnerie, "Réformer le système de remboursement pour les soins de ville, une analyse par microsimulation" (2012) 455 Économie et statistique 89; Franc & Pierre, *supra* note 15.

57 France, Ministères des solidarités et de la santé, *Haut Conseil pour l'avenir de l'assurance maladie. Rapport annuel 2012* (France: Haut Conseil pour l'avenir de l'assurance maladie, 2012).

58 Franc & Pierre, *supra* note 16; Dourgnon, Or & Sorasith, *supra* note 30; Geoffard & Lagasnerie, *supra* note 56.

The solution proposed by successive governments to this concern has been to increase CHI coverage for a larger part of the population, including with public subsidies. Nevertheless, publicly subsidized CHI schemes, which aim on one hand to improve the equity of access and on the other to control cost escalation, are also a source of two-tier treatment in the system. Patients who are part of public schemes (CMU-C, ACS) that do not allow extra-billing can face difficulties in getting an appointment with some physicians. While it is illegal to refuse a patient because of his/her insurance status, some sector 2 doctors could refuse recipients of CMU-C or ACS, using different pretexts.[59]

5.3 Geographical Inequalities in Supply and Access

Notwithstanding the high level of human resources, the unequal geographical distribution of health workers, skewed to the well-off and city centres in urban areas, creates problems of access to care.

The "sacrosanct" principle of "freedom of installation"—that is, health care professionals can practice wherever they wish—results in an unequal distribution of health professionals across regions (see fig. 10.5).[60] The lack of specialists such as gynecologists, ophthalmologists, and anesthetists, as well as generalists in some areas, has become a serious policy concern in the past decade.[61]

While wait times for access to health care is generally considered as satisfactory (95 per cent of the French population can reach a primary-care doctor within fifteen minutes by car[62] and 50 per cent of GP appointments are obtained within forty-eight hours), there are wide variations across regions.[63] Despite the overall high number of specialists, wait times for consulting a specialist became a concern in

---

59   Caroline Després, Stéphanie Guillaume & Pierre-Emmanuel Couralet, "Le refus de soins à l'égard des bénéficiaires de la Couverture maladie universelle complémentaire à Paris" (2009), online (PDF): *CMU* <www.cmu.fr/fichierutilisateur/fichiers/refus_soins_testing2009_rapport.pdf>.

60   Cour des Comptes, *supra* note 23.

61   Sylvie Castaigne & Yann Lasnier, "Les déserts médicaux" (2017) 27 Les avis du Conseil économique, social et environnemental.

62   Magali Coldefy, Laure Com-Ruelle & Véronique Lucas-Gabrielli, "Distances et temps d'accès aux soins en France métropolitaine" (April 2011), online (PDF): *L'Institut de recherche et documentation en économie de la santé (IRDES)* <www.irdes.fr/Publications/2011/Qes164.pdf>.

63   France, Ministères des solidarités et de la santé, *La moitié des rendez-vous sont obtenus en 2 jours chez le généraliste, en 52 jours chez l'ophtalmologiste* by Christelle

recent years. A recent survey suggests that there are important disparities between the specialties: the average appointment wait time was forty-four days for gynecologists, fifty days for cardiologists, and eighty days for ophthalmologists.[64] This survey also suggests that, with the notable exception of dermatologists and ophthalmologists, most patients could get an appointment within a week if their problem was urgent or new, while those for regular checkups often wait three to four months. Nevertheless, these averages hide very different situations between regions. A large number of territories, mostly semi-urban and rural, do not have enough specialists, while other areas have too many. For the three specialties above, the average wait time can exceed six months in some rural zones, on the peripheries of large cities, and in small- and medium-sized municipalities, where physician density is the lowest.[65] A few reports have also shown that, in specializations where there is a shortage of providers, access to physicians who do not extra-bill patients is particularly difficult. For instance, in Île-de-France, for some specialties (e.g., cardiologists, gastroenterologists, gynecologists, pulmonologists) the wait times to visit a specialist who respect SHI tariffs is nearly double that for those who extra-bill.[66]

Several governments have tried to tackle the unequal geographic distribution of physicians and other health care professionals, but given the resistance from health care professionals, they mostly use financial incentives (tax incentives, financial provisions) to encourage physicians to set up practice in underserved areas. These instruments have had limited success in ensuring a fair distribution of human resources. But attempts to introduce quotas for controlling the further addition of doctors in oversupplied zones encounters strong resistance from physicians. More recently, encouraging group practice in primary care has been a lever for increasing the density of GPs in underserved areas, as well as for improving care coordination. Group practice appears to be more attractive for generalists than solo practice in rural or underserved areas.[67]

Millien, Hélène Chaput & Marie Cavillon, Études et Résultats, No 1085 (France: Panoramas de la DREES, 2018).

64   *Ibid.*
65   *Ibid.*
66   Cour des Comptes, *supra* note 23.
67   Guillame Chevillard et al, "Has the Diffusion of Primary Care Teams in France Improved Attraction and Retention of General Practitioners in Rural Areas?"

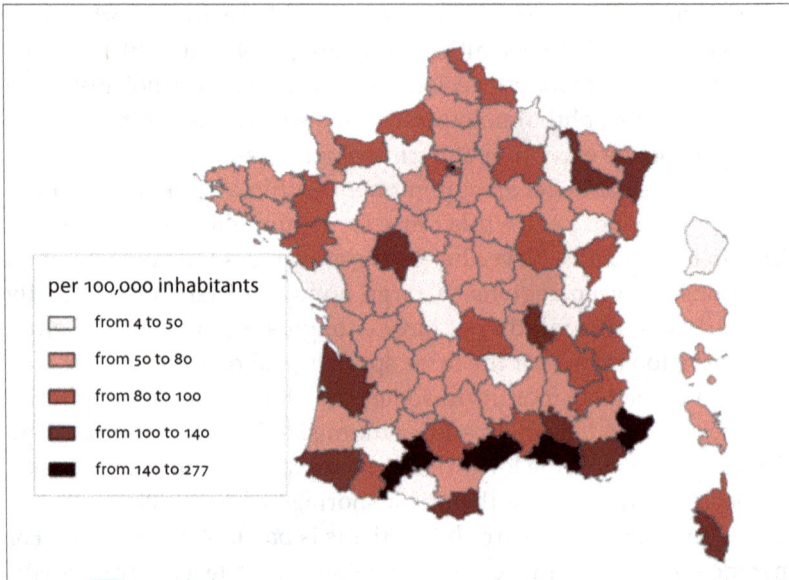

Figure 9.5. Density of specialists across French departments, 2016.
Source: Cour des Comptes, *supra* note 23.

6. Conclusion

The hybrid public-private model in France combines mandatory public insurance (SHI) with widespread (and increasingly mandatory and subsidized) private complementary insurance (CHI), covers effectively the entire French population for a comprehensive set of goods and services. The system requires patients to contribute to the cost of all services included in SHI, and relies heavily on private CHI to ensure access to care. The role of CHI is largely accepted by the public authorities, who have for decades encouraged the extension of CHI coverage, first to the lowest income groups, and gradually to the entire population. Given the increasing constraint on public resources, the private funding of basic health services via complementary insurance is considered as a necessity. However, the greater the entanglement and generalization of CHI, the greater the need for regulation and public intervention to counter the perverse effects of an unregulated insurance market, which is, by construction, less fair, not to mention the cost and complexity of multi-risk management.

Globally, France's experience suggests that reliance on private health insurance for financing essential health services is problematic for equity and solidarity in the system, as well as for cost containment. Complementary insurance is by nature based on contractual freedom, financed partly on the basis of risk without considering ability to pay, and variable in its guarantees. A number of public complementary schemes and regulatory measures were necessary over time to improve equitable access to care and to avoid a two-tier health care system. Therefore, the CHI market is closely controlled, via a mixture of regulatory measures and financial incentives, to reduce the difficulties that would otherwise face the sickest and the poorest in a competitive health insurance market. But pursuing a strategy to provide CHI for the entire population without controlling what is covered has proven to be problematic, both for ensuring equity of access and for cost-efficiency. Therefore, the content of CHI contracts are increasingly monitored and regulated in order to align them with public-sector objectives of controlling health care costs.

At the same time, the French model encourages plurality in health care provision, which relies on a mix of public and private providers. The high number of private hospitals funded by public insurance partly explains the relatively good results concerning waiting times, especially for elective surgery. Nevertheless, the high degree of autonomy (freedom of installation), together with dominant fee-for-service payment for health care providers, results in an unequal distribution of health professionals across regions, and creates problems of care coordination and access. To improve the efficiency and access to health care, new care models have been encouraged, with some promising results, which incentivize collaborative work in multidisciplinary group practices with alternative payment mechanisms.

Overall, the French model has some elements that can inspire the discussion on the role and place of private funding and provision in other countries facing public-budget pressures. The French experience suggests that privately provided health care can support a public health system, but the degree to which it creates a quality differential without endangering equity in access to care is heavily dependent on the way the private insurers and providers are managed, funded, and regulated. The elements of two-tier in France is mainly linked to the fact that there are profound inequalities in the distribution of health professionals across the country, and that many physicians are allowed to extra-bill patients for providing essential services. In areas where access to a physician is difficult, private complementary insurance gives preferential access to those who own a better (more generous) CHI contract, one that covers high extra-billing costs.

CHAPTER 10

Embracing Private Finance and Private Provision: The Australian System

Fiona McDonald and Stephen Duckett

Litigation has commenced in Canada challenging the aspects of the legislation that instantiates the *Canada Health Act* on the basis that a public monopoly in delivering medically necessary services has resulted in Canadians experiencing long wait times for health care, contrary to their *Charter* rights.[1] If the *Cambie* challenge is successful, in whole or in part, federal, provincial, and territorial governments will need to rethink Canadian medicare. In considering health care reforms, they will likely examine how other similar national jurisdictions manage blended public and private health systems. One such country they will likely examine is Australia, given the similarities between the two countries (discussed below). The Australian health system is characterized by a complex division of responsibilities and roles shared between the federal (the Commonwealth of Australia) and state governments,[2] as well as a complicated interplay between public and private sectors (both in terms of funding and delivery). This chapter is divided into two

---

1   See Colleen Flood & Bryan Thomas, "A Successful Charter Challenge to Medicare? Policy Options for Canadian Provincial Governments" (2018) Health Economics, Pol'y & L 1 at 2 [Flood & Thomas]; Colleen Fuller, "Cambie Corp. Goes to Court: The Legal Assault on Universal Health Care" (2015) Canadian Centre for Policy Alternatives at 11–13, online: *Canada Centre for Policy Alternatives* <www.policyalternatives.ca/publications/reports/cambie-corp-goes-court>.

2   We will use the term "state" to refer to both state and territory governments.

parts. In the first part, we analyze constitutional and political factors that have contributed to the federal government financially supporting (directly and indirectly) both public and private health systems. A constitutional provision, prohibiting the "civil conscription" of health professionals, places some limits on the federal government's ability to control health professionals' practice, particularly the extent to which they can work in a duplicative private tier. Politically, one of the major political groupings in Australian politics—a coalition between the Liberal and National Parties (centre-right and right-leaning parties) (the Coalition)—opposed the introduction of a universal public health system and its continuation until the 1990s. The Coalition has now conceded that it cannot survive politically if it continues its opposition to the public financing system known as Medicare, but, despite this, it has maintained an ideological commitment to encouraging a parallel private health sector subsidized directly and indirectly by the federal government. In the second part of this chapter we highlight some of the key challenges experienced by Australia in supporting a two-tier health care system. This includes ongoing issues about the long-term sustainability of both systems due to the direct financial costs of funding both systems, the dispersion of health professionals between systems, and the impact on wait times.

Canada and Australia

Canadian policy-makers may look to the Australian health system because of the many similarities between the two nations, and we begin with a brief analysis of the similarities and differences between the two. Both are geographically large with fairly small, densely concentrated populations. Canada has 9.985 million square kilometres of territory, while Australia has 7.692 million square kilometres. Canada's population is larger, at an estimated 37.5 million,[3] versus Australia's 25.5 million.[4] Both have similar population distributions, with most Canadians living reasonably close to the border with the United States and most Australians close to the coastline.

---

3   See Statistics Canada, *Canada at a glance: Population* (Ottawa: Statistics Canada, 2019) online: <https://www150.statcan.gc.ca/t1/tbl1/en/tv.action?pid=1710000501>.

4   See Australian Bureau of Statistics, "Population Clock" (Canberra: ABS, 2019), online: <https://www.abs.gov.au/ausstats/abs@.nsf/0/1647509ef7e25faaca2568a900154b63?OpenDocument>.

Both are former British colonies, current members of the Commonwealth of Nations, members of the Organisation for Economic Co-operation and Development, and are considered highly developed countries. Their legal systems are similar, based on the English common-law system (with variation in the Canadian province of Quebec). Both are federations, with the primary responsibility for health-system management resting with the provinces in Canada and significant responsibilities at the state level in Australia. Both have similar per capita spending and spend similar amounts of GDP on health care.[5] Finally Australia's Medicare system was adapted from Canada's.[6]

Australia's Constitutional and Legal Framework

It was only in 1973 that Australia reluctantly opened the doors to the creation of a universal, publicly funded health system, and not until 1984 that it was established.[7] In 1901, at the formation of the Commonwealth of Australia, health care was not assigned as a federal responsibility in the Constitution, with the Commonwealth's only direct health-related powers being in respect of quarantine.[8] In 1944, a left-leaning Labor government passed legislation setting up the Pharmaceutical Benefits Scheme to subsidize the costs of selected medications (antibiotics) for Australians.[9] The government of the state of Victoria challenged the legislation, arguing the commonwealth legislation was ultra vires.[10] The High Court of Australia (equivalent to the Supreme Court of Canada) overturned the legislation, finding that the Commonwealth had no powers under the Constitution to pass it.[11] Subsequently, the Commonwealth government convened a constitutional referendum to obtain broader powers in the Constitution in respect of health and welfare. It was

---

5   In 2018, the percentage of GDP on health care (total) was 9.3 per cent in Australia, 10.7 per cent in Canada; the per capita spend was AUD$7,170 and C$6,448. Organisation for Economic Cooperation and Development, OECD HealthData <https://stats.oecd.org/Index.aspx?DataSetCode=SHA>.

6   RB Scotton & CR Macdonald, *The Making of Medibank* (Sydney: School of Health Services Management, University of New South Wales, 1993).

7   *Health Insurance Act 1973* (Cth).

8   *Commonwealth of Australia Constitution Act 1900* (Cth), s 51 (ix) [*Constitution Act*].

9   *Pharmaceutical Benefits Act 1944* (Cth).

10   *Attorney-General (Vic) ex rel Dale v Commonwealth* (1945), 71 CLR 237 at 239.

11   *Ibid* at 266.

successful and the Constitution was duly amended, permitting the Commonwealth to provide hospital benefits and medical and dental services.[12] While the referendum was clear evidence of wide public support for publicly funded health services and pharmaceuticals, the prospect of so-called socialized medicine, as was the characterization of Britain's National Health Service, concerned many members of the medical profession who foresaw losing lucrative private practices.[13] A "civil conscription" sub-provision was added to the section amending the Constitution to protect the interests of medical doctors.[14]

Section 51 of the Australian Constitution states:

> The Parliament shall, subject to this Constitution, have power to make laws for the peace, order, and good government of the Commonwealth with respect to:
>
> (xxiiiA) the provision of maternity allowances, widows' pensions, child endowment, unemployment, pharmaceutical, sickness and hospital benefits, medical and dental services (*but not so as to authorize any form of civil conscription*), benefits to students and family allowances.[15]

There have been three cases before the High Court to determine what the civil conscription sub-clause means.[16] In *General Practitioners*

---

12   *Constitution Act, supra* note 8 at s 51(xxiiiA); *Constitution Alteration (Social Services) 1946*.

13   The Australian Medical Association and many members of the medical profession have shared this opposition, as they see their interests as being "best served by a free enterprise, private practice, fee-for-service model" (George Palmer & Stephanie Short, *Health Care and Public Policy: An Australian Analysis*, 5th ed (South Yarra: Palgrave Macmillan, 2014) at 74); Adrian Kay, "Tense Layering and Synthetic Policy Paradigms: The Politics of Health Insurance in Australia" (2007) 42:4 Australian J Political Science 579 at 585.

14   T Faunce, "*Selim v Lele* and the civil (industrial) conscription prohibition: constitutional protection against federal legislation controlling or privatising Australian Public hospitals" (2008) 16 J Law Med 36 at 40.

15   *Constitution Act, supra* note 8 [emphasis added].

16   See *Federal Council of the British Medical Association in Australia v Commonwealth* (1949) 9 CLR 201; *General Practitioners Society v Commonwealth* (1980) 145 CLR 532; *Wong v Commonwealth; Selim v Professional Services Review Committee* (2009) 236 CLR 573. See also Fiona McDonald "Regulation of Health Professionals" in Ben

Society v Commonwealth,[17] the High Court interpreted the constraints on the Commonwealth's power in respect of doctors to be that the Commonwealth cannot exert any legal or practical compulsion on doctors to provide a service.[18] In short, the Commonwealth cannot stop doctors working in public hospitals or public health systems from also working privately (i.e., it cannot limit dual practice, restricted or prohibited in Canada), and it cannot require doctors to work in the public system.[19] The government has also interpreted the civil-conscription provision to mean that it cannot impose any limitations on the amount charged to patients by doctors working in private practice.[20] This latter interpretation has not been challenged before the High Court. The implications of this for the Australian health system amount to a constitutional guarantee that a private market for health services can exist in parallel to a public health system, largely unrestricted.

Although Commonwealth legislation re-establishing the pharmaceutical benefits scheme, providing universal subsidies for approved pharmaceuticals, was passed in 1947,[21] shortly after the reform to the Constitution, the Labor government lost power, before it could establish universal public health care. The Coalition was then in power in Australia, from 1949 to 1972. The Coalition was opposed to universal health care and believed that the role for government was as a safety net provider for the very poor; everyone else should pay directly for health care. Thus, there was a strong commitment

---

White, Fiona McDonald & Lindy Willmott, eds, *Health Law in Australia*, 3rd ed (Sydney: Thomson, 2018) 647 at 651–653; Faunce, *supra* note 14.

17   *General Practitioners Society v Commonwealth* (1980), 145 CLR 532.

18   *Ibid* at 571.

19   *Wong v Commonwealth; Selim v Professional Services Review Committee* (2009) 236 CLR 573.

20   See, e.g., Australian Commonwealth, Department of Health and Aging, *Submission to the Senate Standing Committee for Community Affairs for the Inquiry into the Health Insurance Amendment (Extended Medicare Safety Net) Bill 2009* (Canberra: Senate Standing Committee, 2009) at 7, online: *Parliament of Australia* <https://www.aph.gov.au/Parliamentary_Business/Committees/Senate/Community_Affairs/Completed_inquiries/2008-10/health_insur_extend_medicare_safety_net_09/submissions/sublist>.

21   *Pharmaceutical Benefits Act 1947 (Cth)*.

by the Coalition to both private financing and provision, even if a public system could be more efficient.[22]

In 1972, a Labor government was elected and sought to create a universal public health system (then called Medibank) based on Canadian medicare, with adaptions for the Australian context.[23] The Labor government could not get the universal public health insurance legislation through a hostile Senate on two occasions. The Labor government then had the Governor-General dissolve both houses of Parliament and call an election.[24] Although Labor was re-elected, with a majority in the lower house, the legislation was again defeated in the Senate; thus, a joint sitting of both houses was required to pass the legislation.[25]

Within months of the universal Medibank scheme being implemented, the Coalition blocked budget legislation in the Senate, a constitutional crisis ensued, and the Governor-General dismissed the Labor government and replaced it with the Coalition. The Coalition won the subsequent election and, despite its pre-election promises, systematically dismantled the public, universal system.[26] In 1983, a Labor government was elected and passed legislation to recreate a universal public health system, renamed as Medicare. In opposition, the Coalition continued to campaign on the basis of repealing Medicare. It was not until 1996 that the Coalition accepted that it could not be re-elected if it continued to oppose universal public health care.[27] It recognized pragmatically that, if it wanted to govern

---

22   Ian McAuley, "Private Health Insurance and Public Policy" (Paper delivered at the 2016 Health Insurance Summit in Sydney, 28 July 2016) at 7 [unpublished], online: <https://cpd.org.au/wp-content/uploads/2016/07/PHI-conference-July-2016.pdf> at 3 [emphasis in the original].

23   Scotton & Macdonald, *supra* note 6.

24   See Stephen Duckett & Sharon Willcox, *The Australian Health Care System*, 5th ed (South Melbourne: Oxford University Press, 2015) 361–364; Anne-Marie Boxall & James A Gillespie, *Making Medicare: The Politics of Universal Health Care in Australia* (Sydney: NewSouth Publishing, University of New South Wales Press, 2013) 36–51.

25   World Bank, 2014, *supra* note 7.

26   Boxall & Gillespie, *supra* note 24, 78–89.

27   The then-Health Minister Wooldridge had studied health policy under the previous Liberal government and had identified the strong public support for Medicare as one reason the Liberals lost elections against Labor in the ensuing period: see Palmer & Short, *supra* note 13. See also Fran Collyer, Kirsten Harley & Stephanie Short, "Money and Markets in Australia's Healthcare System" in Gabrielle Meagher & Susan Goodwin, eds, *Markets,*

again, it must undertake not to repeal Medicare, although it remained ideologically opposed to it.[28] Both the political environment and constitutional constraints have and continue to shape the design of the Australian health systems, and have made a two-tier health care system inevitable. We describe this system in the next section.

The Australian Health System

In Australia, public hospitals are majority funded by the states and partially funded by the Commonwealth under its constitutional power to provide conditional funding to the states.[29] It uses this power, rather than funding public hospitals through its section 51(xxiiiA) ("hospital benefits") power, as the payment was originally structured as support for the states' public hospital systems. The states' grants power (s. 96) has the benefit of the Commonwealth being able to impose conditions on the transfer of funding and thus have a greater control over health policy. Commonwealth funding to the states for public hospitals services is provided pursuant to the National Healthcare Agreement, which is renegotiated regularly.[30] The National Healthcare Agreement funds a base level of activity and payments for additional activity each year, with the Commonwealth funding 45 per cent of the costs of activity.[31]

---

28   *Rights and Power in Australian Social Policy* (Sydney: Sydney University Press, 2015) 257 at 263–64. The current Coalition government has stated that Medicare "is a core Government service" (Jane Norman, "Election 2016: Malcolm Turnbull Says 'Every Element' of Medicare Will Stay in Government Hands," *ABC News* (18 June 2016), online: <www.abc.net.au/news/2016-06-18/medicare-will-never-be-privatised,-turnbull-says/7523242>.

28   *Ibid.*

29   *Constitution Act, supra* note 8 at s 96.

30   Most recently through the Council of Australian Governments: Austl, Commonwealth, Council of Australian Governments, *National Healthcare Agreement 2012* (Canberra: COAG, 2012), online: *Council on Federal Financial Relations* <http://www.federalfinancialrelations.gov.au/content/national_health_reform.aspx>.

31   With the payment for activity varying by type of patient, with payment per patient being standard across the country; the "national efficient price." See Stephen Duckett, "Expanding the breadth of Medicare: learning from Australia" (2018) 13 (Special issue 3/4) J Health Economics Pol'y & L 344–368. The Labor policy was for the cost of growth to be funded initially at 45 per cent by the Commonwealth but phased up to equal funding. The Coalition reversed the phasing-up as a savings measure.

Payments from the states to public hospitals are also generally based on activity, with the activity payment taking the costs of staffing and materials, such as pharmaceuticals, into account.[32] Doctors are permitted constitutionally (as discussed above) and by their terms and conditions of employment to work both in the public and private systems (dual practice) and if they are working in a public hospital their employment contract reflects this. Some doctors may be permitted to offer services to private patients in public hospitals in some circumstances.[33] Primary medical care is overwhelmingly remunerated on a fee-for-service basis and provided by general practitioners (GPs) in small practices, privately incorporated companies or partnerships.

Medicare provides a rebate against the costs of medical services (other than in-hospital medical services provided to public patients and patients covered by compensation schemes, such as transport accident schemes),[34] including approved diagnostic tests (pathology/radiology) and services provided by some other health providers (e.g., nurse practitioners, midwives, etc).[35] The rebate can be claimed for private patients receiving care in public hospitals.[36] The provision of services by public hospitals to private patients provides an additional income stream for public hospitals.[37] Most

---

32   Salaries are negotiated through collective bargaining between the health professional union(s) and the states/territories as the employer. Industrial action, such as strikes, is permitted under certain circumstances. If no agreement is reached, Fair Work Australia (an independent government agency) may make a determination.

33   A professional medical service may be provided under a private-practice agreement entered into between a public hospital and a specialist physician (*Health Insurance Act, supra* note 7 at s 19).

34   All patients presenting at a "public hospital" can elect to be treated as a public patient without any direct financial payment. Medical costs, including diagnostic tests, provided to public patients are covered in the public hospital-funding arrangements.

35   *Health Insurance Act, supra* note 7 at s 4.

36   *Ibid* at s 19. Section 19 of the *Health Insurance Act 1973* states that a Medicare benefit may be paid if the professional service is provided under a private-practice agreement entered into between a public hospital and a specialist.

37   In Queensland, e.g., it is stated that this generates AUD$500 million annually in gross revenue across Queensland. Austl, Queensland, *Private Practice in the Queensland Public Health Sector Framework* (Brisbane: QLD Health, 2015) at 6, online: <https://www.health.qld.gov.au/__data/assets/pdf_file/0024/395700/qh-pol-403.pdf>.

GPs and some specialists bulk-bill the government for patient services, and the Medicare rebate is paid direct to the practice at no
additional cost to the patient. Others bill the patient whatever that
practice determines the cost of the appointment should be, and
then the rebate (which is less than the cost) is paid directly to the
patient. In the March quarter of 2018, 84 per cent of all GP visits
were bulk-billed, meaning that these patients were not extra-billed
by doctors in those practices.[38]

Historically, the Commonwealth has not tested the "civil
conscription" limitation in section 51 (xxiiiA) of the Constitution
and has acted as if it were prohibited by the Constitution from controlling pricing. Doctors providing services privately may, therefore,
extra-bill patients any amount above the amount reimbursed by
Medicare. If a GP visit was not bulk-billed, patients had an average
out-of-pocket cost of AUD$68 per item.[39] Thus, individual doctors
in private practice have full autonomy in determining their own
fees, although consumer/contract law also applies.[40] Medicare
reimbursement rates have been indexed against the Department of
Finance's wage-cost index and the consumer-price index. However,
as a cost-containment measure, the government stopped index-
ation from 2013, although is gradually reintroducing it from 2018.[41]

---

38   Australian Government Department of Health, "Quarterly Medicare Statistics"
     (4 September 2019), online: <http://health.gov.au/internet/main/publishing.nsf/
     Content/Quarterly-Medicare-Statistics>, Table 1.1b.
39   *Ibid.*
40   *Competition and Consumer Act 2010* (Cth). This *Act* is based on a premise that
     competition in markets is desirable. Doctors who mislead patients over fees
     may be subject to sanctions under this *Act*. Fees are also subject to self-regula-
     tion. See the Australian Medical Association, Australian Medical Association
     Code of Ethics (2004) online: <https://ama.com.au/sites/default/files/documents/
     AMA%20Code%20of%20Ethics%202004.%20Editorially%20Revised%202006.%20
     Revised%202016_0.pdf> at 2.7. It addresses fee setting and states: "Set a fair and
     reasonable fee having regard to the time, skill and experience involved in the
     performance of your services, the relevant practice costs and the particular
     circumstances of the case and the patient." A doctor who charged excessively
     could face disciplinary proceedings by the Medical Board of Australia, although
     it appears that these matters tend to be resolved before a disciplinary hearing; I
     Freckelton, "The ethics and regulation of overcharging: issues in the commer-
     ciality of the health practitioner-patient relationship" (2014) 21:3 J Law Med. 497.
41   Austl, Commonwealth, *Budget overview*, (Canberra: Commonwealth of Australia,
     2017) online: <https://www.budget.gov.au/2017-18/content/glossies/overview/
     html/overview-07.htm>.

The Australian Medical Association has stated in any event that the indexing did not keep pace with real cost increases.[42] In summary, Australia's Medicare arrangements remain, as famously characterized more than fifty years ago, as "private practice, publicly supported."[43]

The introduction of Medicare and free public hospital care did not undermine the continued importance of private finance in the Australian system but it did result in a rapid decrease in the number of Australians holding private health insurance (PHI) for public hospital care. Initially insurance for private hospital care remained stable.[44] The Coalition was re-elected in 1996 and wanted to maintain a vigorous private health system because of the ideological position as discussed. Accordingly, from 1996, it progressively instituted a regulatory framework to encourage Australians to purchase PHI covering care in private hospitals.[45] It is important to note that, unlike in Canada or the United States, PHI is not provided through employers as part of an employment package; individuals must choose whether or not to purchase the product.[46] The Coalition argued that such a regulatory framework was necessary for the sustainability of the public health system as a robust privately financed

---

42   Australian Medical Association, *Guide for Patients on how the health care system funds medical care*, (Canberra, AMA, 2015) online: <https://ama.com.au/article/guide-patients-how-health-care-system-funds-medical-care#First>.

43   Theodore Fox, "The Antipodes: Private Practice Publicly Supported" (1963) 281:7286 The Lancet 875–879.

44   Fiona McDonald & Stephen Duckett, "Regulation, Private Health Insurance, and the Australian Health System" (2017) 11:1 McGill JL & Health S31 at S43.

45   *Ibid* at S31; Stephen Duckett & Terri Jackson, "The new health insurance rebate: An inefficient way of assisting public hospitals" (2000) Medical J Austl, 172 (9), 439–444; Stephen Duckett, "Coercing, Subsidising and Encouraging: Two Decades of Support for Private Health Insurance" in Damien Cahill & Phillip Toner, eds, *Wrong Way: How Privatisation and Economic Reform Backfired* (Melbourne: La Trobe University Press in conjunction with Black Inc., 2018), 40–58 at 47.

46   Initially, access to hospital care for poorer people was provided through state government public hospitals; access to general practitioners was supported through friendly society and other "lodge" type arrangements, with these eventually supplanted by voluntary medical-insurance arrangements, often sponsored by medical societies; see Boxall & Gillespie, *supra* note 24. In these circumstances there was no real policy vacuum for employer-sponsored arrangements. Early-twentieth-century industrial relations frameworks focussed on ensuring that all (male) employees had a decent wage to support their family, with health care costs not being separately provided for.

sector would (it was claimed) take pressure off the public system by moving patients into the private system, enable consumer choice of providers, help the private sector, and restore "balance" between the public and private sectors.[47] Since 1953, the Commonwealth has used its constitutional power over insurance[48] to intervene in the PHI market in Australia to require PHI to be community-risk rated rather than individually risk rated. That is to say, private insurers are prohibited by law from fixing a premium price based on an individual' age, gender, or health status.[49]

The first step in the regulatory framework supporting the privately financed sector was for the Commonwealth to subsidize PHI premiums for approved products (i.e., those that offered private hospital cover). From 1 July 2019, the premium subsidy was 25.059 per cent for those under sixty-five years of age, 29.236 per cent for those aged sixty-five to sixty-nine, and 33.413 per cent for those aged seventy and older, on the lowest income tier.[50] The subsidy rate is adjusted annually in an attempt to moderate the rate of growth of government outlays on PHI.[51] The subsidy is also means-tested. For example, for a single person, the subsidy is reduced by about 10 per cent if one earns over AUD$90,000, 20 per cent if one earns over AUD$105,000, and completely eliminated if one earns more than AUD$140,000.[52] The average wage in Australia is approximately AUD$85,000.[53] The premium subsidy, which was more modest when initially introduced, resulted in minimal increased uptake of PHI.[54]

In response, the Commonwealth in 1997 introduced a 1–1.5 per cent taxation penalty (Medicare levy surcharge) on those who do not have PHI after age thirty-one or who cease holding PHI after age

---

47   McDonald & Duckett, *supra* note 44 at S44–45.

48   *Constitution Act, supra* note 8 at s 51(xiv).

49   *Private Health Insurance Act 2007* (Cth), s 55–1.

50   Australian Commonwealth, Australian Taxation Office, "Income Thresholds and Rates for the Private Health Insurance Rebate" (29 June 2017), online: <https://www.ato.gov.au/individuals/medicare-levy/private-health-insurance-rebate/income-thresholds-and-rates-for-the-private-health-insurance-rebate/>.

51   *Private Health Insurance Act, supra* note 49 at ss 22–15(5A) to (5E), 22–30 to 22–45; *Tax Laws Amendment Act (Medicare Levy Surcharge Thresholds) Act (No 2) 2008* (Cth), Schedule 1, ss 2, 7.

52   *Ibid* ss 22–15(2) to (4), 22–35; *supra* note 50.

53   See Austl, Commonwealth, Australian Bureau of Statistics, "Full-time average total earnings" (November 2017), <http://www.abs.gov.au/ausstats/abs@.nsf/mf/6302.0>.

54   McDonald & Duckett, *supra* note 44 at S43.

thirty-one.[55] There is a limited exception in that the Medicare levy surcharge does not apply to singles with incomes under AUD\$90,000 or to families with incomes under AUD\$180,000.[56] However, this too only resulted in minimal increased uptake of those holding approved PHI policies.[57]

Finally, the Commonwealth introduced a scheme called "lifetime health cover loading";[58] if a person does not hold PHI after age thirty-one, or ceases holding it at any point, and then purchases PHI, the insurance companies are required to increase that person's premiums for a ten-year period at a rate of 2 per cent extra on the premium for each year after age thirty that they take out PHI. This policy measure substantially increased the number of persons holding PHI, from 33.5 per cent in 1996,[59] when the lifetime arrangements came into effect, to its 2015/2016 level of approximately 46 per cent.[60] However, while there were increases in the number of Australians who held PHI after 1996, changes introduced in 1995 allowed the development of policies which did not cover all types of care, and fewer people post-1996 thus had a comprehensive PHI policy. More held policies that did not cover certain services, for example, obstetrics, or where there was a policy excess—that is, the policy holder has to pay the first thousand dollars, or where coverage was capped at a specified dollar value, and beyond that the individual had to pay any additional costs.[61] So while 46 per cent of Australians in 2015/2016 held some form of approved PHI (that covers private hospital treatment),[62] the fact that approximately

---

55   *Medicare Levy Act 1986* (Cth), ss 6, 8B–8G.

56   Austl, Commonwealth, Australian Tax Office, *M2 Medicare Levy Surcharge (MLS)* (Canberra: ATO, 2018), online: <https://www.ato.gov.au/ Individuals/Tax-Return/2018/Tax-return/Medicare-levy-questions-M1-M2/ M2-Medicare-levy-surcharge-(MLS)-2018/?=redirected>.

57   McDonald & Duckett, *supra* note 44.

58   *Private Health Insurance Act, supra* note 49 at s 31–1.

59   Austl, Commonwealth, Bills Digest 76, *Private Health Insurance Incentives Bill 1996*, (Canberra: Commonwealth of Australia, 1996/1997), online: <https://www.aph. gov.au/Parliamentary_Business/Bills_Legislation/bd/BD9697/97bd076>.

60   Austl, Commonwealth, Australian Institute of Health and Welfare, *Private Health Insurance Expenditure* (Canberra: AIHW 2015–2016), online: <https://www. aihw.gov.au/getmedia/08320d6a-4ceb-4c75-a16b-aa1a4c9f6d15/aihw-20592-pri- vate-health-insurance-expenditure.pdf.aspx> [Private Health Insurance Expenditure].

61   McDonald & Duckett, *supra* note 44 at S43; *Private Health Insurance Act, supra* note 49.

62   Private Health Insurance Expenditure, *supra* note 60.

32 per cent of those who held approved PHI had non-comprehensive policies[63] implies the purchase thereof was for cost-containment and tax-avoidance reasons, rather than wanting the product.[64] There is increasing dissatisfaction among the Australian population toward the significant annual premium increases being imposed by insurers and "junk" policies that are either non-usable or not usable without significant copayments.[65]

Consequences of Health-System Design

The Commonwealth government is constrained constitutionally to allow a two-tier system,[66] and politically one dominant political grouping, the Coalition (since 1947 it has been in government for, over different periods, approximately fify years), is, as discussed earlier, ideologically predisposed not only to permit but to actively support and subsidize a strong "private" system,[67] no matter if there are more significant efficiencies to be obtained from a different design. In the next section, we turn to examine some of the consequences of the public/private system design in Australia.

Sustainability

The subsidies paid by the Commonwealth for PHI are estimated to cost over AUD$6 billion per annum. Further support for private health provision is provided outside the PHI regulatory framework through Medicare rebates for private hospital care at over

---

63   McDonald & Duckett, *supra* note 44.

64   *Ibid* at S51.

65   Austl, Commonwealth, *Private Health Insurance Consultation* (Canberra: Health, 2015–2016), online: <http://www.health.gov.au/internet/main/publishing.nsf/Content/PHIconsultations2015-16>.

66   Phrased as not allowing "civil conscription" in the *Commonwealth of Australia Constitution Act 1900* (Cth), s 51(xxiiiA).

67   About 70 per cent of all health care funding in Australia is from government; the focus in the public debate has been on how much of that funding should be through public entities ("public provision") compared to through privately incorporated bodies, including privately incorporated medical practices ("private provision"). Despite the very large public subsidy, private providers have extensive autonomy about ownership structures—including listing of the Australian Stock Exchange—and billing arrangements. It is this level of autonomy, rather than their funding, which allows the continued use of the designation "private" for these services.

AUD$3 billion per annum. This comes to a total of approximately AUD$10 billion annually, paid for from the public purse.[68] The federal government subsidy for PHI is expected to grow 7 per cent in real terms over the period from 2015/2016 to 2018/2019.[69] Growth in Commonwealth government spending in health is 3.2 per cent overall, and its spending on public hospitals is expected to grow at 6.7 per cent from 2015/2016 to 2018/2019.[70] The rate of the growth in the PHI subsidy raises concerns about whether this is sustainable in the long term.[71] It also raises concerns about whether the large subsidy for PHI is the most efficient use of taxpayer and private funds, as overheads are higher in the private system.[72]

Cream skimming

A further issue is transfers of high-cost and high-risk patients between private and public hospitals. A recent study found that the incidence of Australian private hospitals transferring patients to public hospitals increased with disease severity and treatment complexity.[73] The authors suggest that this is evidence of a phenomenon referred to as "cream skimming," where there is an incentive for private providers to transfer more expensive patients to the public system.[74] It found that these patients are more likely to stay longer and cost more, even when health conditions and personal characteristics (i.e., higher acuity patients who need the greater post-operative support that can be provided in public hospitals) are controlled for.[75] As Cheng et al note, "the practice of cream skimming by private hospitals

---

68   Duckett, *supra* note 45 at 49–50.
69   See Stephen Duckett, "Aged and Confused: Why the Private Health Insurance Industry is Ripe for Reform" *The Conversation* (10 November 2015), online: *The Conversation* <http://theconversation.com/aged-and-confused-why-the-private-health-insurance-industry-is-ripe-for-reform-50384>; Austl, Commonwealth, *Budget 2015–2016: Budget Strategy and Outlook*, Budget Paper No 1 (Canberra: Commonwealth of Australia, 2015) at 5–13, 5–23, online: <https://budget.gov.au/2019-20/content/bp1/index.htm>.
70   *Ibid.*
71   McDonald & Duckett, *supra* note 44 at S56–58.
72   *Ibid* at S57.
73   TC Cheng, JP Haisken-DeNew & J Yong, "Cream skimming and hospital transfers in a mixed public-private system" (2015) 132 Social Science and Medicine 156 at 160.
74   *Ibid* at 162–163.
75   *Ibid* at 162.

implies that public hospitals will be saddled with difficult and high-cost patients, who are adding strain on an increasingly limited budget."[76] The research also found that the same phenomenon held in reverse, that is, public hospitals were more likely to transfer cheaper (healthier) patients to private hospitals.[77] This was also suggested to be an example of cream skimming but, in this instance, on the part of dual-practice physicians.[78] Given that private-sector work is more lucrative,[79] doctors who work in dual practice are postulated to have an incentive to treat healthier (cheaper) patients in the private system, and hence to transfer those patients from the public system to the private one.[80] This dual practice has significant implications for the sustainability of the Australian public health system.

Workforce implications

McAuley argues that the assumption underlying the PHI regulatory framework—that higher rates of private hospital usage would relieve public hospitals—was flawed, as it considered only demand-side factors.[81] Supply-side factors suggest that human resources, especially specialist doctors, will go where the money is.[82] Research indicates that when medical practitioners allocate more hours of work to the private sector, the number of hours they are available to work in the public sector decreases.[83] As of 2013, remuneration was greater in the private sector in Australia.[84] Canada's system may be less able to compensate for any shift should private practice be made more

---

76   *Ibid* at 163.

77   *Ibid* at 160.

78   *Ibid.*

79   TC Cheng, G Kalb & A Scott, *"Public, Private or Both? Analysing Factors Influencing the Labour Supply of Medical Specialists"* (Melbourne Institute Working Paper No 40/13, 2013), online: <https://melbourneinstitute.unimelb.edu.au/downloads/working-paper-series/wp2013n40.pdf> at 1.

80   Cheng et al, *supra* note 73 at 157.

81   Ian McAuley, "Private Health Insurance and Public Policy" (Paper delivered at the 2016 Health Insurance Summit in Sydney, 28 July 2016) at 7 [unpublished], online: <https://cpd.org.au/wp-content/uploads/2016/07/PHI-conference-July-2016.pdf>.

82   See Cheng et al, *supra* note 79 at 1; McAuley, *ibid.*

83   E Mossialos et al, *International Profiles of Health Care Systems* (Commonwealth Fund, 2017) at 7.

84   Cheng, *supra* note 79 at 9.

available in that country as it has 2.5 practicing physicians per 1,000 population, in comparison with Australia's 3.5.[85]

Wait times

The data in respect of wait times in Australia and Canada are somewhat unclear but show some significant differences. Table 10.1 presents data from Commonwealth Fund comparisons. First and second rows of the table relate to out-of-hospital care. In Australia, PHI does not cover out-of-hospital care by primary-care doctors or specialists (who are all considered private providers in the Australian health system) if those services are covered by Medicare. Some patients will pay a copayment. On the face of it, third row of the table indicates that wait times for elective surgery are less in Australia than in Canada. The Australian data may be average waits for public hospital care—where there are waits—and private hospital care where there are no waits.

Table 10.1. Wait times, 2016

	Australia	Canada
Same-day/next-day appointments	67%	43%
Two months or more to see a specialist	13%	30%
Four months or more for elective surgery[86]	8%	18%

Source: Commonwealth Fund, *International Profiles of Health Care Systems* (Commonwealth Fund 2017) < https://international.commonwealthfund.org/stats/?cat=access_to_care>.

A closer look at the data shows a different picture. About 748,000 Australians on a waiting list were admitted to public hospitals for elective surgery in 2016/2017.[87] Recent data suggests that, in 2016/2017, the median waiting time for elective surgery in Australia was thirty-eight days.[88] The amount of time within which 90 per cent of patients were admitted for elective surgery was 258 days.[89] The national proportion of patients who waited more than 365 days to

---

85   Mossialos et al, *supra* note 83 at 7.

86   The Australian wait time is for public hospital care only; there are essentially no waiting periods for private hospital care in Australia.

87   Austl, Commonwealth, Australian Institute of Health and Welfare, *Elective surgery waiting times 2016–2017 Australian hospital statistics* (Canberra: AIHW, 2017) at vii.

88   *Ibid* at 28.

89   *Ibid.*

be admitted for elective surgery was 1.7 per cent.[90] Table 10.2 presents OECD data by procedure type in the public health systems in Australia and Canada, and indicates that patients wait longer for key elective-surgery categories in Australia.

Table 10.2. Wait times from specialist assessment to treatment, days, 2016

Surgery type	Australia	Canada
Cataract surgery	85	67
Coronary bypass	13	6
Prostatectomy	41	39
Hip replacement (total and partial, including the revision of hip replacement)	110	98
Knee replacement	195	116

Source: OECD, "Health Care Utilisation: Waiting Times" (20 June 2019), online: <https://stats.oecd.org/Index.aspx?QueryId=49344>

While data on waiting lists for elective surgery is kept and reported on nationally in Australia, the hidden wait list is the time it takes to get a specialist appointment and/or appointments for diagnostic procedures through the public system. There is no consistent data on the extent of these hidden waiting lists: some states do not publish anything (e.g., New South Wales) and, for others, the use of different metrics make comparisons difficult.[91] However, media reports suggest that hidden wait times may be significant. In South Australia, one patient was reported waiting sixteen years for an appointment.[92]Australian Capital Territory media reported that the wait time for an initial appointment with a specialist for those at the ninetieth percentile (i.e., those who wait the longest) varied significantly between specialties, with a wait of 1,398 days (3.8 years)

90   *Ibid.*

91   Stephen Duckett, "Getting an initial specialists' appointment is the hidden waitlist," *The Conversation* (7 January 2018), online: *The Conversation* <https://theconversation.com/getting-an-initial-specialists-appointment-is-the-hidden-waitlist-99507>.

92   ABC news, "Some patients waiting more than 16 years for hospital treatment in SA" *ABC News* (1 July 2018) online: <http://www.abc.net.au/news/2018-07-01/patients-waiting-more-than-16-years-for-hospital-treatment-in-sa/9929146>.

to see a urologist and 213 days to see a gynecologist.[93] In Victoria, 2015 data indicated that the median wait in one regional hospital for an ear, nose, and throat specialist was 469 days, and seven days for a gynecologist, although there was significant variation between hospitals.[94] At least one state suggests that they may collect and make public such data in the future.[95]

By comparison, waiting times in the private sector for elective surgery are so small as to be negligible. The absence of lengthy waiting times is a key selling point for private health insurers, who promote "on demand" surgeries as a major benefit of their policies. There is some evidence that the differential between waiting times influences relative levels of demand for public and private hospitals; a 2011 paper by the Melbourne Institute suggested that the two key simultaneous determinants of choice between being treated in a public or private hospital were public health-system waiting times and PHI costs.[96] The implication of the Australian experience is that an extensive private system is not associated with shorter average waits; rather, the reverse is true.

Private health insurance

While PHI may reduce wait times for individuals who hold PHI, McAuley argues that PHI re-assigns queues for services on the basis of ability to purchase a PHI policy, rather than on the basis of clinical need.[97] There is no evidence that the increase in the privately insured population has led to a significant reduction in public-sector waiting times. A Melbourne Institute report states that the empirical data suggests the "impact of private health insurance on alleviating the

---

93   D White, "Hidden data reveals that patients can wait five years to see a special-ist," *Canberra Times* (30 April 2018), online: <https://www.canberratimes.com.au/politics/act/hidden-data-shows-patients-can-wait-five-years-to-see-a-specialist-20180424-p4zbeh.html>.

94   J Medew, "Secret data on hospital waiting times shows public health system is in 'crisis'," *The Sydney Morning Herald* (17 August 2015), online: <https://www.smh.com.au/healthcare/secret-data-on-hospital-waiting-times-shows-public-health-system-is-in-crisis-20150817-gjorwq.html>.

95   White, *supra* note 93.

96   T Cheng & F Vahid, *Demand for hospital care and private health insurance in a mixed public-private system: Empirical evidence using a simultaneous equation modelling approach* (Melbourne: Melbourne Institute of Applied Economic and Social Research, University of Melbourne, 2011) at 2.

97   McAuley, *supra* note 81.

burden on the public hospital system is not expected to be large."[98] Indeed, research from 2005 indicated that a higher proportion of private admissions to hospital is associated with *higher* public hospital waiting times, not lower.[99] The PHI regulatory framework commenced on 1998; however, in 2009, the Commonwealth government entered into an agreement to provide the states with additional funding to manage elective-surgery wait times in the public system.[100] This implies that wait times continued to be a problem—even nearly ten years after the PHI framework of regulation, subsidies, and penalties was introduced.

Other research indicates there was, at best, minimal shifts in private and public shares of hospital admissions.[101] Duckett has suggested that this is not surprising for five reasons.[102] First, few private hospitals provide emergency care, so this type of care cannot be diverted from the public system. Second, some elective surgeries are only performed in public hospitals due to a requirement for extensive post-surgery support than is available in a private hospital. Third, some private patients may have procedures in a private hospital that are not clinically necessary, for which they would not have been admitted into a public hospital. Fourth, some people who purchase PHI are healthy and would, therefore, not affect demand on the public hospital system. Fifth, if a person is taking out PHI for tax-avoidance reasons, they may not hold a product they can use without significant extra costs to them, and would continue to use the free public system.[103]

---

98   Cheng & Vahid, *supra* note 96 at 25.

99   Stephen J Duckett, "Private Care and Public Waiting" (2005) 29:1 Aust Health Rev 87 at 92.

100   Austl, Commonwealth, Council of Australian Governments, *National Partnership Agreement on the Elective Surgery Waiting List Reduction Plan*, (Canberra: COAG, 2009) online: <http://www.federalfinancialrelations.gov.au/content/npa/health/national-partnership/past/elective-surgery-waiting-lists-NP.pdf> [Waiting List Reduction Plan].

101   See R Moorin and C Holam, "Does federal health care policy influence switching between the public and private sectors in Australia?" (2006) 79:2/3 Health Pol'y 284; Kate Brameld, D'Arcy Holman & Rachael Moorin, "Possession of Health Insurance in Australia: How Does it Affect Hospital Use and Outcomes?" (2006) 11:2 J Health Serv Res Policy 94 at 97; Rachael Elizabeth Moorin, Cashel D'Arcy & James Holman, "Modelling Changes in the Determinants of PHI Utilisation in Western Australia across Five Health Care Policy Eras between 1981 and 2001" (2007) 81:2 Health Pol'y 183 at 188; Ian McAuley, "Private Health Insurance: Still Muddling Through" (2005) 12:2 Agenda 159 at 167–68; Duckett, *supra* note 99 at 92.

102   Duckett, *supra* note 45 40–58.

103   See also McDonald & Duckett, *supra* note 44 at S52; McAuley, *supra* note 81.

Wait time initiatives

The initial rhetoric about public subsidies for PHI posited a causal relationship between increased numbers of persons holding PHI and shorter wait times. However, as noted, the reality is the reverse.[104] There are many factors which influence waiting times, and there have been a plethora of initiatives to reduce waiting.

The National Partnership Agreement on the Elective Surgery Waiting List Reduction Plan[105] was entered into by the Commonwealth and the states and territories in 2009 and expired in 2011. The Commonwealth committed funding to reduce the numbers of persons waiting longer than clinically indicated times by improving efficiency and capacity within the public system, with AUD$150 million for an immediate reduction in public waiting lists, AUD$150 million for systems and infrastructure improvement, and a further AUD$300 million for reducing the numbers of "long wait" patients to comply with the National Elective Surgery Urgency Categorisation Guideline[106] and to improve overall efficiency.[107] National Elective Surgery Targets (NEST) were established in 2013.[108] The states agreed to report quarterly data to the Commonwealth about their achievements against NEST, and that that data be made public on the MyHospitals website[109] and on state health department websites. Reports suggest that results from this cash injection were mixed:

---

104 Duckett, *supra* note 45.

105 Waiting List Reduction Plan, *supra* note 100.

106 Australian Health Ministers' Advisory Council, *National Elective Surgery Urgency Categorisation Guideline* (2015), online: <http://www.coaghealthcouncil. gov.au/Portals/0/National%20Elective%20Surgery%20Categorisation%20-%20 Guideline%20-%20April%202015.pdf>.

107 *Ibid* at 3. Essentially, there are target maximum waiting times for different categories of patients, e.g., urgent patients (category 1) should be seen in thirty days, semi-urgent in ninety days. Patients waiting longer than these periods are "long waits."

108 Austl, Commonwealth, *National Partnership Agreement on Improving Public Hospital Services* (2013) online: <http://www.federalfinancialrelations.gov.au/content/ npa/health/_archive/national-workforce-reform/national_partnership.pdf> [Improving Public Hospital Services].

109 See "My Hospitals" (2018), online: *Australian Institute of Health and Welfare* <https:// www.myhospitals.gov.au/>. The data continues to be publicly reported despite the agreement having expired in 2015.

While the total volume of elective surgery under the plan exceeded expectations (41,584 operations were completed against a target of 25,278), the number of "long wait" patients actually increased over the period 2007–2008 to 2009–2010. This means that while some patients were seen within clinically recommended times, the number of people who waited for significant periods of time continued to increase.[110]

This agreement was followed by the National Partnership Agreement on Improving Public Hospital Services (NPA IPHS), which promised the states up to AUD$650 million to meet NEST, up to AUD$150 million in elective surgery capital, up to AUD$500 million to achieve a four-hour National Emergency Access Target (established in the NPA IPHS) in public hospital emergency departments, up to AUD$250 million in emergency-department capital, up to AUD$1.6 billion for new subacute beds, and up to AUD$200 million in a flexible funding pool for capital and recurrent projects across elective surgery, emergency departments, and subacute care.[111] At the state level, Queensland Health reported that NPA IPHS led to it implementing "a range of clinical and process improvements in relation to elective surgery services in response to NPA IPHS. These actions resulted in a significant reduction in the number of people waiting longer than clinically recommended for elective surgery in Queensland."[112] Some states also provided further supplementary funding to reduce elective-surgery wait times; for example, in 2017, New South Wales promised an additional AUD$3 million for some health districts.[113]

110 R de Boer, *Reducing elective surgery waiting times—is more money the answer?* (2011), online: *Parliament of Australia* <https://www.aph.gov.au/About_Parliament/Parliamentary_Departments/Parliamentary_Library/FlagPost/2011/November/Reducing_elective_surgery_waiting_times_-_is_more_money_the_answer>.
111 Improving Public Hospital Services, *supra* note 108 at 3.
112 Austl, Queensland, Queensland Department of Health, *Wait Times Strategy Statewide Consultation Handbook* (Brisbane: Qld Health, 2015) at 4, online: <https://www.health.qld.gov.au/__data/assets/pdf_file/0025/443914/wait-times-strategy-consultation.pdf>.
113 New South Wales Government, Media Release, "Shorter wait times for elective surgery: Local health districts will receive $3 million to help reduce the wait times for common elective surgery" (12 September 2017), online: <https://www.nsw.gov.au/news-and-events/news/shorter-wait-times-for-elective-surgery/>.

As mentioned earlier, doctors in public hospitals in Australia are paid by the hospital, normally, on a salary basis, not on the fee-for-service model as is usual in Canada. This provides policy-makers and administrators with greater authority to require units within the hospitals and health professionals, including doctors, to achieve efficiencies in service provision through measures such as those described above, and through changes to funding models. In 2011, activity-based funding for public hospital services was introduced to pay the states and territories a "national efficient price" for public hospital services so as to encourage efficiencies.[114]

All of the agreements discussed in this section accept that there is capacity for improvement in efficiency across the system and a desire to use mechanisms and invest funding to achieve them. Australia's public health system is more efficient than Canada's.[115] This significant injection of cash into both the direct provision of services to reduce waiting lists and in efficiencies within the system, as well as public reporting, has likely been a significant factor in the current status of wait times for elective surgery in Australia.

Conclusion

The Australian health system is characterized by a complex division of responsibilities and roles shared between the Commonwealth of Australia and state governments, as well as a complicated interplay between public and private sectors. A constitutional provision, prohibiting civil conscription, places some limits on the Commonwealth government's ability to limit the creation and maintenance of a private sector. The Commonwealth's current interpretation of the Constitution is that it is unable to control prices charged by doctors in private practice; an interpretation which has not yet been examined by the High Court of Australia. Although Australia's Medicare

---

114 Austl, Commonwealth, Council of Australian Governments, *National Health Reform Agreement* (Canberra: COAG, 2011), online: <http://www.federalfinancialrelations.gov.au/content/npa/health/_archive/national-agreement.pdf>. Activity-based funding was first introduced in 1993 in Victoria; see S Duckett, "Hospital payment arrangements to encourage efficiency: The case of Victoria, Australia." (1995) 34 Health Pol'y 113–134.

115 Y Varabyova & J Schreyögg, "International comparisons of the technical efficiency of the hospital sector: panel data analysis of OECD countries using parametric and non-parametric approaches" (2013) 112(1/2) Health Pol'y 70.

system was based on Canada's, there are significant differences due to Australia's constitutional framework and political ideologies, which, in effect, guarantees the existence of a two-tier system, regardless of policy merit.

Politically, the Coalition opposed the introduction of a universal public health system until the late 1980s. The Coalition then conceded that it could not politically continue to oppose Medicare, but, despite this, it has maintained an ideological commitment to not just allow but also to encourage and subsidize a parallel private health sector. This active role in promoting a private health sector is different from many other countries that permit a public/private health system but that do not actively promote PHI and the private system to the same extent as seen in Australia.[116] Ireland is an exception to this as it offers subsidies for PHI, also for the expressed purpose of allowing people to access the private system to avoid waiting times. It also imposes penalties on those who do not take up PHI.[117] Some other countries offer subsidies to employers to assist them to provide PHI to their employees, but employers have never played a significant role in providing PHI to employees in Australia. This is a significant difference in tradition between Australia and Canada, as Canada's norm is that employers provide PHI (albeit focused on pharmaceuticals and dental care). Given 66 per cent of Canadians currently hold PHI through their employer, any expectation emerging from the *Cambie* litigation that employers should provide PHI that also covers medically necessary services could have significant implications for productivity and employment rates.[118]

The consequences of Australia's approach to its public/private system provide a number of lessons for Canada. Australia's significant subsidy of PHI raises questions about sustainability in terms of the direct and indirect costs of the subsidy. Similar questions are also raised about the sustainability of the public health system, due to the phenomenon of dual practice and cream skimming, with expensive patients shifted to the public system and less expensive ones to the private.

---

116 McDonald & Duckett, *supra* note 44.

117 S Thomas, "A Comparative Evaluation of Two-Tier Care and the Relationship to Wait Times" (7 February 2018), online: *Centre for Health Law, Policy and Ethics* <http://ottawahealthlaw.ca/twotiercomparative>.

118 Flood & Thomas, *supra* note 1 at 445.

A key argument in the *Cambie* case is that wait times for elective surgery would be better in Canada if it had parallel public and private systems. A superficial look suggests that Australia's system performs substantially better than Canada's with respect to wait times. However, a detailed look at public hospital wait times for particular procedures indicates that wait times in the public system in Australia may be longer than in Canada for some procedures. In other words, Australians may on, aggregate, wait less time for elective surgery but those who rely on the public system wait longer than Canadians. It is important to note that there is also a lack of public information about wait times to get on the public elective-surgical waiting list, or in respect of the public management of non-emergency medical care unconnected to surgery in Australia.

It would seem unlikely than any better performance in terms of wait time management is solely linked to Australia's approach of actively supporting a parallel private health system through using regulatory measures to encourage Australians to purchase PHI. While one of the premises behind the PHI regulatory framework was that higher numbers of people with PHI would reduce waiting times, as this chapter discusses, it is unclear what, if any, positive impact this has had on waiting lists or public hospital utilization more generally. It is, however, clear that Australia did not only rely on the private health system to manage elective-surgery wait times in the public system. The Commonwealth government also provided significant funding targeted at enabling the states to achieve efficiencies within elective-surgery management and the management of the public hospital system more generally, as well as to directly reduce waiting lists by undertaking more surgeries. It accompanied this with accountability mechanisms that set clear targets for elective surgery, and subsequently, emergency-department throughput, required reporting to the Commonwealth of data in relation to certain indicators on a quarterly basis, and placed this data on publicly accessible websites, enabling public scrutiny.

Australia's higher number of doctors per capita may make it easier for it to adjust to the time-sharing of many specialists between the private and public sectors, or the loss of doctors to the private system, in contrast with Canada, which has a significantly lower number of doctors per capita, which could also account for some of the wait time differentials.

CHAPTER 11

Embracing and Disentangling from Private Finance: The Irish System

Stephen Thomas, Sarah Barry, Bridget Johnston,
Rikke Siersbaek, and Sara Burke

The Irish health care system is particularly interesting in that it is one of the few high-income systems that has not achieved significant progress toward universal health care. Indeed, it has only quite recently adopted universality as a formal objective, having been characterized by an entrenched two-tier system for accessing hospitals and market-based general-practitioner access for the majority of the population.[1] Furthermore, the Irish economy battled with the effects of austerity for many years, producing an unhelpful legacy for the Irish health care system in terms of fewer human resources and reduced funding.[2]

In this chapter, we explore the nature and history of the entanglement between public and private financing in the Irish health care system and the impact this has had on system performance. Recent policy proposals to overhaul the Irish health care system, based on the Sláintecare report of 2017, outline a ten-year plan to deliver

---

1   Sara Ann Burke et al, "From Universal Health Insurance to Universal Healthcare? The Shifting Health Policy Landscape in Ireland Since the Economic Crisis" (2016) 120:3 Health Pol'y 235–240.

2   Sara Burke, "Reform of the Irish Healthcare System: What Reform?" in Mary P Murphy & Fiona Dukelow, eds, *The Irish Welfare State in the Twenty-First Century* (London, UK: Palgrave Macmillan, 2016) at 167 [Burke, "What Reform?"]; Des Williams & Stephen Thomas, "The Impact of Austerity on the Health Workforce and the Achievement of Human Resources for Health Policies in Ireland (2008–2014)" (2017) 15:62 Hum Resour Health.

universal health care, expand solidarity funding, and remove private finance from public hospitals.[3] Such proposals are explored and evaluated. The challenge of disentangling private and public finance will be a key focus for policy over the next few years.

Financing the Irish Health Care System

The majority of funding flowing into the Irish health care system comes from general taxation (69 per cent in 2015).[4] This has fallen from a historic high of 76 per cent in 2004 and 2005, at the height of the Celtic Tiger boom, to a low of 68 per cent in 2011–2013, caused by an economic contraction (see fig. 11.1). The other two major sources of funding are out-of-pocket spending (i.e., direct payment to providers when patients access care) and funds flowing through voluntary private health insurers to providers, accounting for 15.4 per cent and 12.7 per cent, respectively, in 2015.[5] The proportion of out-of-pocket payments for health care has remained largely static since 2004, at between 15 per cent and 17 per cent.[6] In contrast, the proportion of financing flowing through private insurers increased sharply over the same period.

Ireland's largely tax-based funding of health care does not bring entitlement to free health care at the point of delivery to the whole population. Unlike most OECD countries, Ireland does not have universal coverage for primary care but instead a safety net system, where those with low incomes are exempted from user fees for key services. The population can be divided into two categories, determined by the 1970 *Health Act*. In category 1 are people with medical cards granted through the General Medical Scheme (GMS), which are primarily allocated on the basis of low income, after a stringent

3   Ireland, Committee on the Future of Healthcare, *Committee on the Future of Healthcare: Sláintecare Report* (Dublin: Houses of the Oireachtas, 2017), online: <https://data.oireachtas.ie/ie/oireachtas/committee/dail/32/committee_on_the_future_of_healthcare/reports/2017/2017-05-30_slaintecare-report_en.pdf> [Committee on the Future of Healthcare, *Sláintecare Report*].

4   Ireland, Central Statistics Office, *Ireland's System of Health Accounts, Annual Results 2014* (Cork, Ireland: Central Statistics Office, 2016), online: <https://pdf.cso.ie/www/pdf/20180720084024_System_of_Health_Accounts_2014_full.pdf> [Central Statistics Office, *Ireland's System of Health Accounts*].

5   *Ibid.*

6   OECD, *Health at a Glance: Europe 2016* (Paris: OECD Publishing, 2016), online: *OECD iLibrary* <www.oecd-ilibrary.org/social-issues-migration-health/health-at-a-glance-europe-2016_9789264265592-en> [OECD, *Health at a Glace: 2016*].

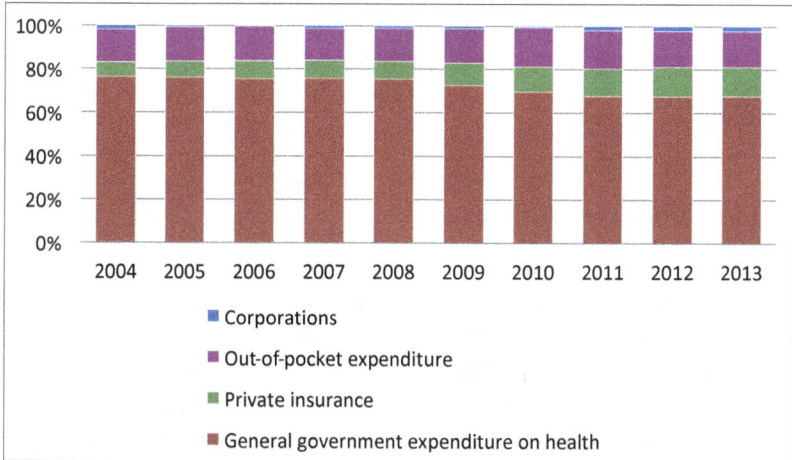

Figure 11.1 Components of total health expenditure, 2004–2013.
Source: "Components of Total Health Expenditure" (2004–2013), online: *World Health Organization* <https://www.who.int/>.

means test. A medical card confers eligibility for free access to GP and hospital services, but this is only available to 36 per cent of the population as of April 2017[7] and, as noted, is based primarily on means.[8] GP visit cards, which confer free GP care, are also separately available but only to a much smaller proportion of the population, based partly on means or age (under age sixty and over age seventy).

In category 2 are those without medical cards, estimated at 64 per cent of the population in 2016,[9] who as a consequence must pay full market prices for GP access, alongside user fees at almost every access point of the system and for prescribed drugs. For example, patients pay an average of €52.50 per GP visit and up to €144 per

7   Centre for Health Policy and Management, Trinity College Dublin, "Pathways Indicators" (2017), online: *Trinity College Dublin: The University of Dublin* <www.tcd.ie/medicine/health_policy_management/research/current/health_systems_research/indicators/> [Trinity College, "Pathway Indicators"].

8   Ireland, Health Service Executive, *July 2017 Management Data Report* (Dublin: Health Service Executive, 2017), online:<https://www.hse.ie/eng/services/publications/performancereports/july-2017-management-data-report.pdf> [Health Service Executive, *July 2017 Management Data Report*].

9   Centre for Health Policy and Management, Trinity College Dublin, "Mapping the Pathways to Universal Health Care," online: *Trinity College Dublin: The University of Dublin* <www.tcd.ie/medicine/health_policy_management/research/current/health_systems_research/overview/> [Trinity College, "Mapping Pathways"].

month for prescription drugs.[10] While everyone is eligible for public hospital care, those in category 2 pay €100 per emergency-department visit (without a GP referral) and €80 a day (capped at ten days per year) for hospital treatment (i.e., €800 annually).[11]

International Comparisons

Ireland spends a significant amount of resources on health care by international standards.[12] This reflects relatively high unit costs for labour and exceptionally high prices for pharmaceuticals.[13] In addition, incentives (such as extra-billing and user charges) and patterns of provision have also tended to promote more expensive modes of delivering care through public hospitals rather than in primary and community settings.[14] This has, in turn, caused significant congestion in hospitals and long waiting lists, spurring yet further private-sector growth. Indeed, a key cause of Ireland's high spending by international standards is also the growth of private health care spending levels, which are now quite high (2.9 per cent of GDP in 2015, the sixth highest of the twenty-eight European Union member states). Indeed, Ireland now has the third-highest proportion of private funding among its EU-15 peers—the fifteen member states before 2004 EU enlargement— exceeded only by Portugal and Greece.[15] Correspondingly, Ireland's share of funding coming from solidarity spending—whether from taxation or compulsory social insurance, where premiums are assessed as a proportion of income—is quite low by EU standards, twentieth among the member states (see the blue bars in fig. 11.2). Across the European Union, the majority of health-system funding is derived from solidarity spending—approximately 79 per cent of total spending in 2014. The remaining portion of expenditure is funded primarily

---

10   Anne Nolan et al, *The Impact of the Financial Crisis on Health System and Health in Ireland* (London: WHO European Observatory on HealtSystems, 2014), online: <www.euro.who.int/__data/assets/pdf_file/0011/266384/The-impact-of-the-financial-crisis-on-the-health-system-and-health-in-Ireland.pdf?ua=1>.

11   *Ibid.*

12   Trinity College, "Mapping Pathways," *supra* note 9.

13   Nolan et al, *supra* note 10.

14   Committee on the Future of Health Care, *Sláintecare Report, supra* note 3.

15   Turner, "The New System of Health Accounts in Ireland: What Does it all Mean?" (2017) 186:3 Ir J Med Sci 533.

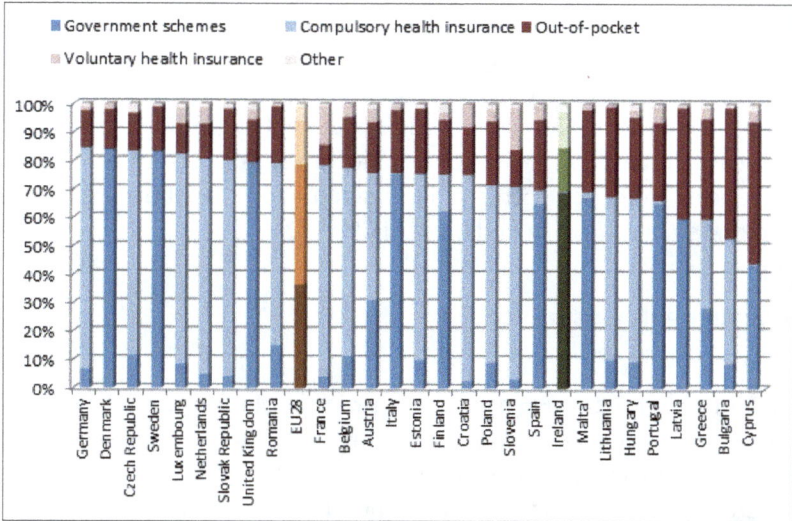

Figure 11.2. Ireland and solidarity funding of health systems in the EU.
Source: OECD, *Health at a Glance: Europe 2018* (Paris: OECD, 2012), online: <read.oecd-ilibrary.
org/social-issues-migration-health/health-at-a-glance-europe-2018_health_glance_eur-
2018-en#page1>.

by household spending on out-of-pocket payments (15 per cent), with private health insurance (PHI) accounting for only 5 per cent.[16]

Current figures suggest that, at 15 per cent, Ireland has the second-highest rate of PHI spending in the European Union as a total proportion of funding, with Slovenia having a marginally higher rate.[17] Moreover, Ireland experienced the greatest growth in PHI as a share of total health spending (7.1 per cent change) across the European Union between 2000 and 2014.[18] This has been a stand-out feature of Irish health financing over the last decade, with PHI as a percentage of total spending increasing 7 per cent in 2004 and 2005, to just under 13 per cent of total funds spent on health in 2015. PHI

---

16   OECD, *Health at a Glance: 2016, supra* note 6.

17   OECD, *Health at a Glance: Europe 2018* (Paris: OECD, 2012), online: <read.oecd-ili-
      brary.org/social-issues-migration-health/health-at-a-glance-europe-2018_health_
      glance_eur-2018-en#page1>; Central Statistics Office, *Ireland's System of Health
      Accounts, supra* note 4.

18   Anna Sagan & Sarah Thomson, *Voluntary Health Insurance in Europe: Role and
      Regulation* (Copenhagen: European Observatory on Health Systems and Policies,
      2016), online: <www.euro.who.int/__data/assets/pdf_file/0005/310838/Voluntary-
      health-insurance-Europe-role-regulation.pdf>.

occupies a unique role in the Irish setting, providing faster access to care in both public and private hospital settings. Perhaps for this reason it expanded its market share during the period of austerity from 2008 to 2014. Nevertheless, it is of note that PHI in Ireland does not cover many out-of-pocket expenditures, as is the case in other European countries with similarly sized supplementary insurance sectors, such as France and Slovenia.[19]

Private Health Insurance

Role

As argued earlier, PHI occupies a unique role in the Irish setting, providing faster access to care in both public- and private-provider settings. However, it does not always cover hospital expenses, and often covers only a fraction or none of non-hospital care, such as outpatient appointments with a specialist, GP visits, or care from allied health professionals. PHI in Ireland does not cover drugs costs, perhaps because there is already a government-reimbursement threshold for households spending more than a fixed amount in a month. Moreover, the benefits of queue-jumping only accrue to those who are able to afford PHI premiums, and there are concerns about the affordability of PHI. In this section, we explore the historical development of PHI in Ireland, its key features currently, and the main causes of its recent growth and resilience.

History

PHI has been available in Ireland since 1957, where it was solely provided by the state-backed Voluntary Health Insurance Board (under the brand name Vhi Healthcare). It was introduced to take the weight off the public sector for those households that could afford it, with quite small initial uptake. Indeed, more generally, government support for PHI has largely been based on it playing this purported role of removing the burden from the public sector.[20]

19   Stephen Thomas, Tamás Evetovits & Sarah Thomson, *Analysis of the Health System in Slovenia: Evaluating Health Financing* (Copenhagen: European Observatory on Health Systems and Policies, 2016), online: <http://www.euro.who.int/__data/assets/pdf_file/0005/336398/Evaluating-health-financing-report-Slovenia.pdf?ua=1>.

20   Francesca Colombo & Nicole Tapay, *Private Health Insurance in Ireland: A Case Study* (Paris: OECD, 2004).

This state-backed monopoly on PHI was effectively ended after EU intervention in the mid-1990s opened up the insurance market for competition. As a consequence of this liberalization, over the last twenty years there have been a number of private insurers that have entered and exited the Irish market. The dominant role of Vhi, the original state-backed PHI, has slowly eroded over this time as other PHI firms joined the market, mainly competing for younger and healthier membership. Vhi has by far the worst risk profile of all the private insurers, although it continues to have around 50 per cent of the PHI market.[21]

The Irish government has attempted to ameliorate problems with PHI through regulation. As a consequence, since 1994, the market has been quite heavily regulated, operating under the principles of intergenerational solidarity, with single-rate community-rating regulations, whereby insurers are required to charge all individuals the same premium per plan (subject to some exemptions). The market is also subject to open enrollment, lifetime cover, and minimum benefit regulations.[22] Market segmentation and diversification of products, though, has nonetheless enabled insurers to cream skim the young and healthy.

Further, the PHI market operated for a long time without a risk-equalization scheme, and when the government attempted to introduce such a scheme in 2005, it was declared unconstitutional by the courts and a fully developed risk-equalization scheme was only introduced in 2013. This replaced a basic system of additional age-related tax credits introduced in 2009.[23] Consequently, for many years little was done to disincentivize risk selection, meaning that a key profit focus for private health insurers was attracting low-risk members rather than seeking to reduce the costs of care. In turn, this contributed to market segmentation, which in turn undermined community-rating regulations.[24] Furthermore, while no risk-equalization

---

21   "Market Figures" (March 2015), online (PDF): *The Health Insurance Authority* <www.hia.ie/sites/default/files/HIA_Mar_Newsletter_2015.pdf>.

22   Conor Kegan et al, "Switching Insurer in the Irish Voluntary Health Insurance Market: Determinants, Incentives, and Risk Equalization" (2016) 17:7 Eur J Health Econ 823.

23   *Ibid.*

24   Brian Turner & Edward Shinnick, "Community Rating in the Absence of Risk Equalisation: Lessons From the Irish Private Health Insurance Market" (2013) 8:2 Health Econ Pol'y L 209.

scheme can entirely remove incentives for risk selection, there are recognized weaknesses in the existing scheme, which could be improved upon to further reduce incentives to cream skim.[25]

Given the increasing popularity of PHI, the Fine Gael–Labour coalition government of 2011 proposed it to be the basis of a universal health insurance, modelled on the Dutch managed-competition system.[26] *The Path to Universal Healthcare*—the white paper on universal health insurance, the legislative basis for the introduction of universal health insurance—was published by the government in April 2014.[27] It proposed an eventual "multi-payer" model of compulsory PHI for all citizens, with for-profit insurance companies operating in competition as per the Dutch approach, but its implementation was delayed until 2019. Despite the plan to universalize PHI and transform it through regulation into the basis of the public plan, a substantial portion of funds was still to come from taxation and to be funnelled through the insurers.[28] In November 2015, long-awaited costings of the proposed model were published, which found that it would require annually between €666 million and €2 billion more than current health spending.[29] The then health minister concluded that this particular model was "not affordable now nor ever."[30] Previous research has predicted that this would be the case, given the experience in the Netherlands.[31]

25   Conor Keegan et al, "Switching Benefits and Costs in the Irish Health Insurance Market: An Analysis of Consumer Surveys" (2019) 19:1 Int J Health Econ Manag 15.

26   Sara Ann Burke et al, "From Universal Health Insurance to Universal Healthcare? The Shifting Health Policy Landscape in Ireland Since the Economic Crisis" (2016) 120:3 Health Pol'y 235.

27   Ireland, Department of Health, *The Path To Universal Healthcare: White Paper on Universal Health Insurance* (Dublin: Department of Health, 2014), online: <health. gov.ie/wp-content/uploads/2014/04/White-Paper-Final-version-1-April-2014.pdf>.

28   *Ibid.*

29   Maev-Ann Wren, Sheelah Connolly & Nathan Cunningham, *An Examination of the Potential Costs of Universal Health Insurance in Ireland* (Dublin: Economic Research Institute, 2015), online: <www.esri.ie/pubs/RS45.pdf >.

30   Ireland, Department of Health, *Statement by Minister Varadkar following Cabinet discussion on UHI* (Dublin: Department of Health, 2015), online: <health.gov.ie/blog/press-release/statement-by-minister-varadkar following-cabinet-discussion-on-uhi/>.

31   P Ryan, S Thomas & C Normand, "Translating Dutch: Challenges and Opportunities in Reforming Health Financing in Ireland" (2009) 178:3 Ir J Med Sci 245.

With the withdrawal of this policy commitment to making PHI the basis of the universal plan, and because of concern about the role and viability of PHI, the outgoing minister for health proposed a policy of lifetime community rating. The aim of this was to bring more young people into the PHI market after the austerity reduction in enrollment to stabilize the market and consolidate the industry. The policy penalized those enrolling for PHI for the first time at age thirty-five and over by imposing late-entry loadings, up to a maximum loading of 70 per cent, subject to some exemptions.[32]

Demand for PHI

The main benefits of PHI in Ireland relate to its role of providing faster access to elective (i.e., non-emergency) hospital care for its beneficiaries. However, it also covers charges for acute care (whether in private or public hospitals). For non-acute services, such as GP and physiotherapist services, PHI cover tends at best to reimburse only part of the cost. Critically, depending on the type of insurance, PHI may not cover part or all of the cost of an outpatient appointment with a specialist.

Recent consumer surveys from the Health Insurance Authority note that key reasons for consumers voluntarily purchasing PHI are perceived poor quality of public care, high cost of private care, and limited access to public care.[33] The last point has been of increasing concern over the past ten years as wait times and lists in Ireland, already poor by international standards, have increased significantly for both inpatient and outpatient treatment, even after the austerity period (see figs. 11.3 and 11.4).

Despite apparent concerns about public care, a key aspect of some PHI funded provision is that it takes place in public hospitals, thus "crowding out" access for public patients in the sense that it takes away potential treatment spots for public-pay patients.[34] Concerns have been raised that individuals with PHI are, in effect, having their access cross-subsidized from the public purse through

---

32   Conor Keegan et al, "Addressing Market Segmentation and Incentives for Risk Selection: How Well Does Risk Equalisation in the Irish Private Health Insurance Market Work?" (2017) 48:1 Econ Soc Rev 61.

33   *Ibid.*

34   BM Johnston et al, "Private Health Expenditure in Ireland: Assessing the Affordability and Sustainability of Private Financing of Health Care" (2019) 123:10 Health Pol'y 963.

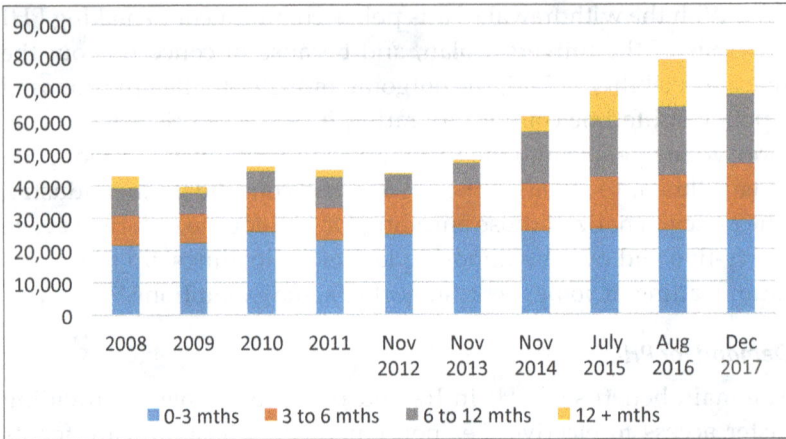

Figure 11.3. Number of adults waiting for inpatient hospital treatment, 2008–2017.
Source: Centre for Health Policy and Management, Trinity College Dublin, "Pathways Indicators" (2017), online: *Trinity College Dublin: The University of Dublin* <www.tcd.ie/ medicine/health_policy_management/research/current/health_systems_research/ indicators/>.

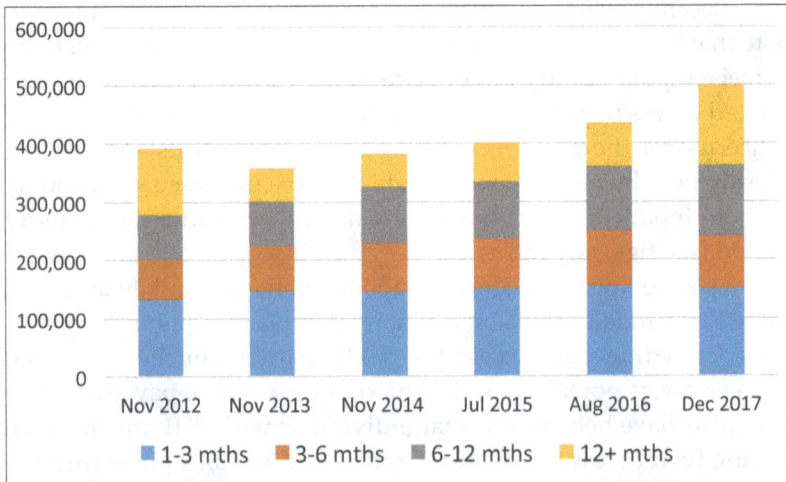

Figure 11.4. Number of adults awaiting outpatient appointments, 2012–2017.
Source: Centre for Health Policy and Management, Trinity College Dublin, "Pathways Indicators" (2017), online: *Trinity College Dublin: The University of Dublin* <www.tcd.ie/ medicine/health_policy_management/research/current/health_systems_research/ indicators/>.

tax breaks and relatively low prices charged by public hospitals to PHI patients. In recent years, however, there has been some unwinding of tax subsidies for those with PHI, and charges for private care in public hospitals have increased substantially to better reflect the full cost of care.

The waits, discussed above, for an initial appointment with a specialist (in the form of an outpatient appointment) and for treatment do not capture waits that happen before these stages. Research carried out with GPs found:

- In the public system 70–80 per cent of GPs have no direct access to CT scans. Even where it is available, there is an average sixteen-week wait. In the private system, 90 per cent of GPs have access to CT scanning, with an average waiting time of 5.5 working days. Furthermore, the average wait for MRI scans in the public system was twenty-two weeks, varying from six days to seventy-two weeks. Virtually all GPs have direct access to an MRI scan in the private sector within seven working days.
- The majority (86 per cent) of GP respondents were of the opinion that increased access to diagnostics would reduce their referrals to emergency departments and improve the quality of their referrals. When questioned regarding outpatient-department referrals, 90 per cent felt that improved access would reduce such referrals, while 92 per cent felt this would improve the quality of these referrals. Overall, 87 per cent believed that improved access to diagnostics would reduce unnecessary admissions.[35]

While this research is over five years old, there is no reason to believe access to diagnostics has improved in the public system, and improving access to diagnostics is a key recommendation in the Sláintecare report.[36] People who privately get these diagnostics tests outlined above either pay wholly or partly out of pocket, or they may be covered by their PHI.

---

35   Margaret O'Riordan, Claire Collins & Gillian Doran, *Access to Diagnostics: A Key Enabler for a Primary Care Led Health Service* (Dublin: Irish College of General Practitioners, 2013).

36   Committee on the Future of Healthcare, *Sláintecare Report, supra* note 3.

Coverage

Over the austerity period, PHI coverage dropped from a high of 52 per cent of the population in 2007 to just under 44 per cent at the end of 2014. By September 2016, the numbers holding PHI had increased slightly, to 44.8 per cent, likely because of the introduction of the lifetime community-rating policy and general economic recovery.[37]

Recent Austerity Context

Ireland experienced a deep and long economic crisis between 2008 and 2014 that led to six austerity budgets. In Europe, the severity of the recession experienced by the Irish economy was only bettered by the Baltic States in the initial years after the 2008 global market crash.[38] However, the duration of the economic slump in Ireland was much worse, and only Greece experienced a longer economic crisis among the EU-15 countries. Ireland was only one of a handful of countries bailed out by the troika of the European Union, the European Central Bank (ECB), and the International Monetary Fund (IMF). Key statistics are that gross national income contracted sharply, by 9 per cent in 2009; unemployment grew quickly, from a low of 4.6 per cent to 14.7 per cent from 2007 to 2012; the country's debt-to-GDP ratio increased from 25 per cent to 124 per cent from 2006 to 2014; and a massive gap in public-sector financing of €2.7bn (a deficit of 17 per cent) opened up by 2014.[39]

The deep and prolonged economic crisis in Ireland had the effect of increasing the importance of private health funding and, in particular, PHI to overall health-system funding patterns. Austerity measures were introduced between 2008 and 2013, and their impact is still being felt, even after the economy recovered and returned to high levels of economic growth.[40]

---

37   Sara Burke et al, "Indicators of Health System Coverage and Activity in Ireland During the Economic Crisis 2008–2014—From 'More With Less' to 'Less With Less'" (2014) 117:3 Health Pol'y 275.

38   Conor Keegan et al, "Measuring Recession Severity and its Impact on Healthcare Expenditure" (2013) 13 Intl J Health Care Fin & Econ 139.

39   Stephen Thomas et al, "A Framework for Assessing Health System Resilience in an Economic Crisis: Ireland as a Test Case" (2013) 13:450 BMC Health Serv Res.

40   Johnston et al, *supra* note 34.

Out-of-pocket payments increased over the austerity period. This increased the financial burden on households as each person had to pay, on average, an additional €120 per person per year to access the same health services.[41] Furthermore, unmet need increased sharply between 2010 and 2014, pushing Ireland above the EU average, suggesting an increased number of people were unable to afford or access care in relation to both general medical and dental examinations.[42]

During the economic downturn, successive budgets sought to shift a greater proportion of the costs of funding health care onto households. Recent research shows that nearly €600 million of the cost of some aspects of health care was transferred from the state onto people between 2008 and 2014.[43] Policies included the introduction of prescription charges for medical card holders, increased emergency-department charges, increased thresholds for reimbursement under the country's Drug Payment Scheme, and reduced medical card eligibility.

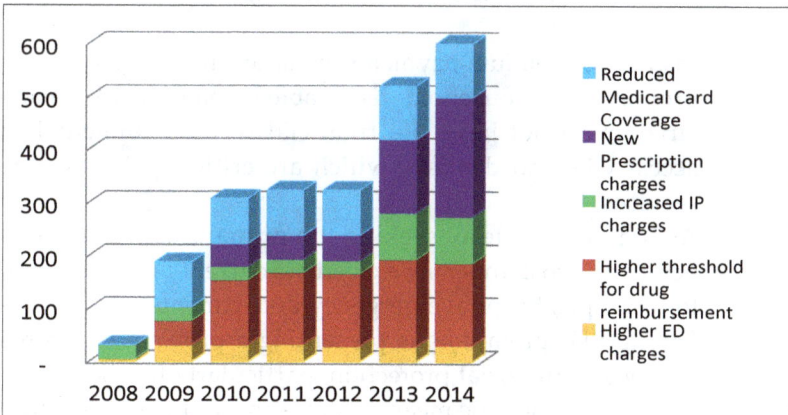

Figure 11.5. Cost shifting from the state to households, 2008–2014.
Source: Centre for Health Policy and Management, Trinity College Dublin, "Pathways Indicators" (2017), online: *Trinity College Dublin: The University of Dublin* <www.tcd. ie/medicine/health_policy_management/research/current/health_systems_research/ indicators/>.

---

41   OECD, *Health at a Glance: Europe 2012* (Paris: OECD, 2012), online: <www. oecd-ilibrary.org/social-issues-migration-health/health-at-a-glance-europe-2012_9789264183896-en> [OECD, *Health at a Glance: 2012*].

42   *Ibid*; OECD, *Health at a Glance: 2016, supra* note 6.

43   Stephen Thomas, Sara Burke & Sarah Barry, "The Irish Health Care System and Austerity: Sharing the Pain" (2014) 383:9928 Lancet 1545.

Ireland was not alone in expanding the role for private finance as a response to the financial crisis—many countries in Europe introduced measures aimed at expanding private finance.[44] These policies are often portrayed as effective mechanisms for improving the efficiency of health systems. However, such arguments may also be a convenient rationale for reducing state spending. They also come to the fore when public-sector budgets are highly constrained. This was exacerbated by the financial bailouts of countries across Europe by the EU/ECB/IMF troika, and their imposed spending constraints. Interestingly, early cutbacks in Ireland may well have had some efficiency dividends in the public sector, but later cuts just reduced service provision and access.[45]

At the same time that many governments in Europe pushed costs on to households, households themselves faced difficult choices over health care payments as a result of reduced disposable income. In Ireland, data from household-spending surveys shows that households prioritized health insurance coverage over out-of-pocket payments.[46] This trend presents three challenges:

- Insurance-premium payments are absorbing and increasing proportion of household disposable income, which means citizens do not have the financial resources needed to access GPs and dentists, which are critical primary-care services.
- As individuals delay seeking the primary care they need because of cost, this may exacerbate current bottlenecks in, for example, hospital emergency departments.
- Paying PHI premiums is presenting a problem of affordability and financial protection, particularly for those with the lowest economic means. Interestingly, there is evidence that significant numbers of the poorest 40 per cent of the population, who are frequently eligible for a medical card

---

44   Marina Karanikolos et al, "Financial Crisis, Austerity, and Health in Europe" (2013) 381:9874 Lancet 1323; Gianluca Quaglio et al, "Austerity and Health in Europe" (2013) 113:1 Health Pol'y 13; Oliver J Wouters & Martin McKee, "Private Financing of Health Care in Times of Economic Crisis: a Review of the Evidence" (2017) 8:23 Glob Pol'y 2.

45   Burke et al, *supra* note 37.

46   Johnston et al, *supra* note 34.

and free care, are taking out PHI, which is causing them financial hardship.

As the Irish government was shifting costs onto households, it was simultaneously reducing its funding of the health care system and, as a consequence, reduced human-resource levels by around 7 per cent.[47] There were 8,027 fewer whole-time equivalent directly employed in the Health Service Executive, the main public sector health care employer, in 2014 than there was in 2008. There was a degree of relative protection for frontline staffing, which only decreased by 2.9 per cent between 2008 and 2014, but, counter to stated policy, the decline in staffing of non-acute care was over double the decline in acute care. Further, the reduction in directly employed staff was largely matched by a marked increase in hospital spending on temporary staff recruited through agencies.

When the economy and the health budget returned to growth in 2015, the recovery in health human resources was again biased away from cost-effective non-acute services, perpetuating the Irish system's over-dependence on hospitals.[48] Figure 11.7 contrasts the human-resource (HR) trends in acute and community services. By December 2016, the levels of acute HR were back to pre-crisis levels, compared to the HR levels for community and primary-care services, which continued to fall far short of needs. Again, such imbalances have tended to exacerbate capacity and cost problems in the Irish health care system.

Staffing levels have continued to grow; by December 2017, there were 110,795 staff in the public health system, akin to pre-crisis staff levels.[49] Nevertheless, the gap between staffing of acute and non-acute services has not been addressed. This will create further pressure on the hospital sector, as it is used for care which should be provided in other parts of the system.

---

47   Des Williams & Stephen Thomas, "The Impact of Austerity on the Health Workforce and the Achievement of Human Resources for Health Policies in Ireland (2008–2014)" (2017) 15:62 Hum Resour Health.

48   Health Service Executive, *July 2017 Management Data Report, supra* note 8.

49   Ireland, Department of Public Expenditure and Reform, *Mid-Year Expenditure Report 2018* (Dublin: Department of Public Expenditure and Reform, 2018), online: <www.per.gov.ie/wp-content/uploads/MYER-2018_-web-version.pdf>.

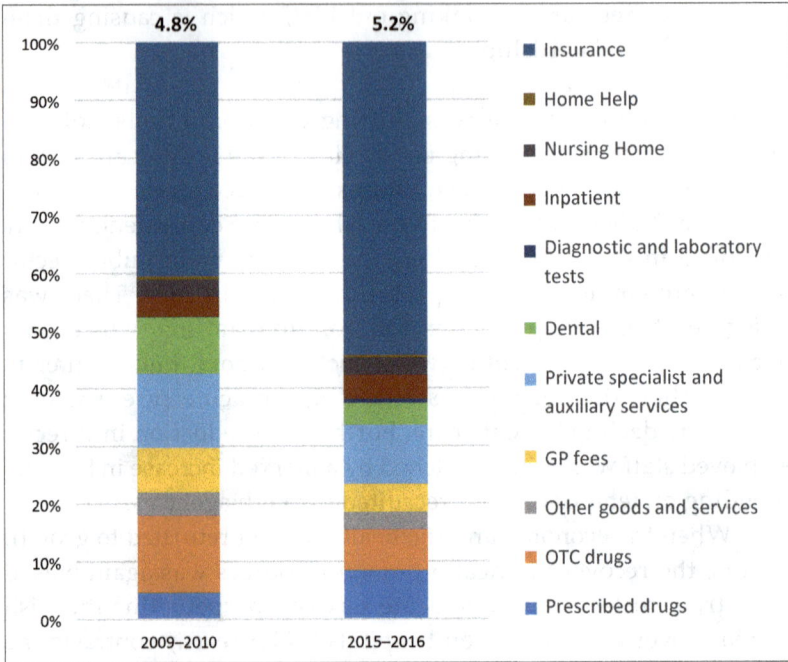

Figure 11.6. Proportion of household private spending on health care by type.
Source: Central Statistics Office, Ireland (2019), online: https://www.cso.ie/en/index.html.

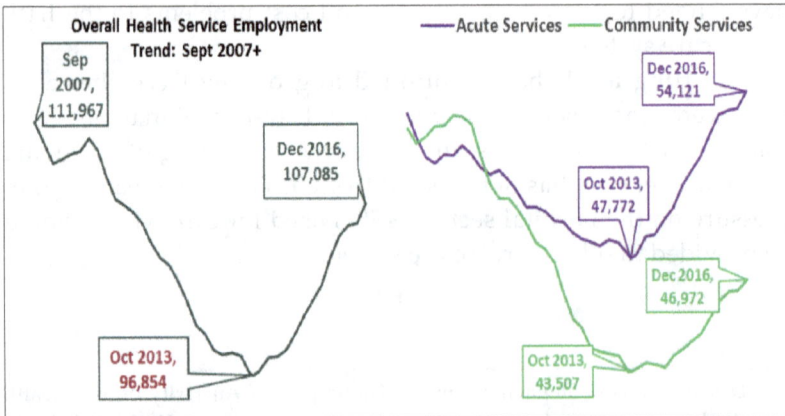

Figure 11.7. Health service employment trends, 2007–2016.
Source: Centre for Health Policy and Management, Trinity College Dublin, "Pathways Indicators" (2017), online: *Trinity College Dublin: The University of Dublin* <www.tcd. ie/medicine/health_policy_management/research/current/health_systems_research/ indicators/>.

Policy Response and Sláintecare

The general election in March 2016 delivered a minority government as voters proved tired of both established parties and austerity policies. The largest party, Fine Gael, with 25 per cent of the vote, was not able to form a stable government coalition despite arrangements with some smaller parties and independents. Instead, a Fine Gael minority government was propped up through a supply-and-confidence arrangement with the main opposition party, Fianna Fáil, and the support of a range of independent members of parliament.[50] As a result, legislation could only be passed through consensus across government and substantial parts of the opposition. This consensus work was dubbed the era of "new politics," and the health care reforms perhaps owe much to this era of joint work and compromise.[51]

In early May 2016, Deputy Roísín Shortall, a former junior health minister and co-leader of a small centre-left party, the Social Democrats, launched an all-party motion on health signed by eighty-nine Teachtai Dála (or TDs, members of Dáil Éireann, the lower chamber of parliament) out of a total of 158. The motion was to establish an all-party committee with a remit of agreeing on a ten-year strategy for health reform, including the delivery of a single-tier universal health service, and switching emphasis to primary and social care.

The day after the motion was introduced, the newly formed government published its Programme for Partnership Government, which included a commitment to "request an Oireachtas All-Party committee to develop a single long-term vision plan for healthcare over a 10 year period. This plan should have cross party consensus."[52]

In the face of continued intractable problems of long waiting lists, massive overcrowding in emergency departments, profound inequities, a backlog of underinvestment, and the absence of his own party's health policy, a new minister for health, Simon Harris, proposed

---

50   Sara Burke, "Achieving a Plan for Universal Healthcare in Ireland Through Political Consensus Post Austerity" (2018) 122:12 Health Pol'y 1278 [Burke, "Achieving a Plan"].

51   *Ibid.*

52   Ireland, Department of the Taoiseach, *A Programme for a Partnership Government* (Dublin: Department of the Taioseach, 2016) at 63, online: <https://assets.gov.ie/3221/231118100655-5c803e6351b84155a21ca9fe4e64ce5a.pdf>.

> an Oireachtas [Irish legislature] all-party committee to develop a
> single long term vision plan for healthcare over a 10 year period
> ... [and concluding that] key to the long-term sustainability of
> our health service and Universal Healthcare ... is the develop-
> ment of a new funding model for the health service.[53]

This is considered the first act of the new politics, as the government
here adopted an opposition motion.[54]

The Oireachtas Committee on the Future of Healthcare was
established in June 2016 and met between July 2016 and May 2017. It
was composed of fourteen TDs across the political spectrum, as specified in the Dáil motion, including Deputy Shortall, who was elected
its chairperson. The committee held thirty public hearings, received
167 submissions from the public and interested bodies, and published
two interim reports. In November 2016, the committee engaged a
team (the authors of this chapter) from the Centre for Health Policy
and Management, in Trinity College Dublin. The Trinity team worked
with the Oireachtas committee in hosting the first-ever expert-led
workshops in the history of the Irish Parliament, where useful health
systems frameworks and international evidence were presented.[55] The
resulting report, Sláintecare, has proved highly influential, not least
because it represented a "unique and historic opportunity for TDs from
across the political spectrum to come together to develop consensus
on a long-term policy direction for Ireland's healthcare system."[56]

The core aims of Sláintecare are to establish:

- a universal, single-tier health service, where patients are
  treated solely on the basis of health need;
- a reorientation of the health system "towards integrated primary and community care, consistent with the highest quality of patient safety in as short a time-frame as possible."[57]

The report outlines a ten-year plan for transformation of the Irish
health system on the basis of key policy recommendations, including:

---

53 Department of the Taoiseach, *supra* note 52.
54 Burke, "Achieving a Plan," *supra* note 50.
55 Committee on the Future of Healthcare, *Sláintecare Report, supra* note 3; Burke, "Achieving a Plan," *supra* note 50.
56 Burke, "Achieving a Plan," *supra* note 50.
57 Committee on the Future of Healthcare, *Sláintecare Report, supra* note 3.

- Introduction of entitlements to care (rather than just eligibility for care).
- Introduction of free care for hospital admissions and GPs, reduction of copayments for medicines, and expansion of public funding.
- Expansion of the primary-care workforce and reorientation toward the primary-care system.
- Removal of private insurance funding from public hospitals (over six years).
- Wait time guarantees, backed up by increased accountability and information.
- A transitional fund to support capacity expansion in the system, and to address the capital backlog acquired over the austerity years.

The report adopts a World Health Organization definition of universal health care and specifies a comprehensive basket of services to be included in a universal health system. In relation to PHI, the report makes the following commitments:

> The Committee also proposes the phased elimination of private care from public hospitals, leading to an expansion of the public system's ability to provide public care. Holders of private health insurance will still be able to purchase care from private healthcare providers.
>
> ...
>
> It recommends a model where private insurance will no longer confer faster access to heal thcare in the public sector but is limited to covering private care in private hospitals.
>
> ...
>
> Reliance on private health insurance may also fall as access to our public healthcare system improves. It is estimated that as the expanded entitlements are phased in, household direct expenditure overall will fall by around €148m each year on average, through reductions in out-of-pocket costs and some reduced private health insurance costs.[58]

---

58   *Ibid* at 17, 25, 132.

The report estimates the costs of the removal of private care from public hospitals to be €649 million per year, and this removal is phased from years two to six of the plan. The committee also "proposed an independent impact analysis of the separation of private practice from the public system with a view to identifying any adverse and unintended consequences that may arise for the public system in the separation."[59] An independent group was established by the government in 2017 to conduct this analysis and submitted its final report in February 2019.

Implications for Private Funding of the Irish Health Care System

There will be substantial implications for the funding of health care in the Irish system if Sláintecare proposals are fully implemented. First, by establishing free care for GPs and hospital inpatient and emergency-department access, and by reducing drug-reimbursement thresholds and lowering prescription charges, out-of-pocket payments will be reduced from 15.4 per cent to 8.5 per cent (fig. 11.8). Instead of patients paying user charges to access care, more funding

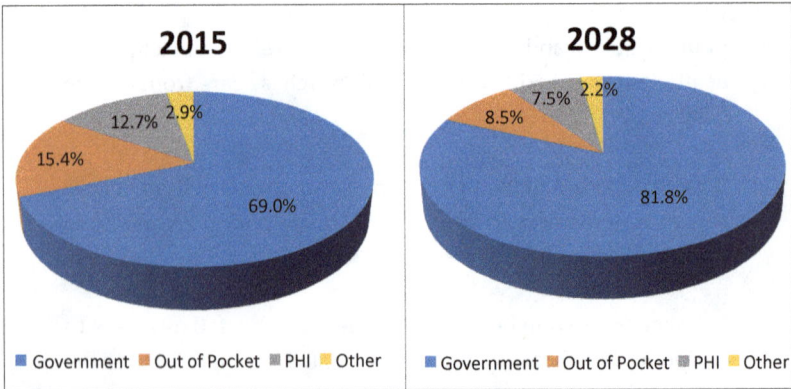

Figure 11.8. Change in shares of health financing as a result of Sláintecare 2015 and 2028.
Source: Central Statistics Office, Ireland, (2019), online: <https://www.cso.ie/en/index.html>; Centre for Health Policy and Management, Trinity College Dublin, "Pathways Indicators" (2017) https://www.tcd.ie/medicine/health_policy_management/research/current/health_systems_research//.

59   Committee on the Future of Healthcare, *Sláintecare Report*, *supra* note 3.

will come from taxation or other public sources. Extra taxation will also fund the gap in public hospital funding caused by the removal of PHI as a funding source. The resultant increase in taxation-based funding will expand its share to almost 82 per cent of aggregate health care funding. In relation to international funding patterns shown in figure 11.2, this would bring Ireland substantially above the EU average, and positioned ahead of the Netherlands, the Slovak Republic, and the United Kingdom. Since PHI would no longer fund faster access to the public hospital system, demand for it would reduce. In this case, it is estimated that the share of PHI of overall funding would fall from 12.7 per cent to 7.5 per cent from 2015 to 2028, which is much closer to the EU average.

It is interesting to note that Sláintecare does not mark the abolition of private financing in the Irish health care system, but it does signify an important shift from allocating access to care on one's ability to pay to medical need. Those with PHI will still be able to access care in public hospitals, but they will not get faster access to that care. They will still be able to seek private care in private hospitals according to the coverage offered by their insurer.

Key Challenges Ahead

For Sláintecare to be successful, careful attention must be given to disentangling the public and private sectors. Key challenges are summarized below.

Changing Financial Incentives

Fee for service for doctors for private activity in public hospitals to be removed. Currently, many consultants have contracts that allow them to work in the private sector over and above their public-sector activity, given a minimum time commitment in their public hospital work. Nevertheless, recent investigative journalism has uncovered that there is a substantial minority of consultants who do not meet their minimum time commitments in public-sector activity.[60] While this may be less important where waiting lists and times are short

---

60   "RTÉ Investigates—Public v Private; The Battle for Care," *RTÉ News* (1 February 2018), online: <www.rte.ie/news/investigations-unit/2017/1122/922105-rte-investigates-public-v-private-the-battle-for-care/>.

for public acute procedures, it is apparent that some consultants both have long waiting lists and also fail to honour their public-sector contracts in relation to minimum hours worked. At face value, removing private funds from public hospitals may impact consultant incomes, though consultants would still be able to practice in private hospitals. Nevertheless, there is concern that there would need to be a change of consultant contracts, and given the history of such negotiations, this may prove to be a difficult and long-winded affair.

PHI insurance payment to public hospitals to be removed. As noted, PHI in some instances covers patients to be treated faster in private beds in public hospitals. With this removed, a small but key source of funding would be taken away from public hospitals at a time when budgets are stretched. Nevertheless, the PHI funding of public hospitals is quite a small proportion of overall acute funding, and its significance has been dropping in recent years. Also, Sláintecare includes an estimate of public compensation of this funding source to be phased in over several years, allowing more patients to be seen publicly (as detailed above).

Resolving Access Problems

Reduce wait times. In order to break the cycle of demand for PHI, the public system must significantly address access problems for public patients. In large part this means addressing the terrible waiting times that patients face for public treatment. Many other countries have achieved great gains in this area over the past decade, primarily through wait time guarantees, enhanced accountability, public engagement with wait time data, and strategic purchasing of care for those experiencing long wait times.

Reduce burden on hospitals. Currently, there is insufficient capacity outside hospitals in primary-, community-, and social-care settings. This tends to suck patients unnecessarily into hospitals, into crowded emergency departments, and into longer hospital stays than necessary. Furthermore, high GP fees do little to encourage earlier access as to time-sensitive health care problems. There is some evidence that crowded emergency departments translate into higher emergency-related admissions, which in turn are crowding out elective care and causing longer wait times. Sláintecare outlines a plan for substantial investment in primary- and community-care staffing and infrastructure, alongside fee removal, toward redefining the appropriate role of hospitals and reducing the demand and perceived need for private financing mechanisms.

Shifting Public Perceptions

Perhaps the most challenging aspect of Sláintecare is to change the pervading public narrative that the public system cannot be trusted to provide quality and timely care. In a recent survey, only 22 per cent of the population thought public care was good enough, and 58 per cent thought PHI was a necessity.[61] The issue of lack of trust in the public sector has, in recent times, been further eroded by periodic scandals around non-disclosure of vital information[62] and poor quality of services.[63] It is further made difficult by powerful interest groups, for example, the Irish Hospital Consultants Association, which has publicly disparaged potential reforms in favour of the status quo, which is to its advantage.[64]

Conclusion

The introduction of PHI in Ireland allowed a two-tier system to develop, with long wait lists in the public system and limited financial protection. The government is now looking at a radical reform program to reorient the system, establish universal health care, and remove private insurance financing from public hospitals. The disentangling of the public and private systems is not an easy task; it will take careful planning, sequencing, coalition building, and

61 Kantar Millward Brown, *A Review of Private Health Insurance in Ireland, 2017* (Health Insurance Authority, 2017), online: <www.hia.ie/sites/default/files/Consumer%20Survey%20on%20the%20private%20health%20insurance%20market%20in%20Ireland%202017.pdf>.

62 Fergal Bowers, "What is the Cervical Check Controversy About?," *RTÉ News* (12 September 2018), online: <www.rte.ie/news/analysis-and-comment/2018/0427/958788-cervical-cancer-q-a/>.

63 Ellish O'Regan, Katherine Donnelly & Ryan Nugent, "Damning Report Highlights Litany of Failures at Maternity Hospital," *Irish Independent* (17 June 2019), online: <www.independent.ie/ca/irish-news/health/damning-report-highlights-litany-of-failures-at-maternity-hospital-36872141.html>.

64 Martin Wall, "State Must Contemplate Perceived Flaws in Sláintecare Policy," *The Irish Times* (7 August 2018), online: <www.irishtimes.com/news/health/state-must-contemplate-perceived-flaws-in-sl%C3%A1intecare-policy-1.3587993>.

changing the public narrative about the nature of the health system. Nevertheless, these are worthwhile challenges to take on in order to deliver a truly universal health care system for Ireland.

While Canada might be considering an expanded role for private health insurance, such a decision needs to be taken with sober judgement. It cannot be easily unwound. PHI was initially introduced in Ireland to take some pressure off the government. However, its introduction has impeded a fair, efficient, and integrated system, and there has been substantial profiteering by smaller insurers since liberalization. It has taken sixty years to develop a plan that will disentangle public and private financing. Implementation will take another ten years at least. It must be questioned as to whether Canada can afford such a lengthy and difficult journey.

CHAPTER 12

Contracting our Way Around Two-Tier Care? The Use of Physician Contracts to Limit Dual Practice

Bryan Thomas

A t the time of medicare's inception, in the early 1960s, Canadian physicians feared becoming employees of the state and staged protests to protect their professional autonomy, securing the ability to operate as independent contractors and bill government on a fee-for-service basis—a status most physicians enjoy to this day.[1] This long-standing professional independence has left some Canadian physicians perennially alive to the temptation of selling their services privately, particularly in high-demand areas of care that frequently carry long wait times. With court challenges like *Chaoulli*[2] and *Cambie Surgeries Corp.*,[3] entrepreneurial physicians have tried to advance this agenda on the coattails of patients, arguing, in effect, that long wait times violate patients' rights to "life, liberty and security of the person"—a problem they claim is best remedied by lifting restrictions on private for-profit care.

To gain some perspective on how Canada's historic concession to physicians' professional independence shapes debate surrounding two-tier care, contrast their situation with that of public-school teachers—another professional group tasked with delivering a universal

1   H. Michael Stevenson & Paul A Williams, "Physicians and Medicare: Professional Ideology and Canadian Health Care Policy" (1985) 11 Canadian Public Pol'y 504.
2   *Chaoulli v Quebec (AG)*, [2005] 1 SCR 791 [*Chaoulli*].
3   *Cambie Surgeries v British Columbia (Medical Services Commission)*, Docket S090663 (Vancouver) [*Cambie*].

public service. Public-school teachers are obliged to work certain hours, instruct the cohort of students assigned to them, and deliver a curriculum tailored by provincial decision makers. Canadians would recoil at the thought of public-school teachers extra-billing students, or shirking their responsibilities to the public-school system for part of the school day as they cater to lucrative private-pay students. The analogy can perhaps be pushed even further: as in the case of health care, students (and their parents) have *Charter* rights in education—notably a right to be educated in accordance to their religious beliefs (within reason).[4] Yet nobody is tempted to conclude—along the logic of the *Cambie* challenge—that public-school teachers must be granted the freedom to sideline in private education during school hours as a way of ensuring that religious students have a "safety valve" from the state monopoly on secular education. We happily restrict all of this behaviour, not through statutory prohibitions on private education—Canada has private schools, after all—but by imposing fairly stringent *contractual* conditions on public-school teachers. Again, this comparison is offered only to highlight the extent to which historical contingencies—related to Canadian physicians' unique employment status—have contributed to the political-economic framing of the *Chaoulli* and *Cambie* legal challenges.

This chapter explores whether and how Canadian physicians might be contractually bound, along similar lines, as an alternative mechanism for limiting the spread of two-tier care. This is an approach taken by some high-performing health care systems around the world—perhaps most notably England—using diverse contractual modalities to prevent or limit public-sector physicians from engaging in private practice. Section 1 provides a brief backgrounder on the legal and historical factors driving Canada's debate over two-tier care. Section 2 explains the policy rationale(s) for limiting physician autonomy contractually—identifying the risks associated with allowing physicians participating in universal public systems to simultaneously participate in private for-profit care (i.e., dual practice). In section 3, I survey how physician contracts have been used in other jurisdictions to limit physician autonomy against the proliferation of two-tier care.

---

4   *Loyola High School v. Quebec (Attorney General)*, [2015] 1 SCR 613.

Canadian Restrictions on Two-Tier Care Explained

As previous chapters have explained in great detail, the legislative framework of Canada's single-payer health care system has come under *Charter* challenge.[5] While the specifics of these challenges vary by province, it is broadly alleged that, given long wait times in Canada's universal health care system (medicare), laws restricting the emergence of a parallel private tier infringe patients' right to "life, liberty and security of the person."[6] As others have observed, there is an air of unreality to the framing of these cases around patients' rights: these challenges are generally funded and championed by physicians—notably specialists in high-demand areas like orthopedic surgery—who stand to profit handsomely from the liberalization of a parallel private tier.[7] It is telling, for example, that the challenge now underway in British Columbia was triggered not by any egregious patient experience, but in response to the BC government's audit of Cambie Surgeries Corporation for surreptitiously extra-billing orthopedic-surgery patients to the tune of hundreds of thousands of dollars annually.[8] The remedies sought in these challenges are likewise indicative of the underlying motivations: the courts are not asked to help fix medicare's wait times for any specific patient(s), let alone for patients generally. All that is asked is that the courts strike down restrictions on physicians and private insurers, which stand in the way of private for-profit care.[9]

---

5   *Chaoulli, supra* note 2; *Cambie, supra* note 3; *Allen v Alberta*, 2015 ABCA 277; *McCreith v. Ontario (A.G.)*, Toronto 07-CV-339454PD3 (Ont. Sup. Ct.).

6   *Canadian Charter of Rights and Freedoms*, s 7, Part 1 of the *Constitution Act, 1982*, being Schedule B to the *Canada Act 1982* (UK), 1982, c 11.

7   Some have likened *Chaoulli* to the infamous *Lochner* case of US constitutional law, where business interests successfully challenged a law limiting the work week to sixty hours, ostensibly in defense of workers' right to freedom of contract. See, Sujit Choudhry, "Worse than *Lochner*?" in Colleen M Flood, Kent Roach & Lorne Sossin, eds, *Access to Care, Access to Justice: The Legal Debate Over Private Health Insurance in Canada* (Toronto: University of Toronto Press, 2005) 75.

8   That audit was completed in 2012, finding that Cambie Surgeries Corp. had extra-billed patients, in violation of British Columbia's *Medicare Protection Act*. See, Ministry of Health, *Specialist Referral Clinic and Cambie Surgeries Corporation: Audit Report* (June 2012), online: <www.bchealthcoalition.ca/sites/default/files/uploads/Specialist%20Referral%20Clinic%20Inc.%20and%20Cambie%20Surgeries%20Corporation%20Audit%20Report.pdf>.

9   Arguably, the focus on "negative rights" was integral to the success of the *Chaoulli* challenge. Courts, wary of overreach, are more comfortable with the tidy

Viewed in this light, these court challenges can be understood as the latest twist in the longer history of physician resistance to "socialized medicine." A segment of Canadian physicians has long bristled against the establishment of medicare, and its implications for their earning power and professional autonomy.[10] At the time of medicare's enactment, physicians' groups across the provinces feared becoming employees of the state, subject to increased managerial oversight and salary restrictions. Doctors' strikes were organized, resisting the rise of "socialism" in the health care sector. This physician resistance was mollified, in large part, by provinces agreeing to allow physicians to retain their status as independent contractors, billing medicare on a fee-for-service basis in an arrangement that persists to this day.[11]

Over time, there was growing concern that physician extra-billing was compromising the accessibility of medicare services. The *Canada Health Act*, passed in 1984, addressed this concern by empowering the federal government to wield its spending power as a carrot and stick, withholding health transfers from provinces that allow extra-billing and user fees, on a dollar-for-dollar basis, and authorizing financial penalties for provinces that breached the core principles of medicare (comprehensiveness, universality, accessibility, portability, and public administration).[12] The provinces complied—against renewed protest from physicians' groups[13]—each enacting their own combination of restrictions drawn from a basic regulatory tool kit: bans on parallel private health insurance, bans on extra-billing and user fees, bans on dual practice (i.e., physicians selling medically necessary care privately must opt out of medicare), and requirements that medically necessary care sold privately be priced at or below

---

work of overturning laws, as opposed to the messy work of solving wait times. See Kent Roach, "The Courts and Medicare: Too Much or Too Little Judicial Activism?" in Colleen M Flood, Kent Roach & Lorne Sossin, eds, *Access to Care, Access to Justice: The Legal Debate over Private Health Insurance in Canada* (Toronto: University of Toronto Press, 2005).

10   See Marchildon, this volume.

11   Gregory P Marchildon, "Physicians Resistance and the Forging of Public Healthcare: A Comparative Analysis of Doctor's Strikes in Canada and Belgium in the 1960s" (2011) 55 Medical History 203.

12   *Canada Health Act*, RSC 1985, c C-6.

13   S Helber & R Deber, "Banning Extra-Billing in Canada: Just What the Doctor Didn't Order" (1987) 13 Canadian Public Pol'y 62.

the public fees rate.[14] With each province enacting one or more of these restrictions, the market for privately financed care has been effectively tamped down. These are the restrictions now under constitutional challenge as infringing patients' *Charter* right to life, liberty and security of the person.

Rationales for Restricting Two-Tier Care

The core issue in these constitutional challenges is whether these restrictions on privatization are necessary to the preservation of public medicare. Critics claim that these restrictions are arbitrary, pointing to the fact that comparator countries manage to sustain high-performing universal health care systems without reliance on such statutory prohibitions.[15] As leading comparativist scholars have been keen to point out, this approach of asking whether high-performing comparator countries employ the *exact same* regulatory modalities as Canada is potentially misleading.[16] After all, no two health care systems are exactly alike, and the unique design features of Canadian medicare may require unique regulatory modalities.[17]

It makes sense, therefore, to begin with more fundamental questions: regulatory modalities aside, does it make sense as a matter of public policy to prevent or limit the emergence of a parallel private tier? For present purposes—anticipating our later discussion of contractual restrictions on physicians engaging in private practice—the core question is this: putting aside the specific regulatory instruments used, does it make sense to restrict the ability of physicians in a universal health care system to moonlight in private/dual practice?

Though it is not possible to conduct controlled experiments in the design of health systems, there are various reasons—both theoretical and empirical—for thinking that a thriving parallel private

---

14   For a province-by-province typology of provincial restrictions on private health-care, see Colleen M Flood & Tom Archibald, "The Illegality of Private Health Insurance in Canada" (2008) 164 CMAJ 825–830.

15   *Chaoulli*, supra note 2 at 834–836.

16   Colleen M Flood & Amanda Haugan, "Is Canada Odd? A comparison of European and Canadian approaches to choice and regulation of the public/private divide in health care" (2010) 5 Health Economics, Pol'y and Law 319.

17   Ted Marmor, Richard Freeman & Kieke Okma, "Comparative Perspectives and Policy Learning in the World of Health Care" (2005) 7 J Comparative Pol'y Analysis 331.

tier may threaten access and quality of care within public health care systems.[18] When extra-billing is combined with dual practice, there is a concern that physicians will prioritize private-sector patients, exacerbating wait times in the public sector—a problem that has been observed, for example, with Australia's experiments with two-tier care.[19] Others suggest that dual practice may result in a kind of brain drain from the public system. The worry here is that private-pay patients will flex their buying power to receive care from leading specialists, while less experienced and/or reputable physicians attend to patients who wait their turn in the public system.[20] Adding to this concern is the further risk that these highly skilled physicians will, in their private practice, attend to patients with easier-to-treat medical conditions—a phenomenon referred to as cream skimming— leaving more complicated cases to the public system (and possibly more junior physicians).[21] Biglaiser and Ma, in their theoretical work on dual practice, worry that a flourishing private tier may have a demoralizing effect on public-sector physicians. Confronted with the fact that dual practitioners earn higher incomes through their private practice, dedicated doctors in the public system may feel underap-preciated, and react by "reducing quality in their public service and by participating in moonlighting [themselves]."[22] Finally, conflicts of interest may arise, as dual-practice physicians have an incentive to see wait times grow in the public system, driving up demand for private care.[23] There is evidence of this problem manifesting itself in Manitoba in the 1990s, when dual practice was allowed for cataract surgery. Public-stream patients of dual-practice physicians faced

---

18   For a more exhaustive discussion, see Hurley, this volume.

19   Stephen J. Duckett, "Living in the Parallel Universe in Australia: Public Medicare and Private Hospitals" (2005) 173 CMAJ 745. See also, P Ferrinho et al, "Dual practice in the health sector: review of the evidence" (2004) 2 Human Resources for Health 14; A Garcia-Prado & P Gonzales, "Whom do physicians work for? An analysis of dual practice in the health sector" (2011) 36 J Health Pol, Pol'y & Law 265.

20   A Garcia-Prado & P Gonzalez, "Whom do physicians work for? An analysis of dual practice in the health sector" (2011) 36 J Health Pol, Pol'y & Law 265 at 282

21   T Iversen, "The effect of a private sector on the waiting time in a National Health Service," (1997) 16 J Health Econ 381.

22   Gary Biglaiser & Ching-to Albert Ma, "Moonlighting: public service and private practice" (2007) 38 Rand J Economics 1113 at 1131.

23   P Ferrinho et al, "Dual practice in the health sector: review of the evidence" (2004) 2 Human Resources for Health 14 at 17.

wait times up to thirteen weeks longer than patients of public-only physicians.[24] A 1994 study of Alberta's experience with cataract surgeons splitting their time between public hospitals and private clinics—charging facility fees in the latter—found similar results.[25]

To be fair, the literature on the effects of dual practice is limited, and suggests arguments both pro and con. On the pro side, for example, permitting dual practice may encourage sought-after specialists to keep one foot in the public sector, rather than opting out entirely to the private sector. Allowing public-sector physicians to dabble in private sector may also provide opportunities to train on new and experimental treatments and technologies that have yet to receive medicare funding.[26] The main argument from proponents of privatization of Canada, it seems, is that dual-practice physicians will not shirk obligations to the public system, but instead will increase their overall volume of care; when confronted by bottlenecks for surgical time in public facilities, the dual practitioner can use their surplus hours to see private patients at no cost to the public system. Indeed, this may have benefits to the public system, it is argued, as patients treated after hours in the private sphere will ease pressures on the public system.[27] The concern, of course, is that, depending on market demand, after-hours dabbling in private practice may grow to pose a real threat to accessible care within the public system.

There is certainly room for more research on these questions. One shortcoming with the literature on dual practice is a lack of attention to the structural features of specific health care systems. For example, the impact of dual practice will surely vary depending on whether physicians are employed on a salaried basis or, as in Canada, on a fee-for-service basis. Under a fee-for-service scheme, physicians can freely migrate their time between the public and private streams, making it difficult to monitor, predict, and control the spillover effects on accessibility within the public system.

---

24 C DeCoster et al, *Surgical Waiting Times in Manitoba* (Winnipeg: Manitoba Centre for Health Policy and Evaluation, 1998), online: <http://mchp-appserv.cpe.uma-nitoba.ca/reference/surgwait.pdf>.

25 W Armstrong, *The Consumer Experience with Cataract Surgery and Private Clinics in Alberta: Canada's Canary in the Mine Shaft* (Alberta: Consumers' Association of Canada, 2009), online: <http://www.albertaconsumers.org/CanaryReportrevised2.pdf>.

26 Garcia-Prado, *supra* note 20 at 265.

27 *Cambie Surgeries*, *supra* note 3 at 229–235.

The Supposed Arbitrariness of Provincial Restrictions on Two-Tier Care

As explained, critics have portrayed Canada as an outlier, internationally, for its reliance upon *statutory prohibitions* to restrict two-tier care. The claimants in *Chaoulli* were at pains to show that many Western European health care systems manage to maintain high-performing universal health care systems while at the same time allowing a parallel private tier. The Supreme Court of Canada was receptive to this argument, with the majority in *Chaoulli* concluding that:

> The evidence adduced at trial establishes that many western democracies that do not impose a monopoly on the delivery of health care have successfully delivered to their citizens medical services that are superior to and more affordable than the services that are presently available in Canada. This demonstrates that a monopoly is not necessary or even related to the provision of quality public health care.[28]

There is much to say about the quality of comparative analysis involved here. Many have reviewed the *Chaoulli* verdict's cursory description of foreign health care systems and complained about a lack of nuance; the decision has spurred debate about Canadian courts' institutional competence to adjudicate complex questions of public policy, involving polycentric trade-offs.[29] A basic concern—brought up elsewhere in this volume—is how Canadian discourse around two-tier care, inside and outside the courts, reliably invokes apples-and-oranges comparisons.[30] For example, Germany is often held up as an example of a high-performing health care system that allows a role for private health care. The comparison is fundamentally misleading, because private health care plays mostly a

---

28   *Chaoulli, supra* note 2 at para 140.
29   Christopher P Manfredi & Antonia Maioni, "Judicializing Health Policy: Unexpected Lessons and an Inconvenient Truth" in James B Kelly & Christopher P Manfredi, eds, *Contested Constitutionalism* (UBC Press, 2009); Kent Roach, "The Challenges of Crafting Remedies for Violations of Socio-economic Rights" in Malcolm Langford, ed, *Social Rights Jurisprudence* (Cambridge: Cambridge University Press, 2009).
30   CM Flood, *supra* note 16.

substitutive role in the German system: patients who "go private" must opt out, irreversibly, from the social health insurance scheme that covers some 90 per cent of the population. The species of privatization on offer in Canadian debates is fundamentally different, with a parallel private tier serving as a purported safety valve for wait times in the public system. The political and economic dynamics surrounding this model are quite unlike those surrounding Germany's two-tier system. For example, there would be a much lower barrier of entry for Canadians entering the private insurance market, absent any requirement of relinquishing public-system coverage.[31]

There is a kind of bait-and-switch in Canadian public discourse around the use of comparative international evidence. Critics of the status quo purport to draw lessons from foreign experiences with two-tier care, but the lesson-drawing ceases the minute it has been established that other countries maintain universal systems while allowing a parallel private tier. There is, in other words, seldom any further inquiry into the alternative approaches employed by these countries to ensure that two-tier care does not lead to serious problems of access and quality of care for patients in the public system.

There is more at play here than a selective use of international evidence by vested interests (though there is that); arguably, the judicialization of these complex questions, by its very nature, encourages a focus on blunt, simplistic answers. As Kent Roach has explained, courts wary of the appearance of judicial activism will be naturally disinclined to explore the nuanced *positive* measures used by foreign health systems to protect universality and accessibility.

> [T]he Court [in *Chaoulli*] considered only the case for an easy remedy—a simple, one-shot negative remedy of holding Quebec's legislative restrictions on private health insurance inoperative— as opposed to more difficult and positive remedies that would give an affected person needed medical treatment or address systemic flaws in the delivery of health care... This makes it even more important that Canadian governments do not take *Chaoulli* as the last word on medicare reform.[32]

---

31   For detailed discussion, see Schmid & Frisina Doetter, this volume.

32   Roach, *supra* note 9.

Roach's exhortation in that last sentence is vitally important. The *Chaoulli* verdict is often misleadingly summarized as holding that restrictions on two-tier care are constitutionally suspect. In fact, the Supreme Court's reasoning is a good deal more open-minded than this: while concluding that Quebec's statutory restrictions on private health insurance are over restrictive, the court alludes open-mindedly to the mechanisms used to protect public plans in other countries. After noting that the United Kingdom does not restrict access to private health insurance, nor restrict a physician's ability to withdraw from the public plan, Justice Deschamps, writing for the majority, observes that "physicians working full-time in public hospitals are limited in the amounts that they may bill in the private sector to supplement income earned in the public sector."[33] At no point does the court imply that these alternative regulatory approaches would run afoul of the *Charter*. While champions of privatization in media discourse portray this issue as a binary choice between allowing or prohibiting private care, international experience—and indeed the very text of *Chaoulli*—suggests that Canadian lawmakers have a possible array of intermediate options at their disposal.[34]

Varying Approaches to Contracting Against Two-Tier Care

As detailed by Quesnel-Vallée et al in chapter 4, the *Chaoulli* decision has not been as disruptive to Quebec's single-payer system as some had initially feared. This is thanks in large part to the province's calibrated response in liberalizing private insurance only for select services identified in the ruling (i.e., total hip or knee replacement, major cataract surgery); meanwhile, access to these services within the public system was shored up with wait time guarantees. The *Cambie* challenge now underway in British Columbia is more expansive—targeting restrictions on extra-billing, dual practice, and user charges. If this complete teardown of restrictions on two-tier care succeeds, Canadian decision makers may wish to go back to the drawing board, and look for regulatory options apart from the statutory restrictions; a good place to start would be by examining the

---

33   *Chaoulli, supra* note 2 at para 80.
34   For a broader discussion, see Colleen M Flood & Bryan Thomas, "A Successful Charter Challenge to Medicare? Policy Options for Canadian Provincial Governments" (2018) 13 (Special Issue) Health Economics, Pol'y & Law 433.

approaches taken by high-performing foreign health care systems, which all sides agree or offer worthwhile guidance.

An approach that is common in Western Europe but little discussed in the Canadian context is to address extra-billing and dual practice through government contracts with physicians. Such contracts could draw from the example of public-school teachers, mentioned above, and stipulate the time physicians must devote to public patients or, alternatively, limit the time that physicians practice privately. What follows is a typology of these contractual approaches.

Exclusivity Clauses in Physician Contracts

One option is to contractually *forbid* private billing by physicians working in the public sector, through an exclusivity clause—an approach equivalent, functionally, to statutory bans on dual practice now in place in some provinces. A concern raised in the literature with this option is that specialist physicians will opt out of the public system altogether or relocate to provinces with more permissive contracts (if such exist). In the mid-1980s, the universal health care system in Greece recognized the "powerful financial incentives to minimise time and effort devoted to salaried institutional practice, and to spend time instead in private work."[35] As a solution, the Greek system imposed exclusivity clauses in physician contracts, offering significant salary increases as a quid pro quo. The strategy was deemed a policy failure, as many senior doctors simply resigned from public practice altogether. (Ireland's restrictions on dual practice are discussed below; for present purposes, it bears noting that a 2018 poll by the Irish Medical Organization similarly found that a majority of hospital-based specialists would leave the public system in the event that existing time-based restrictions on dual practice were strengthened to a full-fledged prohibition.)[36]

Admittedly, there are a host of confounding factors when drawing lessons from Greece's experience for the Canadian context. For one thing, Canadian physicians have never relied on dual practice to supplement their income from medicare; indeed, laws banning dual practice exist in most provinces, and the practice is under challenge

---

35   *Ibid.*
36   Irish Medical Organisation, "Private Practice in Public Hospitals" (February 2018), online: <https://www.imo.ie/news-media/publications/IMO-Submission-to-the-Independent-Review-Group-on-Private-Practice.pdf>.

in the *Cambie* case. From a negotiation standpoint, this would surely have a framing effect, as dual practice was a bird in the hand for senior Greek physicians negotiating in 1985, but would not be for the vast majority of Canadian physicians today (surgeons at the Cambie clinic and other scofflaws excepted). Moreover, Canadian physicians are, according to Marchildon and Sherar's recent analysis, "among the more highly remunerated among OECD countries for which data is available,"[37] which raises the stakes for Canadian physicians contemplating opting out of medicare. Under the existing statutory bans on dual practice now in place in British Columbia and other provinces, we have not seen a significant number of physicians opting out of medicare; indeed, there appears to be a buyer's market for physician services in Canada in recent years.[38] Of course, should court challenges succeed in overturning all of Canada's restrictions on two-tier care in one fell swoop—restrictions on dual practice *as well as* restrictions on parallel private insurance—the economic calculus for physicians considering "going private" would change drastically.

Exclusivity clauses are at the more restrictive end of a spectrum of possibilities for dampening dual practice; other countries, discussed below, rely on milder contractual measures like income and/or time limits on dual practice. A possible concern, therefore, is whether a move by government to impose exclusivity contracts after a (hypothetical) loss in *Cambie* might also be challenged in court under section 7 of the *Charter*. Given there have never been exclusivity contracts within medicare, there is no jurisprudence directly on point, and the matter raises esoteric and untested questions in constitutional law that are beyond the scope of this chapter. On the face of it, it seems highly unlikely that the courts would overturn exclusivity clauses so as to ensure that an adequate supply of physicians is available for the private for-profit health care market. For one thing, this would take the courts far beyond the one-shot remedy of the sort applied in *Chaoulli*. In a world where public-sector physicians are bound by exclusivity contracts, the health care workforce that remains to serve the private sector would be a function of supply and demand. If few physicians are tempted to opt out to the private

---

37   Gregory P Marchildon & Michael Sherar, "Doctors and Canadian Medicare: Improving Accountability and Performance" (2018) 17 Healthcare Papers 14.

38   D Fréchette et al, "What's really behind Canada's unemployed specialists? Too many, too few doctors? Findings from the Royal College's employment study" (Ottawa: The Royal College of Physicians and Surgeons of Canada, 2013).

sector, this reflects the workings of the free market; it is not indicative that negative rights have been violated. Needless to say, the *optics* of the courts intervening to ensure an adequate supply of physicians to the private for-profit sphere would not be ideal, given the courts have almost uniformly refused to intercede to defend patient access in the public system, citing concerns about democratic legitimacy and institutional competence.[39]

Contractual Limitations on Private-Practice Income

Short of demanding exclusivity, provinces might contractually limit private-practice *income*—an approach taken by England until recently.[40] As with exclusivity clauses, income limits may prompt some physicians—particularly senior physicians whose services command higher prices—to opt of the public system altogether, or relocate to jurisdictions with laxer rules around dual practice. There is also evidence of enforcement problems with income limits: data from England shows that its 10 per cent income cap was routinely violated, until it was dropped in 2003 contract renewals.[41] It is unclear whether the problem of lax enforcement is due to some technical impracticality of monitoring (e.g., privacy protections for physicians) or simply a lack of political will. In principle, it seems that compliance could be monitored by auditing physicians' tax returns—a measure unlikely to fly in the Canadian system given the history of physician resistance to restrictions on their autonomy.

Contractual Limitations on Time Spent in Private Practice

A similar option is to contractually limit the *time* that physicians are permitted to spend in private practice. This strategy has been used in Ireland, for example, where public physicians are prohibited from devoting more than 20 per cent of their clinical workload to private-pay patients.[42] An advantage here, from the standpoint of negotiating with physicians, is that time limits impose no hard cap on income earned in the private sector: dual-practice specialists can

---

39   *Auton (Guardian as litem of) v British Columbia (Attorney General)*, [2004] SCJ No 71.

40   N Rickman & A McGuire, "Regulating providers' reimbursement in a mixed market for healthcare" (1999) 46 Scottish J of Political Economy 53.

41   S Morris et al, "Analysis of consultants' NHS and private incomes in England in 2003/2004" (2008) 101 J Royal Society of Medicine 372.

42   J Purcell, *Medical consultants' contract* (Dublin: Office of the Comptroller and Auditor General, 2007).

earn whatever the market will bear for their services, within the time limit.

Here too there are enforcement issues, as a 2016 report from Ireland's auditor general found that the country's 20 per cent time limit has been so routinely breached as to be a "farce."[43] Because Ireland encourages private care, and facilitates its delivery in public hospitals, it has been possible to monitor non-compliance[44] and gain some understanding of its root causes. As the consultants' contract was formed, all parties agreed that a national data-collection system would be used—the Hospital Inpatient Enquiry system—to track public and private activity for inpatient and day cases; a separate system would track outpatient and diagnostic activity.[45] Interestingly, the auditor general's 2017 annual report finds that violations of the 20 per cent rule were not primarily due to shirking per se, but instead due to the country's large quotient of private patients who turn up at hospitals at unpredictable rates:

> In practice, the HSE, hospitals and individual consultants have limited control over the private activity levels as the majority of patients admitted to hospital are maternity admissions or admitted from the hospitals' emergency departments, which must be admitted and treated in order of clinical priority.[46]

There are obvious difficulties in translating Ireland's experience here to the Canadian context. In the event that private for-profit care is

---

43 Martin Wall, "Rules limiting private practice in hospitals 'a farce'- HSE chief" (9 January 2016) *The Irish Times,* online: <www.irishtimes.com/news/health/rules-limiting-private-practice-in-hospitals-a-farce-hse-chief>. An attempt is now underway to audit hospital consultants; see, Martin Wall, "Hospital consultants face audit over private-practice rules" (3 March 2017) *The Irish Times,* online: <https://www.irishtimes.com/news/health/hospital-consultants-face-audit-over-private-practice-rules>.

44 Ireland, Office of the Comptroller and Auditor General, *2017 General Report, Chapter 16: Control of private patient activity in acute public hospitals* (Dublin, 2018) at para 16.9, online: <https://www.audit.gov.ie/en/Find-Report/Publications/2018/2017-Annual-Report-Chapter-16-Control-of-private-patient-activity-in-acute-public-hospitals.pdf>.

45 Health Information and Quality Authority "Hospital In-Patient Enquiry (HIPE)," online: <https://www.hiqa.ie/areas-we-work/health-information/data-collections/hospital-patient-enquiry-hipe>.

46 Ireland, Office of the Comptroller and Auditor General, *supra* note 44.

liberalized by the courts, one question facing government will be whether to allow private care to be carried out in public hospitals, as under the Irish system. While allowing this may facilitate the monitoring of dual practice, it also heightens the risk that private care will be subsidized by the public purse—an approach that Ireland has embraced in various ways but which Canadians are likely to reject. Even modest moves in this direction, such as allowing the administration of privately purchased cancer drugs in public hospitals, have aroused heated debate in Canada.[47]

Limiting Private Practice with Work Plans and Managerial Oversight

As discussed, income-based contractual restrictions were used for decades to bar NHS (National Health Service) consultants (i.e., hospital-based specialists) from earning more than 10 per cent of their income from private practice. The 10 per cent rule was routinely flouted and eventually abandoned with the introduction of a new consultants' contract in 2003 (which operates to this day). However, the autonomy gains from dropping this rule were offset by a barrage of new oversight mechanisms imposed with the 2003 contract—as part of the Blair government's regime of "targets and terror"—which aimed to incentivize consultant productivity and efficiency and curtail private practice.

The new contract requires NHS consultants to negotiate a detailed job plan with their employers, which included quality standards, outcome and efficiency measures, and clinical standards. Under the terms of the new contract, consultants were made answerable to their clinical managers—generally senior consultants—for compliance with these requirements. Poor performance on annual reviews is grounds for denial of pay progression, which had previously been based solely on years served.[48] Compliance with work plans is actively monitored with managerial oversight of a sort unheard of in Canada: practitioners are required to declare to their clinical managers where they practice, what they practice, and when they practice; they must seek approval from their NHS employer before taking up any private work; and conflicts of interests are

---

47   Colleen M Flood & Lorian Hardcastle, "The Private Sale of Cancer Drugs in Ontario's Public Hospitals: Tough Issues at the Public/Private Interface in Health Care" (2007) 1 McGill J Law and Health 5.

48   English National Health Service, *Terms and Conditions—Consultants (England) 2003* (London, National Health Service, 2007).

discouraged by prohibiting physicians from attempting to sell their private services to NHS patients.[49] These myriad restrictions on dual practice were further reinforced through provisions strengthening consultants' commitment to the NHS: in the case of a conflict of interest, NHS commitments are to take precedence over the consultant's private work, and any additional fees that are collected while the consultant is *on-duty* must be remitted to the employing organization (the NHS), unless their collection is expressly authorized by the employer.[50]

A 2013 report by the UK National Audit Office found that many of the benefits intended by the 2003 contract were realized in the years following its implementation.[51] Notably, the percentage of consultants engaged in private practice dropped from 67 per cent in 2000 to 39 per cent in 2012. The report also found that, pursuant to the terms of their contract, most consultants prioritized their NHS work over their private practice. Further objectives, such as increased consultant participation and productivity, were also realized.[52]

Incentive-Based Approaches

Some jurisdictions have offered financial inducements to secure physician loyalty to their public systems. For example, the Spanish government offers salary supplements to physicians who sign restrictive contracts.[53] In Portugal, there are four categories of contract, and remuneration rises with increased time commitment to the public system.[54] In Italy, only physicians who sign exclusive public contracts are eligible for promotion.[55] As we saw, England offers pay progression to consultants who concentrate their work within the NHS.

Incentive-based approaches are touted as fostering public-service values and may appear less draconian than the restrictive

49   *Ibid* at 18–19.
50   *Ibid* at section 9.
51   Amyas Morse, *Managing NHS Hospital Consultants* (London: Department of Health, National Audit Office, 2013) at 21.
52   *Ibid* at 37.
53   P González, "Should physicians' dual practice be limited? An incentive approach" (2004) 13 Health Economics 505.
54   M D Oliviera & C G Pinto, "Health Care reform in Portugal: an evaluation of the NHS experience" (2005) 14 Health Economics S203.
55   A Lo Scalzo et al, "Italy: health system review" in (2009) 11 *Health Systems in Transition* 1, online: <http://www.euro.who.int/__data/assets/pdf_file/0006/87225/E93666.pdf>.

approaches discussed above. Where market demand creates a substantial disparity between public and private remunerations, attempts to buy loyalty to the public system may be very costly, if they are to succeed. Incentive-based approaches may also be difficult to negotiate, as seen in 2003 contract negotiations in the United Kingdom, where physician opposition blocked introduction of an incentive for NHS commitment.[56]

Incentive-based approaches are well-suited to situations where physicians have grown accustomed to engaging in dual practice. In such jurisdictions, physicians may have agreed to lower compensation from the public system with the expectation of augmenting their salaries in private practice. When an attempt is made to roll back or eliminate opportunities for private practice, there is an understandable expectation of compensation. Yet this clearly does not describe the current scenario in Canada, where the vast majority of physicians rely exclusively on medicare for their income, and, by OECD standards, are well remunerated.[57]

Conclusion

Leading Canadian constitutional scholars portray *Charter* jurisprudence as a dialogue between the courts and the legislature, implying that the courts are not to be the *last word* on questions of law and public policy that engage *Charter* protections.[58] Few *Charter* cases call out for dialogic response with the same urgency as *Chaoulli* and, depending on its outcome, *Cambie*. As explained, the fundamental *aim* of regulating two-tier care is perfectly legitimate, supported by available evidence, and commonplace among comparator countries. It is only the *means* by which Canada has chosen to regulate two-tier care that has drawn judicial reproach.

Unfortunately, Canadian discourse around two-tier care has been studiously uninterested in the question of *how to regulate in lieu of present statutory prohibition*. Indeed, public and judicial discourse

---

56   A Oliver, "The English National Health Service: 1979–2005" (2005) 14 Health Economics S75.

57   Gregory P Marchildon & Michael Sherar, "Doctors and Canadian Medicare: Improving Accountability and Performance" (2018) 17 Healthcare Papers 14.

58   Peter W Hogg and Allison A Bushell, "The Charter Dialogue between Courts and Legislatures (Or Perhaps the Charter of Rights Isn't Such a Bad Thing After All" (1997) 35 Osgoode Hall LJ 75.

encourages a naive picture, fostering the mistaken impression that if Canada were simply to do away with its statutory restrictions on two-tier care, our health care system would magically default to something that approximates the high-performing health care systems of Western Europe.

Unfortunately, this is clearly not the case. As this chapter has outlined, many European countries rely on diverse contractual mechanisms to limit dual practice, and attempts to replicate these approaches in Canada would be challenging to implement. The core challenge, arguably, would be the political/economic battle of wrenching Canadian physicians from their long-enjoyed status as independent professionals, free to bill medicare on a fee-for-service basis with limited managerial oversight.

Some of the contractual and administrative tools used in other countries to blunt the deleterious effects of dual practice seem unlikely to work in the Canadian context. For example, Ireland's approach of delivering privately financed care *within* public hospitals, as a way of facilitating managerial oversight over the public-private mix, seems like a non-starter—the optics of private care being delivered in public hospitals are simply at odds with the *Canada Health Act* premise of care being allocated on the basis of medical need. Moreover, as Stephen Thomas and colleagues discuss in chapter 11, the inequities and inefficiencies of Ireland's version of two-tier are spurring reforms that rollback their two-tier system.

Perhaps physician resistance to contractual restrictions on dual practice could be overcome by using an incentive-based approach, offering bonuses to physicians who agree to work exclusively in the public system, or who at least agree to engage in private practice only upon completing a full workweek in the public system. The difficulty here is that these incentives can be costly, and Canadian physicians are *already* generously compensated, even without the option of sidelining in private practice.

Contractual limits on income or time devoted to private-sector work are more readily implemented in countries like the United Kingdom, where physicians are paid on a salaried basis and are subject to greater oversight concerning the nature of their work and their time by administrative agencies. The loosening of dual-practice restrictions in 2003 has come at a cost to consultant autonomy. This quid pro quo has arguably been necessary to ensure consultants discharge their obligations to the NHS and not shirk their contractual duties to the public sector in favour of their more lucrative private practices. The situation in Canada has been different, with dual practice largely nonexistent, while physician autonomy has ruled supreme. Perhaps, should the current litigation in *Cambie* succeed, a similar quid pro quo will come into play, with the introduction to Canada of physician contracts ensuring that practitioners discharge their obligation to the public sector. From the English experience, it can be gleaned that such measures—particularly if combined with other quality-control measures, such as medical audits—would likely cut deep into physicians' clinical autonomy, imposing increased managerial controls and quality standards, which have been foreign to the Canadian health care system to date.

Conclusion:
The Complex Dynamics
of Canadian Medicare
and the Constitution

Colleen M. Flood and Bryan Thomas

An ongoing challenge in British Columbia, launched by Cambie Surgeries Corporation, aims to lift restrictions on private finance so that Canadians can queue-jump to access care ahead of patients in the public system.[1] The case has major implications, not only for Canadian health care but for our broader understanding of how the *Charter* interacts with universal social programs. The global recognition of human rights in health in the mid-twentieth century was meant to offer protections for the most vulnerable, recognizing that health is not a mere commodity to be distributed by market principles. As a society, our commitment to ensuring fair and equal access to medically necessary care is a gauge of our more fundamental commitment to basic human equality.

As we think about the potential of a *Charter* challenge rolling back laws restricting two-tier care, there are political, societal, and legal factors to weigh, not only by the courts but also by

---

1   *Cambie Surgeries v British Columbia (Medical Services Commission)*, Docket S090663 (Vancouver) [*Cambie*]. The Supreme Court of Canada has previously found that Quebec's restrictions on parallel private insurance violated the right to life and security of the person, contained in the Quebec *Charter of Human Rights and Freedom*. *Chaoulli v Québec (Attorney General)*, 2005 SCC 35. *Cambie* seeks to expand on this precedent, sector 7 of the Canadian *Charter* to challenge British Columbia's restrictions on extra-billing, parallel private insurance, and dual practice.

policy-makers, patients, and the public. In this concluding chapter, we discuss some of the issues that emerge including: (i) the reality that Canadian governments have not taken sufficient action to quell Canadians' worries about length of wait times, and through this failure have provided the fuel for *Charter* challenges; (ii) the historic struggles to establish Canadian medicare and prevent two-tier care, and the prospects of governments renewing those struggles in the current political climate; (iii) the challenges involved in transposing international evidence on two-tier care to the Canadian context; and (iv) the appropriate role of the courts in adjudicating these complex issues.

The Basis of *Charter* Challenges to Restrictions on Private Finance

Before we discuss the policy implications, it perhaps behoves us to remind the reader of the basics of the *Charter* challenges that could usher in two-tier care in Canada. The *Cambie* claim engages two core *Charter* arguments. The first (and arguably more central) claim is that BC laws restricting privately financed care unjustifiably infringe patients' section 7 right to "life, liberty and security of the person." Here, it is argued that these laws needlessly trap patients in the medicare system's long wait times, denying them the "safety valve," as the *Cambie* claim puts it, of private care. The second argument is that the current regime disadvantages young, elderly, and disabled patients, in violation of the *Charter*'s section 15 right to "equal protection and equal benefit of the law." Current BC law exempts patients covered by workers' compensation from restrictions on two-tier care, allowing them to jump the queue and receive treatment at private clinics, from medicare-enrolled physicians, at premium fees. It is alleged that this regulatory carve-out prioritizes care for younger, non-disabled patients, and disadvantages patients who do not work due to age (too young or too old) and/or disability status.[2] For both

---

2   This section 15 argument is untested terrain. It is possible that the carve out might be upheld as "reasonably justifiable in a democratic society" under section 1 of the *Charter*, given the costs savings from expediting workers' compensation claims. There is also the question of how the alleged inequality might be remedied: one option is to eliminate the carve out for workers, which amounts to a "levelling down" approach to equality; another option is to create an equivalent carve out for the young, old, and disabled—a hollow remedy, unless these groups

the section 7 and section 15 arguments, even if a court finds that there has been a prima facie infringement of a *Charter* right, the government may defend such infringement pursuant to section 1 of the *Charter*, arguing that any such infringement is "demonstrably justified in a free and democratic society," for example, on the basis that permitting greater privatization of the system will worsen the public health care system, by drawing limited medical manpower from those who need it the most to those with the most resources.

Action on Wait Times

Wait times have become a significant problem for the Canadian health care system. In recent years, Canada regularly scores near the bottom of the Commonwealth Fund's rankings of health care systems in eleven high-income countries.[3] Various factors contribute to Canada's poor performance in the latest rankings, including serious problems of affordability and timeliness of care—especially for lower-income Canadians, for whom systemic wait times are compounded by financial barriers owing to significant gaps in medicare coverage (e.g., skipping doctor visits, treatments, tests, and prescriptions due to out-of-pocket costs). Concerns about wait times are galvanizing *Charter* challenges to laws restricting two-tier care on the grounds that if governments cannot provide timely care they must, in a sense, clear the way for Canadians to use their own private resources.

There have been isolated successes in managing wait times across Canadian provinces, but federal and provincial governments have failed to build on these successes and spread the benefits to all areas of the country and all areas of care.[4] For example, Ontario's Cardiac Care Network (the precursor to CorHealth Ontario) has significantly improved access to care, reducing what were perilously

---

are also offered subsidies to finance private care. The hope for *Cambie* claimants, it seems, is that the courts will not concern themselves with these details, and simply overturn restrictions on two-tier care altogether, leaving government to pick up the pieces. Our hope and expectation is that the courts—which generally approach section 15 claims in health care with skepticism—will give this claim short shrift.

3   E Schneider et al, *Mirror, Mirror 2017: International Comparison Reflects Flaws and Opportunities for Better U.S. Health Care* (New York: Commonwealth Fund, 2017), online: <interactives.commonwealthfund.org/2017/july/mirror-mirror/>.

4   Canada, Advisory Panel on Healthcare Innovation, *Unleashing Innovation: Excellent Healthcare for Canada* (Ottawa: Health Canada, 2015) at 18–19.

long wait times, and improved outcomes for cardiovascular patients.[5] Likewise, the province of Alberta made great strides in one project, streamlining the delivery of knee and hip replacements and creating single-purpose clinics, where care is standardized according to the best available evidence.[6] Yet there has not been an across-the-board effort to reassure all Canadian patients that they will receive care within a reasonable time, regardless of the treatment. In comparison, for example, the United Kingdom implemented a wait time guarantee with a *maximum* of eighteen weeks and definitively tamed their extremely long wait times, particularly for elective surgery.[7]

Canadian efforts to tame the queue have been lukewarm by comparison to the experience in the United Kingdom. Federal funds devoted to this initiative in the 1990s did not achieve the results needed, and, reportedly, new investments for technologies intended to improve access were reportedly used for less pressing purposes, including the purchase of lawn mowers.[8] Governmental inaction in this regard is rooted in part in a deeper problem of Canadian constitutional law and federalism, with the federal government reluctant to enforce conditions on the provinces that are laid out in the *Canada Health Act*, for fear of ruffling provincial feathers.[9] And this reluctance, in turn, may stem from a failure to honour the original pact of medicare, whereby the federal government shares 50 per cent of

---

5   Robert McMurtry, "Patient-centered healthcare could reduce wait times and improve the Canadian health system" (2015), Evidencenetwork.ca, online: <evidencenetwork.ca/patient-centred-healthcare-could-reduce-wait-times-and-improve-the-canadian-health-system/>.

6   Susan Usher & Cy Frank, "One stop shops for assessment and treatment: Alberta Hip and Knee Replacement Project gets results" Health Innovation Forum, online: <www.healthinnovationforum.org/article/one-stop-shops-for-assessment-and-treatment-alberta-hip-and-knee-replacement-project-gets-results/>.

7   Peter C Smith & Matt Sutton, "United Kingdom" in Luii Siciliani, Michael Borowitz, and Valeri Moran eds, *Waiting Time Policies in the Health Sector: What Works* (Paris: OECD, 2013).

8   Raisa Deber, "Canada" in John Rapoport, Philip Jacobs and Egon Jonsson, eds, *Cost Containment and Efficiency in National Health Systems* (Wiley-Blackwell, 2009) 15 at 18.

9   For example, the federal *Canada Health Act* obliges provinces to ensure "reasonable access" to health services. In principle, the federal government could leverage this accessibility principle to hold the provinces to account for long wait times. Of course, the available enforcement mechanism—the withholding of federal transfers—would potentially be politically unpopular, and risk exacerbating wait times.

the costs. As a consequence, provincial governments have an easy scapegoat (federal underfunding) upon which to hang the blame for all problems.[10] Still, given how highly Canadians rank their public health care system, it remains a puzzle why voters are not more demanding of their provincial governments to wrestle down wait times. And, indeed, why provincial governments have not solved this problem in order to win power, particularly since it does not seem (from the successful experiences with reducing wait times in Alberta for hip and knee replacement and for cardiac care in Ontario) that significantly more resources would be required. In other words, the evidence suggests that better management rather than more resources is needed to deal with wait time concerns.

To understand the failure of provinces to act decisively regarding wait times, we need to look not only at the blurred lines of accountability between the federal and provincial governments but also to the history of public medicare and, in particular, the strong role physicians play therein, a history that Greg Marchildon sets out in this volume.[11] In short, tackling the problem of wait times will necessarily require some disruption of the present practices, hierarchies, and power of physicians. Most of us would have experienced a referral from a family doctor, where the reception calls the reception of the selected specialist (hopefully). From this point, one hopes as a patient that the acuity of our situation has an impact on scheduling, but we have no idea. The family doctor refers a patient to one of a handful of specialists that he or she knows, and does not, for example, have any way of knowing if an equally competent specialist has an earlier availability. Instead, the patient must sit in the queue of the anointed specialist even if the system on the whole could meet his or her needs in a far timelier fashion. Lobbying by physicians, nurses, and other health care providers on the topic of health care often refers only to problems of wait times in the most general of ways, and usually does not result in substantive reform proposals but, instead, emphasizes the need not for better management but for more money—always more money. We have many years of experience now to reveal that new monies infused into the health

10   William Lahey, "Medicare and the Law: Contours of an Evolving Relationship" in Jocelyn Downie, Timothy Caulfield and Colleen M Flood, eds, Canadian Health L & Pol'y (2011) 1 at 31–35.

11   See Marchildon, this volume.

care system—which go to paying higher fees and salaries for doctors, nurses, and other health care professionals—do nothing to galvanize change and improvement. We pay more for doing the same thing.[12]

But will a two-tier system help these problems? An important question in the *Cambie* case is whether there is a sufficient link between long wait times and the laws under challenge (e.g., the BC law requiring doctors to either bill the public system in accordance with a negotiated fee schedule or else opt out, to bill privately).[13] The point of these laws is to reduce the incentives that physicians have to practice in the private sector and, thus, ensure a reasonable supply of physicians to public medicare, as well as ensuring access to care is based on need, not ability to pay.[14] The applicants in *Cambie* claim that *but for these laws* the residents of British Columbia (and indeed Canada) would be able to avoid punishing wait times in the public system, or, at least, that these laws can be lifted without worsening wait times in the public system. A similar claim was accepted by the majority of judges in the *Chaoulli* case that, in 2005, overturned a ban on parallel private health insurance in Quebec, enacted to quell two-tier care.

A closer look at the economics of health care, as Jerry Hurley explained comprehensively in this volume, suggests there is zero evidence that laws limiting private finance in any way exacerbate wait times, at least for the vast majority of Canadians. Take, for example, the patient applicant, Mr. Zeliotis, in the *Chaoulli* case. At sixty-five years of age at the time of the trial, and with pre-existing hip and heart conditions, his "right" to buy private insurance is surely a mirage. Private health insurance coverage, were it offered at all to someone of his age and health status, would be prohibitively expensive, and would likely exclude coverage for pre-existing conditions. Unless regulated, private health insurers will not cover people who are very ill, and once existing subscribers become ill, insurers will do their best to find ways to trim or eliminate coverage. Further, as a result of ill health, many people often find their employment prospects diminished or lost, and those who are sick/without income will

---

12   *Supra* note 3 at 28.

13   *Medicare Protection Act*, RSBC 1996, c 286, s 17.

14   The preamble to the impugned legislation reads, "the people and government of British Columbia believe it to be fundamental that an individual's access to necessary medical care be solely based on need and not on the individual's ability to pay." *Ibid.*

find it more and more difficult to pay insurance premiums. Thus, a *Charter* "right" to jump a queue may be viable only for the healthy and wealthy. Moreover, if the laws prohibiting dual practice are overturned, the weight of evidence strongly suggests that physicians will divert their energies and labour increasingly to the private tier, where the patients are likely to be less acute, the rate of pay higher. Although the applicants in *Cambie* strenuously deny such, this would undermine the delivery of care in the public system.

All of this runs counter to the animating spirit of the *Charter*, with its commitment to ensuring that all Canadians have a "right to the equal protection and equal benefit of the law."[15] The Supreme Court of Canada long ago recognized the importance of interpreting the *Charter* in a manner that preserves protections for those less advantaged, with Chief Justice Dickson famously writing that "the courts must be cautious to ensure that it does not simply become an instrument of better situated individuals to roll back legislation which has as its object the improvement of the condition of less advantaged persons."[16] Comparative evidence, particularly from Australia as Fiona McDonald and Stephen Duckett discussed in this volume, suggests that in the absence of significant governmental subsidies and regulations (e.g., mandatory purchase if above a certain income level), private health insurance will only serve a small percentage of the population—the wealthy and the healthy.

History of Medicare and the Power of Physicians

If courts overturn laws protecting public medicare they will do so in the context of a difficult and complex history of government-physician relations in Canada. Public medicare, particularly insurance covering physician services, was a hard-won battle, as physician associations railed against the prospect of being conscripted into public service. The legacy of the physician strike in Saskatchewan in 1962 resulted in a particular Canadian accommodation where physicians are still largely autonomous fee-for-service practitioners. In the light of this history, it is perhaps not surprising that the *Charter* challenges to laws restrictive of two-tier care have been spearheaded by

---

15   Part I of the *Constitution Act, 1982,* being Schedule B to the *Canada Act 1982* (UK), 1982, c 11, s 15.

16   *R v Edwards Books and Art Ltd.* [1986] 2 SCR 713, 35 DLR (4th) 1 at para 141.

physicians themselves—first Dr. Chaoulli, in 2002, and now Dr. Day, the main physician behind the *Cambie* challenge.

The applicants in the *Cambie* case are seeking to persuade the court that they need not deeply consider the policy consequences of a decision to overturn laws protecting public medicare. Their argument will be that, having proclaimed laws limiting two-tier care as unconstitutional, it will then fall to government to respond with a new set of laws, and the court should not worry exactly what those laws or policies may be, provided they are constitutionally compliant,[17] what is known in constitutional parlance as "dialogue theory."[18] On its face, this sounds feasible—that when courts overturn laws governments respond by bringing forth new laws that are constitutionally compliant to achieve their objective. Yet our history reveals not only the very special nature of public medicare relative to all other social programs but also the Sisyphean political work involved in establishing and maintaining public medicare. It is just as likely that if a court tears down laws protective of public medicare, many provincial governments would welcome this outcome given that, as we write, seven of thirteen provinces and territories are led by centre-right governments. Provinces may welcome two-tier care as a way to relieve political pressure on them to improve public medicare and give doctors even more of what they want; namely, more autonomy and more ways of earning extra income. Given the history of medicare, it is naive to assume that governments will respond to a loss in *Cambie* by taking bold steps to tackle wait times while redoubling their commitment to the principle of access according to need.

Complexity and Comparative Evidence

Comparative evidence on how other countries address wait times and restrict two-tier care will be important to the adjudication of *Charter* challenges to laws protecting public medicare. Canadian courts are interested in this kind of evidence to understand to what extent Canada's restrictions on two-tier care are reasonable and proportionate. In other words, it will be easier for a Canadian

---

17   *Cambie* (Plantiffs' Final Argument) at paras 2324–2326.

18   Peter W Hogg & Allison A Bushell, "The *Charter* Dialogue between Courts and Legislatures (Or Perhaps the *Charter of Rights* Isn't Such a Bad Thing After All" (1997) 35 Osgoode Hall LJ 75; Kent Roach, *The Supreme Court on Trial: Judicial Activism or Democratic Dialogue* (Toronto: Irwin Law, 2001).

government to justify restrictions on a two-tier system if other countries have similar laws. For example, Canada's broad restrictions on the advertising and promotion of tobacco products were struck down by the Supreme Court in 1997, in part because they were deemed to be more restrictive than measures taken in other countries.[19] As comparator countries became more restrictive of tobacco advertising, the Supreme Court revisited the issue and upheld wide-ranging restrictions in 2007.[20]

With this kind of approach to constitutional interpretation—where it is a very difficult challenge for a government to justify a *Charter* infringement unless other countries have similar laws—Canada's restrictions on two-tier care are certainly in jeopardy. If one takes a superficial look at Canada's approach to regulating public medicare, it is easy enough to tell a story of Canada as a relative outlier in vigorously suppressing a two-tier system. But this kind of legal reasoning is blind to the particular history, structure, and dynamics of the Canadian health care system. For example, England permits two-tier health care (some 10 per cent of the population have private health insurance and can "jump the queue") and has succeeded in taming wait times (at least until recently). But the fact of two-tier was not *the reason* why wait times were reduced in England: two-tier care has always been a feature of the English system and likely contributed to the problem of long wait times in the first place,[21] and they subsequently had to be tackled with a systematic approach of targets, incentives, and other means *within the public health care system*.[22] Moreover, a key difference between England and Canada is that in England physicians are primarily paid on a salary basis. This means that government has greater managerial oversight over physicians, and can negotiate contractual terms that control work hours, impose systemic fixes for wait times, and so on. By contrast, Canadian physicians enjoy far greater professional autonomy, operating as independent contractors who (mostly) bill government on a fee-for-service basis. In the absence of any restrictions on parallel private practice, Canadian physicians will freely migrate their time

---

19   *RJRMacDonald Inc. v Canada (Attorney General)*, [1995] 3 S.C.R. 199.

20   *Canada (Attorney General) v* JTI-Macdonald Corp., [2007] 2 S.C.R. 610.

21   John Yates, "Lies, Damn Lies and Waiting Lists" (1991) 303 BMJ Clinical Research 802.

22   Carol Propper et al, "Did 'Targets and Terror Reduce Waiting Times in England for Hospital Care" (2008) 8 J Economic Analysis & Pol'y 1.

across the public and private tiers, with financial incentive to cater first and foremost to lucrative private-pay patients.

Perhaps, as in France and Australia, it could be possible to entice some physicians to prioritize the poor or those in high need (e.g., by paying doctors extra benefits such as pensions and such, or restricting the right to work in a parallel private tier to more senior physicians); but it would be incredibly speculative, on the part of Canadian courts, to presuppose that this could come to pass across Canadian provinces. And there is of course the cost to the public purse of paying doctors even more and/or shoring up private insurance to preserve some semblance of equitable access according to medical need. All of this would surely undercut any notion that courts are not wading full square into the world of complex public-policy trade-offs, with significant public resource implications.

Appropriate Role of the Courts

To this point, we have emphasized the importance of applying nuanced historical and comparative analysis to decision making around restrictions on two-tier care. This leads us to a further concern, namely, whether and to what extent *courts* are the appropriate venue for these complex deliberations.

Many have worried that the courts are not well-positioned to adjudicate matters—such as the design of health systems—that involve multifaceted trade-off of scarce resources across the needs of an entire population.[23] The courts' core institutional competence, the argument goes, lies in sorting through past interactions between a plaintiff and a defendant—not in grappling with a half-century of medicare's evolution in a comparative international context.[24] Hopefully, this volume will have impressed upon readers the myriad complexities associated with two-tier care that have not been acknowledged, let alone adequately addressed, in decisions like *Chaoulli*—for example, the fiscal and regulatory challenges that have

---

23   Kent Roach, "Polycentricity and Queue Jumping in Public Law Remedies: A Two-Track Response" (2016) 66 UTLJ 3 at 5.

24   Christopher P Manfredi & Antonia Maioni, "Judicializing Health Policy: Unexpected Lessons and an Inconvenient Truth" in James B. Kelly & Christopher P Manfredi, eds, *Contested Constitutionalism* (Vancouver: University of British Columbia Press, 2009) c. 7 at 137.

arisen in Ireland and Australia as they propped up two-tier care while attempting to avoid glaring inequities in access.

An added wrinkle here is that courts are to some degree *aware* of their own institutional limitations and keen to avoid the appearance of overreach when adjudicating *Charter* challenges to major social programs. In practice, this has meant that courts are especially reluctant to recognize *positive* interpretations of section 7 right to life and security of the person—that is, interpretations that would oblige government to make meaningful, systemic improvements to medicare. With rulings such as *Chaoulli*, recognizing only a *negative* right to be free from unnecessary state interference when purchasing health care privately, the court hopes to avoid dirtying its hands with the messy business of fixing wait times within medicare.

Indeed, this concern with avoiding overreach was a point of underlying consensus in the otherwise pointed argumentation between the minority and the majority in *Chaoulli*. Far from advocating a bold defense of positive rights within medicare, the minority emphasized that even the protection of negative rights would strain the courts' competence. The minority was at pains to highlight all of the questions that were unanswered—and perhaps unanswerable in principle—in the majority's interpretation of section 7:

> What, then, are constitutionally required "reasonable health services"? What is treatment "within a reasonable time"? What are the benchmarks? How short a waiting list is short enough? How many MRIs does the Constitution require? The majority does not tell us. The majority lays down no manageable constitutional standard. The public cannot know, nor can judges or governments know, how much health care is "reasonable" enough to satisfy s 7 of the *Canadian Charter of Rights and Freedoms*. ... It is to be hoped that we will know it when we see it.[25]

As other legal scholars have observed, this tacit judicial preference for recognizing negative rights and denying positive rights is pernicious. It risks creating a "two-tier constitution," where the courts are available to assist those who have the financial means to help themselves (e.g., by purchasing private insurance), but closed off people who

---

25   *Chaoulli* supra note 1 at para 163.

have no choice but to depend on government services.[26] True, there are isolated moments where the courts have expressed openness, in theory, to the possibility that section 7 confers a positive right to, for example, minimal levels of social assistance.[27] But these glimmers of hope are offset by rulings such as *Canadian Doctors for Refugee Care v Canada*,[28] where, in upholding refugees' right to health care, the federal court relied on section 12 protection against cruel and unusual punishment to avoid recognizing positive rights under section 7. And it seems Canadian jurisprudence on this point has verged away from rationality when it leads to the conclusion that governmental failure to fund, for example, life-saving health care for refugee amounts to cruel and unusual punishment under s 12 but cannot trigger a s 7 claim to either life or security of the person.

In the final analysis, this antipathy toward recognizing positive rights in health care may have less to do with the difficulty of finding "manageable constitutional standards," and more to do with brute concerns about fiscal responsibility. Health care is already the largest line item on provincial budgets, and courts may worry that the enforcement of a positive right to reasonable wait times will be an added strain on public funds. As Chief Justice McLachlin and Justice Major begin their concurrence in *Chaoulli*, they express relief that the claimants "do not seek an order that the government spend more money on health care, nor do they seek an order that waiting times for treatment under the public health care scheme be reduced."[29] What gets overlooked here is that recognizing negative rights, and opening the door to two-tier care, may *also* have serious implications for the public purse. We see this in Quebec, where, in its scramble to limit the spread of two-tier care from *Chaoulli*, the government responded with commitments to tackle wait times by, among other things, contracting with private clinics to address overflows. Looking internationally, we see countries like Australia, Ireland, and France

---

26   Lorne Sossin, "Towards a Two-Tier Constitution: The Poverty of Health Rights" found in Colleen M Flood, Kent Roach & Lorne Sossin, eds, *Access to Care, Access to Justice: The Legal Debate Over Private Health Insurance in Canada* (Toronto: University of Toronto Press, 2005) 161 at 171.

27   See *Gosselin v. Quebec (Attorney General)*, 2002 SCC 84, [2002] 4 SCR 429 at paras 78 and 83.

28   *Canadian Doctors for Refugee Care v. Canada (Attorney general)*, 2014 FC 651.

29   *Chaoulli*, supra note 1 at para 103.

devising elaborate Rube Goldberg contraptions of regulations and tax subsidies to sustain two-tier systems.

It is reasonable to ask whether the courts should be involved at all in the redesign of health systems; some esteemed constitutional scholars have pointed to *Chaoulli* as a paradigmatic example where the court should have deferred to government.[30] Having said that, if courts *are* to involve themselves in these complex issues, they must at the very least show an equal willingness to defend the right to timely treatment of patients who seek treatment *within* medicare. As Norman Daniels, a leading thinker on justice within health systems, explains in an oft-quoted passage:

> Rights are not moral fruits that spring from bare earth, fully ripened, without cultivation. Rather, we may claim a right to health or health care only if it can be harvested from an acceptable general theory of distributive justice or from a more particular theory of justice for health and health care.[31]

Anyone claiming that unreasonable wait times are a violation of one's human rights owes us an explanation of how that right will be meaningfully protected for each and every Canadian.

In terms of pragmatics, the notion that positive rights are a *bridge too far* for the courts cannot be sustained. In *Chaoulli*, the majority entrusted the hard work of operationalizing negative rights to government, granting a one year "suspended declaration of invalidity," during which the Quebec government could enact law and policy reforms to address the issue. There is nothing stopping the courts from employing a similar dialogic mechanism to operationalize positive rights to timely care *within* medicare. From its very inception in international law, the right to health has never been conceived of as a trump on the use of public finances. International law has always expressly understood that governments are accountable

---

30   See, e.g., Sujit Choudhry, "Worse than *Lochner*?" in Colleen M Flood, Kent Roach & Lorne Sossin, eds, *Access to Care, Access to Justice: The Legal Debate Over Private Health Insurance in Canada* (Toronto: University of Toronto Press, 2005) 75.

31   Norman Daniels, *Just Health: Meeting health needs fairly* (New York: Cambridge University Press, 2008) at 315.

for the "progressive realization" of these rights, achieving maximal compliance *within* current resource constraints.[32]

In the comparative literature on health rights, a common concern is that the recognition of a positive right to health care will open the floodgates to endless litigation, as patients turn to the courts in an effort to jump queues or secure funding for drugs left off of public formularies. And it is true that this concern has manifested itself in countries such as Colombia[33] and Brazil,[34] threatening the sustainability of public health care systems and skewing the allocation of health care resources toward high-cost drugs sought by wealthier patients, who have the means to litigate. There is no reason whatsoever to suppose that a recognition of positive rights would send Canada down a similar path and indeed recognition of a positive result to health within a Constitution may result in much more incremental attempts by the court to spur governmental action and accountability. Canadian courts could be a force for systems-level accountability—holding governments accountable for establishing fair and efficient *processes* for wait time management and coverage decisions—without opening the floodgates to endless individual claims.[35] Moreover, as we have seen with initiatives in Ontario with cardiac care and in Alberta with hips, knees, and joints, for the courts to insist that governments tackle wait times need not have significant public-resource implications. In doing so, the courts would be insisting on governmental accountability for that which is promised under the *Canada Health Act,* and the various provincial statutes passed in accordance, to ensure *access* to care on the basis of need, not ability to pay, and, further, to hold the federal government accountable for the various commitments they have made in international law to uphold the right to health.

---

32   UN Committee on Economic, Social and Cultural Rights, *General Comment 14: The Right to the highest attainable standard of health,* 22nd Sess, UN Doc E/C.12/2000/4 (2000).

33   Everaldo Lamprea, "Colombia's Right-to Health Litigation in a Context of Health Care Reform" in Colleen M Flood & Aeyal Gross, eds, *The Right to Health at the Public/Private Divide* (New York: Cambridge University Press, 2014)

34   Mariana M Prado, "Provision of Health Care Services and the Right to Health in Brazil: The Long, Winding and Uncertain Road to Equality" in Flood & Gross, eds, *ibid.*

35   Colleen M Flood & Aeyal Gross, "Contexts for the Promise and Peril of the Right to Health" in Flood & Gross, *ibid.*

Concluding Words

Debate over two-tier care is said to be something of a national pastime for Canadians, stretching back long before the courts entered the fray. Interest in the topic is understandable, as most Canadians have some direct experience with wait times, and talk of "solving" the problem through two-tier care excites ideological passions in a way that careful study of comparative evidence does not. Even as this debate continues, Canadians remain ultimately content and protective of medicare: merely to *have* a universal health care system is an ongoing source of pride, it seems, for a country whose primary point of comparison is the United States. The trouble is that these two predilections—fixation on debates over two-tier care and a degree of complacency borne of measuring our system against the low bar of the US health care system—prevents Canadians from demanding of their governments real solutions to the problem of wait times. And as time passes, Canadians may come to accept the creeping advance of privatization and grow complacent about the importance of maintaining high-performing universal health care.

For better or worse, the courts are now a primary locus for debate over the future of two-tier care. It is often thought that intractable political debates can be resolved by handing the issue over to the courts, to be adjudicated by reference to generally accepted *Charter* principles. This approach has worked, arguably, in settling debate over issues like same-sex marriage, medical aid-in-dying, and medical cannabis.[36] Unfortunately, it seems quite unlikely that the judicialization of the two-tier-care debate will bring anything comparable by way of lasting resolution. There are so many moving parts within a health care system, and such a wealth of comparative evidence to be studied and transposed to the Canadian context, that judicial interventions are bound to raise more questions than they resolve.

There are also, in a sense, moving parts *within the legal system* which may preclude any durable judicial resolution of the debate over two-tier care. Judges have differing ideological perspectives, which can subtly influence their framing of questions and subsequent analysis; this framing effect may pass unnoticed in the whirlwind of

---

36 *Reference re Same-Sex Marriage*, [2004] 3 S.C.R. 698.

facts and law stirred up in these sprawling, complex constitutional challenges. We already see variations in judicial framing in the handful of cases that have been adjudicated by provincial courts under the *Chaoulli* precedent. One key variable here is the framing of the plaintiffs' evidentiary burden in establishing a rights infringement. There appear to be two framings in circulation—one individualistic, and the other solidaristic. Under the individualistic framing, the plaintiff must merely demonstrate that their individual section 7 rights have been infringed by restriction on two-tier care. This generous framing has found its way into the case law in interlocutory decisions of the *Cambie* trial, as Justice Winteringham of the BC Supreme Court reasoned that Cambie Surgeries' claim had prima facie merit:

> I am satisfied that the evidence establishes a number of physicians will not perform private-pay medically necessary health services should the MPA Amendments be brought into force. As such, prospective private health care patients will be precluded from accessing health services in a manner that may alleviate their wait time. Furthermore, there is a sufficient causal connection between denying access to private-pay medically necessary health services and ongoing or greater physical and/or psychological harm that the delay may cause.[37]

Under the *solidaristic* framing, plaintiffs face the more onerous burden of establishing that restrictions on two-tier care have contributed to unreasonable wait times for *all* similarly situated patients. We see this framing applied in *Allen v Alberta*,[38] as plaintiff Darcy Allen attempts a cut-and-paste application of *Chaoulli* to overturn Alberta's prohibition on parallel private insurance. Allen's claim was rejected as the court insisted on robust evidence of the causal connection between the prohibition on parallel private insurance and public-system wait times:

> Dr. Allen avoided a deprivation to the security of his person, but I have nothing on the record to show that the deprivation he

---

37   *Cambie Surgeries Corp. v British Columbia* 2018 BCSC 2084.

38   *Allen v Alberta*, 2014 ABQB 184 (CanLII). The ruling was later upheld in *Allen v Alberta*, 2015 ABCA 277, albeit with some hesitation as to whether the trial court had "set too high an evidentiary burden on the appellant." *Ibid* at para 25.

faced in Alberta … was a result of the Prohibition. A vast array
of alternate possibilities come to mind for the added wait times
in Alberta that may have nothing to do with the Prohibition:
under-funding, mis-management, shortage of qualified practitioners, disproportionate incidence of this particular condition
at the relevant times, unexpected population increases or merely
differences in population concentrations and distributions, to
name a few.

Needless to say, the choice of framing will play a major role in the
outcome of these challenges: it is tautological that restrictions on
two-tier care lead to longer wait times for would-be queue-jumpers,
showing that those restrictions contribute to increased wait times
overall which is vastly more challenging. It is not obvious which of
these two framings should predominate. For present purposes, we
simply mean to highlight that judicial resolution of the two-tier care
debate is likely to remain elusive because even the *framing of questions*
admits of enormous ambiguity.

Is two-tier care the future? If there is a thread of optimism
running through this volume, it is that Canada has a wide array of
options at its disposal to address wait times while maintaining the
equity and universality of its public health care system. In our opinion, the highest imperative is that medicare make good—on a systems
level—on the *Canada Health Act*'s principle of accessibility. The courts
can play a meaningful role in this. If long wait times for essential care
are a violation of human rights, then courts should defend that right
whether a patient seeks care privately or within the public system.
Upholding positive rights in this way need not involve the courts
in micromanaging medicare wait times. Significant gains could be
made if the courts simply ordered government to establish a fair
and efficient *process* for managing wait times system-wide—leaving
it to government to design and implement wait time management
systems on the basis of robust and readily available evidence, both
from within Canada and from international experience.

Contributors' Biographies

Sara Allin is Assistant Professor with the Institute of Health Policy, Management, and Evaluation at the University of Toronto, and Director of Operations with the North American Observatory on Health Systems and Policies, a research centre focused on comparative health policy at the sub-national level. Her research focuses on measuring and comparing health-system performance, with a focus on equitable access to care and the interface between health policy and practice.

Sarah E. Barry is Assistant Professor of Health Services Management at the Centre for Health Policy and Management, Trinity College Dublin. Her research focuses on complex systems change and policy implementation for integrated care and other forms of care delivery. She is working on developing methods for the co-production of knowledge that would make a difference in local contexts and contribute to national policy development and design.

Sara Burke, PhD, is a research assistant professor in the Centre for Health Policy and Management, School of Medicine, Trinity College Dublin. Her research interests are health policy, health systems, inequities in health, and access to health care, as well as the politics of health reform. She is currently PI on a project gathering evidence to inform the implementation of major health reform in Ireland.

Danielle Dawson, MA, is a research coordinator at the Centre for Addiction and Mental Health, Nicotine Dependence Clinic, Toronto. Her research areas range from the biopsychosocial determinants of addiction to technology-enabled collaborative care delivery models. Her projects inform the provision of a more satisfying health care delivery experience for patient and provider.

Lorraine Frisina Doetter, PhD, is Senior Researcher and Lecturer at the Research Center on Inequality and Social Policy and Project Director at the Collaborative Research Center 1342, University of Bremen. As a political scientist, her research focuses on comparative social policy and international developments in health and long-term care systems.

Stephen Duckett is Director of the Health Program at Grattan Institute, an independent public-policy think tank based in Melbourne. He served as secretary (deputy minister) of the Australian Department of Health from 1994 to 1996 and was the inaugural president and chief executive officer of Alberta Health Services (2009–2010). An economist, he is a Fellow of the Academy of the Social Sciences in Australia and of the Australian Academy of Health and Medical Sciences.

Noushon Farmanara, at the time of writing, worked with the McGill Observatory on Health and Social Services Reforms, where she supported research projects on the Canadian health care system, including topics related to privatization, primary-care policy, and other health and social-services reforms. She is currently an epidemiologist at the Public Health Agency of Canada, working on research and surveillance of substance-related harms in Canada.

Colleen M. Flood, a Fellow of the Royal Society of Canada (FRSC) and the Canadian Academy of Health Sciences (FCAHS), is the University of Ottawa Research Chair in Health Law and Policy and the inaugural director of the University of Ottawa Centre for Health Law, Policy, and Ethics. Her research focuses on the role of law on the structure and dynamics of health care systems, and her work informs Canadian and global debates over privatization, health system design and governance, and considers the role of the courts in determining rights in health care.

Vanessa Gruben, BSc, LLB, LLM, is an associate professor at the University of Ottawa, Faculty of Law. She is a member of the University of Ottawa's Centre for Health Law, Policy and Ethics. Her research focuses on the legal regulation of assisted human reproduction, and, more generally, health law and language rights in Canada.

Jeremiah Hurley, PhD, is Dean of the Faculty of Social Sciences, a professor in the Department of Economics, and a member of the Centre for Health Economics and Policy Analysis at McMaster University. His research focuses on the economics of health and health care systems, and also addresses physician behaviour, funding models and resource allocation, public and private roles in health care financing, and equity in health systems.

Martha Jackman, LSM, FRSC, is a professor of constitutional law at the University of Ottawa. Her research interests include socio-economic rights, federalism, the Canadian Charter, and health. She is a recipient of the Canadian Health Coalition's Guardian of Public Health Care Award (Academic) and has acted as legal counsel for the Charter Committee on Poverty Issues in a number of test cases, including *Eldridge v British Columbia* (1997) and *Chaoulli v Quebec* (2005).

Bridget Johnston is a health economist focused on applied health systems research, including evaluations of palliative-care interventions across various health care settings and the affordability of health care for households in Ireland. She has experience in engagement with health policy makers in Ireland throughout the Health Service Executive, the Department of Health, and the government. In addition to her research on palliative care in Ireland, she also collaborated on studies in the United Kingdom, United States, and Jordan.

Gregory P. Marchildon, PhD, FCAHS, is Professor and Ontario Research Chair in Health Policy and System Design at the Institute of Health Policy, Management and Evaluation, University of Toronto. The founding director of the North American Observatory on Health Systems and Policies, he has conducted comparative health systems research in numerous jurisdictions. He has also written extensively on the Canadian health system, federalism, and the history of medicare.

Fiona McDonald is the co-director of the Australian Centre for Health Law Research at Queensland University of Technology and is an adjunct associate professor at the Department of Bioethics at Dalhousie University. Her research focuses on legal and ethical issues concerning the delivery of health services, particularly the governance of health systems, organizations, workforce, and technologies.

Rachel McKay is a postdoctoral fellow at the McGill Observatory on Health and Social Services Reforms. Using population data and policy analysis, her work aims to improve the quality and equity of health systems and services.

Jonathan C. R. Mullen, BHSc, MScPH, is a public health student at McGill University. His research focuses on cancer epidemiology and the identification of risk and prognostic factors in lymphoma.

Zeynep Or is a research director at the Institut de Recherche et Documentation en Economie de la Santé and an affiliated professor to the Economics Department of Université Paris-Dauphine. Her research focuses on the impact of institutional designs and policy schemes on health care system performance, involving equity of access, efficiency, and quality of health care provision.

Aurélie Pierre, PhD, is a research fellow at the Institut de Recherche et Documentation en Economie de la Santé. Her work deals with the place of private health insurance in France, focusing on social inequalities and solidarity between healthy individuals and ill patients. She also works on the link between social and spatial inequalities in access to care.

Dr. Amélie Quesnel-Vallée holds the Canada Research Chair in Policies and Health Inequalities at McGill University, where she is a professor with an arts and medicine cross-faculty appointment in the Departments of Sociology and Epidemiology. She is also the founding director of the McGill Observatory on Health and Social Services Reforms. Her research examines the contribution of social policies to social inequalities in health over the life course. She has received numerous awards from professional associations, including the Population Association of America, the American Sociological Association, and the American Public Health Association.

David Rudoler is an assistant professor at Ontario Tech University and a health-services researcher whose research focuses on access to primary care and mental-health and addiction services, health human resources, and the evaluation of community-based interventions.

Achim Schmid is a postdoctoral researcher at the Collaborative Research Center 1342 and the SOCIUM Research Center on Inequality and Social Policy, University of Bremen. His research focuses on comparative health policy and analysis of health and long-term care systems. He has also participated in evaluation projects on the German long-term care insurance which informed the German Ministry of Health.

Rikke Siersbaek is a SPHeRE (Structured Population and Health-Services Research Education) Programme PhD scholar in population health and health services research at Trinity College Dublin. Her work focuses on how health care systems make themselves accessible to socially excluded populations using realist and qualitative approaches.

Bryan P. Thomas is a senior research fellow with the Centre for Health Law, Policy and Ethics and an adjunct professor with the Faculty of Law, University of Ottawa. His research spans a wide range of topics, including Canadian and comparative health law and policy, health-rights litigation, long-term care, global health law, and the role of religious argument in legal and political discourse. Dr. Thomas holds an SJD from the University of Toronto and an MA from Dalhousie University.

Stephen Thomas is Director of the Centre for Health Policy and Management and Director of Health Policy and Engagement for the School of Medicine in Trinity College Dublin. He has a wealth of international experience in policy-oriented health economics and systems research. His research interests include health-system resilience, health care reform, and policy analysis.

Carolyn Hughes Tuohy is Professor Emeritus and distinguished fellow at the Munk School of Global Affairs and Public Policy, University of Toronto. She holds a PhD from Yale University. She specializes in comparative public policy, with an emphasis on social policy. Her most recent book is *Remaking Policy: Scale, Pace and Political Strategy in Health Care Reform* (University of Toronto Press, 2018).

Acknowledgements

First and foremost, we thank our respective partners, Matthew Brougham and Ashleigh Gardner, for all their love and support through the long process of conceiving of and editing this volume. We would also like to thank our research assistant, Kelli White, a JD candidate at the University of Ottawa, who provided amazing support for this project as well as the terrific staff at the University of Ottawa Press. Finally, we gratefully acknowledge financial support from two CIHR Project Grants, "A Comparative Evaluation of Canada's Regulation of Two-Tier Care and the Relationship to Wait Times" (FRN #142418) and "Contracting with Physicians: An Alternative to Legislating Against Dual Practice?" (FRN #119602).

Index

www.ingramcontent.com/pod-product-compliance
Lightning Source LLC
Chambersburg PA
CBHW061233220326
41599CB00028B/5412